Dubai & Abu Dhabi

"All you've got to do is decide to go and the hardest part is over.

So go!"

TONY WHEELER, COFOUNDER – LONELY PLANET

THIS EDITION WRITTEN AND RESEARCHED BY

Andrea Schulte-Peevers and Jenny Walker

Contents

Plan Your Trip 4

Explore Dubai & Abu Dhabi 46

Understand Dubai & Abu Dhabi 191

Survival Guide 213

Dubai Maps 241

(left) Fresh dates on display in Al Ain (p173)

(above) Burj Khalifa (p85), Downtown Dubai

(right) Souvenirs for sale in Dubai's shopping neighbourhoods (p37)

Dubai Marina & Palm Jumeirah p116

Jumeirah & Around p101

Downtown Dubai p83

Bur Dubai p65

Deira p50

Welcome to Dubai & Abu Dhabi

Dubai and Abu Dhabi are a stirring alchemy of profound traditions and ambitious futuristic vision.

Innovation

It's hard not to admire Dubai and Abu Dhabi for their indefatigable verve, gutsy ambition and ability to dream up and realise projects that elsewhere would never get off the drawing board. This is a superlative-craving society that has birthed the world's tallest building, an island shaped like a palm tree, a huge indoor ski paradise, the world's fastest roller coaster and – soon to come – starchitect-designed art museums of international stature. With many more grand projects in the pipeline for World Expo 2020, visiting here often feels like a trip to the future – to two cities firmly in charge of writing their own narrative.

Shopping Haven

Bargain hunter or power shopper, you'll have a fine time spending your dirhams in Dubai and Abu Dhabi. Dubai especially is a top retail haunt that hosts not one but two huge annual shopping festivals. Shopping is a leisure activity here, malls much more than mere collections of stores. Some look like an Italian palazzo or a Persian palace and lure visitors with surreal attractions like an indoor ski slope or a giant aquarium. Traditional souqs, too, are beehives of activity humming with timeless bargaining banter.

Nocturnal Action

After dark, Dubai sometimes seems like a city filled with lotus eaters, forever on the lookout for a good time. Its shape-shifting party spectrum caters for just about every taste, budget and age group. From flashy dance temples, sleek rooftop terraces and sizzling beach clubs to fancy cocktail caverns and concerts under the stars, Dubai delivers hot-stepping odysseys. Much nightlife centres around the fancy hotels, but there's no shortage of more wholesome diversions either, including *sheesha* lounges, community theatre and live-music venues. Although sedate by comparison, Abu Dhabi is no stranger to cutting loose when the moon's high in the sky.

Cultural Dynamism

With Emiratis making up only a fraction of the population, Dubai and Abu Dhabi are bustling microcosms peacefully shared by cultures from all corners of the world. This diversity expresses itself in the culinary landscape, fashion, music and performance. Although rooted in Islamic tradition, this is an open society where it's easy for newcomers and visitors to connect with myriad experiences, be it eating like a Bedouin, dancing on the beach, shopping for local art or riding a camel in the desert.

Why I Love Dubai

By Andrea Schulte-Peevers, Author

Ever since I first set foot in this tiny powerhouse emirate back in 2007, Dubai has fascinated me with its energy, optimism and openness towards people from all over the world. I'm a die-hard foodie, so the staggering variety of authentic global fare is exhilarating, and even the shopping here – which I normally consider a chore – is actually a joy. Dubai is a place that's constantly in flux and it's been exciting to see it grow and mature as a city and as a society. I can't wait to see what the future holds.

For more about our authors, see p264.

Top: 360° bar (p108) with views of the Burj Al Arab (p103)

Dubai & Abu Dhabi's Top 10

1

Burj Khalifa *(p85)*

1 Slicing through the slipstream of the sky's superhighways, there is no more potent a symbol of Dubai's aspiration to position itself as a major global player than its phalanx of futuristic skyscrapers. Above them all looms the Burj Khalifa, shaped like a deep-space rocket and, at 828m, the world's tallest building. Clad in 28,000 glass panels, it also lays claim to several more superlatives, including the highest outdoor observation deck, the most floors, the highest occupied floor and a lift (elevator) with the longest travel distance.

Downtown Dubai

Sheikh Zayed Grand Mosque *(p151)*

2 Abu Dhabi's snow-white landmark mosque was conceived by Sheikh Zayed, the country's 'founding father'. It has truly impressive dimensions with 80 marble domes held aloft by 1000 pillars and space for 40,000 worshippers. Open to non-Muslims, the main prayer hall is a visual extravaganza generously drenched in gold leaf and boasting massive crystal chandeliers, the world's largest hand-woven carpet and pillars adorned with intricate semiprecious stones and floral marble inlays.

Abu Dhabi

ALEXANDER HAFEMANN/GETTY IMAGES ©

2

SUSAN BLICK/GETTY IMAGES ©

3

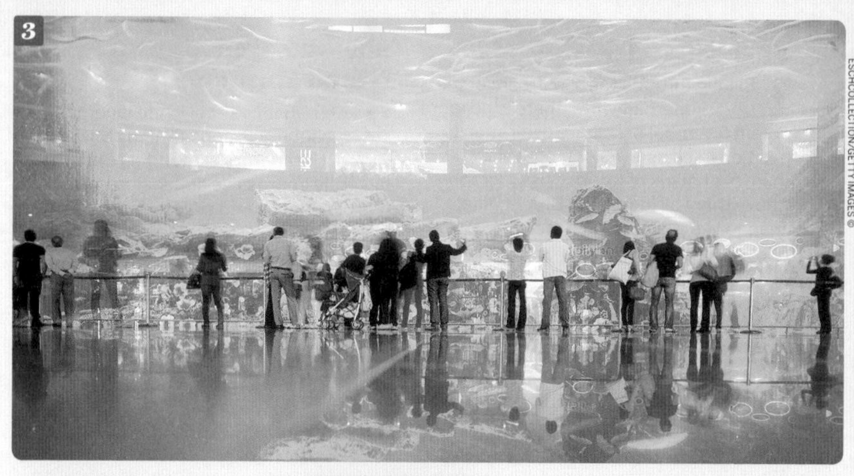

ESCHCOLLECTION/GETTY IMAGES ©

4

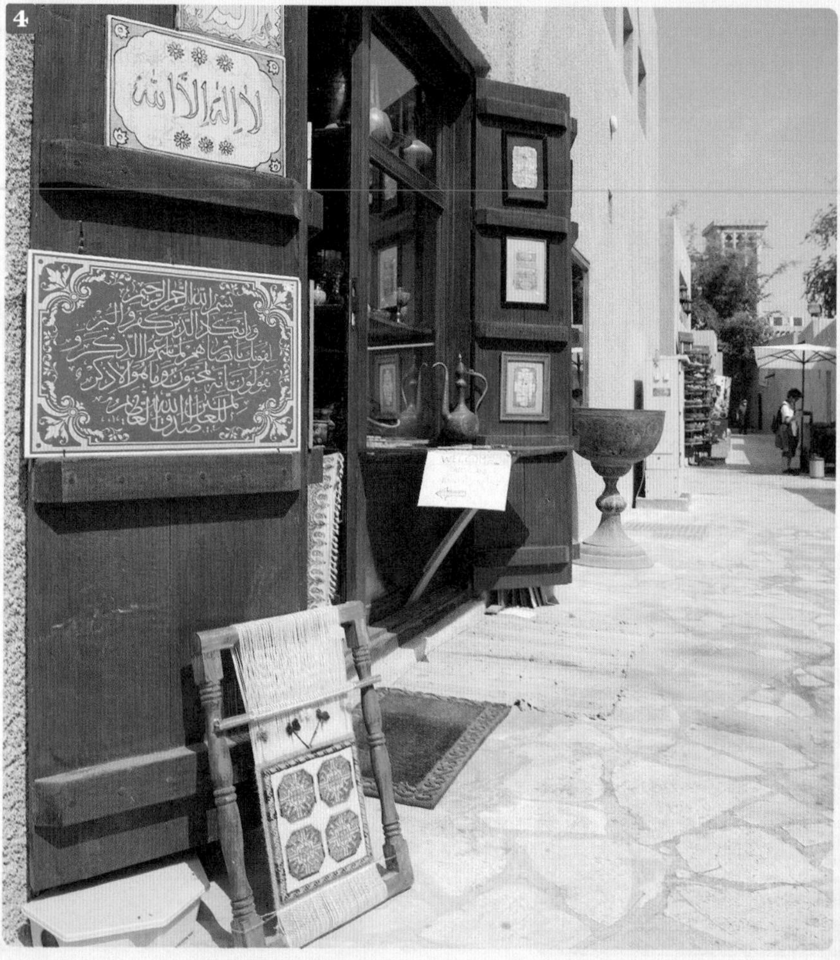

RICHARD NEBESKY/GETTY IMAGES ©

SIMON CHARLTON/GETTY IMAGES ©

Shopping Mall Mania *(p37)*

3 Shopping malls represent an integral part of the culture and lifestyle in Dubai and Abu Dhabi. Many feature eye-popping design and headline-making features such as a ski slope, a giant aquarium and a dinosaur skeleton. Not merely places for maxing out credit cards on fashion, electronics or gourmet foods, malls are also where locals go to socialise in cafes and restaurants, to catch a movie in a state-of-the-art multiplex or to get adrenaline kicks in an indoor theme park or game arcade. DUBAI AQUARIUM, DUBAI MALL (P86)

Shopping

Al Fahidi Historic District *(p68)*

4 Wandering around this restored heritage area in Bur Dubai provides a tangible sense of historic Arabian architecture and culture. Low-lying traditional courtyard buildings flank this quiet labyrinth of lanes, many of them featuring arabesque windows, decorative gypsum screens and wind towers. Some contain craft shops, small heritage museums, art galleries, artsy guesthouses or cafes serving local fare, including Arabic breakfasts and camel-milk smoothies. The Sheikh Mohammed Centre for Cultural Understanding leads guided tours of the quarter.

Bur Dubai

A Night on the Town *(p31)*

5 Dazzling rooftop bars, chill beachfront lounges, glam clubs, classic pubs, funky karaoke joints, outdoor dance venues, snazzy supper clubs – with such variety, finding a party location to suit your mood is hardly a tall order in Dubai. If money is an issue, take advantage of happy hours and ladies' nights. Live-music lovers can keep tabs on the local scene in cool clubs or catch a major star in Dubai or Abu Dhabi's state-of-the-art concert venues.

Drinking & Nightlife

Exotic Souqs *(p53)*

6 For a dose of *Arabian Nights* flair, head to Dubai's historic core and plunge headlong into its charmingly chaotic warren of souqs. Browse for textiles and trinkets in Bur Dubai, then let an *abra* (traditional water taxi) drop you off in Deira, where the pungent aromas of the Spice Souq assault your proboscis in a most pleasant fashion. Even if you don't have a thing for bling, the nearby Gold Souq will feel like a giant Aladdin's cave, while the wriggling bounty at the Fish Market is a shutterbug favourite. SPICE SOUQ (P53)

Deira

Dubai Museum *(p67)*

7 Housed in Bur Dubai's Al Fahidi Fort, the city's oldest surviving structure, this museum provides a well-laid-out introduction to the history of Dubai. Marvel at the turbo-evolution of this city that went from simple desert settlement to futuristic metropolis in just a third of a century. Dioramas re-create traditional scenes in a souq and of life at home, in the mosque, at sea and in the desert. An archaeological exhibition illustrates the ancient history of the region with a display of items unearthed during excavations at local digs.

Bur Dubai

6

CHRIS MELLOR/GETTY IMAGES ©

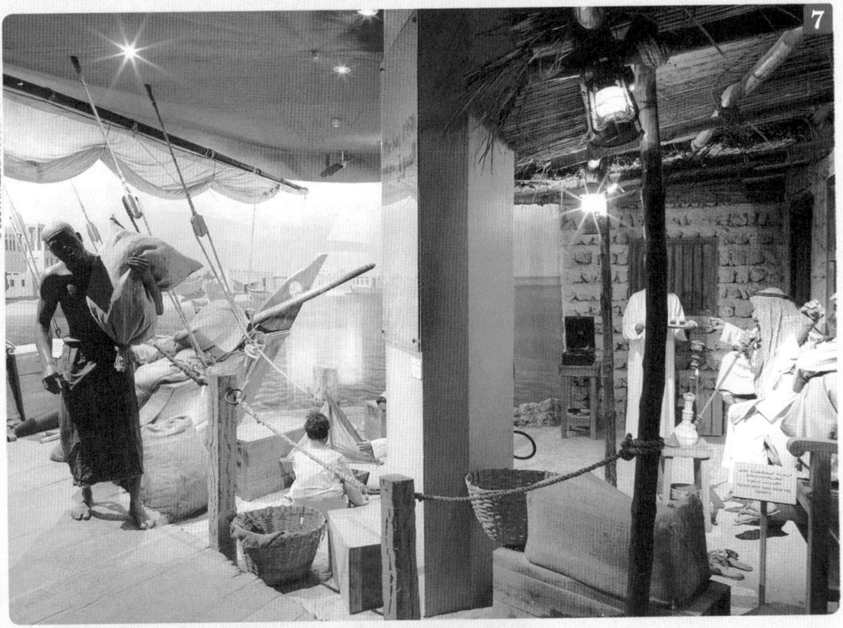

KJELL-ARNE LARSSON/GETTY IMAGES ©

7

8

ALVARO LEIVA/GETTY IMAGES ©

Burj Al Arab *(p103)*

8 This landmark luxe hotel, with its dramatic design that mimics the sail of a ship, floats on its own artificial island and has become the iconic symbol of Dubai's boom years. The interior is all about impact, drama and unapologetic bling, with dancing fountains, gold fittings, giant aquariums and private whirlpool baths your butler can fill with champagne if you so wish. If a stay exceeds your budget, you can still partake in the opulence by making reservations for cocktails, afternoon tea or dinner in the underwater restaurant.

Jumeirah & Around

Emirates Palace *(p137)*

9 One of the world's most expensive hotels ever built, Emirates Palace allegedly came at a price tag of a cool US$6 billion. Surrounded by carefully manicured fountain-laden gardens, it has its own marina, helipad and 1.3km-long sandy beach. The interior is an opulent feast decked out in marble, gold and mother of pearl, hundreds of palm trees and 1000 Swarovski crystal chandeliers. The exterior looks especially magical when illuminated at night.

Abu Dhabi

HOLGER LEUE/GETTY IMAGES ©

BUENA VISTA IMAGES/GETTY IMAGES ©

Desert Escapes *(p170)*

10 The Arabian Desert, with its weathered mountains, undulating sand dunes and wide open spaces, exudes a special mystique that can easily be savoured on a day trip from urbanised Dubai or Abu Dhabi. There are numerous tour operators to set you up with everything from camel treks to sandboarding to overnight safaris. Alternatively, consider renting a 4WD and staying at a desert resort, so you can appreciate the magnificent scenery on your own schedule.

Day Trips from Dubai & Abu Dhabi

What's New

Burj Khalifa 'At the Top Sky'

The Burj Khalifa has outdone itself by opening a new world's highest observation platform on the 148th floor, complete with virtual experiences, a guided tour and refreshments. (p85)

Food Trucks

Mobile kitchens have started making inroads in Dubai, fuelled by ingenuity, delicious cooking and social media. (p106)

Dubai Tram

Getting around Dubai Marina has gotten easier with the launch of the Dubai Tram that shuttles between Dubai Internet City and the Jumeirah Beach Residences.

Dubai Canal

Construction has begun on Dubai's latest mega-project, a 3km canal-style extension of Dubai Creek all the way to the Gulf. (p104)

The Beach at JBR

With smaller outdoor malls all the rage, the opening of this sleek low-rise beachfront contender in Dubai Marina was much anticipated. (p118)

Jumeirah Corniche

The beachfront Jumeirah Corniche stretches for 14km from Dubai Marine Beach Resort to the Burj Al Arab and features a boardwalk, jogging track, kiosks and benches. (p114)

Emirati Cuisine

Sampling local cooking has got easier thanks to the opening of a smattering of restaurants, including Milas, Mama Tani and the Jumeirah branch of Al Fanar. (p27)

Al Quoz Gallery District

More galleries are moving to gritty Al Quoz, drawing cool urban cafes like Tom & Serg in their wake. An extension of the Alserkal Avenue gallery campus is set to open in 2015. (p92)

Frying Pan Adventures

Run by two local sisters, this outfit offers fun, insightful and delicious culinary tours around the backstreets of Bur Dubai and Deira. (p71)

Supper Clubs

The trend of fusing dining and entertainment has arrived in Dubai with the opening of several snazzy supper clubs, most notably The Act, Music Hall and Pacha Ibiza Dubai.

Observation Deck at 300

For a different perspective of Abu Dhabi, head up to this lofty perch 300m above the ground at the Etihad Towers. (p142)

Ripe Farmers Market

Setting up in Za'abeel Park on Fridays in the cooler months, this lively market sells not just locally grown produce but also gourmet products like oil, nuts and honey. (p73)

The Galleria

Part of the Al Maryah Island complex being built to house Abu Dhabi's Central Business District, this magnificent new mall teems with designer outlets. (p150)

For more recommendations and reviews, see **lonelyplanet.com/dubai**

Need to Know

For more information, see Survival Guide (p213)

Currency

United Arab Emirates (UAE) dirhams (Dh)

Languages

Arabic, English

Visas

Citizens of 45 developed nations get free 30-day visas on arrival in the UAE.

Money

ATMs are widely available. Credit cards are accepted in most hotels, restaurants and shops.

Mobile Phones

Mobile phones operate on GSM900/1800. Local SIM cards are easy to find and start at Dh20. Both 3G and 4G networks are available.

Time

Dubai is four hours ahead of GMT/UTC. The time does not change during the summer.

Tourist Information

There are 24-hour tourist information kiosks in Terminals 1 and 3 at Dubai International Airport.

Daily Costs

Budget: Less than Dh600

- Budget hotel room: Dh300–400
- Indie eateries, food courts, supermarkets
- Public transport, happy hours, public beaches

Midrange: Dh600–1200

- Midrange double room: Dh400–700
- Two-course meal in midrange restaurant: from Dh80 without alcohol
- Top attractions and sights: Dh100–200

Top End: More than Dh1200

- Four-star hotel room: from Dh800
- Three-course fine-dining meal with wine: from Dh400
- Drinks in high-end bar: from Dh100

Advance Planning

Three months or more before Double-check visa regulations. Book tickets for high-profile sporting and entertainment events.

One month before Reserve a table at top restaurants, tickets for Burj Khalifa and golf tee times. Check concert-venue websites for what's on during your stay.

One week before Check average daytime temperature and pack accordingly.

Useful Websites

- **Lonely Planet** (www.lonelyplanet.com/dubai) Destination information, hotel bookings, traveller forum and more.
- **Dubai Tourism** (www.definitelydubai.com, www.dubaitourism.ae) Dubai's official tourism site.
- **Zomato** (www.zomato.com) User-generated restaurant reviews.
- **Dubai Explorer** (www.askexplorer.com) Geared towards residents, with lots of practical info.
- **RTA** (www.rta.ae) Public transport information and trip planning.

WHEN TO GO

The best period is November to March, when temperatures are in the low 30°Cs. From June to September, temperatures average 43°C with 95% humidity.

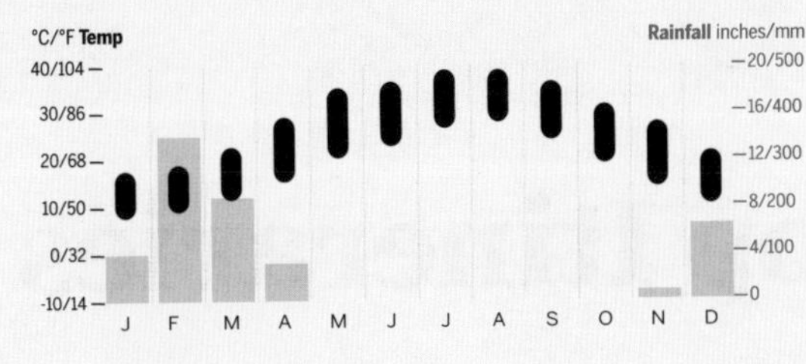

Arriving in Dubai

Dubai International Airport For the metro and buses you need a Nol Card before boarding. Metro service stops around midnight. Taxis have a flagfall of Dh25. Check with your hotel about airport transfers.

Metro The Red Line stops at Terminals 1 and 3 and is the most efficient way to get across town by public transport.

Bus Useful mostly at night when metro service stops. The handiest route is bus C1, which runs 24 hours to Deira, Bur Dubai and Satwa from Terminals 1 and 3.

Taxi A taxi costs between Dh40 (eg Deira) and Dh100 (eg Dubai Marina).

For much more on **arrival**, see p214

Getting Around

Before hopping aboard local transport, purchase a rechargeable pass (Nol Card) from ticket offices or vending machines.

➡ **Metro** The high-tech Red and Green Lines link all major sights and neighbourhoods between 6am and midnight Saturday to Wednesday, and to 1am Thursday and Friday.

➡ **Bus** Slower but useful for going places not served by the metro.

➡ **Tram** Travels along Al Sufouh Rd between Dubai Media City and Dubai Marina.

➡ **Boat** *Abras* (traditional water taxis) cross the Creek. The Dubai Ferry and water buses are good for sightseeing.

➡ **Taxi** Convenient, metered, fairly inexpensive and fast except during rush-hour.

For much more on **getting around**, see p215

Sleeping

Although Dubai has a reputation as a luxury destination, there are plenty of quality midrange hotels away from the beaches and sightseeing hubs like Downtown Dubai. The beach resorts run almost at 100% capacity between November and February, so book far ahead. However, if you're not too picky, finding lodging to match your budget should not be too hard. Considerable discounts are often available through the usual booking engines.

Useful Websites

➡ **Lonely Planet** (www.lonelyplanet.com/united-arab-emirates/dubai/hotels) Reviews of Lonely Planet's top choices.

➡ **Booking.com** (www.booking.com) Wide range of options, with great discounts.

➡ **Direct Rooms** (www.directrooms.com) Competitive site for hotel booking with some good deals.

➡ **Late Rooms** (www.laterooms.com) Especially good for last-minute offers.

For much more on **sleeping**, see p178

RAMADAN

Muslims fast from sunrise to sunset during Ramadan. Foreigners are not expected to follow suit but should not smoke, drink or eat (including chewing gum) in public. Hotels make special provisions by erecting screens for discreet dining. Bars open around 7pm, but clubs remain closed and live music is prohibited. Every night the fast is broken with *iftar* (breakfast), a big communal meal that non-Muslims are welcome to join in.

Top Itineraries

Day One

Bur Dubai (p65)

Start with a cultural breakfast at the **Sheikh Mohammed Centre for Cultural Understanding** for a rare chance to meet locals and eat home-cooked Emirati food. Delve further into local culture and history with a spin around **Al Fahidi Historic District**, dipping in and out of the various small museums and shops before finishing up at the nearby **Dubai Museum**.

Lunch Process impressions over lunch at the Arabian Tea House (p73).

Deira (p50)

Enjoy the short stroll to the breezy **Bur Dubai Souq** via the atmospheric **Hindi Lane**, then catch an *abra* (traditional water taxi) across Dubai Creek to forage for bargains in the bustling Deira souqs. Peruse exotic potions in the **Spice Souq** and dazzling jewellery in the **Gold Souq**, perhaps stopping for a juice or shwarma at **Ashwaq Cafeteria**. Walk along the busy dhow wharves and snap photographs of the colourful cargo vessels.

Dinner Relax during a dinner cruise aboard Al Mansour Dhow (p61).

Deira (p50)

After dinner, take a taxi to **QDs** and wind down with a drink or a *sheesha* (water pipe) while counting the twinkling lights of the Dubai skyline across the Creek.

Day Two

Jumeirah (p101)

Kick off day two with a guided tour of the stunning **Jumeirah Mosque**, then cab it down the coast towards the iconic Burj Al Arab and explore the charming **Madinat Jumeirah** village, perhaps stocking up on camel toys and pashminas at its faux souq or taking an *abra* ride around its network of canals past Arabian-style hotels and lush gardens.

Lunch Enjoy Burj Al Arab views and lunch at Souk Madinat Jumeirah (p112).

Downtown Dubai (p83)

It's the hottest part of the day so make a beeline for the **Dubai Mall** and visit the watery wonderland of the **Aquarium** before giving your credit cards a workout. Watch the sun set from the lofty observation terrace of the **Burj Khalifa** (book way ahead) then enjoy alfresco happy-hour drinks at **Calabar**.

Dinner Marvel at the Dubai Fountain during a meal at Thiptara (p93).

Downtown Dubai (p83)

Check out the killer views and cocktails at **Neos** or belt out your top number at **Harry Ghatto's** at the Jumeirah Emirates Towers.

Day Three

Al Quoz (p88)

(Hint: Pack your beach gear.) Greet the day with strong java and a healthy breakfast at **Tom & Serg**, an ultra-hip industrial loft cafe, before perusing the latest in Middle Eastern art on a gallery hop around the **Alserkal Avenue warehouse complex** in the industrial district of Al Quoz. Afterwards head to **The Beach at JBR** for lunch.

Lunch Try the Counter (p119) or another beachside restaurant.

Dubai Marina (p116)

Dedicate the afternoon to slothdom. Stake out a spot on the beach, either for free at **JBR Open Beach** or by splurging for the sophisticated **Meydan Beach Club**, then spend the afternoon working on your tan and swimming in the crystalline Gulf. There are showers for rinsing off before showing off the day's glow during sundowners at **Bliss Lounge** or **Pure Sky Lounge**.

Dinner Take in glittering marina views over seafood at Aquara (p122).

Dubai Marina (p116)

Follow up with a digestive stroll along the Dubai Marina waterfront past bobbing yachts and glittering futuristic high-rises, perhaps stopping for a nightcap and breathtaking views at the **Observatory** or **Atelier M**.

Day Four

Abu Dhabi (p129)

Begin your tour of Abu Dhabi at the magnificent **Sheikh Zayed Grand Mosque** (closed during prayer times), at the gateway to this capital city. Board the **Big Bus** here and drive past the mangroves off the city's **Eastern Corniche**. Alight at **Manarat Al Saadiyat** to learn about the city's feisty future, built on its pearling past – a past you can encounter at the **dhow harbour**.

Lunch Tuck into a lavish Emirati buffet at Al Arish Restaurant (p158).

Abu Dhabi (p129)

Visit the **fish market** and watch the fishermen mend their nets before leaving Al Mina for the **Corniche**. Hire a bike from **Funride** opposite the Sheraton and cycle part of the 8km to the public beach, passing the city's impressive tower blocks. Enjoy the Gulf breeze with a view of the marina and uninhabited Lulu Island. Rise to the 74th-floor **observation deck** of the Jumeirah at Etihad Towers for the highest high tea in the city.

Dinner Savour seafood at Sayad (p142) in the opulent Emirates Palace.

Abu Dhabi (p129)

Enjoy post-dinner drinks at the glamorous **Etoiles** in the Emirates Palace and then rejoin the real world with a coffee and *sheesha* at one of the late-night Breakwater cafes and watch the city lights dance across the water.

If You Like...

Nightlife

Dek on 8 A chill after-work terrace during the week, this place comes alive with beats on weekends. (p125)

Barasti Dance with sand between your toes or make new friends in the bar at this spirited hot spot, a favourite expat haunt. (p123)

360º Elegant though chilled weekend party playground and the perfect perch for sunsets behind the Burj Al Arab. (p108)

The Act The Dubai offshoot of the Vegas original puts on dazzling shows in a frilly Victorian theatre setting. (p96)

Burlesque Wear red to blend in with the decor at this cabaret, then join the after-show party at the exclusive Yas Island Viceroy. (p164)

A Touch of Luxury

Boating in Style Check out the Creek with glass in hand from the deck of your private yacht. (p42)

High Tea at the Burj Reserve a top table for tea accompanied by sumptuous cakes, a glass of bubbly and heady views, 200m above sea level. (p89)

Bling Thing At the Deira Gold Souq prices are fair, the quality superb and the purchase a glittering investment. (p52)

Go for Gold Sprinkled with 24-carat gold flakes, the Palace Cappuccino at Abu Dhabi's Emirates Palace is the ultimate in delicious decadence. (p137)

Slippers on display, Gold Souq (p52), Deira

Splash Some Cash Make a big entry to Yas Island on board Abu Dhabi's seaplane. The Scenic Island Tour takes 25 minutes. (p166)

Shopping Extremes

Dubai Mall The world's largest mall packs not only a serious retail punch but also provides plenty of family entertainment. (p97)

Deira Souqs Stock up on exotic bargains, from saffron to Kashmiri bed throws and camel-skin slippers to gold necklaces, at this atmosphere-rich antithesis of the modern mall. (p53)

Ibn Battuta Mall This themed mall's stunning decor tracks the journey of a 14th-century Arab scholar from southern Spain to India. (p126)

Central Market Designed by Norman Foster, this modern Arabian bazaar features lots of warm wood and some nifty shops. (p135)

Souk Madinat Jumeirah Even if it's a bit Disney does Arabia, the look is sumptuous and the shops enticing with unusual souvenirs and pleasant refuelling stops. (p112)

Mall of the Emirates Another mall with a dizzying number of shops, as well as the wonderfully incongruous alpine slopes of Ski Dubai. (p110)

Souq Qaryat Al Beri A 21st-century take on an ancient Arab concept, the perfumes, dates and jewellery stores here have a long lineage in Arabia. (p155)

Art & History

Gate Village Smock-and-beret types will love nosing around the exciting contemporary galleries at this posh art hub. (Map p258)

Alserkal Avenue A cutting-edge art campus for predominantly Middle Eastern contemporary art, sculpture and installations. (p92)

Dubai Museum The entire history of Dubai within the confines of Al Fahidi Fort, Dubai's oldest building. (p67)

Al Fahidi Historic District A wander around this restored historic quarter is a journey into Dubai's past. (p68)

Shindagha Historic District Beautifully located along the Creek, these restored residences-turned-museums are where previous generations of Dubai's rulers made their homes. (p69)

Manarat Al Saadiyat With the Abu Dhabi Louvre poised to open in 2015, this exhibition centre introduces the inspiration behind the region's largest cultural project. (p156)

Beaches

Kite Beach This glorious stretch of sand is geared towards active types with kite surfing, volleyball, soap football and other games. (p114)

JBR Open Beach Just off the Walk at JBR, this long sandy strip is flanked by showers, children's fun zones and plenty of restaurants. (p127)

Sunset Beach Overlooking the iconic Burj Al Arab, this is the beach where you shouldn't forget your camera. It's also Dubai's last remaining surfing beach. (p114)

Al Mamzar Beach Park This super-long, pristine and family-friendly beach comes with a pool, playgrounds and water sports but few food outlets, so bring a picnic. (p114)

Corniche, Abu Dhabi Offering 8km of leafy walking track, a separate cycle lane and public and private beaches, this is the city's lungs. (p140)

For more top Dubai and Abu Dhabi spots, see the following:

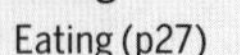

- Eating (p27)
- Drinking & Nightlife (p31)
- Entertainment (p35)
- Shopping (p37)
- Sports & Activities (p42)

Foodie Experiences

Frying Pan Adventures Plunge into the culinary labyrinth of multicultural Bur Dubai and Deira on these fun and educational guided food tours. (p71)

Dubai & Abu Dhabi Food Festivals Discover new trends, meet chefs, take a cooking class and sample fabulous fare during these month-long foodie fairs. (p20)

Al Mansour Dhow dinner cruise For an utterly romantic journey, great hospitality and a generous spread of Indian and Arabic food, take a spin around the Creek on a historic dhow. (p61)

Food Trucks Track down these elusive gourmet mobile kitchens by following their whereabouts via social media. (p106)

Friday Brunch Unleash your inner glutton when faced with a heaping buffet and bottomless sparkling wine at what has become a weekend ritual for many Dubai and Abu Dhabi expats. (p121)

Month by Month

TOP EVENTS

Dubai Shopping Festival, January

Food Festivals in Dubai & Abu Dhabi, February

Art Dubai, March

Abu Dhabi Grand Prix, November

Dubai International Film Festival, December

January

A blissful month here when much of the world is suffering post-holiday doldrums and icy conditions. Expect daytime temperatures averaging a pleasant 25°C.

Dubai Shopping Festival

Held throughout January, this shopping festival (www.mydsf.ae) lures bargain-hunters from around the world. There are huge discounts in the souqs and malls, and the city is abuzz with activities ranging from live concerts to fashion shows and fireworks.

Dubai Marathon

With mild January weather and one of the flattest and fastest courses in the world, this full marathon (www.dubaimarathon.org) attracts pounding participation from all over the globe.

February

Another warm and winning month, with sun-kissed weather and plenty going on, including many outdoor events. Pack a light jacket or pashmina for alfresco evenings.

Swim the Burj

Benefiting the not-for-profit organisation Médecins Sans Frontières (Doctors Without Borders), this charity event sees around 800 swimmers competing in several races around the iconic Burj Al Arab hotel.

Dubai Jazz Festival

This popular festival (www.dubaijazzfest.com) is headlined by such top talent as Sting, John Legend and James Blunt but also gets the crowds toe-tapping with free jazz and blues concerts at various venues around town.

Dubai Duty Free Tennis Championships

Attracting the big serves of the world's top pros, the men's and women's events (www.dubaitennischampionships.com) are a firm fixture on the international tennis circuit.

Dubai Food Festival & Abu Dhabi Food Festival

For several weeks, both Dubai and Abu Dhabi celebrate their astonishing gastronomic diversity with food-related events, entertainment, celebrity chef appearances, dining tours, food trucks and pop-up restaurants (www.dubaifoodfestival.com, www.abudhabievents.ae).

March

The weather might be heating up a fraction, but it is still near perfect in this action-packed month, with warm seas for swimming and plenty of space on the sand.

Festival of Literature

Sponsored by Emirates Airlines, this huge lit-fest

(www.eaifl.com) shines the spotlight on authors and poets from the Middle East as well as international best selling writers.

Art Dubai

Keep tabs on the rapidly evolving art scene in the Middle East and South Asia at this prestigious showcase (www.artdubai.ae) of nearly 100 galleries from the United Arab Emirates (UAE) and around the world exhibiting works at Madinat Jumeirah.

Sikka Art Fair

Some 50 UAE-based artists create site-specific work spanning all media during this 10-day fair (www.sikka.ae) in Bur Dubai's Al Fahidi Historic District.

Taste of Dubai

A feast for foodies, this festival (www.tasteofdubaifestival.com) offers not just delicious bites but also cooking classes, beverage tastings and all sorts of entertainment for young and old.

Dubai World Cup

Dubai's racing season culminates in the world's richest horse race (www.dubaiworldcup.com) but, with no betting allowed, attention also turns to the loony fashion free-for-all of the attendees.

April

It's still warm rather than blistering, but the school holidays mean you'll see more tourists during Easter break. This is a rollicking good month for beach and fashion fans.

Fashion Forward

Models clad in the latest threads by the Middle East's top designers strut the catwalk at this twice-annual fashion fair (www.fashionforward.ae; also held in October) that presents the latest trends in accessories as well as a fashion gallery, cafe and entertainment.

May

Temperatures can nudge 35°C-plus, so air-conditioned malls provide welcome relief.

Al Gaffal Traditional Dhow Race

This traditional dhow race (www.dimc.ae), between the small uninhabited island of Sir Bu Na'air and the Burj Al Arab, has a winner's purse of Dh500,000. Held on the last Saturday of the month, it's a photographer's favourite.

Dubai Summer Surprises

Despite the sizzling time of year, a combination of free kids' entertainment and major sales in shopping malls draws plenty of tourists for the more family-focused little sibling of the Dubai Shopping Festival.

October

Temperatures have started to cool considerably, although you can still expect some toasty warm days early in the month. Nights are perfect for dining alfresco in shirtsleeves or for overnight desert trips.

Abu Dhabi Classics

This series of 12 classical concerts (www.abudhabievents.ae) brings international top talent to various venues around Abu Dhabi between October and May.

Abu Dhabi Film Festival

Stars, directors, critics and cinephiles descend upon Abu Dhabi to meet, mingle and present the latest flicks from around the region in a warm-up to the Dubai International Film Festival (www.abudhabifilmfestival.ae).

Diwali

Lights, candles and firecrackers characterise this magical festival of light, which brings together the ever-growing community of Indian expats in Dubai. Look for traditional sweets in supermarkets and lavishly lit balconies and windows, particularly in Deira and Bur Dubai.

November

Sharjah International Book Fair

This major regional book fair (www.sharjahbookfair.com) presents the latest tomes in Arabic, English and other languages. Readings, workshops and symposia supplement the exhibits.

Abu Dhabi Art

Top regional and international modern and contemporary galleries are joined by collectors, art aficionados and artists for four days of exhibitions, art talks, entertainment and children's programs at Manarat Al Saadiyat (www.abudhabiartfair.ae).

☆ Abu Dhabi Grand Prix

The Formula One racing elite tests its mettle on this wicked track on Yas Island (www.yasmarinacircuit.com).

December

UAE National Day

The birth of a nation in 1971 is celebrated across the country on 2 December with a range of events, from boat parades to fireworks, concerts to horse shows and traditional dances to military parades.

☆ Dubai International Film Festival

This excellent non-competitive film festival (www.dubaifilmfest.com) is a great place to catch international indie flicks as well as new releases from around the Arab world and the Indian subcontinent.

Sheikh Zayed Camel Race Grand Prix Festival

First held in the 1980s, this five-day festival (www.abudhabievents.ae) is the world's largest gathering of Arabian camels with over 10,000 of them participating in races, shows, an auction and even a breeding contest. Held at Al Wathba track, about 45km east of Abu Dhabi. Dates may vary.

(Top) Emirati sweets
(Bottom) Yas Marina Circuit (p161)

TOM LAU/GETTY IMAGES ©

SIMONPRENSON/SHUTTERSTOCK ©

With Kids

Travelling to Dubai and Abu Dhabi with kids can be child's play, especially if you keep a light schedule and involve them in day-to-day planning. There's plenty to do, from waterparks and playgrounds to theme parks and activity centres. Most beach resorts operate kids' clubs.

BUENA VISTA IMAGES/GETTY IMAGES ©

Lost Chambers (p118), Palm Jumeirah

Keeping Cool

Practically all hotels (even cheaper ones) have a swimming pool, while the waterfront resorts have fully developed beach facilities complete with water sports rentals. Among the public beaches Corniche Beach (p145) in Abu Dhabi, Al Mamzar (p114) in Deira and JBR Open Beach (p127) in Dubai Marina have the best family-friendly infrastructure. The latter also has the innovative Beach Water Park (p127), an inflatable offshore playground.

Beach clubs that get a thumbs up from parents include the Jumeirah Beach Hotel (p187), Club Mina (p128) at the Westin and Le Meridien Mina Seyahi, and 25' Beach Club (p128) at the Fairmont Hotel on Palm Jumeirah. Waterparks are a big hit with everyone from tots to teens. For spine-chilling slides, Aquaventure (p127), dramatically positioned at the Atlantis The Palm, is a suitable launch pad, while the original family favourite, Wild Wadi Waterpark (p113), has both options for nervous nellies and adrenaline junkies. The newest and grandest park is Yas Waterworld (p166) in Abu Dhabi which has dozens of slides, rides and pools to get wet.

If liquid water isn't keeping your little ones cool enough, take them to the Olympic-sized ice rink at the Dubai Mall (p86) or do the alpine bit and let them tackle the snow slopes at Ski Dubai (p113) at the Mall of the Emirates.

Theme Parks

Major malls come with kid-oriented activity centres. A treat for smaller children is KidZania (p99) in the Dubai Mall, an interactive miniature city that offers the ultimate in role-play options. Older kids can head to nearby Sega Republic (p99), an indoor amusement park with rides and arcade games. Magic Planet at Deira City Centre and the Mall of the Emirates has similar attractions, as does Fun City (p146) at Abu Dhabi Mall and Marina Mall in Abu Dhabi. A major attraction for older children is Ferrari World Abu Dhabi (p165).

Animal Attraction

Kids fascinated by the underwater world will be enchanted by the Dubai Aquarium & Underwater Zoo (p86) at the Dubai Mall or the labyrinth of underwater tanks and fish-filled tunnels at the Lost Chambers (p118) at Atlantis The Palm. Back on dry land, the Ras Al Khor Wildlife Sanctuary (p87) offers junior birders the chance to observe flamingos and other feathered friends through binoculars. An audience with waddling penguins can be had at Ski Dubai (p113). Abu Dhabi's star animal attraction is the Falcon Hospital (p160). Tour operators like Desert Rangers (p218) and Arabian Adventures (p218) offer camel treks in the desert.

Playgrounds & Parks

Dubai and Abu Dhabi have several parks with picnic areas and playgrounds where children can let off steam. One of the biggest, best and greenest is Creek Park (p70) in Bur Dubai where attractions include a cable-car ride, a botanical garden and a science museum. Skateboard fiends may prefer to swoop by Za'abeel Park (p71), which also has a jogging track. Tots can feed the ducks and enjoy the grassy lawns at Al Safa Park (p104) in Jumeirah (note that sections may be closed for the construction of the Dubai Canal). In Abu Dhabi there are plenty of fun zones along the Corniche, including the excellent Family Park. The best parks for children along the Corniche are Al Khalidiyah Public Park (p141), Al Markaziyah Gardens (p131) and the family beach with a lifeguard. Other fun zones include the Khalifa Park (p153) with a popular splash zone and **Al Mushrif Children's Garden** (Map p132; Al Mushrif Central Park; Al Karama St, Al Mushrif, opp Mushrif Palace, cnr Al Karama St & Mohamed bin Khalifa Sts; admission Dh1, rides Dh2-3; ⌚3-10pm).

NEED TO KNOW

- **Formula & disposable nappies (diapers)** Sold at pharmacies and supermarkets.
- **Babysitting** Ask for a referral at your hotel or try www.dubaimetro-maids.com, www.maidszone.com or www.maid4uae.com.
- **Kids clubs** Many hotels have kids clubs and activities.
- **Strollers & car seats** Bring your own.
- **Transport** Children under five years of age travel free on public transport.

Teen Time

OK, so they've done the ski slopes, disco-danced on the ice rink, splashed around at the waterparks and enjoyed a fashionable strut around the malls. Is there more to prevent teens from succumbing to boredom? For the ultimate holiday pic to impress their pals back home, consider taking them sandboarding, camel riding, on an overnight desert safari or even a trekking trip to the Hajar Mountains. Tours are offered by numerous companies and operate out of both Dubai and Abu Dhabi.

Budding musicians may want to join a drum circle held at a desert camp, while Olympic-runner wannabes can complete a lap or two with the Dubai Road Runners (p115). Scuba diving is another option; young divers over 12 years of age are eligible for open-water dives with Al Boom Diving (p114). There's also tennis (with courts at many midrange to top-end hotels), volleyball and swimming.

Junior Foodies

It's perfectly fine to bring your kids to all but the most formal restaurants, although they (and you) might feel more relaxed at casual cafes, bistros and family restaurants. All the malls boast extensive food courts where kids can browse and pick what they like. Hotels have at least one restaurant suitable for families, usually the 24-hour cafe or the buffet restaurant. Discerning young diners may like to ease themselves into Middle Eastern cuisine with a shwarma, essentially a hot chicken wrap and suitably tasty (and delightfully messy). Ice cream and frozen yoghurt parlours abound as well. There's also a growing crop of kid-geared cafes, including BookMunch Cafe (p106).

For Free

Dubai and Abu Dhabi have the reputation of being among the most luxurious and expensive destinations in the world. Fortunately, some of the best things in life are free (or almost free). Check out this overview of what's on offer to help you stretch your budget.

JOHN ELK/GETTY IMAGES ©

Al Ahmadiya School (p53), Deira

Souq Time

Wandering around the labyrinthine souqs in Bur Dubai and Deira or around the port Al Mina in Abu Dhabi is a fun and eye-opening plunge into local culture and, unless you succumb to the persuasive vendors, it will cost you no more than shoe leather. Browse the textile, perfume, spice, gold, fish, produce and carpet souqs and don't forget to bring your camera. If you're interested in making a purchase, start off the bargaining process by offering half the quoted price.

Waterfront Ramblings

A stroll along Dubai Creek from the Shindagha Tunnel to Al Fahidi Historic District is one of the most authentic and photogenic experiences you can have. Study the architecture of the restored traditional courtyard houses once inhabited by the local ruling family. Watch the wooden *abras* (traditional water taxi) criss-cross the Creek and brightly painted dhows (sailing vessels) bound for Iran and Sudan. Grab a coffee in a waterfront cafe and check out the offerings at the souq. In Abu Dhabi, the Corniche transports the rambler from the past to the present as it weaves from the old dhow harbour to the heart of the modern city at Al Khubeirah.

Museum Cheapies

Dubai has several free or low-cost museums where you can learn about the city's early days. The best of the bunch is the Dubai Museum (p67), which charts the city's turbo-evolution from Bedouin outpost to megalopolis. East of here, Al Fahidi Historic District (p68) harbours a handful of free museums that focus on coffee, coins and art, while the Shindagha waterfront has exhibits on architecture, camels, diving and other cultural facets. Over in Deira, Heritage House (p53) provides a glimpse into the lifestyle of a wealthy family, while Al Ahmadiya School (p53) is Dubai's oldest school. In Abu Dhabi, the Sheikh Zayed Centre for Studies and Research (p139) occupies a cluster of traditional wind tower buildings and displays items belonging to the 'Father of the Nation'.

Mosque Mystique

Mosques in the United Arab Emirates (UAE) are generally closed to non-Muslims, which is why it's such a privilege to be able to tour two of the country's most beautiful houses of worship. In Abu Dhabi, the vast Sheikh Zayed Grand Mosque (p151) is truly a stunner inside and out and can be seen entirely for free on your own or on guided tours. In Dubai, it's possible to admire the beauty of the Jumeirah Mosque (p104) on guided tours costing Dh10.

Freebie Attractions

A top freebie sight in Dubai is the choreographed dancing fountain at the Dubai Mall (p86), with the lit-up drama of the Burj Khalifa as a soaring backdrop. The Dubai Mall itself is filled with attractions, most famously the Dubai Aquarium and a giant dinosaur skeleton. Across town at the Mall of the Emirates (p104), you can look in on the winter wonderland of Ski Dubai through panoramic windows. Nearby, the iconic Burj Al Arab (p103) is best admired from Sunset Beach or Madinat Jumeirah, whose Arabian architecture and mock-souq are attractions in their own right. In Abu Dhabi, even paupers can feel like kings while wandering around the Emirates Palace (p137), one of the most expensive hotels ever built.

Gallery Hopping

Don your sunhat and sunblock, shift into exploring mode and head to Alserkal Avenue (p92) in industrial Al Quoz to keep tabs on what's happening in artist studios around the Middle East. Some 20 cutting-edge galleries call the pimped-up warehouses of this arts and cultural campus their home, with more dotted around surrounding streets. It also costs nothing to check out canvases at Gate Village at the Dubai International Finance Centre. In Abu Dhabi's Manarat Al Saadiyat (p156), a permanent display charts the growth of the city and the inspiration behind the award-winning architecture of the evolving cultural district. The centre's contemporary art gallery and the sand-dune-shaped UAE pavilion also have free exhibits.

NEED TO KNOW

- **Happy Hour & Ladies' Nights** Offered by many bars, especially on Tuesdays.
- **Wi-fi** Most cafes, restaurants, spas, bars and malls offer free wi-fi for their customers.
- **Self-Catering** Hotel apartments are a good option for self-caterers.
- **Transport** The Dubai metro is fast, clean and inexpensive.

Great Outdoors

Some of the finest stretches of sand may have been gobbled up by luxe resorts and beach clubs, but there's still miles of coastline where you can take a dip for free, including Al Mamzar, Kite Beach, Sunset Beach and JBR Open Beach in Dubai (p114), as well as the Corniche beaches in Abu Dhabi. Of Dubai's parks, the nicest ones are Creek Park (p70), which has pleasant views, a cable car and botanical gardens, and Za'abeel Park (p71), which brims with picnic areas and a lake. Bird lovers can head for the Ras Al Khor Wildlife Sanctuary (p87), home to flamingos and other winged critters. In Abu Dhabi, the newly landscaped Eastern Corniche (p153) offers miles of safe walking and running tracks with views across the city's expansive mangrove forests.

Off to the Races

Admission is free and there is no betting, so the only dirhams you may have to spend are for the cab ride out to the Meydan Racecourse (p99) in Dubai to watch some of the world's finest thoroughbreds and most famous jockeys sweat it out on the turf. The state-of-the-art stadium is impressive in itself and the vibe can be electric. For a quintessential Arabian experience, there's nothing like attending a camel race. Seeing these ungainly beasts galumphing by the hundreds at top speeds makes for fantastic memories (not to mention photographs). Head to the Al Marmoun track south of Dubai or the Al Wathba track east of Abu Dhabi.

Eating

Filling your tummy in Dubai and Abu Dhabi is an extraordinarily multicultural experience with a virtual UN of cuisines to choose from. Lebanese and Indian fare are most prevalent, but basically you can feast on anything from Afghan kebabs to fish and chips in the cities' myriad eateries. These run the gamut from simple street kitchens and fast-food franchises to family restaurants and luxe dining temples.

What's Trending Now?

LOCAL INGREDIENTS

Taking global fare local is not a trend unique to Dubai and Abu Dhabi, but it's arrived here with a vengeance. A new generation of chefs lets the trio of 'seasonal-regional-organic' ingredients steer their menus, thereby adding pizzazz to time-tested recipes by making them lighter, healthier and more creative. Classic dishes are reinterpreted and elevated through new techniques and daring flavour combinations. Following the farm-to-table credo, many chefs now grow their own herbs or vegetables, pick up fresh produce from the local farmers market and source their eggs from farms in nearby Al Ain and fish from the northern emirate of Ras Al Khamaih.

FOOD TRUCKS

The export hit from the US and the UK finally started rolling into Dubai and Abu Dhabi in 2014. A growing crop of colourful mobile kitchens can be spotted throughout the city, usually at parties, concerts, events or open-air markets, with exact dates and locations posted via social media. For background and to find out who's the talk of the town, turn to Meals on Wheels (p106).

EMIRATI CUISINE

Restaurants serving Emirati food used to be rare but, thankfully, this is changing. Modern Emiratis are accustomed to an international diet, but there are also a number of traditional plates rooted in the Bedouin tradition that have, over time, become infused with spices and ingredients from trading partners throughout Asia and Arabia. Dishes are typically one-pot stews featuring a combination of rice or some form of wheat, vegetables and/or meat or fish. Many are flavoured with cinnamon, saffron and turmeric and topped with nuts or dried fruit. During Ramadan, traditional dishes feature strongly in the *iftar* (breaking of the fast), the big feast served after sundown.

A popular dish you'll likely encounter is *harees*, a porridge-like stew made from cracked wheat and slow-cooked chicken or lamb. *Fareed* is a lamb stew layered with flat bread, while *makbous* is a casserole of meat or fish, rice and onions cooked in a spicy sauce. Fish features prominently on local menus and is usually served grilled, fried or baked. The salt-cured variety is used in a local dish called *madrooba*.

CAMEL MILK

Bedouins have known it for centuries, but of late the health benefits of camel milk have started to make international headlines. The closest substitute to mothers' milk, camel milk is lower in fat and has triple the amount of vitamin C and iron when compared to cow's milk. The number of cafes offering 'camelccinos' (camel milk cappuccino), milkshakes, smoothies and other camel-milk-based beverages is growing at a steady clip. Camel cheese, chocolate and ice cream are other products showing up on supermarket shelves. Restaurants have also started to put camel burgers on their menus, although camel meat is not actually a staple in Emirati cuisine.

NEED TO KNOW

Price Ranges

The symbols below indicate the average cost per main course at restaurants listed throughout this book.

$	under Dh50
$$	Dh50–Dh100
$$$	over Dh100

Opening Hours

As a guideline, figure on hotel restaurants being open from noon to 3pm and 7pm to 11pm daily. Many low-key indie eateries remain open throughout the day except on Friday when some don't open until the afternoon.

Reservations

➡ Reservations are essential at the top restaurants and recommended for mid-range eateries, especially for dinner. Be prepared to give your mobile number, and expect a call if you're late.

➡ For top tables, make weekend bookings – Thursday and Friday nights, and Friday brunch – at least a week ahead.

Tipping

Many restaurants, particularly in hotels, tack on a 10% service charge, but depending on the hotel, the employees may never see this money. Leave an additional 10% to 15% in cash, under the ticket, particularly at low-end restaurants. If service is perfunctory, it's OK to leave a mere 5%.

Vegetarians & Vegans

Dubai and Abu Dhabi are good for vegetarians, with lots of Asian and subcontinental cuisine on offer. Health-conscious cafes and restaurants have been sprouting faster than alfalfa and serve up inspired menus that leave the old veggie and tofu burgers in the dust. The idea of organic food too is catching on quickly, although it's still not as widely available as in other countries and – due to the harsh climate – much of it has to be imported at the expense of a sizeable carbon footprint.

Many of the Indian restaurants, particularly in Deira and Bur Dubai, have extensive vegetarian menus. Even those that are not dedicated vegetarian restaurants still do fantastic things with vegetables, paneer (cheese) and rice. You can also fill up fast at Lebanese restaurants with all-veg mezze, while Thai places have plenty of coconut-and-chilli spiced veg curries and soups. Vegans may be more challenged, but certainly won't be limited to a few lettuce leaves and a carrot stick. Many fine-dining restaurants have dedicated vegetarian menus as well.

Fast-Food Faves

Dubai and Abu Dhabi are fast-food havens, and we're not talking golden arches (although they're here as well). If there ever was a local snack food with cult status, it would have to be the shwarma, strips of marinated meat (usually chicken or lamb) and fat roasted on a rotating grill, slivered and stuffed into a pita bread.

The selection of Middle Eastern mezze is simply stunning, ranging from humble hummus (chickpea dip) and creamy *muttabal* (aubergine/eggplant dip) to *kibbeh* (meatballs) and tabbouleh (parsley-based salad). India contributes not only its famous curries and biryanis (rice dishes) but also various *chaat* (street-food snacks) such as *bhaji* (fritters), *samosa* (savoury pastries), *puri* (deep-fried bread) and *dosa* (fermented crêpes). Kebabs are also a fast-food staple.

Self-Catering

Both Dubai and Abu Dhabi have big international supermarket chains with a bewildering selection of high-quality, international food items. Carrefour is probably the best stocked but the quality tends to be better (and prices higher) at Spinney's and Waitrose. Both stock many products from the UK, North America and Australia and are predictably popular with Western expats. Some branches have separate 'pork rooms' that are off limits to Muslims. Choithram is cheaper and caters more to the South Asian communities. Many markets are open until midnight; some never close.

Farmers markets are also making inroads. In the winter months you'll find a Friday market in Za'abeel Park (p71) and a small courtyard market in Souk Madinat Jumeirah (p112). The fruit and vegetable market next to the fish market (p60) in Deira is open daily. There's also a second fish market in Jumeirah.

Dubai: Eating by Neighbourhood

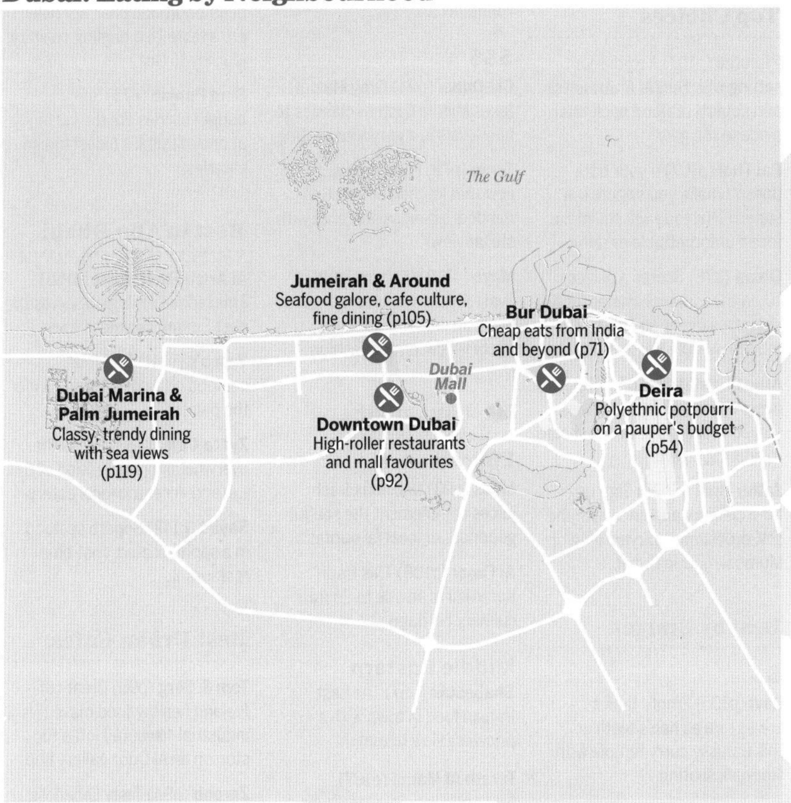

Food Bloggers

Dubai is a fast-changing city and so it's only natural that the gastro scene also develops at lightning speed. Fortunately, there are a number of passionate foodie bloggers keeping an eye on great eats and new openings. Here are our top three, but there's plenty more you can link to via the portal www.fooderatiarabia.com.

FooDiva (www.foodiva.net) The best of the bunch is run by Greek-Cypriot-British expat Samantha Wood who's also a regular contributor to *The National* newspaper and CNN. Her insightful and impartial reviews show that she really knows the scene inside and out.

I Live in a Frying Pan (www.iliveinafryingpan.com) Local Arva Ahmed is obsessed with ferreting out the best among Dubai's authentic hole-in-the-wall eateries. She not only blogs about her discoveries but also takes curious budget gourmets on food tours through her company Frying Pan Adventures (p71).

The Hedonista (www.thehedonista.com) Australian Sarah Walton has spent half a lifetime working around food and wine and now shares her extensive expertise on eating her way around Dubai and beyond in independent reviews.

Lonely Planet's Top Choices

Pierchic (p107) A to-die-for setting with Burj Al Arab views and superb seafood pack this place to the gills.

Pai Thai (p107) If your date doesn't make you swoon, the superb Thai food will still make for an unforgettable evening.

Qbara (p78) Scores a perfect 10 on the romance-meter for its sensuous decor and matching modern Middle Eastern cuisine.

Aroos Damascus (p55) Seriously delicious Syrian staples served with a smile in a vast cafe to adoring crowds.

Jaffer Bhai's (p73) Sign up for a culinary audience with the self-proclaimed 'biryani king of Mumbai', now in Dubai.

Eric's (p73) Unassuming neighbourhood charmer delivers a taste-bud tingling culinary journey to Goa.

Sind Punjab (p73) Spicy budget curries are the currency at one of Dubai's oldest Indian eateries.

Best by Budget

$

Ravi (p105) Empty tables are as rare as hen's teeth at this unfussy curry temple with sidewalk seating.

Special Ostadi (p73) Sheiks to shoeshiners clutter this funky been-here-forever Iranian kebab joint.

Al Tawasol (p55) Sit on the floor Bedouin-style and figure out how to feast on Yemeni classics without cutlery.

$$

Samad Al Iraqi (p107) A top place to try woodfire-roasted fish called *masgouf*, Iraq's national dish.

Leila (p93) Beirut import delights with updated Lebanese home-cooking in a nostalgic setting.

Baker & Spice (p93) Healthy and delicious salads and other cafe fare with a view of the Dubai Fountain.

$$$

Clé Dubai (p94) Greg Malouf takes Middle Eastern classics to new levels in a gorgeous setting.

Tomo (p78) Eponymous gourmet kitchen of tradition-minded Japanese star chef with stellar views.

Maya (p120) Richard Sandoval reinterprets time-honoured Mexican dishes in modern Michelin-decorated fashion.

Best by Cuisine

Emirati

Milas (p93) Delicious fresh juices complement the soulful goodness of local favourites.

Al Fanar (p106) This traditional lair is an ode to Emirati culinary heritage.

Middle Eastern

Shabestan (p57) The best Iranian food in town with a priceless view to match.

Turath Al Mandi (p107) Authentic Yemeni eatery where the chicken *mandi* will have you lickin' your fingers, guaranteed.

European

BiCE (p122) Fabulous wine complements meals that have all the flavours of Italy locked inside.

Picante (p77) Diverse and sometimes surprising ingredients find their destination in superb Portuguese creations.

Traiteur (p60) Richly satisfying French cuisine amid a theatrical setting.

Indian

Indego by Vineet (p120) Michelin man Vineet Bhatia seduces diners with contemporary spins on Indian classics.

Best in Abu Dhabi

Al Arish Restaurant (p158) This hidden Arab gem serves the best Emirati cuisine in town.

Vasco's (p141) Fabulous seafood on a cosy terrace under the palms.

Zyara Café (p133) Red is the overwhelming impression of this fun and eccentric local eatery.

Sayad (p142) Superb seafood in a sophisticated, cool-blue restaurant.

Best Urban Cafes

Tom & Serg (p95) Great coffee and healthy food make this industrial-flavoured loft a top stop on an Al Quoz gallery hop.

Zaroob (p94) Tasty Lebanese street food in a setting so perky it may get you off your Prozac.

Fümé (p119) Dubai Marina views are gratis at this rustic city slicker trading in global comfort food.

Best Meals with a View

Aquara (p122) Sleek yachts bobbing against a backdrop of skyscrapers in Dubai Marina.

Rivington Grill (p94) Watch the fabulous dancing fountains while you dine.

Thiptara (p93) Dine on a lakeview deck beneath the world's tallest tower.

Drinking & Nightlife

Dubai may be famous for its glitzy-glam clubs, but of late it's also been growing a more low-key underground scene. The busiest nights are Thursday and Friday – Dubai's weekend nights – when party animals let off steam in the bars and on the dance floor. Alcohol is served in hotels and some licensed venues only. Many Emiratis prefer going out for sheesha (water pipes), mocktails or coffee.

Bars & Pubs

Snug pubs, beachside lounges, DJ bars, dive bars, cocktail temples, hotel lounges – with such variety finding a libation station to match your mood or budget is not exactly a tall order in Dubai. Generally, the emphasis is on style and atmosphere and proprietors have often gone to extraordinary lengths to come up with unique design concepts.

Venues in Downtown Dubai, Jumeirah, Dubai Marina and Palm Jumeirah tend to be on the fancy side and appeal mostly to well-heeled visitors and expats. Beachfront lounges and rooftop bars are all the rage these days, as is the supper club concept that wraps dining, drinking and dancing into one fabulous night. Away from the five-star hotels, bars and pubs in Bur Dubai and Deira are more of a low-key, gritty affair. Note that prostitution, though officially illegal, is tolerated in many establishments in all parts of town.

Sheesha & Mocktails

Most Emiratis don't drink alcohol, preferring to socialise over coffee, juice and mocktails. If you're not up for drinking, follow the locals to a mellow *sheesha* cafe and play a game of backgammon. Even if you don't smoke, it's tempting to recline languorously and sample a puff of the sweet flavours. *Sheesha* cafes are open until after midnight, later during the winter months. The going rate is Dh30 to Dh75 for all you can inhale. For inspiration, see www.shisha-dubai.com.

Clubbing

DJs spin every night of the week with the top names hitting the decks on Thursdays and Fridays. Partying is not restricted to night-time with plenty of beach clubs like Blue Marlin Ibiza UAE and Nasimi Beach kicking into gear in the early afternoon on weekends in the cooler months. The sound repertoire is global – funk, soul, trip-hop, hip-hop, R&B, African, Arabic and Latino – although the emphasis is still clearly on house and other EDM (electronic dance music).

Globetrotting big-name DJs like Ellen Allien, Carl Craig, Ricardo Villalobos, DJ Koze, Roger Sanchez and Ben Klock occasionally jet in for the weekend to whip the crowd into a frenzy in the top venues and at megaparties like Groove on the Grass or White Dubai. But there's plenty of homegrown talent as well. Names to keep on the radar include Raxon, Danny Neville, Shadow, Beatz, Adam, Bliss, Hoolz, Haidz, Smokinggroove, Kay Tek, Sufyan and Miss PM, MrMr, Vas Floyd, Julian Jinx and JC.

Some top EDM parties are put on by local record label and event agency Audio Tonic, which also owns the Friday 'Sunset Sessions' residency at 360° at the Jumeirah Beach Hotel. Another successful club night is Jamrock, which introduced reggae, soca and dancehall artists to the region. For more of an underground vibe, check out Electric

NEED TO KNOW

Costs

- Drinking is expensive in Dubai because of high taxes. A pint of beer will set you back Dh20 to Dh40, a glass of wine around Dh50 and a cocktail Dh75.
- Clubs charge from Dh50 to Dh300 for big-name DJs. Women get free admission at many venues.

Opening Hours

- Many bars and clubs are open seven days a week, although some close one day a week.
- Bars and pubs also serve food. Hotel bars tend to open from midday until midnight or 1am, although some of the trendiest only welcome barflies from 6pm or 7pm.
- Clubs open around 9pm, get going around 11pm and close at 3am.
- During Ramadan bars are open at night, but clubs and live-music venues are closed.

Club & Party Listings

- www.residentadvisor.net
- www.infusion.ae
- www.platinumlist.net
- www.timeoutdubai.com

Night, currently at Tamanya Terrace, and such promoters as Plus Minus (deep house and techno), Globalfunk (drum and bass), Superheroes (house, garage, drum and bass), Bassworx (drum and bass, dubstep, garage), Catch (underground EDM) and Aurora (house) who put on party nights at current club faves like The Dek on 8, The Basement, Zero Gravity, Blue Marlin Ibiza UAE and Casa Latina.

For up-to-date details on what's happening in the club world, check out *Hype* magazine, which is available at bars, boutiques, gyms and spas around town. The digital edition is available for free from the iTunes app store or sign up with **Magzter** (www.magzter.com) and read it online.

Dress Code & Door Policies

Doors are tough at many clubs, and anyone bouncers feel does not fit in with the crowd may be turned away. Many venues have a dress code (check Facebook or the website if unsure) that is strictly enforced, so make sure you've ironed that shirt and leave your jeans, sneakers and flats at home. Beachside venues are more relaxed, although even these only allow women, couples and mixed groups. Underground clubs tend not to have a door policy.

Some clubs have been accused of racist policies, particularly against South Asians, while others turn away groups of single men, especially on busy nights.

If a top DJs is at the decks, you can usually buy advance tickets online. For some club nights, you need to get on the guest list, usually via Facebook.

Happy Hour & Ladies' Nights

One way to stretch your drinking budget is by hitting the happy hours offered by a wide roster of bars, from dives to five-star lounges, either on specific days of the week or even daily. Discounts range from 50% off drinks to two-for-one deals or double measures on selected beverages. Most start early in the evening, usually around 5pm or 6pm and run for two or three hours. They're hugely popular with the after-work crowd and also a good way to ring in a night on the town. Some venues also have a second happy hour later at night.

Women have yet more options for liquoring up on the cheap during ladies' nights. Many bars and pubs go to extraordinary lengths to lure the 'fairer gender' with free cocktails, bubbly and nibbles. Of course, they don't do this out of the goodness of their hearts; after all, where there are tipsy women, men (who pay full price) follow. Some ladies' nights run all night, others only during certain hours. The best night is Tuesday, with fewer deals on other nights and hardly any on the weekend. Check www.ladiesnightdubai.com for a round-up.

Buying Alcohol

One of the most common questions among first-time visitors is: 'Can I buy alcohol?' The answer is yes – in some places. When arriving by air, you can, as a non-Muslim visitor over 18, buy 4L of spirits, wine or beer in the airport duty-free shop. With the exception of the 'dry' emirate of Sharjah (just north of Dubai), where alcohol and even *sheesha* smoking is banned, you can also purchase alcohol in bars and clubs that are generally attached to four- and five-star

Dubai: Drinking & Nightlife by Neighbourhood

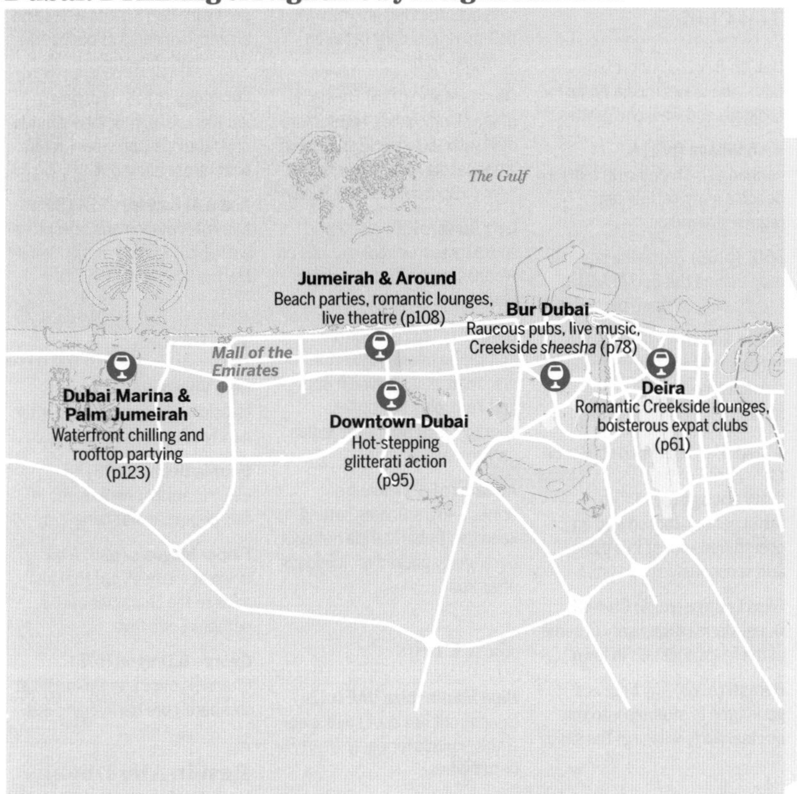

hotels for on-site consumption. Expat residents can acquire an alcohol licence, which entitles them to a fixed monthly limit of alcohol sold in such places as the African & Eastern liquor stores and some branches of Spinney's. Note that visitors are *not* permitted to legally purchase alcohol in these places and staff is supposed to ask to see the licence.

The only store where visitors can officially buy alcohol without a licence is at the Barracuda Beach Resort in the emirate of Umm al Quwain, about an hour's drive north of Dubai. Note that you are not officially allowed to transport alcohol through Sharjah, although most people just seem to take the risk anyway.

Zero Tolerance

Dubai and Abu Dhabi have zero tolerance when it comes to drinking and driving. And we mean zero: under no circumstances should you ever get behind the wheel of a car if you've had even one sip of alcohol. Getting caught could get you a one-month stint in jail, a fine and deportation. Even just being drunk in public is illegal and may also result in jailtime and a fine of several thousand dirham. Also note that even if you are the victim of a crime (eg sexual assault or robbery), police protection may be limited if you are found to be under the influence. See Legal Matters (p220) for more.

Lonely Planet's Top Choices

Dek on 8 (p125) Unpretentious vibe draws media types for cocktails and weekend parties.

Irish Village (p61) A congenial Irish pub with blarney decor, a leafy setting and regular live music.

360° (p108) Watch the sun drop behind the Burj Al Arab at this sizzling offshore party den.

Music Room (p79) Top place in town to keep tabs on the local music scene.

Best Beachfront Bars

Jetty Lounge (p123) Sip artful potions tucked into an overstuffed sofa at this classy and sensuously styled bar.

Bliss Lounge (p124) Chilled Dubai Marina dispensary of some of the finest cocktails in town.

Barasti (p123) Any time is a good time to stumble into the original party village in the sand.

Best Rooftop Bars

Siddharta (p124) Cocktails with a view of the glittering Dubai Marina at this ab-fab lounge by the pool.

40 Kong (p96) Power players and desk jockeys loosen their ties and inhibitions at this swank outdoor lair.

Atelier M (p124) Stylish new entry has a stellar perch atop the Pier 7 building in the Marina.

Best for Happy Hour & Ladies' Nights

Calabar (p95) Kickstart the night with half-price drinks daily from 6pm to 8pm at this sleek Downtown alfresco lounge.

Pure Sky Lounge (p124) Sunsets over the Gulf go well with half-off drinks daily between 5pm and 7pm.

Observatory (p125) The home of the skinny ladies' night (Monday) with 150-calorie drinks and a happening happy hour from 5pm to 8pm daily except Friday.

Left Bank (p109) Women score three free vodka drinks on Wednesdays at this canalside Madinat outpost.

Barasti (p123) Beachfront institution offers 30% drink discounts daily between 4pm and 7pm, plus bottomless sparkly for Dh50 for the ladies on Tuesdays.

Aquara (p122) Three free drinks and a stunning setting keep this Dubai Marina hot spot perennially packed on Tuesdays after 8pm.

Best Clubs

Blue Marlin Ibiza UAE (p124) Beachfront hot spot spins electronic sounds for party-hearty hard bodies.

Basement (p124) Plug into the local DJ scene keeping it real with an eclectic sound range.

N'Dulge (p125) Mega-club at the Atlantis brings big-time DJs to the turntables.

The Act (p96) Newcomer shakes things up with mildly risque cabaret acts amid Victorian theatre lushness.

Cavalli Club (p96) Bling brigaders should strap on those heels and make a beeline to this sparkling dancing den.

Best for Sheesha & Mocktails

Kan Zaman (p73) Count the colours of the Creek while puffing away at this waterfront lounge.

Kris Kros (p95) Urban outpost with Burj Khalifa views and an encyclopaedia of booze-free drinks and *sheesha*.

Mazology (p108) Hipsters get high on high-octane sounds and fabulous Gulf views at this beachfront hang-out.

Reem Al Bawadi (p124) Spin tales of romance and adventure while kicking back in this Dubai Marina lair.

Best Pubs

Irish Village (p61) The classic is still going strong after nearly 20 years in business.

Double Decker (p96) An electric atmosphere reigns in this popular expat hang-out.

Fibber Magee's (p96) A bit down at the heel, but that just adds to the character of this perennial pub fave.

George & Dragon (p78) Channel your inner Bukowski at this hard-core barfly hang-out.

Best in Abu Dhabi

Iris (p163) This Yas Marina favourite has a relaxed and rustic atmosphere despite the high-tech destination.

O1NE (p164) Turn up at this graffiti-decked nightclub in a matching graffiti-clad limo and enjoy 3D projections.

Cooper's (p154) Almost every night is ladies' night at this classic brass-trimmed watering hole.

Etoiles (p143) Perfect for post-dinner drinks, this is one of the most stylish bars in town.

Chameleon (p155) With names like Flaming Rosemary Gimlet and Watermelon Rita, cocktails are an art form at this bar.

Entertainment

Dubai and Abu Dhabi's cultural scene is growing in leaps and bounds with thriving expat communities and two major developments on the horizon – the Dubai Opera and the Abu Dhabi Performing Arts Centre – fuelling the local music and theatre scenes. International A-list entertainers regularly make the cities' state-of-the-art venues a stop on their concert tours.

Live Music

Alongside plenty of cover bands ranging from cheesy to fabulous, Dubai also has a growing pool of local talent performing at festivals and such venues as the Music Room, Chi, Barasti, the Fridge and the Irish Village in Dubai. Rock and metal dominate but sounds from punk to pop to hip-hop are also making appearances.

Homegrown bands to keep on the radar include rock groups the Boxtones, Kicksound and Nikotin; the metal bands Nervecell, Tartarus and Riff Raff; the hip-hop collective the Recipe; Arabic folk trio Dahab; reggae rock by Sho and alternative rock by Daisygrim. A major success story is Dubai-based Juliana Down who became the first local artists to sign with a major label (Sony) in 2011 and who've opened for Justin Timberlake, Guns N' Roses, Maroon 5 and other headliners. Big international acts like these perform at such venues as the Dubai Media City Amphitheatre, the Meydan Racecourse as well as Yas Arena in Abu Dhabi.

One initiative nurturing local talent is **Freshly Ground Sounds** (www.freshlygroundsounds.com). Founded in 2013 by Ismat Abidi, the collective puts on acoustic and lo-fi sessions in small, indie community venues like the Archive in Dubai or Café Arabia in Abu Dhabi.

Local and imported talent also rocks the many festivals, including mega-events like Party in the Park, Sandance and Sensation. Hipsters flock to the alternative music nights put on by Dubai-based promoter Ohm Events, such as The Chill Out Festival, Boombox, Unplugged and Muzik.

Classical music is not terribly prevalent, although that is likely to change once the Dubai Opera taking shape as part of a new cultural district in Downtown Dubai is open for business. For now, you can catch the occasional concert at Dubai Community Theatre and Arts Centre (DUCTAC) and the Madinat Theatre. The Dubai Concert Committee puts on the World Classical Music Series with concerts held at the One&Only Royal Mirage. Abu Dhabi hosts top talent during the Abu Dhabi Classics series taking place at Manarat Al Saadiyat.

At the Movies

Catching a movie is a favourite local pastime with most cinephiles flocking to mall-based high-tech multiplexes for the latest international blockbusters. Indie and art-house cinemas are still rare, although Reel Cinemas at the Dubai Mall dedicates one screen to non-mainstream fare. **Bollywood Cinema** (Map p260; www.alquozmall.com; Al Quoz Mall, 17B St, Al Quoz Industrial Area 3; Ⓜ First Gulf Bank) at Al Quoz Mall screens Indian movies on weekends. There's also a smattering of indie film clubs, including **Loco'Motion** (www.facebook.com/locomotionuae) and the **Scene Club** (www.thesceneclub.com), founded by Emirati filmmaker Nayla Al Khaja. Both screen alternative flicks in cultural venues such as the XVA Cafe in Bur Dubai, Creekside in Deira and

NEED TO KNOW

Listings

Keep tabs on what's on and upcoming via www.timeoutdubai.com, www.infusion.ae and www.whatson.ae. Look for flyers in bars, cafes and the Virgin Megastore. Another excellent source is the weekly *Hype* magazine, available for free in print and digitally on iTunes and **Magzter** (www.magzter.com).

Tickets

The easiest way to buy tickets for big-name concerts, parties and events is online through www.platinumlist.net, www.itp.net/tickets and www.ticketmaster.ae.

Costs

Costs vary wildly. You can hear a jazz trio in a snazzy bar for the cost of a glass of wine or shell out Dh350 or more for a big-name artist.

Music Bans

Dancing and loud music in public places is strictly forbidden. This includes beaches, parks and residential areas; dancing is restricted to licensed venues only.

the **Archive** (Map p254; ☎04-349 4033; www.facebook.com/TheArchiveDubai; Al Safa Park; Ⓜ Business Bay) in Al Safa Park. Also check out the schedule of the **Alliance Française** (☎04-335 8712; www.afdubai.org), which shows weekly films in French and occasionally hosts festivals.

For movies under the stars head to the outdoor cinema at The Beach in Dubai Marina or the free Sunday screenings at Rooftop Gardens in Wafi City. The two most important film festivals are the Abu Dhabi International Festival in October and the Dubai International Film Festival in December.

Theatre & Dance

Dubai's performing arts scene is slowly evolving with the best productions being put on at DUCTAC and the Madinat Theatre in Souk Madinat Jumeirah. Both present their own productions and visiting troupes, both in theatre and dance, especially ballet. New on the scene is the community theatre Courtyard Playhouse in Al Quoz, home of the Dubai Drama Group.

The most popular traditional dance in the region is the *ayyalah*. The United Arab Emirates (UAE) has its own variation, performed to a simple drumbeat, with anywhere between 25 and 200 men standing with their arms linked in two rows facing each other. They wave walking sticks or swords in front of themselves and sway back and forth, the two rows taking it in turn to sing. It's a war dance and the words expound the virtues of courage and bravery in battle. You can see the dance on video at the Dubai Museum or during festivals at the Heritage Villages in Dubai and Abu Dhabi.

Dubai Mall (p97), Downtown Dubai

PETER UNGER/GETTY IMAGES ©

Shopping

Shopping is a favourite pastime here – especially in Dubai, which boasts not only the world's largest mall but also shopping centres that resemble ancient Egypt or an Italian village and feature ski slopes, ice rinks and giant aquariums. Souqs provide more traditional flair, and a growing crop of Euro-style outdoor malls, indie boutiques and galleries beckon as well.

Where to Shop

Dubai and Abu Dhabi have just about perfected the art of the mall, which is the de facto 'town plaza': the place to go with friends and family to hang out, eat and be entertained as well as shop. Most are air-conditioned mega-malls anchored by big department stores like Bloomingdale's or Galeries Lafayette and filled with regional and international chains, from high-street retailers to couture fashion labels. Almost all have at least one large supermarket like Carrefour, Spinney's or Waitrose.

A recent fad has seen the arrival of outdoor malls like The Beach in Dubai Marina or the City Walk in Downtown Dubai, with a smaller selection of stores calibrated to the needs and tastes of neighbourhood residents. There's also a growing number of indie designer boutiques, especially along Jumeirah Road, as well as a bustling monthly flea market. Small Indian- or Asian-run department stores are great for picking up bargain basics.

NEED TO KNOW

Opening Hours

- Most major malls are open from 10am to 10pm Saturday to Wednesday and until 11pm or midnight on Thursday and Friday (weekends), and later during the Dubai Shopping Festival and Ramadan (often until 1am).
- Traditionally, souqs (markets) and non-mall stores close a few hours during the afternoon for prayer, lunch and rest, and don't open on Fridays until late afternoon, but that's changing. These days many remain open all day, although business is slow in the afternoon.
- Malls get packed on Friday nights. Some supermarkets and convenience stores are open 24 hours.

Returns

Try before you buy and ask about return policies, especially for gifts. Many stores offer returns for store credit only. When in doubt, consider a gift certificate, which generally has an extensive expiration period and with international chains can often be used online.

Websites

- **www.littlemajlis.com** Specialises in handmade and artisanal items from around the region.
- **www.quickdubai.com** Great for gifts, including last-minute needs such as cakes and flowers.
- **www.sukar.com** Big discounts on known brands.
- **www.souq.com** A local version of eBay with some top bargains and plenty of variety.
- **www.emiratesavenue.com** Great for the latest electronics, including TVs and iPhones.

If you're looking for local character, head to the souqs (markets) in Bur Dubai and Deira or the port area in Abu Dhabi. In these colourful, cacophonous warrens you can pick up everything from a gram of saffron to an ounce of gold, usually at good prices. It helps to sharpen your haggling skills. You may also be tempted by touts trying to sell knock-off designer perfumes and handbags – it's up to you to ignore them or accept their offer. Note that there is no bargaining in such modern souqs as Souk Madinat Jumeirah in Dubai or Souq Qaryat al Beri in Abu Dhabi. Evocatively designed to look like something out of *Arabian Nights*, they're filled with tourist-geared souvenirs of varying quality.

What to Buy

BEDOUIN JEWELLERY

Bedouin jewellery is a brilliant buy and, given the steady popularity of boho-ethnic chic, makes a great gift. Look for elaborate silver necklaces and pendants, chunky earrings and rings, and wedding belts, many of which incorporate coral, turquoise and semiprecious stones. Very little of the older Bedouin jewellery comes from the Emirates; most of it originates in Oman, Yemen and Afghanistan (cheaper stuff usually hails from India).

PASHMINAS

These feather-light shawls handmade by weavers in Kashmir from genuine pashmina (goat hair) or shahtoosh (the down hair of a Tibetan antelope) are a great buy. They come in hundreds of colours and styles, some beaded and embroidered, others with pompom edging – you'll have no trouble finding one you like. Although the cheaper ones are machine-made, they're also pretty.

CARPETS

Dubai and Abu Dhabi are a carpet lover's paradise. Fine Persian carpets, colourful Turkish and Kurdish kilims and rough-knotted Bedouin rugs are all widely available. Dubai has a reputation in the region for having the highest-quality carpets at the best prices. Bargaining is the norm. If you can't secure the price you want, head to another store. When you buy a carpet, ask for a certificate of authentication guaranteed by the Dubai Chamber of Commerce & Industry, so you can be sure that the carpet actually comes from where the vendor says it does.

ARABIAN HANDICRAFTS & SOUVENIRS

Arabian handicrafts are as popular with visitors as carpets, gold and perfume. The Oriental decor of top-end hotels and restaurants seems to inspire travellers to pack away little pieces of exotica to recreate their own little genie bottles back home. Head to the souqs for Moroccan coloured lanterns,

Dubai: Shopping by Neighbourhood

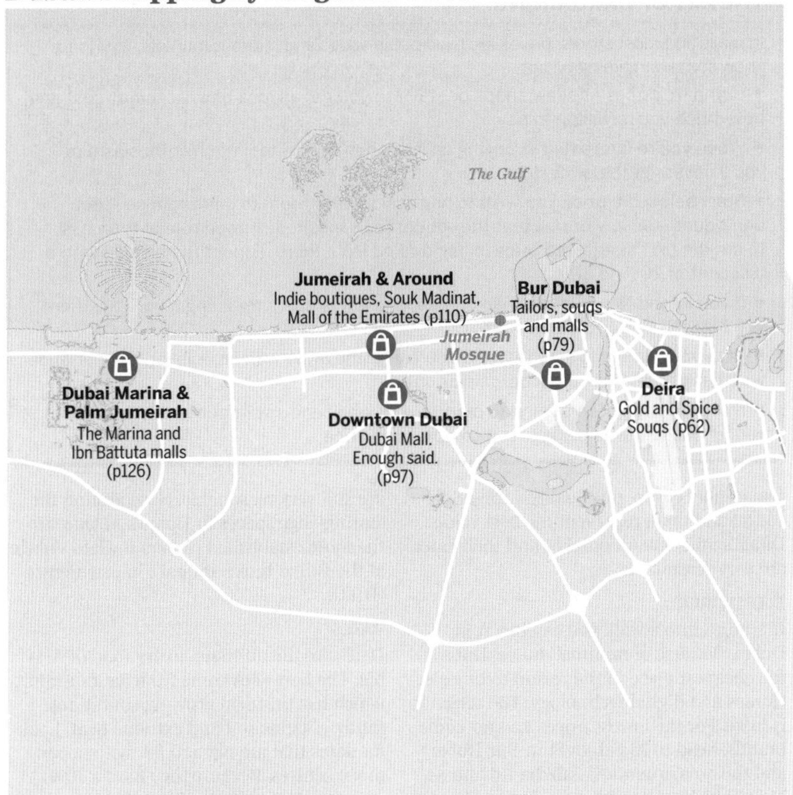

Syrian rosewood furniture inlaid with mother-of-pearl, Arabian brass coffee pots, Turkish miniature paintings, and embroidered Indian wall hangings and cushion covers dotted with tiny mirrors.

PERFUME & INCENSE

Attars (Arabian perfumes) are spicy and strong. Historically, this was a necessity: with precious little water, washing was a sometimes-thing, so women smothered themselves in *attars* and incense. As you walk past Emirati women (and men), catch a whiff of their exotic perfume. You can find Arabian-perfume shops in all Dubai's malls, but for more authentic flair visit the Perfume Souq, a small stretch lined with perfume stores along Sikkat al Khail and Al Soor Sts in Deira, just east of the Gold Souq.

Shopping for perfume can wear out your sense of smell. If you're in the market for Arabian scents, do what top perfumers do to neutralise their olfactory palate: close your mouth and make three forceful exhalations through your nose. Blast the air hard, in short bursts, using your diaphragm. Blowing your nose first is probably a wise idea… Some people incorrectly say to smell coffee grounds, but all this practice does is numb your sense of smell.

EXOTIC DELICACIES

Fragrant Iranian saffron costs far less here than it does back home. Buy it in the souqs or in supermarkets. Honey from Saudi Arabia, Yemen and Oman is scrumptious. Look for it in speciality shops in Satwa, in the Spice Souq and in supermarkets. Its colour ranges from light gold to almost black.

FABRIC

Vendors at Bur Dubai Souq and along nearby Al Fahidi St carry vibrant, colourful textiles from India and South Asia. They're

THE ART OF BARGAINING

In malls and most stores, prices are fixed but in souqs and outdoor markets, it pays to know some bargaining basics.

- Compare prices at a few shops or stalls so you get an idea of what things cost and how much you're willing to pay.
- When you're interested in buying an item, don't show too much enthusiasm or you'll never get the price down.
- Start below the price you wish to pay so you have room to compromise – but don't quote too low or risk that the vendor feels insulted. A good rule of thumb is to cut the first suggested price in half and go from there. Expect to finish up with a discount of 20% to 30%.
- If you intend to buy more than one item, use this as a bargaining chip – the more you buy, the better the discount.
- Take your time and stay relaxed. You can come away with an enjoyable experience whether you end up with a bargain or not.
- If negotiations aren't going to plan, simply smile and say goodbye – often the vendor will follow and suggest a compromise price.

remarkably cheap, but quality varies. Silk, cotton and linen represent the best value. Dubai's tailors work quickly, and their rates are very reasonable.

ELECTRONICS

If it plugs into a wall, you can buy it in Dubai. Because of minimal duties, Dubai is the cheapest place in the region to buy electronics and digital technology. The selection is huge. For the lowest prices and no-name brands, head to Al Fahidi St in Bur Dubai and the area around Al Sabkha Rd and Al Maktoum Hospital Rd, near Baniyas Sq, known as the Electronics Souq. If you want an international warranty, shell out the extra money and head to a mall or Jumbo Electronics.

GOLD & GEMS

Calling itself the 'City of Gold', Dubai's glistening reputation grows from low prices and the sheer breadth of stock. There are a whopping 700 jewellery stores around town, with nearly 300 at the Gold Souq and about 90 at the Gold & Diamond Park.

ART

With new galleries springing up all the time and the scene becoming increasingly diverse, it's easier than ever to snap up a piece of original art created by a local or regional artist, especially since prices are still very reasonable. Nose around the cutting-edge spaces in Dubai's Al Quoz or the more established players in Gate Village at the Dubai International Finance Centre (DIFC).

DATES

Dates are the ultimate luxury food of Arabia. The best ones come from Saudi Arabia, which has the ideal growing conditions: sandy, alkaline soil and extreme heat. Look for dates that are big and fat, with gooey-moist centres. Because they have a 70% sugar content, dates technically have a very long shelf life, but you'll find they taste best around the autumn harvest. A major purveyor of quality dates is Bateel whose boutiques look like jewellery stores.

SOUVENIRS

The quintessential kitsch souvenir used to be a mosque clock with a call-to-prayer alarm. Now the souqs and souvenir shops overflow with wacky, kitsch gifts – glass Burj Al Arab paperweights, Russian nesting dolls in Emirati national dress, key rings strung with miniature towers, camel-crossing-sign fridge magnets, and coffee mugs and baseball caps with Sheikh Zayed or Sheikh Mohammed waving to the crowd.

Lonely Planet's Top Choices

Ajmal (p81) Exotic Arabian essential oils and perfumes sold in exquisitely beautiful bottles.

S*uce (p111) Sassy avant-garde fashions from a wide range of young international designers.

United Designers (p64) Flip through racks of original fashion by exciting young local designers.

Gold Souq (p52) Pageant of glitter and craftsmanship that's fun to see even without buying.

Candylicious (p98) Willy Wonka would feel right at home in this super-sized sweets store with candy kitchen.

Best Bookshops

Kinokuniya (p98) The enormous assortment at this Japanese mother lode of books almost catapults you back to the pre-digital age.

House of Prose (p112) Quirky but well-assorted purveyor of new and used English-language books.

BookMunch (p106) Children's books in multiple languages plus a cafe and play section make this a popular family hang-out.

Bookshop at DIFC (p98) Community hang-out with strong coffee and hand-picked books about the Middle East.

Best Markets

Ripe Food & Craft Market (p73) Happening market with quality local produce alongside artsy-crafty stuff and global snack stands.

Marina Market (p126) Lots of homemade arty knick-knacks to beautify self and home.

Dubai Flea Market (p79) True bargains abound at this monthly market on the beautiful grounds of Za'abeel Park.

Best for Fashion

The Cartel (p99) Avant-garde fashions by local and international designers in the warehouse district.

West LA Boutique (p112) The holy grail for fashionistas wanting to dress like young Hollywood royalty.

O-Concept (p111) This edgy Jumeirah boutique has young things looking good at reasonable price tags.

O' de Rose (p113) Provides a platform for regional indie designers with a love for bold colour.

Fabindia (p81) His-and-hers fashion created by Indian villagers perks up any outfit.

Best Shopping Malls

Dubai Mall (p97) A power shopper's Shangri-La, the Dubai Mall is the largest shopping mall in the world.

Mall of the Emirates (p110) Get lost amid the ample temptations of this mega-mall famous for its indoor ski slope.

Ibn Battuta Mall (p126) Shopping goes exotic amid gorgeous decor in six country-themed courts, including Persia, India and Spain.

Dubai Festival City Mall (p63) Shop till you drop then relax in one of many cafes set around a pretty marina.

Abu Dhabi Mall (p149) A tempting choice of boutiques, designer stores and international chains.

Best for Gifts

Camel Company (p112) Go camel-crazy at this multi-outlet boutique starring cuddly camels on everything from mugs to notepads.

Bateel (p80) Delicious dates presented like precious jewels in an elegant boutique setting.

Lata's (p112) Quality souvenirs from around North Africa and the Middle East.

Gallery One (p127) Makes regional art accessible and affordable to all with framed prints, notebooks, calendars and other art products.

Tehran Persian Carpets & Antiques (p98) A mind-boggling bonanza of quality souvenirs from Iran, beyond carpets and antiques.

Yasmine (p112) Fabulous assortment of quality pashminas, including precious hand-embroidered ones.

Best Modern Souqs

Souk Al Bahar (p87) Across from the Dubai Mall, this richly decorated Arabesque souq teems with restaurants and souvenir stores.

Souk Madinat Jumeirah (p112) Following a harmonious rhythm of courtyards, alleyways and outdoor areas, this souq also has a theatre and lots of cafes and restaurants fronting the Madinat canals.

Souq Khan Murjan (p79) Part of Wafi Mall, this exotically styled labyrinthine souq takes its design cue from the bazaar in Baghdad.

Central Market (p135) Abu Dhabi's exquisite modern souq was designed by Norman Foster and combines luxury boutiques with cafes and craft-based stores.

Sports & Activities

No matter what kind of activity gets you away from the pool, beach or shopping mall, you'll be able to pursue it in Dubai and Abu Dhabi, be it on or in the water, on the ice, in the desert, on the ski slopes or in the spa. Spectator sports too are huge, reflecting the interests of the diverse population and including numerous prestigious international events.

Water Sports

DIVING & SNORKELLING

Diving around Dubai means mostly nosing around shipwrecks on the sandy seabed of the Gulf at a depth of between 10m and 35m. The better sites are generally a long way offshore and mostly for experienced divers. Creatures you might encounter include clownfish, sea snakes, Arabian angelfish, rays and barracuda. Snorkellers and novices should head to the section of Jumeirah Beach behind the Sunset Mall which is sheltered by a rocky breakwater. For more exciting dives, you need to head to the East Coast (Khor Fakkan and Dibba) or north to the rugged Musandam Peninsula, which is actually part of Oman. A well-established local company leading guided dives, tours and certification courses is Al Boom Diving (p114).

SURF SPORTS

Dubai ain't Hawaii (waves average 0.67m) but that's not stopping a growing community of surfers from hitting the waves at Sunset Beach next to the Jumeirah Beach Hotel. Prime months are from December to February, although October, March and April may also bring decent swells. If there are no waves, you can still hit the water on a stand-up paddle board, a sport that's increasingly enjoying popularity in Dubai. Rent equipment or get lessons in either sport at Surf House Dubai (p115).

Kitesurfers congregate at northwest-facing Kite Beach which also has two outfits – Dubai Kite School (p115) and Dukite – that offer lessons and courses.

MOTORISED WATER SPORTS

Practically all of the large beach resorts maintain state-of-the-art water-sports centres that offer both guests and non-guests a range of ways to get out on the water. The menu may include waterskiing, jet-skiing, wakeboarding, parasailing, and power boating. Priority is given to hotel guests; visitors can expect to pay higher rates or a beach access fee.

BOAT CHARTER

For a glorious perspective of Dubai from the water, rent your own skippered boat: try the Dubai Creek Golf & Yacht Club (p64). Options include a one-hour Creek cruise for Dh325, but for the full experience book at least a four-hour trip that passes the World islands, Palm Jumeirah and the Burj Al Arab (Dh1500). Rates are good for up to six passengers. Fishing trips cost Dh2000 for four hours and Dh375 per additional hour.

WATERPARKS

Dubai has two waterparks, Wild Wadi Waterpark (p113) in Jumeirah and Aquaventure (p127) at Atlantis The Palm, but the newest and grandest is Yas Waterworld (p166) in Abu Dhabi.

Golf

Golf is huge in the Gulf, and nowhere more so than in the United Arab Emirates (UAE), which boasts 21 golf courses, including several championship courses designed by big names such as Greg Norman, the man behind Jumeirah Golf Estates (p128). Overall, clubs don't require memberships but green fees can soar to Dh1100 for 18 holes during the peak winter season (November to March), although they drop the rest of the year, especially in summer. Proper attire is essential. If you're serious about golf, reserve your tee times as soon as you book your hotel and flight.

Running

The winter months are cool enough for running nearly anytime during the day; in summer you've got to get up with the sun to jog without fear of heatstroke. There are excellent jogging tracks in Za'abeel Park (p71), along the Jumeirah Corniche, The Beach on JBR and in Al Barsha Park. Prefer running with company? Check out Dubai Road Runners (p115) or **Dubai Creek Striders** (Map p258; ☎04-321 1999; www.dubaicreekstriders.com). If you're into the more social aspects of running (read: drinking afterwards), look into DH3, aka the **Desert Hash House Harriers** (www.deserthash.org). The Dubai Marathon takes over city streets in January.

Desert Driving

Off-road driving in the desert (also disturbingly known as 'dune bashing') is hugely popular. At weekends (Friday and Saturday), the city's traffic-tired workers zip down the Dubai–Hatta road and unleash their pent-up energy on the sand dunes, such as the ruby-red heap of sand nicknamed 'Big Red'. All the major car-hire companies provide 4WD vehicles. Expect to pay around Dh500 for 24 hours for a Toyota Fortuner or a Honda CRV, plus insurance. If you have no experience in driving off-road, we strongly recommend first taking a desert driving course such as those offered by Desert Rangers (p218).

Day Spas & Massage

Though you can get a good rub-down at most sports clubs, for the proper treatment book a dedicated spa. Ask if a spa treatment includes use of the pool and grounds. If it does, make a day of it – arrive early and relax poolside. Most spas offer manicures and pedicures, but if you want a dedicated nail salon, try Nail Spa; there are several branches, including one at the Dubai Mall and another at Abu Dhabi's Eastern Mangroves Promenade.

Skiing

The largest indoor ski slope in the world, Ski Dubai (p113), located at the Mall of the Emirates, is an incongruous but delightful stop for winter-sports enthusiasts. You can also take lessons and learn how to snowboard.

Spectator Sports

HORSE RACING

Horse racing has a long and vaunted tradition in the Emirates. Racing season kicks off in November and culminates in March with the Dubai World Cup, the world's richest horse race. It's held at the superb Meydan Racecourse, a futuristic stadium with a grandstand bigger than most airport terminals. In Abu Dhabi, races take place at the Abu Dhabi Equestrian Club. For the full low-down, see Dubai at the Races (p99).

CAMEL RACING

Camel racing is deeply rooted in the Emirati soul and attending a race is hugely popular with locals and visitors alike. It's quite an exhilarating sight when hundreds of one-humped dromedaries fly out of their pens and onto the dirt track, jostling for position in a lumbering gallop with legs splayed out in all directions, scrambling towards the finish line at top speeds of 40km/h. Fastened to their backs are 'robot jockeys' with remote-controlled whips operated by the owners while driving their white SUVs on a separate track alongside the animals. The camels used to be piloted by child jockeys but this practice was outlawed in the UAE in 2005 for humanitarian concerns.

Racing season runs between October and early April. The closest track to Dubai is Al Marmoun, about 40km south of town en route to Al Ain. The other major track is Al Wathba, about 45km east of Abu Dhabi. For the schedule, check www.dubaicalendar.ae (search for 'camel'). Admission is free.

MOTOR RACING

Motor sports are exceedingly popular in the UAE with the Abu Dhabi Grand Prix, a Formula One race held in November at the Yas Marina Circuit on Yas Island, being the most prestigious event. One of the oldest races is the Abu Dhabi Desert Challenge held in March that has brought top car and motorcycle rally drivers to the UAE since 1991. Dubai is also a stop on the 24 Hour Race series, an endurance race held in January at the Dubai Autodrome. Also look for events hosted by the **Emirates Motor Sports Federation** (EMSF; www.emsf.ae), which inaugurated the Emirates Desert Championship in 2003.

FOOTBALL (SOCCER)

Attending a local football match can be great fun as up to 10,000 spectators crowd into the stadiums to passionately cheer on their favourite team while a singer and a band of drummers lead song and dance routines to further inspire the players. Fourteen clubs compete in the country's league – called the **Arabian Gulf League** (www.agleague.ae) – which was founded in 1973 and went pro in 2008. These include four teams from Dubai (Al Ahli, Al Nasr, Al Shahab and Al Wasl) and three from Abu Dhabi (Al Dhafra, Al Jazira and Al Whada). The season runs from mid-September to mid-May. Check the league's website for the schedule and venues

JOCHEN TACK/GETTY IMAGES ©

Dubai Marathon

TOP ANNUAL SPORTING EVENTS

Dubai and Abu Dhabi host some top sporting events throughout the year and it's crucial to book tickets far in advance, especially for such grand-slam events as Abu Dhabi's Grand Prix. For tickets, check the event websites or try www.platinumlist.net.

Dubai Marathon (www.dubaimarathon.org) Sweat it out in January with thousands of other runners or just cheer them on during this popular street race with a prize fund of a million dollars. Less-energetic types can enter a 10km run or a 3km 'fun run'.

Dubai Desert Classic (www.dubaidesertclassic.com) The golfing elite comes to town for this February tournament held at the Emirates Golf Club (the US$2.5-million purse doesn't hurt). There have been some thrilling finishes over the past couple of years – the 18th hole has become legendary on the PGA circuit.

Dubai Duty Free Tennis Championships (www.dubaidutyfreetennischampionships.com) Big-name players like Serena Williams and Novak Djokovic volley away at this two-week pro event in February at the Aviation Club. The women play the first week, men the second. It's a big opportunity to see some great hitting in a relatively small stadium.

Dubai World Cup (www.dubaiworldcup.com) The horse-racing season culminates in March with the world's richest event held at the Meydan Racecourse. Prize money rings up at a record-holding US$10 million. While there's no betting, this is the city's biggest social event.

Dubai Rugby Sevens (www.dubairugby7s.com) Held in November or December, this is the first round of the eight-leg International Rugby Board Sevens World Series. The three-day event features 16 international squads, various amateur teams and live entertainment. Up to 150,000 spectators make the pilgrimage to The Sevens stadium, about 30 minutes south of Dubai on the road to Al Ain.

DP World Tour Championship (www.europeantour.com) This golfing championship held in November is the crowning tournament of the Race to Dubai that pits the PGA European Tour's top players against each other in 49 tournaments in 26 destinations over the course of one year. Held since 2008, it comes with a purse of US$7.5 million. It's played on two Greg Norman–designed courses at Jumeirah Golf Estates.

Abu Dhabi Grand Prix (www.yasmarinacircuit.ae) Since 2009, the Formula One racing elite, including Sebastian Vettel and Lewis Hamilton, descend upon the wicked 5.5km-long Yas Marina Circuit on Yas Island in early November.

Sports & Activities by Dubai Neighbourhood

- **Deira** Good boating, golfing, tennis and spas.
- **Bur Dubai** Running in Za'abeel Park or Creek Park.
- **Downtown Dubai** Ice skating at the Dubai Mall, fancy spas in the hotels and horse racing at Meydan.
- **Jumeirah & Around** Swimming, boating, diving, water sports, Wild Wadi Waterpark, running along the beach.
- **Dubai Marina & Palm Jumeirah** Swimming, water sports, golfing, boating, diving, Aquaventure waterpark.

GARY MCGOVERN/GETTY IMAGES ©

Explore Dubai & Abu Dhabi

DUBAI & ABU DHABI'S TOP SIGHTS

Neighbourhoods at a Glance

❶ Deira p50

Deira feels like a cross between Cairo and Karachi. Dusty, crowded and chaotic, it's a world away from the slick and sanitised city piercing the clouds along Sheikh Zayed Road and in Dubai Marina. Along the Creek, colourful wooden dhows engage in the time-tested trading of goods destined for Iran, Sudan and other locales. Nearby, the bustling souqs are atmospheric ancestors to today's malls, where you can sip sugary tea and haggle for bargains with traders whose families have tended the same shop for generations.

❷ Bur Dubai p65

Bustling Bur Dubai is home to the restored historical districts of Al Fahidi and Shindagha, wonderful for late afternoon and evening strolls. Bur Dubai Souq is just as lively as the Deira souqs, with the aesthetic plus of

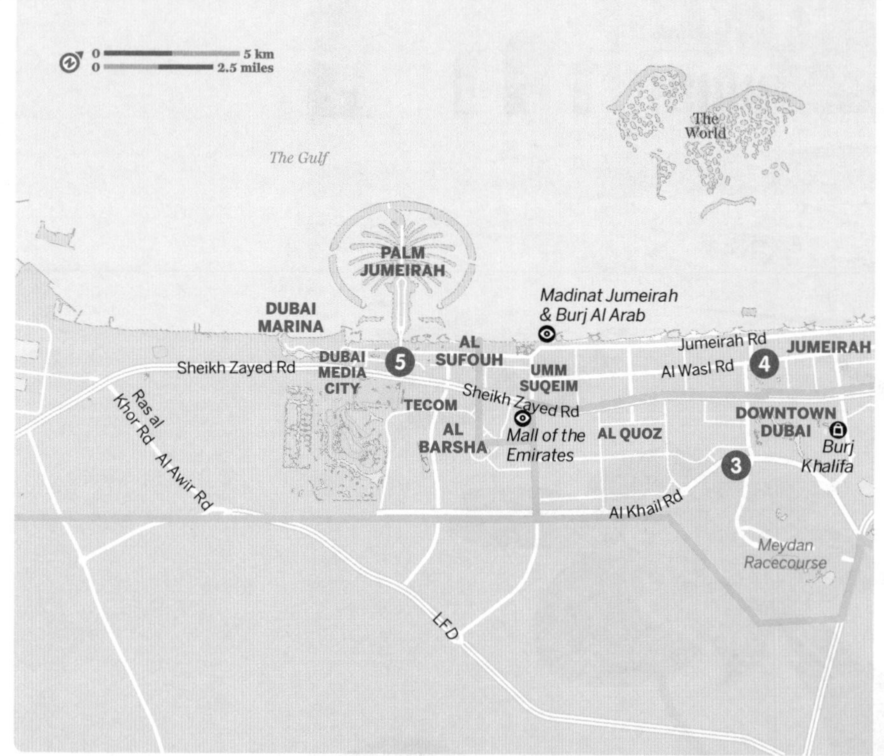

wooden arcades and a waterfront location. Meena Bazaar in the surrounding streets is Dubai's Little India, where textile and sari stores and Indian eateries can easily absorb a couple of fascinating hours. Bur Dubai may not be as sleek and sophisticated as the newer townships, but it has a real community spirit that can be hard to find elsewhere.

3 Downtown Dubai p83

Dubai's main artery, Sheikh Zayed Road travels past the architecturally distinguished skyscrapers of the Financial District and the 828m-high Burj Khalifa, the world's tallest structure and anchor of glamorous Downtown Dubai, the new urban district that encompasses high-end hotels, residences, office buildings and the gargantuan Dubai Mall with its dancing Dubai Fountain. Further south, sections of the industrial district of Al Quoz are evolving into Dubai's main alternative arts and creative hub.

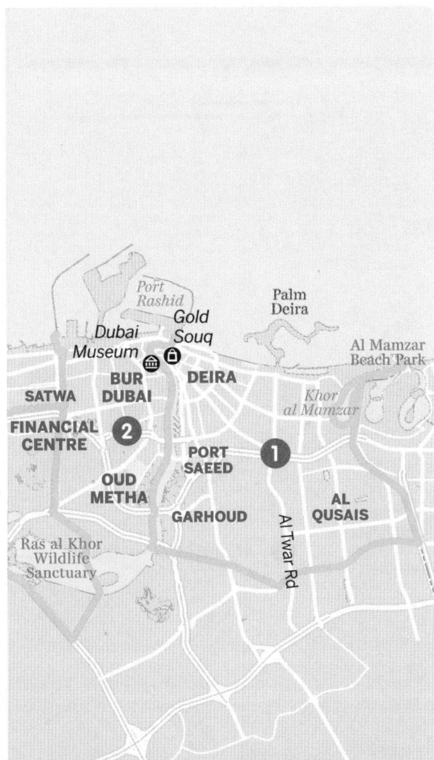

4 Jumeirah & Around p101

Before there was the Palm Jumeirah and Dubai Marina, Jumeirah was the place where everybody went to realise their Dubai dreams. It's the emirate's answer to Bondi or Malibu, with excellent public beaches, boutique shopping, copious spas and health clubs, and a mix of Mercedes and expensive 4WDs in villa driveways. The actual boundaries can seem confusing as the name crops up all over the place, attached to hotels that are actually situated in Dubai Marina or the famous Palm 'Jumeirah' Island. In reality, on its northern edge Jumeirah rubs up against vibrant Satwa, while to the south the neighbourhood encompasses Madinat Jumeirah and the iconic Burj Al Arab.

5 Dubai Marina & Palm Jumeirah p116

Dubai's newest district consists of several different areas. In Dubai Marina you find bobbing yachts, the group of buttercream-yellow towers known as the Jumeirah Beach Residence (JBR) and two attractive promenades with cafes and shopping: the Marina Walk and the Walk at JBR. North of here, Al Sufouh encompasses some of the most upmarket hotels in town, as well as the free zones of Dubai Internet City, an information technology park, and Dubai Media City, home to CNN, BBC World, Bloomberg and other outlets. Jutting into the Gulf is the Palm Jumeirah, the smallest of three planned artificial islands off the coast of Dubai, and the only one to see fruition (and likely to stay that way).

Deira

Neighbourhood Top Five

❶ Plunging headlong into the **souqs** (p53) for a sensory dose of *Arabian Nights* flair: pungent aromas at the Spice Souq, glittering gold at the Gold Souq, heady Arabian *attars* at the Perfume Souq, wriggling ocean critters at the Fish Souq and local dress and accessories at the New Naif Market.

❷ Feeling mesmerised by the Dubai skyline across the glistening Creek from the lounge at **QDs** (p61).

❸ Strolling down leafy **Al Muteena St** (p55) and stopping for *masgouf* (grilled fish) in an Iraqi restaurant.

❹ Checking out Dubai's first school, **Al Ahmadiya** (p53), housed in an exquisite traditional building.

❺ Crossing **Dubai Creek** (p54) in an *abra* (traditional water taxi), enjoying an atmospheric journey unchanged for decades.

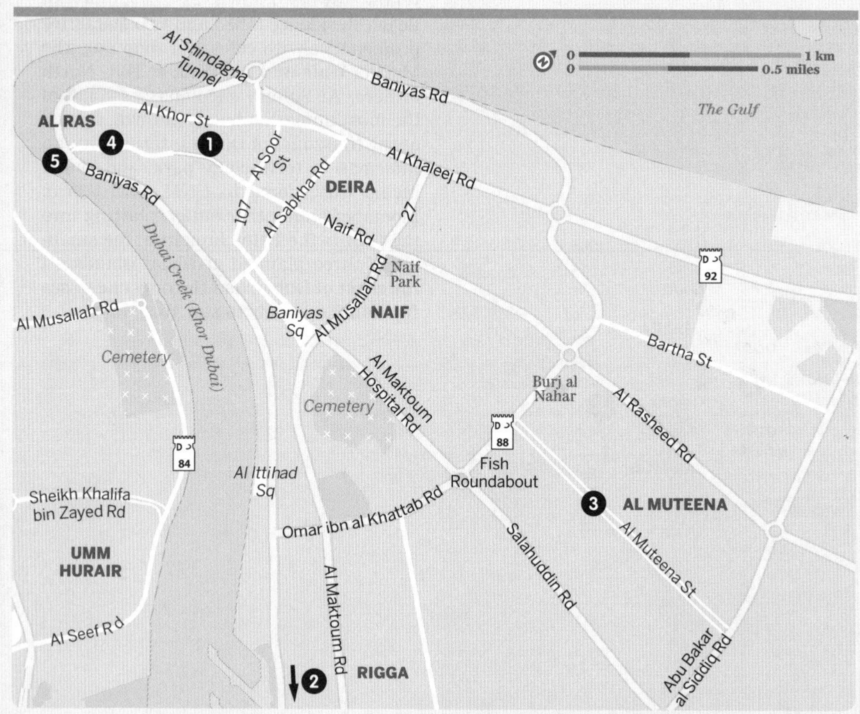

For more detail of this area, see Map p244 and p246

Explore Deira

Hugging the northern side of the Creek, Deira is one of Dubai's oldest and most charismatic neighbourhoods, a world apart from the sky-piercing towers of modern Dubai. The most historic area is Al Ras, near the mouth of the Creek, where sightseeing highlights include a restored pearl trader's home and the city's first school. Nearby, brightly painted dhows (traditional sailing vessels) still dock along the waterfront as they have since the 1830s. But Deira's biggest asset is its cluster of atmospheric souqs (spice, gold, perfume, fish, produce); a tangle of narrow lanes heaving with a cacophony of sounds and smells that bursts to life in the late afternoon.

The souq area is also Dubai's most dazzlingly multicultural neighbourhood, a bustling cauldron peacefully shared by immigrants from around the globe. Many operate little restaurants perfect for soaking up the local colour and for sampling authentic fare from such far-flung locales as India, Syria, Lebanon, Ethiopia, Iraq and Afghanistan. For a more upscale experience, book a dinner cruise aboard a dhow, festively decorated with twinkling lights, or head to a Creekside alfresco lounge in one of the high-end hotels. Deira also brims with Russian, Filipino, Lebanese, Indian and Pakistani nightclubs, usually found in budget or midrange hotels. They typically feature enthusiastic house bands, cheap beers and, yes, some illicit and seedy goings-on.

Southeast of the souqs along the Creek, Deira gets increasingly modern. There are big shopping malls like the Deira City Centre and Dubai Festival City Mall, as well as such architectural landmarks as the Etisalat Tower, easily recognised by the giant 'golf ball' at its top.

Local Life

- **Haggle** Enjoy bargaining in the souqs. It's a favourite local pastime and, as long as you're comfortable with a little lighthearted confrontation, it's good fun.
- **Traditional coffee** Kick-start your day by ducking into a tucked-away cafe for a shot of Arabic coffee.
- **Exotic meals** Take a culinary journey to Yemen, Lebanon or wherever your nose leads you in the souqs and around Al Rigga and Salah Al Din metro stations.

Getting There & Away

- **Metro** Deira is served by both the Red and Green Lines; they intersect at Union station. The Red Line travels to the airport.
- **Boat** *Abras* link the souqs in Deira and in Bur Dubai. A water bus travels further southeast to Baniyas from the Dubai Old Souq station.

Lonely Planet's Top Tip

A cheap and easy way to get a feel for the atmospheric Dubai Creek is by crossing it aboard an *abra*, a traditional water taxi, for a mere Dh1. If you want a more in-depth experience, consider hiring a private *abra* to sail past various Creek communities with the wind in your hair and seagulls cheering you on. Boats can be hired at all *abra* stations; the going rate is Dh100 per hour.

Best Places to Eat

- Al Tawasol (p55)
- Traiteur (p60)
- Shabestan (p57)
- Aroos Damascus (p55)
- Ashiana by Vineet (p60)

For reviews, see p54.

Best Places to Drink

- QDs (p61)
- Cielo Sky Lounge (p61)
- Irish Village (p61)

For reviews, see p61.

Best Places to Shop

- Deira City Centre (p62)
- Gold Souq (p52)
- Dubai Festival City Mall (p63)

For reviews, see p62.

JOHN BORTHWICK/GETTY IMAGES ©

TOP SIGHT
GOLD SOUQ

'Dubai: City of Gold' screams the banner atop the rainbow-coloured LED display at the wooden entrance gate to Dubai's Gold Souq. Moments later you'll feel as though you've just entered a latter-day Aladdin's cave. Lining a wooden-latticed central arcade and its spidery side lanes are hundreds of jewellery shops spilling over with gold, diamonds, pearls, silver and platinum. Simple rings to intricate golden Indian wedding necklaces, it's a dazzling display and a must-see even if you're not part of the bling brigade.

Gold has been big business in Dubai since the 1940s. Today, the emirate is one of the world's largest gold markets, accounting for roughly 25% of the global trade. The quality of the gold is government-regulated, so you can be fairly confident that the piece of jewellery you've got your eye on is genuine (unlike the Rolex watches and Prada bags touts are trying to tempt you with). The price is determined by weight based on the official daily international rate as well as by the artistry and the intricacy of the item. Sharpening your bargaining skills should make merchants drop the initial asking price by 20% to 30%.

If you're not buying, stop by the Kanz jewellery store at the northern souq entrance to snap a selfie with the world's largest and heaviest gold ring, as certified by none other than Guinness World Records. Called the Najmat Taiba (Star of Taiba), the 21-carat beauty weighs in at nearly 64kg and is worth a hefty US$3 million.

Simply watching the goings-on at the souq is another treat, especially in the evening. Settle down on a bench and take in the colourful street theatre of hard-working Afghan men dragging heavy carts of goods, African women in bright kaftans balancing their purchases on their head and chattering local women out on a shopping spree.

DON'T MISS

- World's largest gold ring
- Strolling down the central arcade

PRACTICALITIES

- Map p244
- Sikkat al Khail St
- 10am-1pm & 3-10pm
- M Palm Deira

SIGHTS

The main sights of Deira are all within easy walking distance of each other around the atmospheric mouth of Dubai Creek.

GOLD SOUQ
MARKET

See p52.

SPICE SOUQ
MARKET

Map p244 (btwn Baniyas Rd, Al Ras Rd & Al Abra St; roughly 9am-10pm Sat-Thu, 4-10pm Fri; M Al Ras) Steps from the Deira Old Souq *abra* station, the sound of Arabic chatter bounces around the lanes of this small covered market as vendors work hard to unload aromatic frankincense, dried lemons, medicinal herbs and exotic seasonings all photogenically stored in burlap sacks alongside dried fruit, nuts, fragrances and knick-knacks.

Since this is a working souq, not a tourist attraction, the tiny shops also sell groceries, plastics and other household goods to locals and sailors from the dhows. Good buys include incense burners, saffron, rose water, henna kits and *sheesha* (water pipes).

HERITAGE HOUSE
MUSEUM

Map p244 (04-226 0286; Al Ahmadiya St; 8am-7.30pm Sat-Thu, 2.30-7.30pm Fri; M Al Ras) FREE This 1890 courtyard house offers a rare opportunity to peek inside the one-time residence of a wealthy pearl merchant. Built from coral and gypsum, it wraps around a central courtyard flanked by verandahs to keep direct sunlight out. Most rooms have audiovisual displays and use dioramas to recreate traditional aspects of daily life.

The house once belonged to Sheikh Ahmed bin Dalmouk, the founder of the adjacent Al Ahmadiya School, Dubai's oldest learning pens. You're free to explore on your own and pop into such rooms as the *majlis* (meeting room), the kitchen, the bride room (with distinctly unhappy-looking bride and groom mannequins), a bathroom and a traditional larder or 'store'. The upstairs room was originally used for family gatherings but displays traditional children's games.

AL AHMADIYA SCHOOL
MUSEUM

Map p244 (04-226 0286; Al Ahmadiya St; 8am-7.30pm Sat-Thu, 2.30-7.30pm Fri; M Al Ras) FREE Dubai's first public primary school was founded by the pearl merchant Sheikh Ahmed bin Dalmouk and welcomed its first pupils (all boys) in 1912. Decades later, Dubai's current ruler, Sheikh Mohammed, was among those who squeezed behind the wooden desks to learn the Holy Quran, grammar, Arabic calligraphy, mathematics, literature and astronomy. The classroom is still there today but overall exhibits are pretty basic, explanations meagre and the audiovisual components often not working.

However, the building itself is lovely. Note the exquisite detail, especially the intricate carving within the courtyard arches, the heavy ornamented doors and the decorative gypsum panels outside the entrance. It remained in use as a school until the student body outgrew the premises in 1963.

DHOW WHARFAGE
HARBOUR

Map p244 (along Baniyas Rd; M Al Ras) For a glimpse of Dubai's long trading history, stroll down the Creek for photogenic close-ups of brightly coloured dhows, precariously loaded to the hilt with everything from air-conditioners to chewing gum to car tyres. This type of long flat wooden vessel used in the Indian Ocean and the Gulf has docked here since the 1830s when the local Maktoum rulers established a free-trade port, luring merchants away from Persia.

KEEPING COOL INDOORS – NATURALLY

The Al Ras neighbourhood in Deira and the Shindagha and Al Fahidi Historic Districts in Bur Dubai are great places to see and enter traditional houses, such as Heritage House or Sheikh Saeed Al Maktoum House. Built from gypsum and coral, they typically wrap around a central courtyard flanked by verandahs to keep direct sunlight out of the rooms. Another distinctive feature are the wind towers (*barjeel* in Arabic), a form of non-electrical air-conditioning unique to the region. Towers typically rise 5m or 6m above the building and are made of wood, stone or canvas. Open on all four sides, they can catch even the tiniest of breezes which are then channeled down a central shaft and into the room below. In the process the air speeds up and is cooled. The cooler air already in the tower shaft pulls in and subsequently cools the hotter air outside through a simple process of convection.

Today's dhows trade with Iran, Iraq, Pakistan, Oman, India, Yemen, Somalia and Sudan. Most of the wares are re-exported after arriving by air or container ship from countries like China, South Korea and Singapore.

Try to chat to the sailors if you can – if you find one who speaks English, you may learn that it takes a day to get to Iran by sea and seven days to Somalia, or that dhow captains earn as little as Dh400 a month. If your sailor friend is in a chatty mood, he may even regale you with real-life pirate stories. The pirates that stalk the waters off Yemen and Somalia sometimes make life very tough for Dubai's hard-working dhow sailors.

PERFUME SOUQ MARKET

Map p244 (Sikkat al Khail & Al Soor Sts; M Palm Deira) Several blocks of perfume shops stretching east of the Gold Souq hardly warrants the title 'souq', yet these bustling stores sell a staggering range of Arabic *attars* (perfumes), *oud* (fragrant wood) and incense burners.

COVERED SOUQ MARKET

Map p244 (btwn Al Sabkha Rd, 107th St & Naif Rd; M Palm Deira) Despite the name, this souq is not really covered at all and more a warren of small shops in narrow lanes crisscrossing a few square blocks. Even if you're not keen on cheap textiles, faux Gucci, *kandouras* (long traditional robes), washing powder and cheap trainers, you're sure to be wowed by the high-energy street scene.

NAIF SOUQ MARKET

Map p244 (btwn Naif South, 9a & Deira Sts; 8.30am-11.30pm; M Baniyas Sq) Although the historic Naif Souq burned down in 2008 and was replaced by this mall-style version, it's still an atmospheric place to shop for bargain-priced fabrics, henna products, hair extensions, costume jewellery and local dresses, including *abeyyas* and colourful kaftan-style 'maxi' (ie full-length) dresses.

EATING

Deira has a great street scene: snag a pavement table beneath flickering neon and soak up the local colour. This is where many expat workers live, and there's a wealth of excellent budget-priced restaurants here – Chinese, Arabic, African and especially Indian. Upmarket restaurants can be found in the five-star hotels and in Wafi City.

DUBAI CREEK

What the Tiber is to Rome and the Thames is to London, the Creek is to Dubai: a defining stretch of water at the heart of the city and a key building block in its economic development. Known as Al Khor in Arabic, the Creek was the base of the local fishing and pearling industries in the early 20th century and was dredged in 1961 to allow larger cargo vessels to dock. The first bridge, Al Maktoum Bridge, opened two years later.

The broad waterway used to end 15km inland at the Ras Al Khor Wildlife Sanctuary, but was extended 2.2km to the new Business Bay district in 2007. Another 3km extension – dubbed Dubai Canal – kicked off in December 2013 and will link the Creek and the Gulf.

To this day, many people have a mental barrier when it comes to crossing the Creek over to Deira. It's a bit akin to some Londoners' aversion to going 'south of the river' or Manhattanites' reticence to head across to Queens. While it's true that traffic can be horrible during rush hour, congestion eased in 2007 with the opening of the 13-lane Business Bay Bridge near Dubai Festival City, and a six-lane Floating Bridge (open 6am to 10pm) near Creek Park. A fourth bridge, Al Garhoud Bridge, was widened to 13 lanes. There's also the Shindagha Tunnel near the mouth of the Creek, which is open for both vehicles and pedestrians.

Using public transport, you have three options for crossing the Creek. The fastest and easiest is by Dubai metro. Both the Red Line and Green Line link the banks via underwater tunnels. The most atmospheric way to get across, though, is the Dh1 ride aboard a motorised *abra*, a wooden boat that connects the Bur Dubai and Deira souqs in a quick five minutes. In summer, you might prefer the air-conditioned comfort of the water buses, which cost Dh2 per trip.

See Transport (p215) for details on all services.

LOCAL KNOWLEDGE

GETTING LOST: DEIRA

Sometimes it pays to rip up the script and improvise. Some of the most fascinating parts of town aren't home to a single tourist attraction worth recommending, but are brimming with the soul the city is so frequently accused of lacking. Dubai is considered a safe city – there aren't any no-go areas and even the scariest-looking alleyways will usually be quite harmless. Be adventurous and spontaneous. Put away the maps and follow your instinct. The following are some of the best areas in Deira in which to get hopelessly, joyously lost.

Naif The area between Naif Rd and Al Khaleej Rd is a labyrinthine muddle of slim, cluttered streets and one of the best places in town for urban photography. Walk past old men smoking *sheesha* and playing backgammon on the pavements; pockets of Ethiopia and Somalia; hilariously awful fake Rolexes; games consoles; heady perfumes; blindingly bright shop facades; and the occasional goat, walking nonchalantly down the centre of the street. You just don't get this on the Palm Jumeirah...

Al Muteena Easily reached by metro (get off at Salah Al Din), Al Muteena St is one of the most enticing walking streets in town, with wide pavements, palm trees and a park-like strip running along its centre. In the Iraqi restaurants and cafes you'll see *masgouf* – a whole fish sliced in half, spicily seasoned and barbecued over an open flame. And the *sheesha* cafes have to be seen to be believed: check out the rock gardens, dangling fronds and artificial lakes. Nearby Al Muraqqabat Rd brims with superb Syrian, Lebanese and Palestinian eateries. A bit south of here, Al Rigga Rd is also packed with promising eateries and also boasts a lively street scene.

★AL TAWASOL — YEMENI $

Map p246 (☎04-295 9797; Abu Bakar al Siddiq Rd; mains Dh23-45; ⏰11-1am; Ⓜ Al Rigga) At this gem, the best seats are on the carpeted floor of your private Bedouin-style tent with a thin sheet of plastic serving as a 'table cloth'. It's famous for its chicken *mandi*, a spice-rubbed and oven-roasted bird served over a bed of rice and eaten with your hands (they'll bring a spoon upon request). It's next to the Ramee Hotel.

AROOS DAMASCUS — SYRIAN $

Map p244 (☎04-227 0202; cnr Al Muraqqabat & Al Jazeira Sts; sandwiches Dh4-20, mains Dh15-60; ⏰24hr; Ⓜ Salah Al Din) A Dubai restaurant serving Syrian food to adoring crowds since 1980 must be doing something right. One of our favourite dishes is *arayees* – a pita pocket stuffed with spice-laced ground lamb and grilled to crunchy perfection. Great tabbouleh, huge outdoor patio, cool flickering neon. Busy until the wee hours.

XIAO WEI YANG — CHINESE $

Map p244 (☎04-221 5111; Baniyas Rd; hotpots from Dh26, ingredients Dh2-15; ⏰noon-2am; Ⓜ Union) Near Twin Towers, Xiao Wei Yang works like this: pick a bubbling herb-based or spicy hotpot base that's placed on a hot plate on your table. Create a dipping sauce from a mix of satay, garlic, coriander, chilli and spices. Choose a few ingredients (fish balls, crab, tofu, lotus root, beef slices) to cook in the cauldron. Dip and enjoy! Cash only.

QWAIDER AL NABULSI — ARABIC $

Map p244 (☎04-227 7760; Al Muraqqabat St; snacks Dh10-17, mains Dh28-50; ⏰7.30am-1am; Ⓜ Al Rigga, Salah Al Din) Behind the Vegas-style neon facade, this place looks at first like a sweets shop but actually has a full menu of Arabic delicacies. A top menu pick is the felafel *mahshi* whose crunchy and sesame-seed-coated skin seals in a fluffy filling coloured green from the addition of parsley and other herbs. It's located near Al Jazeira St.

ABESINIAN RESTAURANT — ETHIOPIAN $

Map p244 (☎04-273 7432; 10 Somali St; mains Dh25-35; ⏰10am-midnight; Ⓜ Abu Baker Al Sidiqque) The staff are welcoming and warm at this homey Ethiopian restaurant, where the big platters of curry and stews are scooped up with *injera*, a spongy flatbread of native grain. Tricky to find (it's opposite the Hyatt Regency Hotel) but worth it.

ASHWAQ CAFETERIA — ARABIC $

Map p244 (☎04-226 1164; cnr Al Soor & Sikkat al Khail Sts; mains Dh4-7; ⏰8.30am-11.30pm; Ⓜ Palm Deira) In a prime people-watching spot near the Gold Souq, Ashwaq may be just a hole-in-the-wall with a few sidewalk

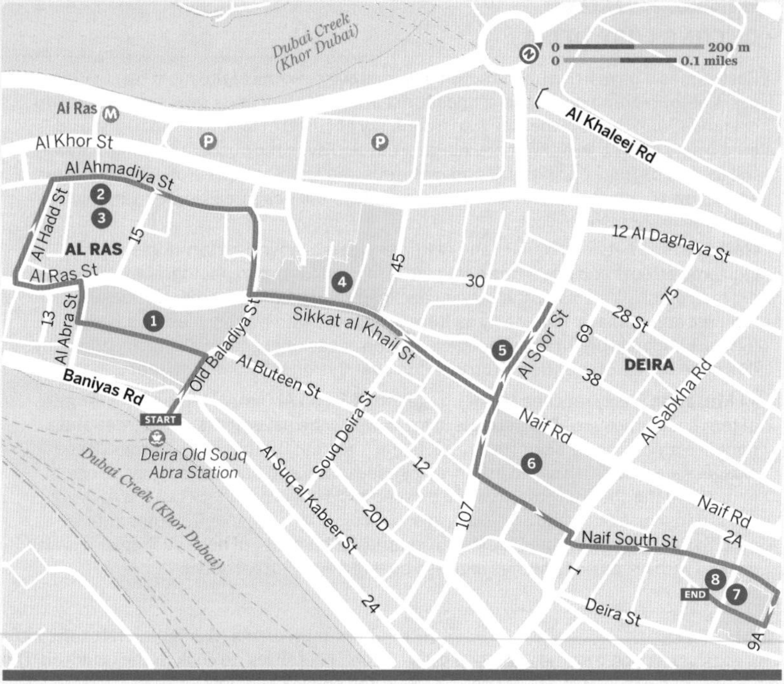

Neighbourhood Walk
Deira Souq Stroll

START SPICE SOUQ
END AFGHAN KHORASAN KEBAB HOUSE
LENGTH 2KM; THREE HOURS

As soon as you step off the *abra* (water taxi) at Deira Old Souq Abra Station, heady scents will lure you across to the ❶**Spice Souq** (p53). Take some time to explore. Turn right as you exit on Al Abra St, then left on Al Ras St and right again on Al Hadd St. At the end of Al Hadd St turn right and follow Al Ahmadiya St to the beautifully restored ❷**Heritage House** (p53) for intriguing insights into Dubai's history and culture.

Behind Heritage House is Dubai's first school, ❸**Al Ahmadiya School** (p53). Look around, then continue along Al Ahmadiya St, turning right into Old Baladiya St, where you'll find wholesalers trading in *gutras* (men's white headcloths), sandals and Chinese products.

Ahead, to the left, is the wooden latticed archway entrance to Dubai's famous ❹**Gold Souq** (p52). Pop into the small shops to look at over-the-top gold pieces created for brides' dowries and duck into the narrow lanes to suss out tiny teashops, simple cafeterias, busy tailors and barber shops.

Exit the Gold Souq, follow Sikkat al Khail St to Al Soor St and turn left. This is the heart of the ❺**Perfume Souq** (p54), a string of shops selling pungent Arabian *attars* (perfumes) and *oud* (fragrant wood). Backtrack and continue straight on what is now 107th St, with hawkers selling cut-price clothes, Chinese-made shoes and kitschy souvenirs.

Tucked east of 107th St are the tiny alleys of the ❻**Covered Souq** (p54), a warren of little shops selling everything from textiles to *sheesha* pipes. Cross Al Sabkha Rd, head into Naif South St and turn right into 9A St. Keep going until you arrive at the ❼**New Naif Market** (p54), which has risen from the ashes of the historic Naif Souq.

If you've worked up an appetite, a carnivorous feast at ❽**Afghan Khorasan Kabab** (p57) will keep you sated for ages. Find it by turning right into a little alley about half a block past the Naif Mosque.

tables, but its shwarma rocks the palate. Wash them down with a fresh juice.

AFGHAN KHORASAN KABAB AFGHANI $

Map p244 (☎04-234 0999; off Deira St; mains Dh22-39; ⏰noon-1am; Ⓜ Baniyas Sq) Big hunks of meat – mutton or chicken – charred on foot-long skewers are paired with Afghan pulao (rice pilaf), chewy bread and sauces. That's it. Think caveman food. Eat with your hands. For added authenticity, sit upstairs in the carpeted *majlis*. It's located in an alley behind Naif Mosque, off Deira St.

AL BAGHDADI HOME IRAQI $$

Map p244 (☎04-273 7064; Al Muteena St; mains Dh35-85; ⏰7am-1am; Ⓜ Salah Al Din) On Al Muteena, one of Dubai's best, if lesser-known, walking streets, Al Baghdadi is one of several restaurants specialising in the national Iraqi dish called *masgouf*, a local carp seasoned with salt, tamarind and turmeric and spit-roasted in a round fire pit. This takes about 30 to 45 minutes, giving you ample time to nibble on the mezze. It's near the Sheraton Deira Hotel.

CHINA CLUB CHINESE $$

Map p244 (☎04-205 7333; www.radissonblu.com; Radisson Blu Hotel, Baniyas Rd; yum cha Dh99, mains Dh45-165; ⏰lunch & dinner; 📶; Ⓜ Union, Baniyas Sq) Sensuous silks and embroidered tapestries provide a classy backdrop for the authentic Cantonese and Sichuan cuisine at this 'club'. Feast on such standouts as Sichuanese spicy wok-fried lamb or crispy Peking duck carved and rolled tableside. The deep-fried ice cream is a delicious finish. Lunchtime brings great-value yum cha.

YILDIZ SARAY TURKISH $$

Map p244 (☎04-252 2142; www.yildizsaray.ae; Emirates Concorde Hotel, Al Maktoum Rd; mains Dh45-100; ⏰10am-11pm; Ⓜ Al Rigga) Tucked into a ho-hum hotel is this gem of a restaurant where complimentary bread and *ezme* (a spicy tomato-pepper spread) are the mere overture to the full symphony of classic Turkish fare. Menu standouts include *ali nazik* (grilled lamb chunks in smoky eggplant yoghurt sauce), *iskender kebab* (slivers of beef and lamb in tomato sauce) and the syrup-soaked *kunafa* (pastry).

SPICE ISLAND INTERNATIONAL $$

(☎04-262 5555; Crowne Plaza Dubai Hotel, Salahuddin Rd; buffet with soft/house/premium drinks Dh199/259/329; ⏰6.30-11.30pm; 👪; Ⓜ Salah Al Din, Abu Baker Al Siddique) With dishes from China, Japan, India, Italy, Mexico and Mongolia, plus seafood and loads of desserts, Spice Island is not just a visual feast, it's one of the best all-round buffets in town and popular with families. The kiddie play area with supervised activities like face painting doesn't hurt either. Friday brunch is busy – best book ahead.

GLASSHOUSE BRASSERIE INTERNATIONAL $$

Map p244 (☎04-227 1111; Hilton Dubai Creek, Baniyas Rd; mains Dh75-135; ⏰7am-midnight; 📶; Ⓜ Al Rigga, Union) As the name suggests, Glasshouse has vast picture windows overlooking palms and the Creek beyond. The kitchen does not attempt pyrotechnics here, relying instead on pimping up such comfort-food faves as onion soup, Caesar salad, chicken tikka masala, prawn linguine and fish and chips.

THAI KITCHEN THAI $$

Map p246 (☎04-602 1234; www.dubai.park.hyatt.com; Park Hyatt Dubai; small plates Dh38-65, Friday brunch from Dh240; ⏰dinner; Ⓜ Deira City Centre) The decor is decidedly un-Thai, with black-lacquer tables, a swooping wave-form ceiling and not a branch of bamboo. But the Thai chefs know their stuff: dishes are inspired by Bangkok street eats and served family-style, perfect for grazing and sharing. The Friday brunch gets a major thumbs up. It's located next to the Dubai Creek Golf & Yacht Club.

YUM! ASIAN $$

Map p244 (☎04-205 7333; www.radissonblu.com; Radisson Blu Hotel, Baniyas Rd; mains Dh45-65; ⏰noon-11.30pm; 👪; Ⓜ Union, Baniyas Sq) Though not as dynamic or sophisticated as some Asian restaurants, Yum! is a good pick for a quick bowl of noodles when you're wandering along the Creek – you can be in and out in half an hour.

★SHABESTAN IRANIAN $$$

Map p244 (☎04-222 7171; Radisson Blu Hotel, Baniyas Rd; mains Dh105-155; ⏰lunch & dinner; Ⓜ Union, Baniyas Sq) Dubai's top Persian outpost also scores high on the romance meter with a panorama of glittering lights unfolding over the Creek. Take your sweet time as you tuck into slow-cooked lamb, charcoal-grilled kebabs or chicken dressed in a walnut-pomegranate sauce. Traditional ice cream with saffron and rose water makes a worthy coda to a superb meal.

JOHN ELK/GETTY IMAGES ©

BRENT WINEBRENNER/GETTY IMAGES ©

1. Heritage House (p53)
The former home of a wealthy pearl merchant, this 1890 courtyard house was built from coral and gypsum.

2. Dubai Creek (p54)
A man on board a dhow (traditional sailing vessel), which frequently travel along Dubai Creek.

3. Spice Souq (p53)
Loose spices and pottery are just some of the goods you'll find for sale at this working souq.

4. Middle Eastern cuisine (p27)
Hand prepared pita bread is often used in the preparation of delicious shwarmas.

GALLO IMAGES/GETTY IMAGES ©

3

SIMON MCGILL/GETTY IMAGES ©

LOCAL KNOWLEDGE

DEIRA FISH MARKET

Follow your nose to Dubai's largest and busiest **fish market** (off Al Khaleej Rd; 5am-1pm Sat-Thu, 4-10pm daily; M Palm Deira), near the Shindagha Tunnel, where treasures of the sea have been hawked since 1988. This may not be the kind of place to pick up souvenirs but the wriggling lobsters, shrimp the size of small bananas, metre-long kingfish and mountains of blue crabs are undeniably photogenic. There's also a section of salt-preserved fish called *maleh* and considered a delicacy in the Gulf. Much of the fish is caught right off the coast of the UAE, especially off Sharjah and Ras al Khaimah, the two emirates just to the north of Dubai. Shellfish is usually imported from neighbouring Oman.

Even if you're not buying, it's fun to simply listen to the cacophonous din and to observe the wild haggling between the blue-suited fishmongers and their customers. Come either early in the morning or in the evening (avoid the afternoon siesta hours), and wear sneakers or other waterproof shoes. If you're buying, avoid overfished species like hammour and kingfish and ask to have the fish cleaned. If you can't cook it up yourself, take it over to Grill & Shark, an Egyptian-run cookery in the adjacent building, and ask the cooks to prepare your fish for a few dirham. There's no seating here but shell out a few more coin to sit at the tables of the little Indian kiosk next door. While your fish is being cooked, you could swing by the adjoining fruit and vegetable market to stock up on neatly stacked and bargain-priced produce, including lots of delicious dates.

Note that a new, larger fish market has been under construction near Dubai Hospital, about 3km east on Al Khaleej Rd. There are rumours that it may finally open in summer 2015.

ASHIANA BY VINEET — INDIAN $$$

Map p244 (04-207 1733; www.ashianadubai.com; Sheraton Dubai Creek Hotel & Towers, Baniyas Rd; mains Dh75-205; lunch Sun-Thu; dinner daily; ; M Union) The brainchild of Vineet Bhatia, India's first Michelin chef, Ashiana is one of Dubai's top ambassadors of modern Indian cuisine. Instead of run-of-the-mill curries, your taste buds will be treated to such delicately spiced concoctions as *raan lucknowi* (slow-cooked, 48-hour marinated lamb) and *kukkad biryani* (pastry-encrusted chicken tikka with pomegranate-mint raita), all beautifully presented.

TABLE 9 — INTERNATIONAL $$$

Map p244 (04-212 7551; www.table9dubai.com; Hilton Dubai Creek, Baniyas Rd; 3-/4-/6-course dinner Dh300/350/425; 6.30-11pm; ; M Al Rigga, Union) After incarnations under Gordon Ramsay and his protégés Scott Price and Nick Alvis, Table 9 is now capably helmed by British-born chef Darren Velvick. Each carefully chosen ingredient plays off each other nicely – without getting too tricky – in such compositions as mackerel tartare with lime and avocado. Tasting menus include one fully vegetarian version.

TRAITEUR — FRENCH $$$

Map p246 (04-317 2222; www.dubai.park.hyatt.com; Park Hyatt Dubai; mains Dh130-270; dinner Sun-Fri; M Deira City Centre) A meal at Traiteur is pure drama, both on the plate and in the striking 14m-high dining room and raised show kitchen, where a small army of chefs elevates classic French bistro fare into a fine-dining experience. The rotisserie duck and the seafood platter are both outstanding. The menu indicates which fish are sustainable options so you can order responsibly. Superb Friday brunch. It's next to the Dubai Creek Golf & Yacht Club.

MIYAKO — JAPANESE $$$

Map p244 (04-279 0302; www.dubai.regency.hyatt.com; Hyatt Regency Dubai; set lunch Dh80-95, dinner Dh65-270; lunch & dinner; ; M Palm Deira) The cool minimalist dining room of this excellent Japanese eatery feels very Tokyo, with sleek surfaces of stainless steel, shoji screens and a traditional tatami room. The sushi is super fresh and expertly cut, from the dark-red tuna to the marbled salmon. For an entertaining experience (read: knife-juggling chefs), grab a seat at a communal teppanyaki table.

AL DAWAAR — INTERNATIONAL $$$

Map p244 (04-317 2222; www.restaurants.dubai.hyatt.com; Hyatt Regency Dubai, Al Khaleej Rd; buffet lunch/dinner Dh185/235; lunch & dinner; M Palm Deira) In a city that likes to teeter on the cutting edge, this revolving restaurant on the Hyatt's 25th floor is endearingly old school. The decor is quite sophisticated, the vibe serene, the buffet a bounty of European, Middle Eastern, Asian and Japanese dishes, and the views of the city predictably impressive, especially at night.

AL MANSOUR DHOW INTERNATIONAL $$$

Map p244 (☎04-222 7171; www.radissonblu.com/hotel-dubaideiracreek; Baniyas Rd; 2hr dinner cruise Dh195; ⏲8pm; Ⓜ Union, Baniyas Sq) For a traditional (albeit touristy) experience, book a table on this old wooden dhow cheerfully decorated with bands of twinkling lights and operated by the Radisson Blu Hotel. A house band plays on as you graze on the lavish buffet spread that's heavy on Middle Eastern and Indian choices before reclining with a *sheesha* in the upper-deck lounge. Board outside the hotel.

SUMIBIYA JAPANESE $$$

Map p244 (☎04-205 7333; www.radissonblu.com; Radisson Blu Hotel, Baniyas Rd; set menu Dh125; ⏲dinner; ; Ⓜ Union, Baniyas Sq) At Dubai's first *yakiniku*-style restaurant is interactive foodie fun for families or groups. Every stone table has a recessed gas grill where you cook your own meat, then pair it with sauces and condiments. The set menus featuring either beef, chicken, fish or lamb along with salad, rice, soup, kim chi and dessert, are good value.

DRINKING & NIGHTLIFE

★QDS BAR, SHEESHA

Map p246 (☎04-295 6000; www.dubaigolf.com; Dubai Creek Golf & Yacht Club, Garhoud; ⏲5pm-2am Sun-Wed, to 3am Thu & Sat, 1pm-3am Fri; Ⓜ Deira City Centre) Watch the ballet of lighted dhows floating by while sipping cocktails at this always-fun outdoor Creekside lounge deck where carpets and cushions set an inviting mood. In summer, keep cool in an air-conditioned tent. Great for *sheesha*, but skip the food (except for the pizza and Friday afternoon barbecue).

CIELO SKY LOUNGE BAR

Map p246 (☎04-416 1800; www.cielodubai.com; Dubai Creek Golf & Yacht Club; ⏲4pm-2am; Ⓜ Deira City Centre) Looking very much like a futuristic James Bond–worthy yacht, Cielo flaunts a sultry, romantic vibe helped by the bobbing yachts below and the cool Creek views of the Dubai skyline. It's a great spot to ring in the night with tapas (great ceviche!) and sundowners (the sangria is a signature drink). Tuesday is ladies' night.

IRISH VILLAGE PUB, BEER GARDEN

Map p246 (☎04-282 4750; www.theirishvillage.com; 31st St, Garhoud; ⏲11-1am Sat-Wed, to 2am Thu & Fri; ; Ⓜ GGICO) This always buzzy pub, with its Irish-main-street facade made with materials imported straight from the Emerald Isle, has been a Dubai institution since 1996. There's Guinness and Kilkenny on tap, lawns around a petite lake, the occasional live concert and plenty of cheap, cheerful pub grub to keep your tummy happy (and brain balanced). It's located next to the Dubai Tennis Stadium.

DUBLINERS PUB

Map p246 (☎04-702 2455; www.dubliners-dubai.com; Le Meridien Dubai Hotel, Airport Rd; ⏲noon-2am; ; Ⓜ Airport Terminal 1) This airport-adjacent Irish pub staple has become even better and bigger after a recent refurb. There's eight beers on tap, above-average pub grub and a crowd that's chatty and friendly. On game nights and during the Friday brunch (Dh75 per person, including two drinks) the place is usually elbow-to-elbow. Happy hour 5pm to 8pm.

JUICE WORLD JUICE BAR

Map p244 (☎04-299 9465; www.juiceworld.ae; Al Rigga St; ⏲1pm-2am; Ⓢ Al Rigga) Need some A.S.S., Man Kiwi or Viagra? Then head down to this upbeat Saudi juice bar famous not only for its 150 fantastically creative liquid potions but also for its outrageous fruit sculptures. There's an entire room of them: must be seen to be believed. The big outdoor terrace offers primo people-watching. It's next to Al Rigga metro station.

ISSIMO SPORTS BAR

Map p244 (☎04-227 1111; Hilton Dubai Creek, Baniyas Rd; ⏲3pm-1am; ; Ⓜ Al Rigga, Union) Illuminated blue flooring, black-leather sofas and sleek chrome finishing lend an edgy look to this sports-and-martini bar. If you're not into sports – or TV – you may find the giant screens distracting. Good for an *aperitivo* before dinner at the hotel's highly regarded Table 9 (p60) or Glasshouse Brasserie (p57) restaurants.

LOCAL KNOWLEDGE

PASHMINA: TELLING REAL FROM FAKE

Pashmina shawls come in all sorts of wonderful colours and patterns. Originally made from feather-light cashmere, there are now many cheaper machine-made synthetic versions around. Before forking over hundreds of dirham, how can you make sure you're buying the real thing? Here's the trick. Hold the fabric at its corner. Loop your index finger around it and squeeze hard. Now pull the fabric through. If it's polyester, it won't budge. If it's cashmere, it'll pull through – though the friction may give you a mild case of rope burn. Try it at home with a thin piece of polyester before you hit the shops; then try it with cashmere. You'll never be fooled again.

TERRACE BAR

Map p246 (04-317 2222; www.dubai.park.hyatt.com; Park Hyatt Dubai; noon-1.30am; Deira City Centre) With its sleek design, floor-to-ceiling windows and canopy-covered deck, the Terrace provides plenty of eye candy before you've even taken in the chic crowd or the dreamy sunset views across the Creek. A raw seafood bar provides a major protein kick, while the big selection of top-shelf vodka should help loosen any inhibitions. It's next to the Dubai Creek Golf & Yacht Club.

KU-BU BAR, CLUB

Map p244 (04-222 7171; Radisson Blu Hotel, Baniyas Rd; 7pm-3am; Union, Baniyas Sq) A resident DJ spins funky tunes at this windowless, tattoo-themed pick-up joint with secluded nooks that are made even more private with plush draperies. A good choice for drinks before or after dinner at the Radisson Blu's restaurants.

JULES BAR CLUB

Map p246 (04-702 2455; www.julesbar-dubai.com; Le Meridien Dubai, Airport Rd; 11am-3am; Airport Terminal 1) Rotating house bands belt out 'It's Raining Men' and other chart toppers as an eclectic mix of burly oil workers, Asian expats and flight crews grind shoulder-to-shoulder on the dance floor. Watch out for different theme nights, including Filipino Mondays and Tuesdays and Corona Wednesdays. For sustenance there's a decent line-up of Tex-Mex and Filipino bar bites.

SHOPPING

DEIRA CITY CENTRE MALL

Map p246 (04-295 1010; www.deiracitycentre.com; Baniyas Rd; 10am-10pm Sun-Wed, to midnight Thu-Sat; Deira City Centre) Though other malls are bigger and flashier, Deira City Centre remains a stalwart for its wide selection of shops, from big-name chains like H&M and Zara to locally owned stores carrying quality carpets, souvenirs and handicrafts. There's also a huge branch of the Carrefour supermarket, food courts, a textile court selling Indian and Middle Eastern clothes and fabrics, and a multiplex cinema.

AL WASHIA ACCESSORIES

Map p246 (04-295 0221; www.alwashia.com; Deira City Centre, Baniyas Rd; 10am-10pm Sat-Wed, to midnight Thu & Fri; Deira City Centre) Has all that bling got to you yet? If so, then you can glitter along with the best of them by picking up some accessories here, including twinkling tiaras, jewelled hairpins, dangly earrings, fancy clutch bags and a few surprises, such as cushion-cover embroidery sets with Middle Eastern themes.

MANGO TOUCH ACCESSORIES

Map p246 (04-295 7712; Deira City Centre, Baniyas Rd; 10am-10pm Sat-Wed, to midnight Thu & Fri; Deira City Centre) The stylish Spanish Mango chain has cleverly bagged a corner of the market with this boutique store which specialises in original, reasonably priced bags, mostly handmade with prices dangling at the Dh120 mark. There are a few leather numbers closer to the Dh600 tag.

LUSH BEAUTY

Map p246 (04-295 9531; Deira City Centre, Baniyas Rd; 10am-10pm Sat-Wed, to midnight Thu & Fri; Deira City Centre) This natural soap and cosmetics shop is full of all kinds of organic body-beautiful products, such as lip balms made with natural oils, foot lotion with ginger oil and cloves, lemon cuticle butter, coconut deodorant, vanilla puff talc and some wonderful perfumes.

MIKYAJY COSMETICS

Map p246 (04-295 7844; www.mikyajy.com; 2nd fl, Deira City Centre, Baniyas Rd; 10am-10pm Sat-Wed, to midnight Thu & Fri; Deira City Centre) You feel like you're walking into a chocolate gift-box at tiny Mikyajy, the Gulf's home-grown make-up brand. Although developed for Middle Eastern skin tones, the vivid colours brighten up any face.

AJMAL PERFUME

Map p246 (☎04-295 3580; www.ajmalperfume.com; Deira City Centre, Baniyas Rd; ⏲10am-10pm Sat-Wed, to midnight Thu & Fri; ⓂDeira City Centre) *The* place for locally made traditional Arabic perfumes and scented oils, family-owned Ajmal was founded in India in the early 1950s. Its stores are always crowded with local women keen on finding their favourite among the 200 heady and complex fragrances filled into equally fancy jewel-encrusted bottles. Check the website for additional branches.

VIRGIN MEGASTORE MUSIC

Map p246 (☎04-295 8599; 2nd floor, Deira City Centre, Baniyas Rd; ⏲10am-10pm Sat-Wed, to midnight Thu & Fri; ⓂDeira City Centre) The enthusiastic sales staff are great at suggesting Middle Eastern music to take back home, from traditional *oud* music to Oriental chill-out. The selection is huge. Also check out the Arabian and Iranian DVDs.

EARLY LEARNING CENTRE TOYS

Map p246 (☎04-295 1548; www.elc.com; Deira City Centre, Baniyas Rd; ⏲10am-10pm Sat-Wed, to midnight Thu & Fri; ⓂDeira City Centre) This UK-based chain stocks great quality games and toys designed to get little ones from age zero to six thinking and developing key learning skills. And because they're not always easy to figure out, they'll keep children busy for hours. There are additional branches around town, including at the Mall of the Emirates and Souk Madinat Jumeirah.

DAMAS JEWELLERY

Map p246 (☎04-295 3848; Deira City Centre, Baniyas Rd; ⏲10am-10pm Sun-Wed, 10am-midnight Thu-Sat; ⓂDeira City Centre) Damas may not be the most innovative jeweller in Dubai, but with over 50 stores, it's essentially omnipresent. Among the diamonds and gold, look for classic pieces and big-designer names such as Fabergé and Tiffany.

WOMEN'S SECRET LINGERIE

Map p246 (☎04-295 9665; 1st fl, Deira City Centre, Baniyas Rd; ⏲10am-10pm Sun-Wed, to midnight Thu-Sat; ⓂDeira City Centre) This sassy Spanish label is popular for its global-pop-art-inspired underwear, swimwear and nightwear. Expect anything from cute Mexican cross-stitched bra-and-pants sets to Moroccan-style kaftan-like nightdresses.

AL GHURAIR CITY MALL

Map p244 (☎04-295 5309; www.alghuraircentre.com; cnr Al Rigga & Omar ibn al Khattab Rds; ⏲10am-10pm Sat-Thu, 2-10pm Fri; ⓂUnion, Salah Al Din) If seeing all those flowing robes has made you want your own *gutra* (white headcloth worn by men in the Gulf States), grab yours at this ageing mall. The place to shop for national dress, it offers stylish *abeyyas* (full-length black robes worn by women) and *shaylas* (headscarves), quality leather sandals, and *dishdashas* (men's traditional long robes) in shades of ivory, brown and grey. There's also some specialty shops selling everything from Arabic jewellery to handwoven rugs, and international fashion outlets such as Mexx and Guess.

DUBAI FESTIVAL CITY MALL MALL

(www.festivalcentre.com; Al Rebat St, Festival City; ⏲10am-10pm Sun-Wed, to midnight Thu-Sat; ⓂCreek) Southwest of the airport, near

HENNA

Henna body tattooing is a long-standing tradition dating back 6000 years, when women in central Turkey began painting their hands in homage to the Mother Goddess. The practice spread throughout the eastern Mediterranean, where the henna shrub grows wild. Today, Emirati women continue the tradition by decorating their hands, nails and feet for special events, particularly weddings. A few nights before the nuptials, brides-to-be are honoured with *layyat al-henna* (henna night). This is a women-only affair, part of a week of festivities leading up to the big day. The bride is depilated, anointed head-to-toe with perfumes and oils, and shampooed with henna, jasmine or perfume. Her hands, wrists, ankles and feet are then tattooed with intricate floral designs, which typically last around six weeks. Lore has it that the duration of the tattoos is an indication to the mother-in-law of what kind of wife the bride will become. If she's a hard worker – and thus a more desirable daughter-in-law – the henna will penetrate deeper and remain longer. Want to give it a try? Henna tents are all over the city. Look for signs depicting henna-painted hands in Deira City Centre, BurJuman Centre, Souk Madinat Jumeirah and hotel lobbies.

WORTH A DETOUR

MIRDIF CITY CENTRE

It's a bit of a trek to this vast mall, but you'll be rewarded with some cool stores mixed between the usual global chains. Entertainment options include a VOX multiplex cinema and the massive Magic Planet indoor family entertainment centre with a small waterpark, a skydiving simulator, a bowling alley and an amusement arcade.

Decathlon Huge selection of sportswear and sporting goods by in-store and international brands at wallet-friendly prices.

Pottery Barn The first Middle East branch of this US purveyor of stylish stuff for home and hearth.

Crate & Barrel Similar to Pottery Barn, but a bit more contemporary and upscale.

Hamley's The mothership of all toy stores, from the UK.

United Designers Showcases local UAE-based fashion designers with the aim of supporting young emerging talent.

Balmain Stylish menswear from French fashion guru Christophe Decarnin.

Ajmal Family-owned since the 1950s, Ajmal sells Middle Eastern oils and perfumes that are well priced and exquisitely bottled.

To get to Mirdif City Centre, head southeast of the airport on Airport Rd for around 10km. The mall is well signposted. Alternatively, take the metro Red Line to the Rashidiya terminus and continue by taxi or mall shuttle.

Business Bay Bridge, this behemoth has all the standard shops, plus Ikea – a big draw for locals and expats. Its main plus is the picturesque location around a circular marina, which is lined with 50 bars and restaurants. You can also take an *abra* float here, ogle at the yachts or just enjoy a waterside stroll.

GIFT VILLAGE — DEPARTMENT STORE

Map p244 (☎04-294 6858; www.gift-village.com; Baniyas Sq; ⏰9am-1am Sun-Thu, 9am-noon & 2pm-2am Fri; Ⓜ Baniyas Sq) If you've spent all your money on Jimmy Choo shoes and at the Gold Souq and need a new inflight bag, this cut-price place has a great range. It also stocks cosmetics, shoes, clothing, toys, sports goods, jewellery and kitsch souvenirs, all imported from China, Thailand and Turkey and sold at wallet-friendly prices.

SPORTS & ACTIVITIES

AMARA SPA — SPA

Map p246 (☎04-602 1234; www.dubai.park.hyatt.com; Park Hyatt Dubai; day pass weekdays/weekends Dh300/350; ⏰9am-10pm Sun-Thu, 7.30am-10pm Fri & Sat; Ⓜ Deira City Centre) One of Dubai's top spas, Amara has eight treatment suites, including three for couples, all with their own private walled gardens and outdoor rain showers. A popular package is 'Spirit of Amara' (Dh895), a two-hour regimen involving a scrub down with Aleppo soap enriched with laurel oils followed by a full-body massage using the spa's signature oil of frankincense, amber, myrrh and sandalwood. Afterwards, you can relax in the steam bath or sauna or by the palm-tree-shaded pool.

BLISS RELAXOLOGY — SPA

Map p246 (☎04-286 9482; Shop 11, Emirates Blvd, G Block; 1hr Thai massage Dh150; ⏰9am-midnight; Ⓜ GGICO) It's not quite pampering fit for a queen, but if you're in bad need of working out the kinks without spending buckets of money, this relaxation station might just do the trick. Treatments range from a traditional Thai massage to foot reflexology, and start at Dh110 for 30 minutes. The spa is near the airport and next to Wellcare Hospital.

DUBAI CREEK GOLF & YACHT CLUB — GOLF

Map p246 (☎04-295 6000; www.dubaigolf.com; green fees Sun-Thu Dh825, Fri & Sat Dh725; Ⓜ Deira City Centre) Gorgeously located on the Creek, the par 71 Creek course measures 6,967 yards set amid beautiful landscaping, with water hazards and manicured coconut and date palm-lined fairways. After dark, you can hit the floodlit par 3 course or the driving range. Note the clubhouse looks like a miniature Sydney Opera House.

Bur Dubai

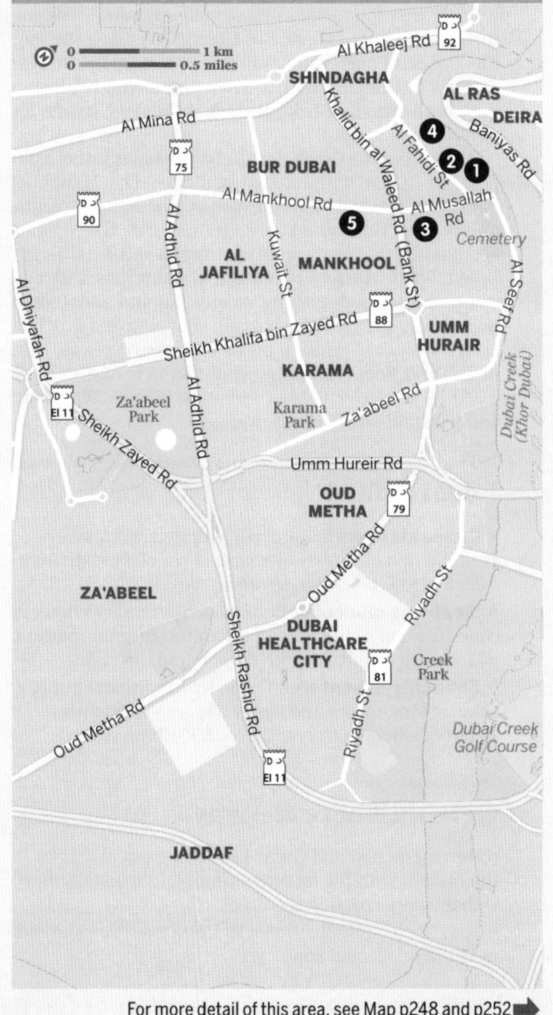

For more detail of this area, see Map p248 and p252

Neighbourhood Top Five

❶ Soaking up Dubai's history on a wander along Dubai Creek from the atmospheric **Al Fahidi Historic District** (p68) to the waterfront Shindagha Historic District. Many of the beautifully restored buildings house small museums that provide further insight into pre-oil times.

❷ Visiting **Dubai Museum** (p67) for an entertaining introduction to the city's turbo-evolution.

❸ Chowing down with expat workers at Meena Bazaar eateries like **Special Ostadi** (p73).

❹ Bargaining for souvenirs at the lively **Bur Dubai Souq** (p69) before exploring the surrounding bustling streets.

❺ Keeping tabs on Dubai's music scene with a concert at the **Music Room** (p79).

Lonely Planet's Top Tip

For an astonishing immersion in Bur Dubai's multiethnic food and culture, book a guided walking tour with local blogger and foodie extraordinaire Arva Ahmed, founder of Dubai's first culinary tour company, Frying Pan Adventures (p71). Enjoy exotic nibbles as she takes you through the bewildering tangle of Bur Dubai's narrow lanes.

Best Places to Eat

- Special Ostadi (p73)
- Qbara (p78)
- Tomo (p78)
- Jaffer Bhai's (p73)
- Arabian Tea House (p73)

For reviews, see p71.

Best Places to Drink

- Music Room (p79)
- George & Dragon (p78)

For reviews, see p78.

Best Museums

- Dubai Museum (p67)
- Sheikh Saeed Al Maktoum House (p70)
- Traditional Architecture Museum (p70)

For reviews, see p68.

Explore Bur Dubai

Modern Dubai so dominates the city's image that it's easy to forget there was life here before the petro-dollar era. Thankfully, there's Bur Dubai to provide an eye-opening journey into the city's past. It was on the western bank of the Creek where the 800 members of the Al Bu Fasalah tribe from Abu Dhabi first settled in 1833. Their leader, Maktoum bin Butti, was the founder of the Al Maktoum dynasty that rules Dubai to this day.

Although Bur Dubai stretches from the Creek to the World Trade Centre at the beginning of Sheikh Zayed Road, the neighbourhood's most intriguing area is a conveniently compact section hugging the Creek. Peek into the city's past on a wander around the restored historic districts of Shindagha and Al Fahidi, passing through the atmospheric Bur Dubai Souq along the way. The tangle of narrow lanes in this area teems with local eateries feeding expats from Nepal, India and Pakistan with authentic fare from their homelands. Nirvana for adventurous foodies!

Away from the Creek, Bur Dubai becomes rather nondescript, if not without its highlights. The Mankhool district is stacked with inexpensive hotel apartments, quirky nightlife, good restaurants and the upmarket BurJuman Centre mall. Across Sheikh Khalifa bin Zayed Road, densely populated Karama has a strong community feel due to its mostly Filipino and Indian population. It's great for bargain shopping and bustling eateries serving princely meals at paupers' prices. East of Za'abeel Road, sprawling Oud Metha is easily recognised by the eye-catching Egyptian-themed Wafi Mall and pyramid-shaped Raffles Hotel.

Local Life

- **Creekside views** Settle down with a creamy avocado smoothie or a *sheesha* (water pipe) at one of the waterfront cafes and look on as wooden *abras* cross the Creek.
- **Meat-free munching** Bur Dubai has the city's highest concentration of Indian vegetarian restaurants, many of which are a beehive of activity well into the night.
- **Shopping adventures** Try on the traditional Punjabi dress of long tunics and baggy trousers in brightly coloured silk or cotton at the local clothing stores.

Getting There & Away

- **Metro** The Red and Green Lines intersect at BurJuman, with the latter continuing into historic Bur Dubai before crossing the Creek.
- **Boat** *Abras* link Bur Dubai to Deira from two stations near the Bur Dubai Souq.

TOP SIGHT
DUBAI MUSEUM

Unless some mad scientist invents a time travel machine, this museum is your ticket to learning about Dubai's stratospheric rise from Bedouin village to megalopolis and global centre of trade and tourism. It's housed in Al Fahidi Fort, built in 1799 and the oldest surviving structure in town. The crenellated citadel served as the residence of the local rulers until 1896 and went through stints as a prison and a garrison before becoming a museum in 1971.

Past the ornate gates, a walkway culminates in a central courtyard dotted with bronze cannons, small wooden fishing boats and traditional dwellings, including a *barasti*, a hut made of mud and palm fronds that was the kind of traditional summer home most locals lived in until the middle of the 20th century. Pop behind the heavy carved wooden doors to check out modest displays of instruments and handcrafted weapons before heading down a spiralling ramp to the main galleries.

After watching a slick multimedia presentation charting Dubai's impressive development, visitors cross the deck of a dhow to enter a mock souq with endearing dioramas depicting shopkeepers and artisans at work. Some are enhanced with light effects and historical photos and film footage. Other scenes illustrate traditional life at home, at the mosque, in the desert and at sea. The latter includes an extensive pearl-diving exhibit where you can marvel at the fact that these men wore only nose clips while descending to extraordinary depths.

The highlight for many will be the final archaeology section which showcases finds from ancient settlements at Jumeirah, Al Qusais and other local archaeological sites. Most are believed to have been established here between 2000 and 1000 BC. Don't miss the large well-lit gallery opposite the gift shop, with its displays of unearthed artefacts from the numerous tombs in the area.

DON'T MISS

- Multimedia presentation
- Archaeology exhibit
- Pearl-diving exhibit

PRACTICALITIES

- Map p248
- ☎04-353 1862
- Al Fahidi St
- adult/child Dh3/1
- ⌚8.30am-8.30pm Sat-Thu, 2.30-8.30pm Fri
- Ⓜ Al Fahidi

SIGHTS

Bur Dubai's main historic sights handily cluster in a compact strip flanking the western bank of Dubai Creek.

DUBAI MUSEUM
MUSEUM

See p67.

AL FAHIDI HISTORIC DISTRICT
NEIGHBOURHOOD

Map p248 (btwn Al Fahidi St & Dubai Creek; MAl Fahidi) Traffic fades to a quiet hum in the labyrinthine lanes of this nicely restored heritage area formerly known as the Bastakia Quarter. Its narrow walking lanes are flanked by sand-coloured houses topped with wind towers, which provide natural air-conditioning (see p53). Today, there are about 50 buildings containing crafts shops, cultural exhibits, courtyard cafes, art galleries and two boutique hotels.

The quarter was created in the early 1900s by pearl and textile merchants from the Persian town of Bastak who came to Dubai to take advantage of tax breaks granted by the sheikh. After most residents moved out in the 1970s, the buildings housed migrant workers and gradually fell into disrepair but were ultimately saved from the wrecking ball and restored. Hidden within the maze is a short section of the **old city wall** from 1800, which looks a bit like a dinosaur tail. The compact area is easily explored on an aimless wander, but for a more in-depth experience, sign up for a guided tour with the Sheikh Mohammed Centre for Cultural Understanding.

AL SERKAL CULTURAL FOUNDATION
GALLERY

Map p248 (04-353 5922; Heritage House No 79, off Al Fahidi St; 9.30am-8pm Sat-Thu; MAl Fahidi) FREE This rambling courtyard building in Al Fahidi Historic District provides a fitting setting for traditional and cutting-edge works by local and international artists. Exhibitions change monthly. In the workshop in front, you can often see a master engraver at work.

MAJLIS GALLERY
GALLERY

Map p248 (04-353 6233; www.themajlisgallery.com; Al Fahidi St; 10am-6pm Sat-Thu; MAl Fahidi) FREE Majlis was founded in 1989, making it Dubai's oldest fine art gallery. It presents mainly paintings and sculpture created by international artists inspired by the region as well as high-quality pottery, glass and other crafts. It's located in an old wind-tower house on the edge of Al Fahidi Historic District. The central courtyard surrounds a magnificent henna tree.

XVA GALLERY
GALLERY

Map p248 (04-353 5383; www.xvagallery.com; XVA Guesthouse, off Al Fahidi St; 10am-6pm; MAl Fahidi) Tucked into Al Fahidi Historic

EMIRATI CULTURE DEMYSTIFIED

Anyone keen on delving deeper into Emirati culture and history should take advantage of the activities and tours offered through the nonprofit **Sheikh Mohammed Centre for Cultural Understanding** (Map p248; 04-353 6666; www.cultures.ae; House 26, Al Mussalah Rd; tours Dh65, breakfast/lunch/dinner & brunch Dh80/90/100; 9am-5pm Sun-Thu, 9am-1pm Sat; MAl Fahidi), based on the edge of Al Fahidi Historic District. Guided by the motto 'Open Doors, Open Minds', this unique institution was founded in 1995 by Dubai's current ruler, Sheikh Mohammed bin Rashid, in order to build bridges between cultures and to help visitors and expats understand the traditions and customs of the United Arab Emirates (UAE).

The centre regularly runs highly informative 90-minute guided heritage tours of Al Fahidi Historic District and can also organise more comprehensive 2½-hour tours for groups of 10 or more people. These include a peek inside a mosque, an *abra* (traditional water taxi) ride and a spin around the textile, spice and gold souqs in Bur Dubai and Deira. All tours conclude with a Q&A session and Arabic coffee, tea and dates.

If you're interested in the culinary side of Emirati life, join one of the centre's traditional Bedouin-style meals. At breakfast you'll get to taste *balaleet* (sweetened crunchy vermicelli) and *chabab* (cardamom-spiced pancakes), while at lunchtime your belly will be filled with *saloona* (a stew) or *machboos* (a rice and meat/fish dish).

The centre also runs hugely popular tours of Jumeirah Mosque (p104).

All tours and meals must be booked in advance. Check the website for the schedule.

District since 2003, XVA's curators have a knack for ferreting out top-notch up-and-comers from around the Middle East. Works often express the artists' cultural identities and challenge viewers' preconceptions. It also shows at prestigious art fairs such as Art Basel and Art London.

COFFEE MUSEUM — MUSEUM

Map p248 (☎04-380 6777; www.coffeemuseum.ae; off Al Fahidi St; ⊙10.30am-6pm Sat-Thu; Ⓜ Al Fahidi) FREE This small private museum in a historic Emirati home offers an aromatic bean-based journey around the world and back in time. Learn about the origins of coffee, examine centuries-old grinders, pots, roasters and other implements, and sample traditional Ethiopian or Turkish coffee prepared by staff in traditional costume. Upstairs is a reading room, a children's corner and a modern cafe.

COIN MUSEUM — MUSEUM

Map p248 (off Al Fahidi St; ⊙8am-2pm Sun-Thu; Ⓜ Al Fahidi) FREE Near Al Farooq Mosque in Al Fahidi Historic District, this small museum presents a collection of nearly 500 rare coins from throughout the Middle East, including Egypt, Turkey and Morocco.

HINDI LANE — STREET

Map p248 (off Ali bin Abi Talib St; Ⓜ Al Fahidi, Al Ghubaiba) The only place of worship for Dubai's sizeable Hindu community is the Shiva and Krishna Mandir, a temple complex just behind the Grand Mosque. From here you'll quickly reach a colourful alleyway that expats refer to as 'Hindi Lane' where vendors sell religious paraphernalia and offerings to take to the temples: baskets of fruit, garlands of flowers, gold-embossed holy images, sacred ash, sandalwood paste and packets of bindis (the little pendants Hindu women stick to their foreheads).

GRAND MOSQUE — MOSQUE

Map p248 (Ali bin Abi Talib St; Ⓜ Al Fahidi, Al Ghubaiba) Dubai's tallest minaret (70m high) lords over more than 50 small and large domes that give the city's largest mosque its distinctive silhouette. Today's building was only completed in 1998 but is, in fact, a replica of the historic house of worship from 1900. As with all Dubai mosques except Jumeirah Mosque, it's off limits to non-Muslims.

As well as being the centre of Dubai's religious and cultural life, the original was also home to the town's *kuttab* (Quranic school), where children learned to recite the Quran from memory. It's opposite the Dubai Museum.

FUN FACTS ABOUT CAMELS

Camels...

- can reach a top speed of 40km/h
- are pregnant for 13 to 15 months
- can go up to 15 days without drinking
- soak up water like a sponge when thirsty, guzzling up to 100L in 10 minutes
- have a life expectancy of 50 to 60 years
- in Arabia are one-humped dromedaries
- can travel 160km without drinking
- move both legs on one side of the body at the same time

BUR DUBAI SOUQ — MARKET

Map p248 (btwn Bur Dubai waterfront & Ali bin Abi Talib St; Ⓜ Al Ghubaiba) This covered souq may not be as old as the Deira souqs but it can be just as atmospheric – although be prepared for pushy vendors. Friday evenings here are especially lively, as it turns into a virtual crawling carnival with expat workers loading up on socks, pashminas, T-shirts and knock-off Calvins on their day off. In a section known as the **Textile Souq** you can stock up on fabrics – silk, cotton, satin, velvet – at very reasonable prices.

SHINDAGHA HISTORIC DISTRICT — NEIGHBOURHOOD

Map p248 (Shindagha Waterfront; Ⓜ Al Ghubaiba) With a strategic location at the mouth of Dubai Creek, Shindagha was the Beverly Hills of Dubai in the first half of the 20th century. This is where the ruling sheikhs, their families and the city elite lived in stately coral and gypsum homes wrapped around a central courtyard and cooled by wind towers (see p53). The entire area has been given a major facelift and is now a heritage district.

A wide promenade paralleling the Creek links the handsomely restored buildings. A stroll along here is especially atmospheric at sunset with the lights reflected in the water against the dhows heading out to sea. In fact, it's possible to continue walking along the waterfront past the Shindagha Tower (a former defensive watchtower), the *abra* stations and the Bur Dubai Souq all the way to Al Fahidi Historic District, Bur Dubai's other heritage quarter.

TRADITIONAL ARCHITECTURE MUSEUM — MUSEUM

Map p248 (Shindagha Historic District; ⌚8am-8pm Mon-Sat, 8am-2pm Sun; Ⓜ Al Ghubaiba) FREE This magnificent courtyard house has seen stints as a residence, jail and police station. Today it houses a thorough exhibit on traditional Arab architecture. This is the place to learn how those wind towers really work and why there are different dwelling types along the coast, in the mountains and in the desert.

Most galleries feature entertaining and informative videos, which the caretaker will be happy to play for you.

SHEIKH SAEED AL MAKTOUM HOUSE — MUSEUM

Map p248 (☎04-393 7139; Shindagha Historic District; adult/child Dh3/1; ⌚8am-8.30pm Sat-Thu, 3-9.30pm Fri; Ⓜ Al Ghubaiba) The grand courtyard house of Sheikh Saeed, the grandfather of current Dubai ruler Sheikh Mohammed bin Rashid, is the crown jewel of the restored Shindagha Historic District. Built in 1896, it served as Sheikh Saeed's private residence until his death in 1958. Aside from being an architectural marvel, the building is now a museum of pre-oil times with an excellent collection of photographs of Dubai taken in the 1940s and '50s on the Creek, in the souqs and at traditional celebrations.

Other rooms feature coins, stamps and documents dating back as far as 1791, as well as an interesting display on pearl diving.

CAMEL MUSEUM — MUSEUM

Map p248 (☎04-392 0368; Shindagha Historic District; ⌚8am-2pm Sun-Thu; Ⓜ Al Ghubaiba) FREE This exhibit raises the humble camel to celebrity status. It explains how and why the animals are held in such high regard in Arabian culture and depicts the historical importance of camels in the region and their prominence in Arabic literature. There are sections on camel racing and on the history of camels in region.

CROSSROADS OF CIVILIZATIONS MUSEUM — MUSEUM

Map p248 (☎04-393 4440; www.themuseum.ae; Al Khaleej Rd; admission Dh30; ⌚10am-5pm Sun-Thu, 10am-4pm Sat; Ⓜ Al Ghubaiba) This private museum, opened in January 2014, in a traditional home in the Shindagha Historic District, pays homage to Dubai's history as a trading link between East and West. On display are hundreds of historic maps, manuscripts, weapons, ceramics, coins and other artefacts from the cultures and civilisations that passed through the region. Highlights include a 7500-year-old bull-shaped Ubaid vase, ancient Greek silver coins and Roman glass vessels.

HERITAGE VILLAGE — MUSEUM

Map p248 (Shindagha Historic District; ⌚8.30am-10.30pm Sat-Thu, 4.30-10.30pm Fri; Ⓜ Al Ghubaiba) FREE This outdoor museum is a well-meaning attempt at recreating a village from pre-oil times and features various styles of houses (coastal and mountain), a small souq, historic exhibits and crafts stations. From October to April, there are occasionally activities and demonstrations, although most of the time the place seems sadly neglected.

DIVING VILLAGE — MUSEUM

Map p248 (☎04-393 7139; Shindagha Historic District; ⌚8.30am-10pm Sat-Thu, 3.30-10pm Sun; Ⓜ Al Ghubaiba) FREE At this outdoor museum, you can delve into Dubai's maritime history and learn about the harsh realities of life as a pearl diver and the importance of diving and trading to the region. There's a smattering of old boats to help visitors take a step back in time.

The Diving Village is affiliated with the adjacent Heritage Village, which focuses on Dubai's Bedouin heritage.

CREEK PARK — PARK

Map p252 (☎04-336 7633; off Riyadh St; admission Dh5, cable-car ride adult/child Dh25/10; ⌚8am-11pm Sat-Wed, 8am-midnight Thu & Fri; 👪; Ⓜ Oud Metha, Dubai Healthcare City) This large and lovely park teems with family-geared attractions, from playgrounds and carousels to pony and camel rides, and a children's museum. Come here to explore and relax in the gardens or to give the barbecue pits a workout. A hugely popular feature is the 2.5km **cable-car ride** which delivers fabulous vistas of the park and waterfront from 30m in the air.

CHILDREN'S CITY — MUSEUM

Map p252 (☎04-334 0808; www.childrencity.ae; Gate 1, Creek Park, off Al Riyadh St; adult/child 2-15yr Dh15/10, plus park entrance Dh5; ⌚9am-8pm Sat-Thu, 3-9pm Fri; 👪; Ⓜ Oud Metha,

LOCAL KNOWLEDGE

HITTING THE 'OLD DUBAI' FOOD TRAIL

Far from glim-glam Dubai Marina and Downtown Dubai, the narrow lanes of Bur Dubai and Deira are a feast for foodies, a beehive of shoebox-sized restaurants where expat cooks whip up comfort food from home for their brethren. To many the food may be unfamiliar, the places easily overlooked or perhaps a bit intimidating. In comes Arva Ahmed to break down the barriers on her food walking tours, where she'll introduce you to some of the most delicious fare from such far-flung locales as Yemen, Nepal, India, Morocco, Ethiopia, Iran and Palestine.

Arva had already made a name for herself as a well-respected food blogger when she came up with the concept of **Frying Pan Adventures** (www.fryingpanadventures.com; tours Dh280-520), the first food tours in Dubai. Pick your favourite from her expanding roster that includes the 'Middle Eastern Food Pilgrimage' and 'Little India on a Plate'. On each tour you'll enjoy nibbles at five or six hidden gems while Arva or her sister Farida shower you with fascinating tidbits about the food, the restaurant and the culture.

Tours run three to five hours and involve walking distances from 1.5km to 3km. Check the website for the schedule and to book a tour.

Dubai Healthcare City) This colourful cluster of Lego-style buildings in Creek Park is jam-packed with dozens of interactive and inspiring learning stations where kids between ages two and 15 can playfully explore scientific concepts, the human body, space exploration and natural wonders. One of the most popular exhibits is a simulator where you can fly on a magic carpet or ride a camel. All signs are in English and Arabic.

Luddites (of any age) may like to try their hand sending a message from the giant computer, while toddlers can retreat to a special play area. Staff also puts on a busy schedule of educational workshops and planetarium shows.

WAFI CITY — NEIGHBOURHOOD

Map p252 (www.wafi.com; Oud Metha & Sheikh Rashid Rds; MDubai Healthcare City) Ancient Egypt gets a Dubai-style makeover at this lavishly designed hotel, residential, restaurant and shopping complex complete with pyramids, hieroglyphs and statues of Ramses and Anubis. The best time to visit is during the light-and-sound show that kicks off nightly at 9.30pm. In the cooler months, free outdoor movie screenings take over the Rooftop Gardens on Sunday nights at 8.30pm.

There are several excellent restaurants here, including Tomo (p78) at the Raffles Hotel, Qbara (p78) at the Wafi Fort Complex and Asha's (p77) at the Pyramids.

ZA'ABEEL PARK — PARK

Map p252 (04-325 9988; Gate 1, off Sheikh Khalifa bin Zayed Rd; admission Dh5; 8am-10pm Sun-Wed, to 11pm Thu-Sat; ; MAl Jafiliya) This sprawling park is hugely popular with families and filled with activity zones, including a pretty lake with cascades and a restaurant as well as interactive themed areas such as a Technology Zone, a Barcode Garden, an Alternative Energy Zone and a Space Maze. Views are great from the 45m-high Panoramic Tower.

The park hosts a farmers market every Friday (p73) and a flea market (p79) on the first Saturday of the month (October to May).

EATING

Bur Dubai is possibly Dubai's most eclectic area: restaurants run the gamut from dirt-cheap curry joints to white-tablecloth restaurants worthy of a Michelin star. Meena Bazaar (around the souq) and Karama are both good bets.

GOVINDA'S — VEGETARIAN $

Map p252 (04-396 0088; www.govindasdubai.com; 4A St; mains Dh22-35; lunch & dinner Sat-Thu; ; MBurJuman) Jains run this super-friendly, super-healthy vegetarian Indian restaurant where the cooking is rich in character even though the chefs shun oil, onion and garlic. Dishes to try include the velvety *paneer makhanwala* and the rich *dal makhani*. Do save room for the homemade Tru Frut natural ice cream from the attached parlour. Also tops for mocktails. It's behind the Regent Palace Hotel in Karama.

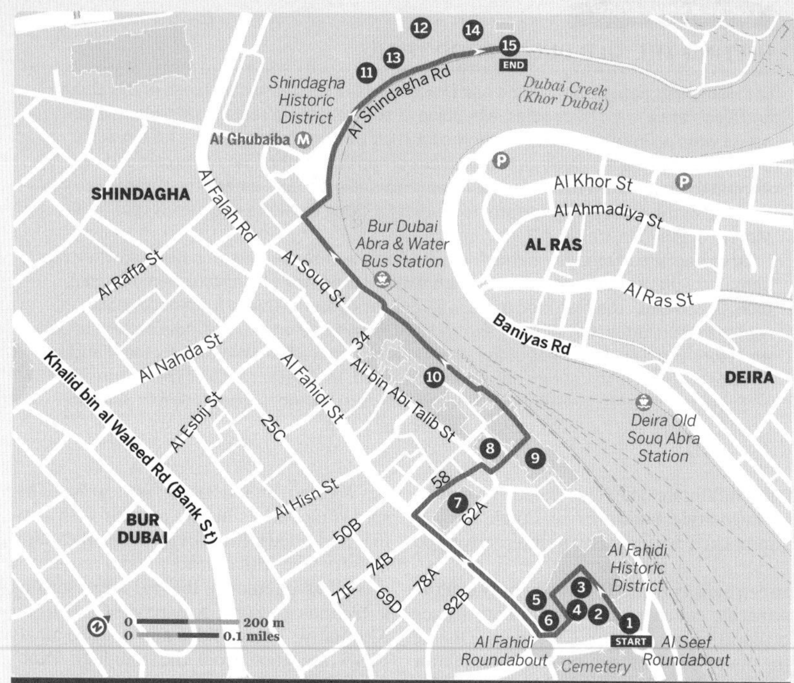

Neighbourhood Walk
Bur Dubai Waterside Walk

START AL FAHIDI HISTORIC DISTRICT
END KAN ZAMAN
LENGTH 3KM; TWO HOURS

Kick off your tour with a wander along the narrow lanes of ❶ **Al Fahidi Historic District** (p68), one of Dubai's oldest neighbourhoods. Check out the traditional wind-tower architecture. Pop into small exhibits like the ❷ **Coffee Museum** (p69) or the ❸ **Al Serkal Cultural Foundation** (p68) and stop for refreshments in the courtyard of ❹ **XVA** (p73) or the enchanting walled garden of the ❺ **Arabian Tea House** (p73).

Thus fortified, stop by the ❻ **Majlis Gallery** (p68), the oldest art space in Dubai, before continuing west along bustling Al Fahidi St to the ❼ **Dubai Museum** (p67), which introduces the history, heritage and development of this burgeoning city. Continue north from the museum and study the architectural details of the ❽ **Grand Mosque** (p69), which boasts Dubai's tallest minaret. Take the lane to the mosque's right-hand side and continue straight ahead for a few steps, then duck left into teensy ❾ **Hindi Lane** (p69), a vibrant and colourful alley with pint-sized stores selling religious paraphernalia.

Exiting Hindi Lane takes you to the wooden arcades of ❿ **Bur Dubai Souq** (p69) and its colourful textile and trinket shops. After arriving at Bur Dubai Abra Station, follow the waterfront to the Shindagha Historic District, which is lined with the restored residences of Dubai's ruling family. Several of them now house themed exhibits, such as the ⓫ **Traditional Architecture Museum** (p70) and the ⓬ **Camel Museum** (p70). The key building along here, though, is the ⓭ **Sheikh Saeed Al Maktoum House** (p70) which displays an intriguing collection of old photographs of Dubai. If you're visiting during Eid or the Dubai Shopping Festival, the ⓮ **Heritage and Diving Villages** (p70) will be a hive of activity, providing an authentic glimpse into Emirati traditions. Ponder all that you've just seen while relaxing with a fresh juice or traditional meal at the waterfront ⓯ **Kan Zaman** (p73).

SPECIAL OSTADI IRANIAN $

Map p248 (☎04-397 1469; Al Musallah Rd; mains Dh20-40; ⊙noon-4pm Sat-Thu, 6.30pm-1am daily; ⓂAl Fahidi) Everybody feels like family at this been-here-forever (since 1978) spit-and-sawdust eatery presided over by the magnificently mustachioed Mohammed. Amid walls plastered in photographs of happy guests, a fleet of swift servers brings out heaping plates of rice and kebabs into a dining room humming with chatter and laughter.

SIND PUNJAB INDIAN $

Map p248 (☎04-352 5058; Bukaz Bldg, Al Esbij St, Meena Bazaar; mains Dh11-35; ⊙8am-1.30pm; ⓂAl Fahidi, Al Ghubaiba) Like a fine wine, some restaurants only get better over time and such is the case with Sind Punjab, the first family eatery to open in Meena Bazaar in 1977. Since then, the low-frills eatery has garnered a feverishly loyal following for its finger-lickin' butter chicken and *dal makhni* (a rich lentil and kidney bean stew).

JAFFER BHAI'S INDIAN $

Map p252 (☎04-342 6467; Za'abeel Rd; mains Dh19-43; ⊙noon-midnight Sat-Thu, from 1pm Fri; ⓂADCB) Jaffer Bhai, the self-crowned 'biryani king of Mumbai', now feeds his soulful fare to adoring crowds in this modern Karama eatery decorated with a timeline of his career. The chicken biryani gets tops marks and the mutton *nihari* (the house speciality) is quite good as well, although perhaps a bit oily. Finish up with *maharani rabdi*, the Indian spin on crème brûlée. It's near the Karama post office.

ERIC'S INDIAN $

Map p252 (☎04-396 5080; 10b St, Sheikh Hamdan Colony, Karama; mains Dh18-32; ⊙lunch & dinner; ⓂBurJuman, ADCB) Prints by Goan cartoonist Mario Miranda decorate the simple but buzzing dining room of this purveyor of magically spiced dishes from this tropical Indian island. The menu has few false notes but popular items include the chicken 'lollipops' (drumsticks), the Bombay duck (which is actually a fish!) and the chicken *xacuti*, a mouth-watering curry with poppy seeds.

JAMBO'S GRILL EAST AFRICAN $

Map p252 (☎04-358 3583; www.jambosgrill.com; Za'abeel Rd; mains Dh18-109; ⊙noon-3pm & 7pm-midnight Tue-Thu, Sat & Sun, 1-4pm & 7pm-midnight Fri; ⓂADCB) Study the colourful mural of East Africa while taking your taste buds on a safari around Kenya and Tanzania at this upbeat Karama eatery. This is the place to try *mishkaki* (super-tender chunks of beef served with two chutneys and a fiery hot sauce), the coconut-based *kuku paka* roast chicken curry and the intensely spiced prawn *pili-pili*. Nice mocktails, too.

RIPE FOOD & CRAFT MARKET MARKET $

Map p252 (☎04-380 7602; Gate 1, Za'abeel Park; ⊙9am-2pm Fri Nov-Mar; ⓂAl Jafiliya) With the local-seasonal-organic trend finally engulfing Dubai, it's no surprise that the city has sprouted a proper weekly farmers market. Held every Friday in beautiful Za'abeel Park, it features not only fruit and veg but also local honey, nuts, spices and eggs, plus arts and crafts, food stations and locally roasted gourmet coffee. Pretty much all you need for a picnic under the palms.

ARABIAN TEA HOUSE CAFE $

Map p248 (☎04-353 5071; www.arabiantea-house.com; Al Fahidi St; mains Dh30-45; ⊙7am-11pm; ⓂAl Fahidi) A grand old tree, white wicker chairs, turquoise benches and billowing flowers create a sun-dappled refuge in the courtyard of an old pearl merchant's house. The food is respectable cafe fare – salads, sandwiches, quiches – but it's the vast selection of quality teas that makes this place so special. For a local treat, try the Arabic breakfast.

XVA CAFÉ CAFE $

Map p248 (☎04-353 5383; www.xvahotel.com/cafe; off Al Fahidi St; mains Dh20-35; ⊙9am-7pm Sat-Thu, 10am-5pm Fri Nov-Apr; 🖉; ⓂAl Fahidi) Tucked into the historic Al Fahidi district, this cultured courtyard cafe set within the eponymous boutique hotel and gallery puts the emphasis on meat-free fare such as eggplant burgers, burghul salad and *mor-jardara* (rice topped with sautéed veggies and yoghurt). The mint lemonade is a great energy booster on a hot day.

KAN ZAMAN MIDDLE EASTERN $

Map p248 (☎04-393 9913; Shindagha Historic District; appetisers Dh10-36, grills Dh35-59, sheesha Dh30; ⊙5pm-2am; ⓂAl Ghubaiba) This traditional Creekside hang-out is perfect for watching the sunset over a juice and mezze, but to see it at its bustling best you need to come later in the evening when *sheesha* aficionados invade to relax with a view of the dhows heading out to sea. It's near Shindagha Tunnel.

JOHN ELK/GETTY IMAGES ©

BRENT WINEBRENNER & DEGELIA/GETTY IMAGES ©

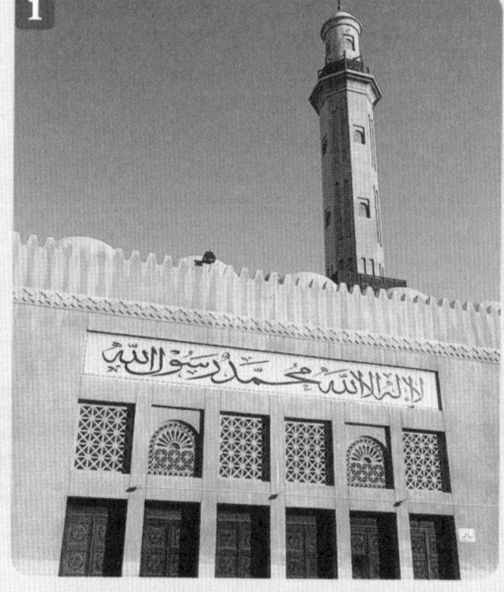

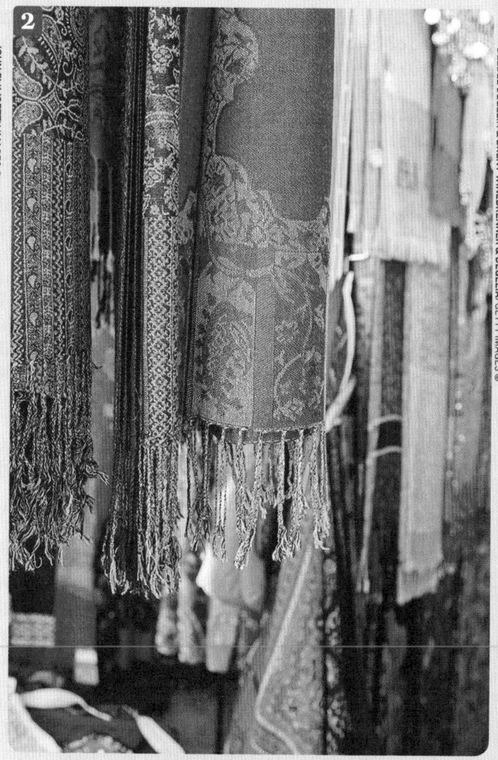

1. Grand Mosque (p69)
Dubai's tallest minaret (70m high) attracts visitors to the city's largest mosque.

2. Bur Dubai Souq (p69)
Colourful pashminas entice shoppers at this busy souq.

3. Sheikh Mohammed Centre for Cultural Understanding (p68)
A guide in traditional men's clothing demonstrates how he prays in the Centre's mosque.

4. Al Fahidi Historic District (p68)
The buildings that make up this heritage area contain craft shops, cultural exhibits, cafes and art galleries.

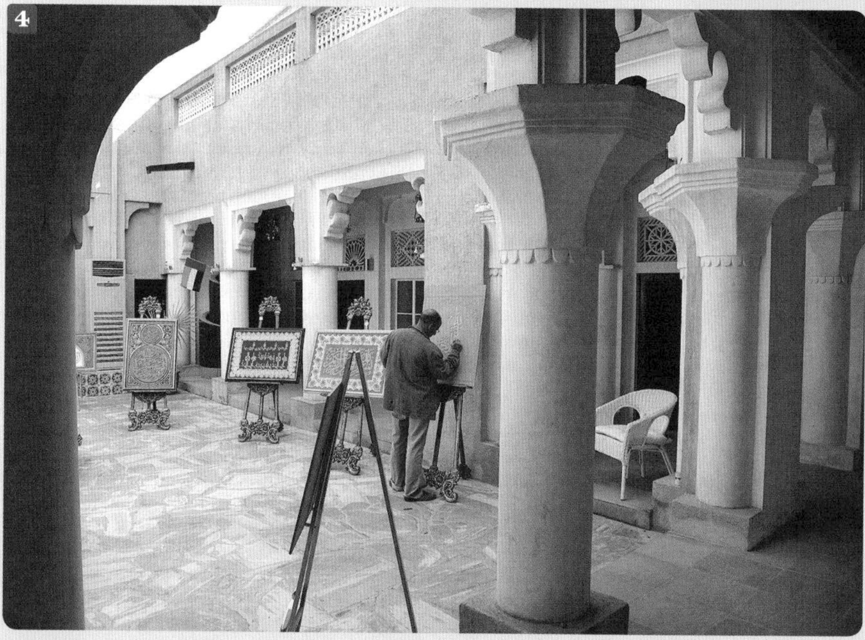

GALLO IMAGES/GETTY IMAGES ©

3

VAIBHAV INDIAN $

Map p248 (☎04-353 8130; www.vaibhav.ae; Al Fahidi St; snacks Dh3-17; ⏰7.30am-11pm; ✎; Ⓜ Al Fahidi) This always bustling all-veg Indian street-food haven and bakery may be tucked into a lane in Meena Bazaar, but might as well be in Mumbai. It does a roaring trade in *pav bhaji* (thick tomato-based sauce served with a fresh bread roll), *dosas* (savoury wraps) and stuffed *parathas* (pan-fried flatbread), all prepared right in front of you in a Bollywood-worthy spectacle. It's behind the National Bank of Dubai.

NEPALIKO SAGARMATHA NEPALI $

Map p248 (☎04-393 9775; off Al Fahidi & 11th St; mains Dh10-20; ⏰noon-midnight; Ⓜ Al Ghubaiba) A favourite gathering place of Dubai's Nepali expats, this small joint serves fabulous *momos* (dumplings), including a version filled with buffalo meat, paired with two spicy dipping sauces. It's run by a former trekking guide.

LEMONGRASS THAI $

Map p252 (☎04-334 2325; www.lemongrassrestaurants.com; ground fl, Bu Haleeba Bldg; mains Dh26-69; ⏰noon-11.30pm; Ⓜ Oud Metha) Lemongrass' soothing mango-and-lime-coloured dining room is an ideal backdrop for brightly flavoured cooking that spans the arc from pad thai (nicely presented in an omelette wrapper) to curries with a marvellous depth of flavour. If you like spicy, say so; the kitchen can be shy with the heat. Located next to Lamcy Plaza.

BACCHANALIAN BOATING

A great way to experience the magic of 'Old Dubai' is during a dinner cruise along the Creek. Feed tummy and soul as you gently cruise past historic waterfront houses, sparkling high-rises, jutting wind towers and dhows bound for India or Iran. Dining rooms are air-conditioned and alcohol is served. **Bateaux Dubai** (☎04-814 5553; www.bateauxdubai.com; Al Seef Rd, next to Rulers Court, Bur Dubai waterfront; per person 2½hr dinner cruise Dh400; ⏰8.30-11pm; Ⓜ Al Fahidi) is a good choice, especially if food is as important to you as ambience. Indulge in a four-course à la carte feast aboard this stylish contemporary boat with panoramic windows, linen-draped tables and live music. The other recommended dinner cruise is Al Mansour Dhow (p61) in Deira.

LOCAL HOUSE ARABIC $

Map p248 (☎04-354 0705; www.localhousedubai.com; Al Fahidi St; mains Dh25-55; ⏰11am-10pm; Ⓜ Al Fahidi) This lovely courtyard restaurant on the edge of Al Fahidi Historic District made headlines in 2010 when it became the first in the United Arab Emirates (UAE) to serve camel burgers. Vegetarians can stick to the camel-milk shakes.

KARACHI DARBAR PAKISTANI $

Map p252 (☎04-334 7272; 33B St, Karama Market; mains Dh7-28; ⏰4-2am; Ⓜ ADCB) A favourite pit stop of expats and Karama Market shoppers with an eye for a biryani bargain, this local chain puts tummies into a state of contentment with a huge menu of Pakistani, Indian and Chinese dishes. Reliable picks include shrimp masala, mutton kadai and butter chicken. The chef can be a bit too generous with the oil or ghee (clarified butter). It's near Lulu Supermarket.

SARAVANA BHAVAN INDIAN, VEGETARIAN $

Map p248 (☎04-353 9988; www.saravanabhavan.com; 4-5 Khalifa bin Saeed Bldg; dishes Dh7-16; ⏰7am-11pm Sat-Wed, to 11.30pm Thu & Fri; ✎; Ⓜ Al Ghubaiba) Head a block back from the Bur Dubai Abra Station to find this superb no-frills place, one of the best Indian vegetarian restaurants in town. If you thought vegetarian was restrictive, think again. The vast menu includes wonderfully buttery paneer vegetarian dishes, rogan josh, biryanis, *dosas* and a medley of side orders. It's near HSBC Bank.

LEBANESE VILLAGE RESTAURANT LEBANESE $

Map p248 (☎04-352 2522; Al Mankhool Rd; mains Dh30-50; ⏰noon-2am; Ⓜ Al Fahidi) Tastes are vivid and fresh at this tried-and-true eatery where the best seats are under a shady umbrella on the sidewalk terrace (more appealing than the bright diner-style interior). The menu has few surprises but that's OK because it does staples like grills, hummus and tabbouleh dependably well. Also handy for takeaway if you're staying in a nearby hotel apartment. It's near the Ramada Hotel.

CURRY LEAF SRI LANKAN $

Map p248 (☎04-397 8940; Al Mussalla Tower; mains Dh9-52; ⏰9am-11pm; Ⓜ Al Fahidi) A gem hidden in the food court of a badly ageing mall, Curry Leaf is a local favourite for genuine Sri Lankan fare. The signature hoppers (crispy rice-flour pancakes with fried egg) go well with the smoky-hot curries, while *lumpries* (spiced rice baked with meat, egg and aubergine) is a delicious Dutch-colonial culinary treat. It's next to Al Fahidi metro station.

ASHA'S MODERN INDIAN $$

Map p252 (☎04-324 4100; www.ashasrestaurants.com/dubai; 1st fl, Pyramids, Wafi City; set lunch Dh75, mains Dh55-225; ⊙lunch & dinner; MDubai Healthcare City) Namesake of legendary Bollywood singer Asha Bhosle, this sensuously lit, tandoori-orange dining room shines the spotlight on contemporary northwest Indian fare. The extensive menu includes the hilariously named Same Old Chicken Curry, which is anything but thanks to the addition of rose water and saffron. Dine in or on the terrace overlooking the Wafi City courtyard.

PICANTE PORTUGUESE $$

Map p248 (☎04-397 7444; www.picantedubai.com; Four Points by Sheraton Bur Dubai, Khalid bin al Walid Rd; mains Dh70-160; ⊙lunch & dinner; 📶; MAl Fahidi) Picante is decked out in orange and blue, the dominant colours of the bluffs and the sea of the Algarve beaches on the south coast of Portugal whose cuisine it celebrates. Typical dishes include *bacalhau* (salt cod fillet), *estufado* (chicken stew) and *pastel de nata* (egg custard) for dessert.

AWTAR ARABIC $$

(☎04-317 2222; Grand Hyatt Dubai, Al Qataiyat Rd; mains Dh55-130; ⊙7.30pm-3am; MDubai Healthcare City) Locals love the opulent Bedouin tent-like atmosphere and warm welcome of this formal Lebanese restaurant, complete with belly dancer and live band. The menu presents a veritable lexicon of mezze perfect for grazing and sharing, while carnivores can tuck into the grilled meats (the lamb is excellent). Round up a posse and come at 10pm, when the scene gets rockin'.

CHUTNEYS INDIAN $$

Map p252 (☎04-310 4340; Mövenpick Hotel Bur Dubai, 19 St; mains Dh60-80, thali Dh55-80; MDubai Healthcare City, Oud Metha) Chutneys provides a richly nuanced culinary journey to northern India. There's lots of familiar feel-good fare including juicy kebabs and fluffy biryanis, but if you want to branch out, try the *tawa murgh rayyan* – a chicken- and tomato-based curry. Dinners get downright romantic if you close the curtains around your table. The lunchtime-only thalis (set meals) are superb as well.

A QUESTION OF PORK

Pork is available for non-Muslims in a special room at some larger supermarkets such as Spinneys. In many hotel restaurants, pork is a menu item and is clearly labelled as such. For those used to eating pork, the 'beef bacon' and 'turkey ham' alternatives that are commonly available are often nothing more than a reminder of how tasty the real thing is.

BAIT AL WAKEEL ARABIC $$

Map p248 (☎04-353 0530; Waterfront, Bur Dubai Souq; mezze Dh12-30, mains Dh35-120; ⊙noon-11pm; MAl Ghubaiba) Teeming with tourists lured by the romantic Creekside setting, this restaurant occupies one of Dubai's oldest buildings (from 1935) and has a great wooden dining deck that used to be a boat landing. Come for coffee, juice or mezze and enjoy the view. Secret tip: for an even better perspective, head up to the roof via the stairs in the back of the restaurant.

KHAZANA INDIAN $$

Map p252 (☎04-336 0061; www.khanakhazanadubai.net; 10th St, Al Nasr Leisureland; mains Dh55-175; ⊙lunch & dinner; 🖉; MOud Metha) Celebrity chef Sanjeer Kapoor's first signature joint is still one of the best Indian restaurants in town, if the loyal following of regulars is any indication. Everything from curries to tandoor dishes tastes genuine, fresh and inflected with an authentic medley of spices. Ample bamboo and rattan creates a relaxed feel-good ambience, helped along by the friendly servers.

ANTIQUE BAZAAR INDIAN $$

Map p248 (☎04-397 7444; Four Points by Sheraton Bur Dubai, Khalid bin al Waleed Rd; mains Dh42-90; ⊙lunch & dinner; 📶; MAl Fahidi) Resembling an exotic Mogul palace, Antique Bazaar's decor is sumptuously ornate with carved-wood seats, ivory-inset tables and richly patterned fabrics. Thumbs up to the *machli mirch ka salan* (fish with coconut, tamarind and curry) and the *gosht awadhi biryani* (rice with lamb, saffron and nuts).

At dinnertime, a music and dance show competes with the food for your attention.

PAUL CAFE $$

Map p252 (04-327 9669; Wafi Mall, Sheikh Rashid Rd; mains Dh30-100; 10am-10pm Sat-Wed, to midnight Thu & Fri; ; Dubai Healthcare City) This French cafe is an upmarket mall staple that's beloved for its scrumptious freshly baked goods (great almond croissants!). The menu features a large variety of dishes, from ample-sized breakfasts to crisp salads, bulging sandwiches and such satisfying mains as cod with ratatouille or classic steak and fries. There are additional branches at several other malls.

★QBARA MIDDLE EASTERN $$$

Map p252 (04-709 2500; www.qbara.ae; Wafi Fort Complex, near 13th & 28th Sts; mains Dh90-250; 6pm-1am; Dubai Healthcare City) Qbara gets our vote for most beautiful restaurant in Dubai. Think dark, mysterious and sensuous with a 10m-long bar leading to the circular dining room punctuated with a huge glass-bubble chandelier. The bar is backed by a wall carved with Islamic motifs reaching all the way to the upstairs lounge. The innovative modern Arabic cuisine can easily compete with the stunning decor.

★TOMO JAPANESE $$$

Map p252 (04-357 7888; www.tomo.ae; Wafi City, Raffles Hotel; mains Dh70-550; 12.30-3.30pm & 6.30pm-1am; ; Dubai Healthcare City) Visiting celebs aren't the only ones who love this gorgeously formal lair where Chitoshi Takahashi serves top Japanese cuisine. No gimmicky fusion here, just perfect super-fresh cuts of sushi and sashimi, delectable Wagyu beef, feathery tempura and other treasured morsels served on the 17th floor of the Raffles Hotel. Snag a table on the 360-degree terrace with the entire city glittering below.

PEPPERCRAB SINGAPOREAN $$$

(04-317 2222; Grand Hyatt Dubai, Al Qataiyat Rd; dishes Dh40-175, crab per 100g Dh45; 7-11.30pm Sat-Wed, to midnight Thu & Fri; Dubai Healthcare City) If you've never had Singaporean food, Peppercrab is perfect for surrendering your culinary virginity. Prepare your palate with wasabi shrimp and wok-fried duck, then don an apron and get ready to do battle with the main event, the eponymous 'peppercrab' – a succulent, tender crustacean prepared in your choice of half a dozen ways.

> **TIME FOR A CUPPA?**
>
> **Meena Bazaar** is ideal for a pick-me-up in the form of a steaming cup of masala chai (also called kadak chai). It's a blend of black tea boiled with milk, sugar and spices (typically cardamom, cloves, peppercorns, cinnamon or a combination thereof) that was brought to the Gulf by expats from India and Pakistan and is popular even at the height of summer. Pop into any of the local cafes around here and treat yourself to a cup or two.

DRINKING & NIGHTLIFE

BOX CLUB

Map p248 (04-355 6600; Al Rolla Rd; 10pm-3am Mon-Sat; Al Fahidi) It remains to be seen if this new kid on the block at the Raintree Rolla Hotel can grow wings, but the early signs are pretty promising, especially during ladies' night on Wednesdays when R&B, hip-hop, soul and funk rule the dance floor.

VELVET UNDERGROUND CLUB

Map p248 (04-355 8500; Khalid bin al Waleed Rd; 10.30pm-3am; BurJuman) Global locals keep it cool and attitude-free while letting loose on the dance floor to a gamut of sounds from house to R&B and Bollywood tunes at this popular club at the Royal Ascot Hotel (not to be confused with the Ascot Hotel).

GEORGE & DRAGON PUB

Map p248 (04-393 9444; Al Falah Rd, Meena Bazaar; 7pm-3am; Al Ghubaiba) Keeping barflies boozy for over 15 years, this quintessential British dive comes with the requisite dart board, pool table, greasy fish and chips, cheap beer and a painted window of St George jousting with the dragon. In the Ambassador, Dubai's oldest hotel (since 1971), it's fun and full of character(s) but perhaps not the ideal place for date night.

ROCK BOTTOM CAFÉ PUB

Map p248 (04-396 3888; Regent Palace Hotel, Sheikh Khalifa bin Zayed Rd; noon-3am; ; BurJuman) This been-here-forever place has a '70s-era American roadhouse feel, with a cover band blaring out Top-40 hits and a DJ filling in the breaks with gusto. By day it's a regular cafe serving Tex-Mex, but with a mob of friends and a bottle of tequila gone, it's the quintessential ending to a rollickin' night on the town.

COOZ BAR

(04-317 2222; www.dubai.grand.hyatt.com; Grand Hyatt Dubai, Al Qataiyat Rd; 9-3am; Dubai Healthcare City) Sip a martini at this dimly lit, stylish cocktail bar and enjoy some smooth live jazz by the resident singer and pianist.

PEOPLE BY CRYSTAL CLUB

Map p252 (050-297 2097; www.dubai.raffles.com; Raffles Dubai, Sheikh Rashid Rd; 11pm-3am Thu-Sat; Dubai Healthcare City) On the two top floors of the pyramid-shaped Raffles, this see-and-be-seen club boasts made-to-impress decor, panoramic city views and world-class DJs. There are lots of nooks and lounges for quiet tête-a-têtes if you need a break from the dance floor.

ENTERTAINMENT

★MUSIC ROOM LIVE MUSIC

Map p248 (04-359 8888; www.themusicroomdubai.com; Majestic Hotel, Al Mankhool Rd; 8pm-3am; Al Fahidi) Arab hip-hop queen Malikah and English metal band Salem are among the many artists who've played gigs at Dubai's best place for indie and alt-sounds from local, regional and international talent. Great for dipping into the local music scene, it's the kind of spot that appeals to music aficionados who keep attitude to a minimum.

CREEKSIDE CAFE CULTURAL SPACE

Map p248 (04-359 9220; www.creeksidedubai.me; Waterfront, Bur Dubai Souq; 10am-10pm; Al Fahidi) New on the scene, this contemporary cultural space and cafe puts on all sorts of workshops (pottery, marbling, silkscreen etc) as well as hosting film screenings, book presentations and readings. It's also a good place to simply swing by for a cup o' java with a view of the Creek.

LOCAL KNOWLEDGE

TAILOR-MADE FASHION

The backstreets of Bur Dubai are filled with talented Indian tailors who will run up a dress or suit for you in a couple of days. Some also sell material, although you'd be better off paying a visit to the nearby Textile Souq (within the main Bur Dubai Souq; p69), where you can ponder over endless swatches of wonderful fabrics. The best street for choice is Al Hisn (off Al Fahidi St, near the Dubai Museum), where reliable tailors include poetically named Dream Girls and Hollywood Tailors. Expect to pay about Dh150 for a dress and allow at least three days for your garment to be sewn up.

SHOPPING

DUBAI FLEA MARKET FLEA MARKET

Map p252 (www.dubai-fleamarket.com; Gates 1, 2 & 3 Za'abeel Park; admission Dh5; 8am-3pm every 1st Sat Oct-May; Al Jafiliya) Flea markets are like urban archaeology: you'll need plenty of patience and luck when sifting through other people's trash and detritus, but oh, the thrill when finally unearthing a piece of treasure! Trade malls for stalls and look for bargains amid the piles of pre-loved stuff that's spilled out of local closets.

WAFI MALL MALL

Map p252 (04-324 4555; www.wafi.com; Sheikh Rashid & Oud Metha Rds; 10am-10pm Sat-Wed, to midnight Thu & Fri; Dubai Healthcare City) At the heart of Wafi City, a hotel, retail and residential complex designed in the style of ancient Egypt, is one of Dubai's older but architecturally most stunning malls. Alas, eclipsed by bigger and more central ones, it's often sadly deserted. Its biggest eye-catchers are the stained-glass pyramids and a vast dome. In the basement, the Souq Khan Murjan sells crafts from around the Arabian world and was modelled after the original Baghdad bazaar.

THE ONE HOME FURNISHINGS

Map p252 (04-324 1224; www.theone.com; Wafi Mall; 10am-10pm Sat-Wed, to midnight Thu & Fri; Dubai Healthcare City) Nirvana for design-minded home decorators, this airy showroom unites funky, innovative and top-quality items from dozens of international manufacturers. Even everyday items get a

DUBAI'S SHOPPING FESTIVALS

Every year in January, the month-long **Dubai Shopping Festival** (www.mydsf.com) draws hordes of bargain-hunting tourists from around the world. This is a good time to visit Dubai: in addition to the huge discounts in the souqs and malls, the weather is usually gorgeous and the city is abuzz. Outdoor souqs, amusement rides and food stalls are set up in many neighbourhoods. There are traditional performances and displays at the Heritage and Diving Villages (p70), family entertainment across the city, concerts, fireworks and events in the parks. **Dubai Shopping Surprises**, a related event, is held during the unbearably hot months of July and August; it mainly attracts visitors from other Gulf countries. Insider tip: for the best bargains at either festival, come during the last week, when retailers slash prices even further to clear out their inventory.

The carnival-like **Global Village** (☎04-362 4114; www.globalvillage.ae; Hwy E311, exit 37; admission Dh15; ⏲4pm-midnight Sat-Wed, to 1am Thu & Fri) runs from late November to late March, about 13km south of Sheikh Zayed Road. Think of it as a sort of 'world fair' for shoppers. Each of the 30-something pavilions showcases a specific nation's culture and – of course – products. Some favourites: the Afghanistan pavilion for fretwork-bordered stone pendants and beaded-silver earrings; Palestine for traditional cross-stitch *kandouras* (casual shirt-dresses worn by men and women) and ever-popular cushion covers; Yemen for its authentic *khanjars* (traditional curved daggers); India for spangled fabrics and slippers; and Kenya for its kitsch bottle-top handbags.

Aside from shopping, there's also lots of entertainment – from Chinese opera to Turkish whirling dervishes – as well as a funfair with dozens of rides from tame to terrifying. Other fun zones may include a heritage village, a 3D haunted house, huge sand sculptures and a prehistoric oceanarium. Global Village is off Hwy 311, exit 37. Bus 103 travels here from Union metro station in Deira, bus 104 from Al Ghubaiba metro station in Bur Dubai.

zany twist here, like pearl-beaded pillows, tigerprint wing-back chairs or vintage-style pendant lamps.

BURJUMAN — MALL

Map p248 (☎04-352 0222; www.burjuman.com; Sheikh Khalifa bin Zayed Rd; ⏲10am-10pm Sat-Wed, to 11pm Thu & Fri; 📶; Ⓜ BurJuman) This high-end mall was in the process of large-scale remodelling at the time we visited. Once completed, it will boast a new 14-screen multiplex cinema, an expanded food court and a vast Carrefour supermarket branch in addition to an eclectic mix of stores from high-street chains to couture brands.

SAKS FIFTH AVENUE — FASHION

Map p248 (☎04-501 2700; www.saksme.com; BurJuman Mall, Sheikh Khalifa bin Zayed Rd; ⏲10am-10pm Sun-Wed, to 11pm Thu & Fri; Ⓜ BurJuman) Founded in 1898 in New York City, the Dubai branch of this luxury department store has kept label-loving Dubai residents and visitors looking good for over a decade. Racks brim with both classic designers like Balmain and Cerruti as well as the latest shooting stars, including some regional contenders like Feiruza Mudessir's label Finchitua.

SUN & SAND SPORTS FACTORY OUTLET — SPORTING GOODS

Map p248 (☎04-351 6222; www.sunandsand-sports.com; Khalid bin Al Waleed Rd, near 18th St; ⏲10am-10pm; Ⓜ BurJuman) This is the factory outlet branch of one of the biggest sporting goods retailers in the region with a storeroom jam-packed with shoes, rackets, jackets and more from major international brands. Prices tend to be a bit lower than usual, but it's the big selection that gives this place an additional edge.

BATEEL — FOOD

Map p248 (☎04-359 7932; www.bateel.com; BurJuman Mall, Sheikh Khalifa bin Zayed Rd; ⏲10am-10pm Sun-Wed, to 11pm Thu & Fri; Ⓜ BurJuman) Old-style traditional Arabian hospitality meant dates and camel milk. Now Emiratis offer their guests Bateel's scrumptious date chocolates and truffles, made using European chocolate-making techniques. Staff are happy to give you a sample before you buy. Check the website for additional branches, and if you fancy a date cake or pastry, check out Cafe Bateel on the same level.

COMPUTER PLAZA @ AL AIN CENTRE
ELECTRONICS

Map p248 (☎04-352 6663; www.alaincentre.com; Al Mankhool Rd; ⏰10am-10pm Sat-Thu, 2-10pm Fri; Ⓜ Al Fahidi) Jam-packed with small shops selling every kind of software, hardware and accessory for PCs, this computer and electronics mall also has a good range of digital cameras and mobile phones. On the ground floor, a handful of fast-food outlets and an ice-cream counter keep tummy rumblings in check. It's next to Spinneys.

FABINDIA
FASHION

Map p248 (☎04-398 9633; www.fabindia.com; Al Mankhool Rd; ⏰10am-10pm Sat-Thu, 4-10pm Fri; Ⓜ ADCB) In business since 1950, Fabindia is one of India's biggest retail chains and sells mostly products made by Indian villagers using traditional skills and techniques. There's a huge selection of fashion, furnishings and handicrafts, including colourful *kurtis* (tunics), elegant shawls, patterned silk cushions and organic teas and chutneys, all sold at very reasonable prices. It's near the EPPCO petrol station.

AJMAL
PERFUME

Map p248 (☎04-351 5505; www.ajmalperfume.com; BurJuman Mall, Sheikh Khalifa bin Zayed Rd; ⏰10am-10pm Sat-Wed, to 11pm Thu & Fri; Ⓜ BurJuman) The place for traditional Arabian *attars* (perfumes), Ajmal custom blends its earthy scents and pours them into fancy gold or jewel-encrusted bottles. These aren't frilly French colognes – they're woody and pungent perfumes. Ask for the signature scent 'Ajmal', based on white musk and jasmine. Other branches are in Deira City Centre, the Mall of the Emirates and the Dubai Mall.

KARAMA MARKET
SHOPPING AREA

Map p252 (18B St; Ⓜ ADCB) A visually unappealing concrete souq, Karama's bustling backstreet shopping area is crammed with stores selling handicrafts and souvenirs. Vendors may also likely offer to take you to 'secret rooms' in the back of the building that are crammed with knock-off designer bags and watches. Quality varies, so it pays to have a keen eye and to know what the originals look like. Prices are low, but bargaining lowers them further.

ROYAL SAFFRON
SPICES

Map p248 (Al Fahidi Historic District; Ⓜ Al Fahidi) This tiny shop tucked into the quiet lanes of Al Fahidi Historic District is a photogenic find. It's crammed full of spices like cloves, cardamom and cinnamon, plus fragrant oils, dried fruits and nuts, frankincense from Somalia and Oman, henna hair dye – and quirky salt and pepper sheikh and sheikhas.

SILK WONDERS
SOUVENIRS

Map p248 (☎04-351 3251; www.silkwonder.com; Atheryat Mall, Al Fahidi St; Ⓜ Al Fahidi) Near the Dubai Museum, this is one of several pick-and-mix stores filled with inexpensive stuff to bring the folks back home. Max out your luggage allowance with shawls, perfumes, embroidered clutches, sequined bedspreads and pillows, woven silk-and-wool rugs, ornaments from India, Iranian carved boxes and plenty of other neat trinkets.

LOCAL KNOWLEDGE

CRICKET CRAZY

The enormous Indian and Pakistani communities in Dubai l-o-v-e cricket. You'll see them playing on sandy lots between buildings during their lunch breaks, in parks on their days off, and late at night in empty car parks. In contrast, you won't see Emiratis playing: cricket in Dubai belongs to the subcontinental nationalities. If you want to get under the skin of the game, talk to taxi drivers. But first ask where your driver is from – there's fierce competition between Pakistanis and Indians. Each will tell you that his country's team is the best, and then explain at length why. (Some drivers need a bit of cajoling; show enthusiasm and you'll get the whole story.) When Pakistan plays India, the city lights up. Remember: these two nationalities account for about 45% of Dubai's population, far outnumbering Emiratis. Because most of them can't afford the price of satellite TV, they meet up outside their local eateries in Deira or Bur Dubai to watch the match. Throngs of riveted fans swarm the pavements beneath the crackling neon – it's a sight to behold.

MINI-CRUISES

A great way to see the sights is by taking a mini-cruise offered by **Dubai Ferry** (Map p248; ☎800 9090; www.rta.ae; Al Ghubaiba Water Station, Shindagha Waterfront; gold/silver tickets Dh75/50, children 2-10yr half-price; Ⓜ Al Ghubaiba). Boats leave several times daily from landing docks next to Al Ghubaiba metro station. The 90-minute one-way trip along the coast to Dubai Marina travels past Jumeirah, the Burj Al Arab and the Palm Jumeirah and leaves at 11am, 1pm and 6.30pm. There's also a one-hour afternoon tea round-trip cruise going down Dubai Creek as far as the Floating Bridge at 3pm and a one-hour sunset cruise to Jumeirah Beach leaving at 5pm. The boats are quite comfortable with an air-conditioned interior and an open deck in case you want to stick your nose into the breeze. Soft drinks and snacks are available.

SPORTS & ACTIVITIES

PHARAOHS' CLUB — GYM

Map p252 (☎04-324 0000; www.cleopatrasspaandwellness.com; Wafi Mall, Sheikh Rashid Rd; gym/pool per day Dh200/130; ⏲6.30am-10pm Sat-Thu, 9am-9pm Fri; Ⓜ Dubai Healthcare City) Pump it up at this top-notch fitness club which has some serious weight-lifting equipment (including 100lb dumbbells), a superb climbing wall (measuring up at a dizzy 13.5m) and various fitness classes. The best amenity is the enormous, free-form 'lazy-river' rooftop swimming pool, which is available for one-day drop-ins and is great for kids.

WONDER BUS TOURS — BOAT TOUR

Map p248 (☎04-359 5656; www.wonderbusdubai.net; ground fl, BurJuman Centre; adult/child 3-11yr Dh160/115; ⏲several times daily; Ⓜ BurJuman) These unusual sightseeing tours have you boarding the bright yellow amphibious Wonder Bus at the BurJuman Centre, driving down to the Creek, plunging into the water, cruising past historic Bur Dubai and Deira and returning to the shopping mall, all within the space of one hour.

AL NASR LEISURELAND — ACTIVITY CENTRE

Map p252 (☎04-337 1234; www.alnasrll.com; 12A St, Oud Metha; adult/child 3-9yr Dh10/5; ⏲9am-11pm; 👪; Ⓜ Oud Metha) Open since 1979, Leisureland is definitely old school, but it's got a bit of character and lots of facilities under one roof, including tennis and squash courts, a bowling alley and an ice rink. Non-members pay admission plus a fee for whatever sporting activity they fancy. Rates are very reasonable.

Of the several eateries, Viva Goa (Indian restaurant) is the best pick. Tuesdays are reserved for women and children. It's behind the American Hospital.

Downtown Dubai

DOWNTOWN DUBAI | FINANCIAL DISTRICT | AL QUOZ

Neighbourhood Top Five

❶ Craning your neck to take in the entire length of the elegantly tapered **Burj Khalifa** (p85), which pierces the sky at 828m, making it the world's tallest building. A superfast elevator drops you at observation platforms on the 124th and 148th levels.

❷ Shopping at the mother of all malls: **Dubai Mall** (p97), with a record-breaking 1200 shops.

❸ Keeping tabs on the latest in Middle Eastern art at the galleries in **Alserkal Avenue** (p92).

❹ Spotting flamingos and migratory birds at **Ras Al Khor Wildlife Sanctuary** (p87).

❺ Feeling hypnotised by the beautifully choreographed singing and dancing **Dubai Fountain** (p86).

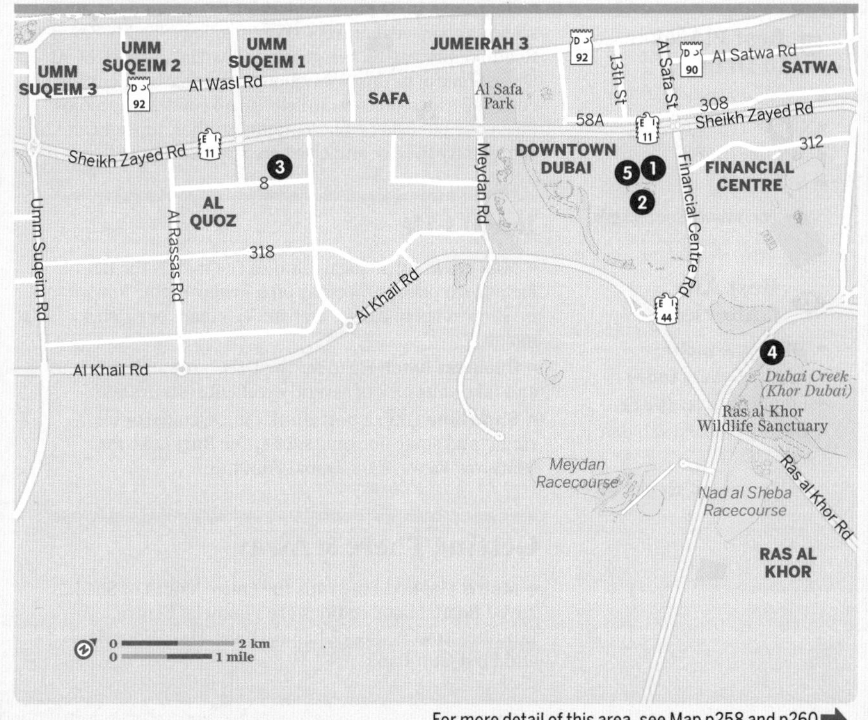

For more detail of this area, see Map p258 and p260

Lonely Planet's Top Tip

The trip to the world's highest observation platform in the world's tallest building – the Burj Khalifa – is one of the hottest tickets in town. Unless you fancy paying a premium for an on-the-spot fast-track ticket, book your preferred time slot online as early as possible to avoid disappointment, especially if you're in Dubai on a short stay.

Best Places to Eat

- Thiptara (p93)
- Zaroob (p94)
- Clé Dubai (p94)
- Baker & Spice (p93)
- Tom & Serg (p95)

For reviews, see p92.

Best Places to Drink

- Calabar (p95)
- Cabana (p95)
- The Act (p96)
- Neos (p95)

For reviews, see p95.

Best Art Galleries

- Third Line (p89)
- Ayyam Gallery (p87)
- Empty Quarter (p87)
- Gallery Isabelle van den Eynde (p88)

For reviews, see p88.

Explore Downtown Dubai

Downtown Dubai is the city's vibrant urban hub and a key destination for visitors. Its literal pinnacle is the Burj Khalifa – the world's tallest building – which overlooks the Dubai Mall. The world's biggest shopping temple, it also teems with crowd-pleasing attractions, including a massive aquarium, an ice rink and a complete dinosaur skeleton. The mall flanks the Burj Lake where the mesmerising Dubai Fountain erupts in choreographed dance, music and light shows nightly. For front-row views, book a table at a restaurant in the mall, in the Arabian-themed Souk Al Bahar or at one of the five-star hotels ringing the lake. Still under construction is Downtown Dubai's 'Opera District' which will be anchored by a 2000-seat opera house.

Dubai's financial heart, meanwhile, beats north of Downtown along Sheikh Zayed Road, the city's main artery. Banks, investment companies and the stock exchange make their home at the Dubai International Financial Centre (DIFC). There's little reason to visit unless you're interested in architecture, in which case the Gate Building and the Jumeirah Emirates Towers (where Dubai's ruler Sheikh Mohammed keeps his offices) make appealing photo-ops. Art fans can scan the prestigious galleries at DIFC's Gate Village for the latest in Middle Eastern art.

To tap in to Dubai's underground art and creative scene, ur ban adventurers should follow Sheikh Zayed Road sout hwest to the gritty, industrial district of Al Quoz. Some of its dusty warehouses now harbour cutting-edge galleries alongside an eclectic mix of design studios, magazine publishers, photography studios, hipster cafes, community theatre and other creative enterprises.

Local Life

- **Mall crawling** To local families the mall is the de facto town plaza, especially on a Friday night. Join in: shop, relax in a cafe, grab an ice cream or catch a movie.
- **Business lunch** Head for the DIFC around lunchtime and take your pick of several excellent restaurants.
- **Showtime** Grab a post-dinner juice, coffee or ice cream and stake out your spot at the Burj Lake for front-row views of the Dubai Fountain.

Getting There & Away

- **Metro** The Red Line runs the entire length of Sheikh Zayed Road. Major stations are Financial Centre, Emirates Towers, Burj Khalifa/Dubai Mall, Noor Bank and First Gulf Bank.

TOP SIGHT
BURJ KHALIFA

The Burj Khalifa is a ground-breaking feat of architecture and engineering, with two observation decks on the 124th and 148th floors and a restaurant-bar on the 122nd. The world's tallest building (828m), it opened in 2010, only six years after excavations began. Up to 13,000 workers toiled day and night, putting up a new floor in as little as three days.

Taking in the views is a deservedly popular experience and, aside from making a reservation at the At.mosphere restaurant (p94), there are two ways to go about it. The most popular ticket is the one to the 'At the Top' observation deck on the 124th floor (452m), where high-powered telescopes help bring even distant developments into focus and cleverly simulate the same view at night and 35 years back in time. Getting to the deck means passing various multimedia exhibits until a double-decker lift whisks you up at 10m per second.

To truly be on the world's highest observation platform, though, you need to buy tickets for 'At the Top Sky' on the 148th floor (555m). A visit here is set up like a hosted VIP experience with refreshments, a guided tour and an interactive screen where you 'fly' to different city landmarks by hovering your hands over high-tech sensors. Afterwards, you're escorted to the 125th floor to be showered with Burj trivia and to engage with another virtual attraction called 'A Falcon's Eye View'.

Timed tickets are available at the ticket counter or online up to 30 days in advance. Get your ticket early, especially if want to go up at sunset, or risk having to pay for expensive fast-track admission.

DON'T MISS

- Buying tickets in advance!
- Views, views, views
- Multimedia exhibits

PRACTICALITIES

- Map p258
- ☎800-2884 3867
- www.atthetop.ae
- 1 Sheikh Mohammed bin Rashid Blvd, entry lower ground fl, Dubai Mall
- At the Top adult/child 4-12yr/fast track Dh125/95/300, surcharge 3-7pm Dh25, At the Top Sky Dh500
- ⏲8.30am-midnight, last entry 45min before closing
- Ⓜ Burj Khalifa/Dubai Mall

SIGHTS

Downtown Dubai proper has most of the must-see sights, including the Burj Khalifa, Dubai Mall and Dubai Fountain. Art lovers need to head to the gallery quarters in the Financial District and Al Quoz.

Downtown Dubai

BURJ KHALIFA — LANDMARK

See p85.

DUBAI FOUNTAIN — FOUNTAIN

Map p258 (Burj Lake; shows 1pm & 1.30pm Sat-Thu, 1.30pm & 2pm Fri, every 30min 6-11pm daily; M Burj Khalifa/Dubai Mall) FREE This choreographed dancing fountain is spectacularly set in the middle of a giant lake against the backdrop of the glittering Burj Khalifa, the world's tallest building. Water undulates as gracefully as a belly dancer, arcs like a dolphin and surges as high as 150m, all synced to stirring soundtracks from classical, Arabic and world music.

There are plenty of great vantage points, including from some of the restaurants at Souk Al Bahar, the bridge linking Souk Al Bahar with the Dubai Mall, and the Dubai Mall waterfront terrace. For even closer views, book a cruise aboard a wooden *abra* (traditional water taxi) that sets sail between 5.45pm and 11.15pm (Dh65).

DUBAI MALL — MALL

Map p258 (04-362 7500; www.thedubaimall.com; Sheikh Mohammed bin Rashid Blvd; 10am-midnight; M Burj Khalifa/Dubai Mall) The mother of all malls is much more than the sum of its 1200 stores: it's a veritable family entertainment centre with such crowd magnets as a huge aquarium, an amusement park with thrill rides and arcade games, an Olympic-sized ice rink and a genuine dinosaur skeleton. It also boasts a gorgeous souq, a designer fashion avenue with catwalk and its own glossy monthly magazine. And as if that wasn't enough, the mall was undergoing expansion at the time of writing.

DUBAI TROLLEY

Getting around Downtown Dubai has never been easy, which is why we're happy to see the arrival of the Dubai Trolley. Its first section, which covers 1km with three stops at the Dubai Mall, the Address Downtown and the Vida Downtown Dubai hotels, should have rolled out by the time you're reading this. When completed, the nostalgic double-decker streetcars, which are powered by electricity, will run for 7km along Mohammed bin Rashid Blvd, linking the mall with the Burj Khalifa, other hotels and the Dubai Metro station.

DUBAI AQUARIUM & UNDERWATER ZOO — AQUARIUM

Map p258 (04-448 5200; www.thedubaiaquarium.com; ground fl, Dubai Mall; tunnel & zoo adult/child 3-12yr Dh70/55; 10am-10pm Sun-Wed, to midnight Thu-Sat; M Burj Khalifa/Dubai Mall) The Dubai Mall's most mesmerising sight is this gargantuan aquarium where thousands of beasties flit and dart amid artificial coral. Sharks and rays are top attractions, but other popular denizens include sumo-sized groupers and massive schools of pelagic fish. You can view quite a lot for free from the outside or pay for access to the walk-through tunnel. Tickets also include access to the Underwater Zoo upstairs whose undisputed star is a 5m-long Australian crocodile named King Croc.

The giant lizard is 40 years old and weighs in at an impressive 750kg. He's joined by a menagerie of other rare and unusual critters, including air-breathing African lungfish, cheeky archerfish that catch insects by shooting water, spooky giant spider crabs and otherworldly sea dragons.

Various add-on aquatic experiences give you the opportunity to get close-ups of many of these animals. The most thrilling is a shark dive (from Dh675), the tamest a glass-bottom boat ride (Dh110, including tunnel and zoo).

Budget at least 30 minutes each for the tunnel and the zoo.

DUBAI DINO — EXHIBIT

Map p258 (www.thedubaimall.com; Souk Dome, ground fl, Dubai Mall; 10am-midnight; M Burj Khalifa/Dubai Mall) FREE The Jurassic era meets the future in the Dubai Mall's Souk Dome, the new home of *Amphicoelias brontodiplodocus*, an almost complete 155-million-year-old dinosaur skeleton unearthed in Wyoming in 2008. The long-necked lizard stands nearly 8m tall and measures

WORTH A DETOUR

URBAN BIRDING

Right in the heart of the city, **Ras Al Khor Wildlife Sanctuary** (04-606 6822; www.wildlife.ae; cnr Oud Metha Rd & Ras Al Khor St; 9am-4pm Sat-Thu; Dubai Healthcare City) FREE is an amazing nature preserve within view of the skyscrapers. Pretty pink flamingos steal the show in winter but avid birdwatchers can spot more than 170 species in this pastiche of salt flats, mudflats, mangroves and lagoons spread over an area of around 6.2 sq km (2.4 sq miles).

Bordering Dubai Creek, the sanctuary is an important stopover on the east African–west Asian flyway. There are common sightings of broad-billed sandpipers and Pacific golden plovers; in winter great spotted eagles and other raptors may be patrolling the skies.

There are currently two accessible hides (platforms) with fantastically sharp binoculars: the Flamingo Hide on the sanctuary's western edge near the flamingo roost off the junction of Al Wasl and Oud Metha Rds and the Mangrove Hide overlooking the mangrove forest off Ras Al Khor Rd on the southern edge.

Admission is free and no advance registration is required for groups under five people. It's a 6km taxi ride from the nearest metro station.

24m long – including its whip-like tail – thus filling up the better part of the exotic arched and dramatically lit atrium.

SOUK AL BAHAR MALL

Map p258 (04-362 7012; www.soukalbahar.ae; Downtown Dubai; 10am-10pm Sat-Thu, 2-10pm Fri; Burj Khalifa/Dubai Mall) Designed in contemporary Arabic style, this attractive mall is Downtown Dubai's answer to Madinat Jumeirah. Meaning 'Market of the Sailor', it features natural-stone walkways, high arches and front-row seats overlooking Dubai Fountain from several of its restaurants and bars, including Baker & Spice (p93), Left Bank and Karma Kafé (p94). It's located next to the Dubai Mall.

Financial District

Anchored by the iconic twin Jumeirah Emirates Towers, the Financial District is the domain of the business brigade. At its heart is the Dubai International Finance Centre (DIFC), a minimalist 15-storey triumphal arch that houses the Dubai Stock Exchange. Two wooden bridges link DIFC to the Gate Village, a modernist cluster of 10 mid-rise stone-clad towers built around walkways and small piazzas.

AYYAM GALLERY GALLERY

Map p258 (04-439 2395; www.ayyamgallery.com; Bldg 3, Gate Village; 10am-10pm Sun-Wed, 2-10pm Thu & Sat; Emirates Towers) With branches at Gate Village and in Al Quoz as well as in Damascus, Beirut, Jeddah and London, this top gallery's main mission is to promote emerging Middle Eastern artists and to introduce their often provocative, political and feminist work and voices to a wider audience outside the region itself.

EMPTY QUARTER GALLERY

Map p258 (04-323 1210; www.theemptyquarter.com; Bldg 2, Gate Village; 10am-8pm Sun-Thu; Emirates Towers) It's always worth stopping by this top-notch gallery focused entirely on fine-art photography created by accomplished shutterbugs from around the globe. Shows often capture the zeitgeist with evocative, provocative or political themes such as Miguel Angel Sanchez' recent exhibition, *The Faces of Gaza*.

ART SAWA GALLERY

Map p258 (04-386 2366; www.artsawa.com; Bldg 8, Gate Village; 10am-6pm Sat-Thu; Emirates Towers) One of the Village's smaller galleries, Art Sawa provides a platform for young Middle Eastern artists but also showcases widely collected established ones such as Syria's most famous sculptor, Mustafi Ali.

CUADRO GALLERY

Map p258 (04-425 0400; www.cuadroart.com; Bldg 10, Gate Village; noon-6pm Sat, 10am-8pm Sun-Thu; Emirates Towers) In a fabulous space taking up the entire ground floor of Gate Village's Building 10, this highly regarded gallery shines the spotlight on contemporary artists and sculptors from both the West and Middle East and also presents lectures, workshops and panel discussions.

OPERA GALLERY GALLERY

Map p258 (☎04-323 0909; www.operagallery.com; Bldg 3, Gate Village; ⏰10am-8pm Sun-Thu; Ⓜ Emirates Towers) More an art showroom than a classically curated gallery, Opera caters to collectors of artistic heavyweights in genres as varied as pop art, calligraphy and landscapes. One section of the beautiful bi-level space is reserved for contemporary artists from the Middle East.

Al Quoz

The most cutting-edge galleries within Dubai's growing art scene are in an industrial area called Al Quoz south of Sheikh Zayed Road. There are two main clusters: one in and around the Courtyard on 6th St and the main hub called Alserkal Avenue (p92) on 8th St.

The district is not directly served by the Dubai metro and you'll need to take a taxi from either Noor Bank or First Gulf Bank stations. Tell the cabbie to take exit 43 off Sheikh Zayed Road, follow Al Manara Road southeast, turn right on 8th St and continue just past 17th St when you'll see the entrance to Alserkal Avenue on your right. The website www.artinthecity.com is an excellent source.

GALLERY ISABELLE VAN DEN EYNDE GALLERY

Map p260 (☎04-323 5052; www.ivde.net; Alserkal Ave; ⏰10am-7pm Sat-Thu; Ⓜ Noor Bank, First Gulf Bank) This edgy gallery has lifted some of the most innovative and promising talent from the Middle East, North Africa and South Asia from obscurity into the spotlight. The mythology-laced installations, videos and collages of Cairo-based Lara Baladi and the distorted photography of Iranian-born Ramin Haerizadeh are among the works that have attracted collectors and the curious since 2006. Enter from 8th St near 17th St.

GREEN ART GALLERY GALLERY

Map p260 (☎04-346 9305; www.gagallery.com; Alserkal Ave; ⏰10am-7pm Sat-Thu; Ⓜ Noor Bank, First Gulf Bank) Specialised in painters, photographers and sculptors from the Middle East, Green Art became one of the first Gulf galleries to participate in Art Basel in 2012. It recently expanded its roster to include international artists such as Alessandro Balteo Yazbeck from Venezuela and the painter Zsolt Bodoni from Hungary. Enter from 8th St near 17th St.

CARBON 12 GALLERY

Map p260 (☎04-340 6016; www.carbon12dubai.com; Alserkal Ave; ⏰11.30am-7pm Sat-Thu; Ⓜ Noor Bank, First Gulf Bank) A minimalist white-cube space presents the gamut of contemporary forms of expression created by established international artists. Some of them have roots in the Middle East, such as Tehran-born New York resident Sara Rahbar, whose textile art has made it into the British Museum. Enter from 8th St near 17th St.

GREY NOISE GALLERY

Map p260 (☎04-379 0764; www.greynoise.org; Alserkal Ave; ⏰11am-7pm Sat & Mon-Thu; Ⓜ Noor Bank, First Gulf Bank) This contemporary gallery has built up its reputation as a go-to space for experimental and cutting-edge art from the region, South Asia and Europe since 2008. Representing only 10 artists, including Caline Aoun and Michael John Whelan, it's a small but carefully curated roster. Enter from 8th St near 17th St.

LAWRIE SHABIBI GALLERY

Map p260 (☎04-346 9906; www.lawrieshabibi.com; Alserkal Ave; ⏰10am-6pm Sat-Thu; Ⓜ Noor Bank, First Gulf Bank) Relative newcomer Lawrie Shabibi arrived in 2011 and has since energised the local art scene by promoting the works of innovative contemporary talent from the Middle East, North Africa and South Asia. Art education is another focus and frequent artist talks and screenings are held both at the gallery and in nonprofit spaces around Dubai. Enter from 8th St near 17th St.

SALSALI PRIVATE MUSEUM GALLERY

Map p260 (SPM; ☎04-380 9600; www.salsalipm.com; Alserkal Ave; ⏰11am-6pm Sun-Thu, 1-5pm Sat; Ⓜ Noor Bank, First Gulf Bank) SPM is the first private museum for contemporary Middle Eastern art in the region. It presents the collection of prominent Iranian collector Ramin Salsali who bought his first piece at age 21. Today he owns some 800 paintings, sculptures, video art and installations. Enter from 8th St near 17th St.

DUBAI'S ICONIC BUILDINGS

Burj Khalifa (p85) The world's tallest building stacks up at a cloud-tickling 828m. For the design, American architect Adrian Smith found inspiration in the desert flower *Hymenocallis*, whose patterning systems are embodied in Islamic architecture. The tower is designed as three petals arranged around a central core. As it rises from the flat base, the petals are set back in an upward-spiralling pattern.

Burj Al Arab (p103) The Burj was completed in 1999, and is set on an artificial island 300m from the shore. The 60-floor, sail-shaped structure is 321m high. A translucent fibreglass wall serves as a shield from the desert sun during the day and as a screen for an impressive light show each night. It remains *the* iconic symbol of Dubai.

Dubai Creek Golf & Yacht Club (p64) When you cross the bridges over the Creek from Bur Dubai South, you'll notice the pointed white roof of the clubhouse set amid artificial, undulating hillocks. The idea behind this 1993 design was to incorporate a traditional element – the white sails of a dhow (traditional sailing vessel) – into the form and style of the building.

Dubai International Financial Centre (Map p258; Sheikh Zayed Rd; Ⓜ Financial Centre) Dubai's stock exchange and leading international financial institutions are housed in a complex of six buildings surrounding a central 80m-high triumphal arch called the Gate. Designed by the American firm Gensler Associates, it sits on an axis with the Jumeirah Emirates Towers and the World Trade Centre, effectively framing these two landmarks.

Dusit Thani Dubai (p184) Sheikh Zayed Road features many modern skyscrapers, but few are as eye-catching as this one. The 153m-high building has an inverted 'Y' shape – two pillars that join to form a tapering tower. It's meant to evoke the Thai joined-hands gesture of greeting, which is appropriate for this Thai hotel chain, but some feel it looks more like a giant tuning fork. It's next to Interchange No 1.

Jumeirah Emirates Towers (p186) Designed in an ultramodern style, the twin, triangular, gunmetal-grey towers soar from an oval base on Sheikh Zayed Road and are among the world's tallest. The taller of the two (355m) houses offices, while the other (305m) is a hotel. Balanced by the curvilinear base structure, the curved motif is also repeated in the upper storeys of the buildings.

Jumeirah Beach Hotel (p187) This curvaceous S-shaped construction represents a wave, with the Gulf as its backdrop. The glimmering facades of the hotel and its close neighbour, the Burj Al Arab, are achieved by the use of reflective glass and aluminium. The two structures combined – a huge sail hovering over a breaking wave – symbolise Dubai's maritime heritage.

National Bank of Dubai (Map p244; Ⓜ Union) This shimmering building located by Sheraton Dubai Creek Hotel & Towers in Deira has become another quintessential symbol of Dubai. Designed by Carlos Ott and completed in 1997, it combines simple shapes to represent a dhow with a billowing sail. The bronze windows reflect the activity on the Creek.

THIRD LINE
GALLERY

Map p260 (☎04-341 1367; www.thethirdline.com; 6th St near 17th St; ⏰10am-7pm Sat-Thu; Ⓜ Noor Bank, First Gulf Bank) A pioneer on Dubai's gallery scene and one of the city's most exciting spaces for contemporary Middle Eastern art, Third Line represents around 30 artists. Trying to raise the profile of Middle Eastern art outside the region, the gallery also regularly exhibits at international art fairs, including Art Cologne and Art Basel.

COURTYARD
ARTS CENTRE

Map p260 (☎04-347 5050; www.courtyard-uae.com; 6th St near 17th St; Ⓜ Noor Bank, First Gulf Bank) This arts complex wraps around its eponymous courtyard, flanked by an eccentric hodgepodge of buildings that makes it look like a miniature movie-studio backdrop: here an Arab fort, there a Moorish facade or an Egyptian tomb. It contains design shops, galleries, a community theatre and other creative businesses.

GALLO IMAGES - FRANK MARITZ/GETTY IMAGES ©

ED NORTON/GETTY IMAGES ©

1. Souk Al Bahar (p87)
This attractive mall features many natural-stone corridors with high arches.

2. Dubai Mall (p97)
The stunning interior of the world's largest mall is just one of its draws; 1200 stores, an aquarium, an ice rink and a variety of food outlets also captivate the masses.

3. Dubai Fountain (p86)
The Burj Khalifa (p85) makes a fine backdrop to the spectacular Dubai Fountain.

4. Dubai Aquarium & Underwater Zoo (p86)
People flock to the Dubai Mall to check out its spectacular aquarium.

PETER UNGER/GETTY IMAGES ©

3

THOMAS KURMEIER/GETTY IMAGES ©

LOCAL KNOWLEDGE

ALSERKAL AVENUE ARTS DISTRICT

Contemporary art from the Middle East and beyond has found a home in Dubai thanks to the vision of Abdelmonem Alserkal. The local developer and arts patron has turned a sprawling warehouse complex in dusty Al Quoz into a buzzing gallery campus called **Alserkal Avenue** (Map p260; www.alserkalavenue.ae; near 8th & 17th Sts, Al Quoz 3; M Noor Bank, First Gulf Bank). Although some warehouses are still in industrial use, about 20 of the high-ceilinged spaces have already morphed into pristine, white-walled art galleries.

They will soon be joined by an extension taking shape in an adjacent former marble factory where more galleries, studios and other creative enterprises are expected to open in 2015. A walkway will also connect the art campus with the galleries on 6th Ave, which should make the entire area more pedestrian-friendly. All this, Alserkal hopes, will ultimately create an alternative creative district that will also host concerts, talks, film screenings and other events.

A spin around Alserkal Avenue and 6th St is easily combined with a meal at one of the urban cafes, like Tom & Serg (p95) and the **Lime Tree Cafe** (Map p260; 04-325 6325; www.thelimetreecafe.com; 4B St, Al Quoz; snacks Dh20-55; 8am-6pm; ; M Noor Bank), that have been popping up around here lately. Note that galleries are closed on Friday and that many don't open until the afternoon on Saturdays (despite their advertised timings).

1X1 ART GALLERY — GALLERY

Map p260 (04-341 1287; www.1x1artgallery.com; Warehouse No 4, off 8th St near Al Marabea Rd; 11am-8pm Sat-Thu; M First Gulf Bank, Noor Bank) Tucked into a driveway, this gallery is helmed by the energetic Malini Gulrajani who has brought some of the foremost names in India's art scene to Dubai. With shows featuring heavyweight painters such as Bose Krishnamachari and Chittrovanu Mazumdar and the sculptor N N Rimzon, this grand and elegant gallery has become a fixture on the radar of collectors.

CARTOON ART GALLERY — GALLERY

Map p260 (04-346 6467; www.cartoonartgallery.org; 4B St, off Sheikh Zayed Rd; 10am-6pm Sat-Thu; M Noor Bank, First Gulf Bank) This bi-level space is the first gallery in the Middle East dedicated to cartoon and animation art. A typical exhibition might feature artwork and posters illustrating the world of Tintin or present animated cartoons by such illustrious names as Japanese artist Hayao Miyazaki.

MEEM GALLERY — GALLERY

Map p260 (04-347 7883; www.meemartgallery.com; Umm Suqeim Rd, off Interchange No 4; 10am-6pm Sat-Thu; M Mall of the Emirates, First Gulf Bank) A co-venture by two Emirati business tycoons and British art dealer Charlie Pocock, this blue-chip gallery is dedicated to presenting the masters of modern Arab art. As such, it usually exhibits some pretty big names, such as Libyan calligrapher Ali Omar Ermes, the pop art of Jordan's Jamal Abdul Rahim or paintings by modern Arab art pioneer Dia Azzawi from Iraq.

EATING

Downtown Dubai is the purview of high-roller restaurants, with most of them holding forth in the five-star hotels and the Dubai International Financial Centre (DIFC). For a funky antidote, check out the urban cafes in Al Quoz.

Downtown Dubai

ELEVATION BURGER — AMERICAN $

Map p258 (04-330-8468; www.elevationburger.com; ground fl, Dubai Mall; burgers Dh25-42; 10am-midnight Sun-Wed, to 1am Thu-Sat; M Burj Khalifa/Dubai Mall) This Virginia-based chain proves that there is such a thing as guilt-free fast food by serving burgers made entirely from organic, grass-fed and free-range beef. There are a dozen toppings to choose from, including caramelised onions and smoky 'elevation' sauce. Carbophobes can trade the bun for lettuce. It's above the ice rink.

MORELLI'S GELATO — CAFE $

Map p258 (04-339 9053; www.morellisgelato.com; lower ground fl, Dubai Mall; per scoop Dh17; 10am-midnight; M Burj Khalifa/Dubai Mall) The family that introduced Italian ice cream to the UK in 1907 now also serves their wonderfully creamy flavours to gelato fans in Dubai. Order just a scoop to go or find a table in the cheerful purple-and-white cafe for a sit-down sundae.

MILAS EMIRATI $$

Map p258 (☎04-388 2313; www.milas.cc; ground fl, Dubai Mall, Denim Village; mains Dh57-95; ⏰9.30am-11.30pm Sun-Wed, to 12.30am Thu-Sat; Ⓜ Burj Khalifa/Dubai Mall) Milas is how Emiratis pronounce *majlis* – the traditional guest reception room. This particular *majlis* has a contemporary look (wood, glass, neon) that goes well with updated riffs on such traditional local dishes as *harees* (sugar-sprinkled cooked wheat) and *makhboos* (beef stew). Thoughtful perks: wet handcloths, the complimentary *danqaw* (chickpea) appetiser and a post-meal perfume tray.

MAYRIG DUBAI ARMENIAN $$

Map p258 (☎04-279 0300; www.mayrigdubai.com; Sheikh Mohammed bin Rashid Blvd; mains Dh57-85; ⏰noon-12.30am; 📶; Ⓜ Burj Khalifa/Dubai Mall) Mayrig's Armenian menu may borrow heavily from Lebanese cuisine, but not without setting its own distinctive flavour accents. Menu stars include *sou beureg* (a flaky cheese-filled pastry), the mouth-watering *fishnah kebab* topped with wild sour cherry sauce, and the lemon zest chocolate cake. There's no alcohol but you can enjoy *sheesha* (water pipe) on the terrace. It's opposite Al Manzil Hotel.

LEILA LEBANESE $$

Map p258 (☎04-448 3384; Sheikh Mohammed bin Rashid Blvd; mains Dh28-78; ⏰9.30am-11pm Sat-Wed, to midnight Thu & Fri; Ⓜ Burj Khalifa/Dubai Mall) This Beirut import serves grannie-style rural Lebanese cafe cuisine adapted for the 21st century: light, healthy and fresh. The homey decor more than dabbles in the vintage department with its patterned wallpaper, crisp tablecloths and floral dishes. Don't miss the spicy potato cubes and the *jebneh mtabbaleh* (white cheese with tomato and oregano).

BAKER & SPICE INTERNATIONAL $$

Map p258 (☎04-425 2240; www.bakerandspiceme.com; Souk Al Bahar; mains Dh45-145; ⏰8am-11pm; 📶; Ⓜ Burj Khalifa/Dubai Mall) The colourful salad bar is the undisputed star at this charming, country-style cafe. Presented in mouth-watering fashion, it's a seasonal bounty of intriguingly paired organic ingredients (eg lentils perked up with pumpkin cubes and pomegranate seeds). The mains are more conventional but just as tasty. Also a good spot for breakfast.

EATALY ITALIAN $$

Map p258 (☎04-330 8899; www.eataly.com; lower ground fl, Dubai Mall; mains Dh39-119; ⏰9am-midnight; Ⓜ Burj Khalifa/Dubai Mall) Italy's popular shop-cum-cafe has landed in the Dubai Mall, bringing artisanal morsels from around the boot to discerning palates. Stock up on pesto from Liguria, balsamico from Modena, olive oil from Sicily and pasta made right in the store, then fill your stomach with a hearty *panino* (sandwich), crisp *insalata* (salad) or spaghetti *al pomodoro* (with tomatoes).

HOI AN VIETNAMESE $$$

Map p258 (☎04-405 2703; www.shangri-la.com; Shangri-La Hotel, Sheikh Zayed Rd; mains Dh104-176; ⏰dinner; Ⓜ Financial Centre) Teak latticework, plantation shutters and spinning wooden ceiling fans evoke colonial-era Vietnam at this upmarket restaurant, where the tastes are lively and bright. Start with the crispy crab rolls, then move on to lotus-leaf-wrapped sea bass or seafood wok-fried in intricate and fragrant sauces. Low lighting and genteel service make this a good date spot.

THIPTARA THAI $$$

Map p258 (☎04-428 7888; www.theaddress.com; Palace Downtown Dubai, Sheikh Mohammed bin Rashid Blvd; mains Dh110-200, set menus from Dh299; ⏰dinner; Ⓜ Burj Khalifa/Dubai Mall) Thiptara means 'magic at the water' – very appropriate given its romantic setting in a lakeside pagoda with unimpeded views of the Dubai Fountain. The food is just as impressive, with elegant interpretations of classic Thai dishes perked up by herbs grown by the chef himself.

ASADO ARGENTINIAN $$$

Map p258 (☎04-888 3444; www.theaddress.com; Palace Downtown Dubai, Sheikh Mohammed bin Rashid Blvd; mains Dh130-290; ⏰7-11.30pm; Ⓜ Burj Khalifa/Dubai Mall) Meat lovers will be in heaven at this rustic-elegant lair with stellar views of the Burj Khalifa from the terrace tables. Start with a selection of deliciously filled *empanadas*, the traditional Argentinian fried dumplings, before treating yourself to a juicy grilled steak or the signature baby goat, slowly tickled to succulent perfection by a charcoal fire. Reservations essential.

KARMA KAFÉ ASIAN $$$

Map p258 (04-423 0909; www.karma-kafe.com; Souk Al Bahar; mains Dh75-150; 3pm-2am Sun-Thu, noon-2am Fri & Sat; Burj Khalifa/Dubai Mall) At this hip outpost a large Buddha oversees the dining room dressed in sensuous crimson and accented with funky design details. Though Japan-centric, the menu actually hopscotches around Asia with special nods going to the teriyaki tenderloin, the lava prawns and the Thai calamari. The terrace has grand Dubai Fountain views. Reservations essential.

AT.MOSPHERE INTERNATIONAL $$$

Map p258 (04-888 3828; www.atmosphereburjkhalifa.com; 122nd fl, Burj Khalifa; mains Dh200-650; 12.30-2.30pm & 3pm-2am; ; Burj Khalifa/Dubai Mall) The food may not be out of this world, but the views are certainly stellar from the world's highest restaurant (442m) in the Burj Khalifa. Richly decorated in warm mahogany, limestone and thick carpets, the dining room oozes a hushed and sophisticated ambience while the compact menu lets quality meats and seafood shine.

RIVINGTON GRILL BRITISH $$$

Map p258 (04-423 0903; www.rivingtongrill.ae; Level 3, Souk Al Bahar; mains Dh95-260; Burj Khalifa/Dubai Mall) This London transplant serves classic British food in a couldn't-be-more-Dubai location with a candlelit terrace overlooking the Dubai Fountain. Not only homesick Brits give a keen thumbs up to the fish and chips with poshed-up mushy peas, beef Wellington with all the trimmings and the smoked haddock fishcakes. Traditional Sunday roast is served here on Saturday (Dh175).

Financial District

ZAROOB LEBANESE $

Map p258 (04-327 6060; www.zaroob.com; ground fl, Jumeirah Emirates Towers; dishes Dh8-26; 24hr; ; Emirates Towers) With its open kitchens, baskets billowing with fruit, colourful lanterns and steel shutters festooned with funky graffiti, Zaroob radiates the earthy integrity of a Beirut alley filled with street-food stalls. Feast on such delicious but no-fuss food as felafel, shwarma, flat or wrapped *manoush* sandwiches, *alayet* (tomato stew) or tabbouleh, all typical of the Levant region.

NOODLE HOUSE ASIAN $$

Map p258 (04-319 8088; lower level, The Boulevard, Jumeirah Emirates Towers; mains Dh40-90; noon-midnight; ; Emirates Towers) The concept at this reliably good multi-branch pan-Asian joint is simple: sit down at long wooden communal tables and order by ticking dishes on a tear-off menu pad. There's great variety – roast duck to noodle soups and pad thai – and a spice-level indicator to please disparate tastes. Some dishes come in two sizes to match tummy grumbles.

IVY INTERNATIONAL $$$

Map p258 (04-319 8767; www.theivy.ae; ground fl, The Boulevard, Jumeirah Emirates Towers; mains Dh120-360, 2-/3-hour business lunch Dh120/150, brunch Dh300-600; noon-11pm Sat-Wed, to 11.30pm Thu & Fri; ; Emirates Towers) Dark oak floors and stained glass set a retro-chic scene at the Dubai edition of this London institution. Aside from a few classic British dishes (such as the signature shepherd's pie), the menu has a distinctly international brasserie bent with everything from gazpacho to foie gras and Sri Lankan lamb curry making appearances. Reservations essential.

ZUMA JAPANESE $$$

Map p258 (04-425 5660; www.zumarestaurant.com; Gate Village 06; set lunches Dh130, mains Dh75-160; lunch daily, dinner Sat-Wed, to 2am Thu & Fri; ; Emirates Towers) Every dish speaks of refinement in this perennially popular bi-level restaurant that gives classic Japanese fare an up-to-the-minute workout. No matter if you go for the top-cut sushi morsels (the dynamite spider roll is a serious eye-catcher!), meat and seafood tickled by the robata grill, or such signature dishes as miso-marinated cod, you'll be keeping your taste buds happy.

CLÉ DUBAI MIDDLE EASTERN $$$

Map p258 (04-352 5150; www.cle-dubai.com; Al Fattan Currency House; sharing dishes Dh30-285, 2-/3-course lunch Dh95/130; noon-2am; ; Financial Centre) Australian-born Michelin chef Greg Malouf has decamped to Dubai to open this sensuously styled haven for dedicated foodies and power diners. In his signature approach, he deconstructs the flavour-intense mystique of traditional Middle Eastern dishes and reassembles it into thoroughly contemporary culinary symphonies like goat tagine, salmon kibbeh or hazelnut felafel. The terrace delivers views of the Burj Khalifa.

EXCHANGE GRILL STEAKHOUSE **$$$**

Map p258 (☎04-311 8316; www.fairmont.com/dubai; Fairmont Hotel, Sheikh Zayed Rd; steaks Dh215-565; dinner; ; M World Trade Centre) One of Dubai's premier steakhouses, Exchange Grill has a clubby feel, with oversized leather armchairs orbiting linen-draped tables and big-picture windows overlooking the glittering strip. You'll have a fine time spiking your cholesterol level with trendy Wagyu beef (marble score 6–7) or the less pricey but actually more flavourful Angus prime. Seafood rounds out the menu, but beef is definitely the big draw.

AL NAFOORAH LEBANESE **$$$**

Map p258 (☎04-319 8088; www.jumeirah.com; ground fl, The Boulevard, Jumeirah Emirates Towers; mezze Dh36-125, mains Dh65-135; lunch & dinner; ; M Emirates Towers) In this clubby, wood-panelled dining room the vast selection of delectable mezze is more impressive than the kebabs, but ultimately there are few false notes on the classic Lebanese menu. Even in summer you can sit on the terrace beneath an air-conditioned marquee.

RIB ROOM STEAKHOUSE **$$$**

Map p258 (☎04-319 8088; www.jumeirah.com; ground fl, Jumeirah Emirates Towers; mains Dh100-525; lunch Sun-Thu, dinner daily; ; M Emirates Towers) Surrender to your inner carnivore at this power-player hang-out where the air is practically perfumed with testosterone. The yummy cuts of Angus and Wagyu steaks and juicy prime rib speak for themselves.

Al Quoz

★TOM & SERG CAFE **$$**

Map p260 (☎056-474 6812; www.tomandserg.com; 15th St; mains Dh36-89; 8am-4pm Sun-Thu, to 5pm Fri & Sat; ; M Noor Bank, First Gulf Bank) An instant hit with Dubai hipsters, this loft-style urban cafe with concrete floors, exposed pipes and an open kitchen would fit right into London or Melbourne and is a great stop on an Al Quoz gallery hop. The menu teems with feel-good food like homemade muesli, quinoa-felafel wraps and a Reuben made with Wagyu salt beef. Great coffee, too. It's near Ace Hardware.

DRINKING & NIGHTLIFE

Downtown Dubai

CABANA BAR, LOUNGE

Map p258 (☎04-888 3444; www.theaddress.com; 3rd fl, Address Dubai Mall Hotel; 9am-midnight Sun-Thu, to 12.30am Fri & Sat; ; M Burj Khalifa/Dubai Mall) A laid-back poolside vibe combines with urban sophistication and stellar views of the Burj Khalifa at this alfresco restaurant and terrace lounge. A DJ plays smooth tunes that don't hamper animated conversation. Cap a Dubai Mall shopping spree during happy hour, which runs from 4pm to 8pm. On Tuesdays, women can drink at half price.

CALABAR BAR

Map p258 (☎04-888 3444; www.theaddress.com; ground fl, Address Downtown Dubai Hotel; 6pm-2.30am; ; M Burj Khalifa/Dubai Mall) You'll have plenty of time to study the space-age Burj Khalifa, the eye-candy crowd and the sexy cocktail bar setting while you're waiting…and waiting…for a pricey but potent cocktail at this Latino-themed bar. It's a popular post-work and post-mall-crawl pit stop with a handy daily happy hour from 6pm to 8pm.

NEOS BAR

Map p258 (☎04-888 3444; www.theaddress.com; Address Downtown Dubai Hotel; 6pm-2.30am; ; M Burj Khalifa/Dubai Mall) At this glamour vixen, you can swirl your cosmo with the posh set 63 floors above Dubai Fountain. It takes two lifts to get to this urban den of shiny metal, carpeted floors, killer views and a DJ playing house.

KRIS KROS SHEESHA, MOCKTAILS

Map p258 (☎04-453 9994; Sheikh Mohammed bin Rashid Blvd; sheesha Dh47, mocktails Dh20-25; ; M Burj Khalifa/Dubai Mall) Tucked into an office tower with a side view of the Burj Khalifa, funkily furnished Kris Kros does its name justice, as its menu criss-crosses the globe (buffalo wings, burritos, pizza, shwarma etc). What makes the place special, though, is the extensive selection of mocktails and *sheesha*, including such unusual flavours as mango vanilla and bubblegum.

MAJLIS CAFE

Map p258 (056-287 1522; www.themajlisdubai.com; Souk, Dubai Mall; 10am-midnight; ; Burj Khalifa/Dubai Mall) If you ever wanted to find out how to milk a camel (and who doesn't?), watch the video on the interactive iPad menu of this pretty cafe while sipping a camelccino (camel-milk cappuccino) or date-flavoured camel milk. Nibbles, desserts, chocolate and cheese, all made with camel milk, beckon as well.

Financial District

THE ACT CABARET, CLUB

Map p258 (04-355 1116; www.theactdubai.com; Shangri-La Hotel, Sheikh Zayed Rd; 8.30pm-3am Sun & Thu, to 1am Mon-Wed; Financial Centre) To create his Dubai edition of The Box, his burlesque dinner theatre in Vegas, London and New York, entertainment impresario Simon Hammerstein had to think, well...outside the box. So no raunchy performances here but still a mighty good time featuring artistic and often sexy variety acts to go with your plate of ceviche or *anticuchos de lomo* (beef skewers). The setting is just as special, a lush Victorian-styled theatre draped in dark red walls, velvet curtains and baroque mirrors. Dancing after dinner. No phones, no cameras.

40 KONG BAR

Map p258 (04-355 8896; www.40kong.com; 40th fl, H Hotel, Sheikh Zayed Rd; 6pm-3am; ; World Trade Centre) Finance moguls and corporate execs mix it up with cubicle hotties at this intimate rooftop cocktail bar perched atop the 40th floor of the H Hotel with views of the World Trade Centre and Sheikh Zayed Road. The twinkling lanterns and palm trees set romantic accents for post-work or -shopping sundowners, paired with Asian bar bites.

DOUBLE DECKER PUB

Map p258 (04-321 1111; Al Murooj Rotana Hotel, cnr Financial Centre & 312th Rds; noon-3am; ; Financial Centre) You'll feel quite Piccadilly at this boozy, boisterous bi-level pub that's decked out in a London transport theme. Drinks promotions, quiz nights, English Premier League football and better-than-average (by far) pub grub attract a boisterous expat crowd.

ZINC CLUB

Map p258 (050-151 5609; www.zinc.ae; Crowne Plaza Hotel, Sheikh Zayed Rd; 10pm-3am; ; Emirates Towers) This reliable standby has a killer sound system and spins mostly house, R&B, hip-hop and dancehall. It gets a good crowd nightly, including many regulars, and lots of cabin crew. There's a nightly happy hour from 10pm to midnight. Admission for women is free; men pay between Dh50 and Dh100, depending on the event.

FIBBER MAGEE'S PUB

Map p258 (04-332 2400; www.fibbersdubai.com; Sheikh Zayed Rd; 8am-2am; ; World Trade Centre) Scruffy Fibbers is an all-day pub that isn't about seeing and being seen – quite frankly, it's a bit too dark for that. It's Irish through and through, with all-day breakfast, Irish stew and liver and onions on the menu and Guinness and Kilkenny on tap. Also great fun on game nights. It's behind Saeed Tower One.

HARRY GHATTO'S KARAOKE BAR

Map p258 (04-319 8088; Jumeirah Emirates Towers Hotel, Sheikh Zayed Rd; noon-3am Sat-Thu, 4pm-3am Fri; ; Emirates Towers) Karaoke kicks off at 10pm, just when happy hour ends oh-so-conveniently in case you need to knock back a couple of drinks to loosen your nerves before belting out your best Beyoncé or 'Bohemian Rhapsody'. There's 1000 songs to choose from, Japanese munchies on the menu and a lively mix of people to (hopefully) cheer you on.

CAVALLI CLUB CLUB

Map p258 (050-991 0400; http://dubai.cavalliclub.com; Fairmont Hotel, Sheikh Zayed Rd; 9.30pm-3am; ; World Trade Centre) Black limos jostle for position outside Italian designer Roberto Cavalli's over-the-top lair where beaus and socialites keep the champagne flowing amid a virtual Aladdin's cave of black quartz and Swarovski crystals. Girls, wear those vertiginous heels or risk feeling frumpy. Boys, dress snappy or forget about it. The entrance is behind the hotel.

Al Quoz

RAW COFFEE COMPANY CAFE

(04-339 5474; www.rawcoffeecompany.com; 8am-5pm Sat-Thu, 9am-5pm Fri; ; Noor Bank) A keen java radar is required to track down this coffee roastery in a hidden alley amid the dusty warehouses of Al Quoz. The building houses not only the roasting operation but also a cafe where local latterati gather for a chat and some of the best organic and fair-trade bean-based drinks in town.

ENTERTAINMENT

FRIDGE LIVE MUSIC

Map p260 (☎04-347 7793; www.thefridgedubai.com; Alserkal Ave, 8th St near 17th St; Ⓜ Noor Bank, First Gulf Bank) Now part of the Alserkal gallery campus, this music promoter hosts regular concerts (usually on Fridays) that shine the spotlight on local talent still operating below the radar. The line-up defines eclectic and may hopscotch from swing to opera, jazz to pop, sometimes all in one night.

BLUE BAR BAR, LIVE MUSIC

Map p258 (☎04-332 0000; Hotel Novotel World Trade Centre Dubai, Za'abeel Rd 2nd; ⏲2pm-2am; 📶; Ⓜ World Trade Centre) Cool cats of all ages gather in this relaxed joint for some of the finest live jazz and blues in town along with reasonably priced cocktails named after jazz greats (try the Louis Armstrong–inspired Wonderful World). The mostly local talent starts performing at 10pm (Wednesday to Friday only).

COURTYARD PLAYHOUSE THEATRE

Map p260 (☎050-986 1761; www.courtyardplayhouse.com; Courtyard Bldg, 6th St near 17th St; Ⓜ Noor Bank, First Gulf Bank) In late 2013, the curtain was raised on this 58-seat community theatre, the brainchild of husband-and-wife team Kemsley Dickinson and Tiffany Schultz and made possible through crowdfunding, fundraising and donations. The intimate space is the city's first improv stage and also the permanent home of the Dubai Drama Group. Creative and acting workshops are also on the menu.

REEL CINEMAS CINEMA

Map p258 (☎04-449 1988; www.reelcinemas.ae; 2nd fl, Dubai Mall; 2D/3D films Dh35/45, Platinum Movie Suite Dh130/160; Ⓜ Burj Khalifa/Dubai Mall) With 22 screens (including one featuring a state-of-the-art Dolby Atmos sound system), Reel is one of the top flick-magnets in town. The fare is mostly Hollywood blockbusters, except in the Picturehouse, which screens art-house films. VIP seats in the Platinum Movie Suite come with reclining leather chairs and table service.

SHOPPING

★**DUBAI MALL** MALL

Map p258 (☎04-362 7500; www.thedubaimall.com; Sheikh Mohammed bin Rashid Blvd; ⏲10am-midnight; 📶; Ⓜ Burj Khalifa/Dubai Mall) With around 1200 stores, this is not merely the world's largest shopping mall – it's a small

LOCAL KNOWLEDGE

HOW TO 'DO' THE DUBAI MALL

The Dubai Mall is a shopper's nirvana, but its size can be somewhat intimidating. Here are some tips to help cut down on the confusion:

➡ Pick up a map and directory from one of the 18 information desks strategically positioned near entrances and throughout the four floors. All are staffed by friendly multilingual folk happy to point you in the right direction. Alternatively, use the interactive electronic store finders to show you your current location and the way to a particular store.

➡ The four levels are divided into 'precincts' with clusters of product categories. For instance, go to Fashion Ave (which has marble floors and silver resting divans) for high-end designers, to the ground floor for high-street fashions, next to the ice rink for active-wear, to the 2nd floor for electronics and to the lower ground floor for food products.

➡ The mall is busiest on Thursday night and Friday after 4pm, so avoid these times if you don't like crowds.

➡ Wi-fi is free, but for now you need a United Arab Emirates (UAE) mobile-phone number to register for the service.

city unto itself, with a giant ice rink and aquarium, a dino skeleton, indoor theme parks and 150 food outlets.

There's a strong European label presence here, along with branches of the Galeries Lafayette department store from France, Hamley's toy store from the UK and the first Bloomingdale's outside the United States.

KINOKUNIYA BOOKS

Map p258 (☎04-434 0111; www.kinokuniya.com/ae; 2nd fl, Dubai Mall; ⊙10am-midnight; Ⓜ Burj Khalifa/Dubai Mall) This bookstore-in-the-round (founded in 1927 Japan) is El Dorado for bookworms. Shelves are stocked with a mind-boggling half a million tomes plus 1000 or so magazines in English, Arabic, Japanese, French, German and Chinese.

NAYOMI LINGERIE

Map p258 (☎04-339 8820; www.nayomi.com.sa; 1st fl, Dubai Mall; ⊙10am-midnight; Ⓜ Burj Khalifa/Dubai Mall) One of Dubai's sexiest stores stocks push-up bras, baby dolls, high-heeled feathery slippers, slinky night gowns and other nocturnal niceties made in – of all places – Saudi Arabia. In fact, Nayomi, which means 'soft' and 'delicate' in Arabic, is a major brand all over the Middle East with 10 branches around Dubai alone.

CANDYLICIOUS FOOD

Map p258 (☎04-330 8700; www.candylicious-shop.com; ground fl, Dubai Mall; ⊙10am-midnight; Ⓜ Burj Khalifa/Dubai Mall) Stand under the lollipop tree, watch the candymakers at work or gorge yourself on gourmet popcorn at this colourful candy emporium stocked to the rafters with everything from jelly beans to halal sweets and gourmet chocolate. Sweet bliss. Just don't tell your dentist. You'll find it next to the Dubai Aquarium.

SUPER HERO FASHION, TOYS

Map p258 (☎04-355 8226; 2nd fl, Dubai Mall; ⊙10am-midnight; Ⓜ Burj Khalifa/Dubai Mall) The planned Marvel City Theme Park may still be on the drawing board, but in the meantime you can channel your inner superhero at this fun store while posing with the Hulk or snagging a Batman bikini, a Superman T-shirt or a Spiderman baby bib.

DAISO GENERAL STORE

Map p258 (☎04-388 2902; www.daisome.com; lower ground fl, Dubai Mall; ⊙10am-midnight; Ⓜ Burj Khalifa/Dubai Mall) Millionaires to wallet-watchers shop at Daiso, Japan's equivalent of the '99 cents' or 'One Euro' store and nirvana for fans of fun, kitsch and cute trinkets – almost all developed in Japan by Daiso itself. The huge inventory (up to 90,000 items) also includes plenty of practical stuff like pens, paper towels and packing material.

SOUK AL BAHAR MALL

Map p258 (www.soukalbahar.ae; Old Town Island; ⊙10am-10pm Sun-Thu, 2-10pm Fri; Ⓜ Burj Khalifa/Dubai Mall) Translated as 'Market of the Sailor', Souk Al Bahar is a small Arabesque-style mall next to the Dubai Mall that sells mostly tourist-geared items. It's really more noteworthy for its enchanting design (arch-lined stone corridors, dim lighting) and Dubai Fountain–facing restaurants, some of which are licensed. Also handy: a branch of Spinney's supermarket in the basement.

TEHRAN PERSIAN CARPETS & ANTIQUES GIFTS

Map p258 (☎04-420 0515; 1st fl, Souk Al Bahar; Ⓜ Burj Khalifa/Dubai Mall) The name is misleading, because although it does sell carpets and a handful of antiques, the inventory is especially strong when it comes to Iranian decorative items including delicately carved boxes made from gorgeous peacock-coloured turquoise or turquoise-blue decorative plates, fancy stained-glass lamps and plenty of colourful silver jewellery and trinkets.

BOOKSHOP AT DIFC BOOKS

Map p258 (☎050-874 9671; www.bookshop-dubai.me; DIFC, Precinct 2 Bldg, main lobby; ⊙8am-6pm Sun-Thu; Ⓜ Emirates Towers) This bookshop, cafe, workspace and overall convivial hang-out has a handpicked selection of new and used books about the Middle East and North Africa and also does killer coffee, cookies and croissants.

GOLD & DIAMOND PARK JEWELLERY

Map p260 (☎04-362 7777; www.goldanddiamondpark.com; Sheikh Zayed Rd; ⊙10am-10pm Sat-Thu, 4-10pm Fri; Ⓜ First Gulf Bank) An air-conditioned, less atmospheric alternative to the Deira Gold Souq, this buttoned-up business mall houses some 90 purveyors of bling. No bargaining here. If you can't find what you want, it's possible to commission a bespoke piece.

WORTH A DETOUR

DUBAI AT THE RACES

A passionate love of Arabian thoroughbreds courses through the blood of Emiratis. The royal Maktoum family's own Godolphin horse-racing stables in England have produced many winners and are well known to horse-racing enthusiasts worldwide (despite a 2013 doping scandal that resulted in the ban of the lead Godolphin trainer).

Dubai racing's home is the spectacular **Meydan Racecourse** (04-327 0077, tickets 04-327 2110; www.dubairacingclub.com; Al Marqadh; general admission free, premium seating Dh50; Nov-Mar), about 5km southwest of Downtown Dubai. Spanning 1.5km, its grandstand is bigger than most airport terminals and lidded by a crescent-shaped solar-panelled roof. It can accommodate up to 60,000 spectators and integrates a five-star hotel, restaurants and an IMAX theatre and a racing museum.

Racing season starts in November but doesn't heat up until January, when the Dubai World Cup Carnival brings top horses and jockeys to Dubai. It culminates in late March with the elite Dubai World Cup, the world's richest horse race, with prize money of a dizzying US$10 million.

Even if you don't like horse racing, attending a race presents great people-watching opportunities, because it attracts fans from a wide range of nationalities, ages and social backgrounds.

Meydan has a free-admission area where dress is casual. For the grandstand you'll need tickets and may want to dress up. Most races start at 6.45pm but it's best to check the website for the exact schedule and tickets.

There are also **stable tours** (04-381 3405; stabletours@meydanhotels.com; 7.30am-noon Tue & Wed Oct-Apr) that let you meet the trainers and horses and also get close-ups of the jockey's dressing room and the parade ring.

THE CARTEL FASHION

Map p260 (04-388 4341; www.thecartel.me; Alserkal Ave; 10am-8pm Sun-Thu, noon-8pm Sat; M Noor Bank, First Gulf Bank) Deep in the industrial Al Quoz arts district, this concept boutique pushes the boundaries when it comes to fashion and accessories. Look for 'wearable art' by an international roster of avant-garde designers, including such local ones as Amber Feroz, Gia Mia, Reemami, Muse Maison and Maria Iqbal. Enter from 8th St near 17th St.

SPORTS & ACTIVITIES

DUBAI ICE RINK ICE SKATING

Map p258 (04-437 1111; www.dubaiicerink.com; ground fl, Dubai Mall; per session incl skates Dh60-80; 10am-midnight; M Burj Khalifa/Dubai Mall) This Olympic-sized ice rink is ringed with cafes and restaurants and can even be converted into a concert arena. Sign up for a private or group class if you're a little wobbly in the knees. There are also nighttime disco sessions for moving and shaking it up on the ice.

KIDZANIA AMUSEMENT PARK

Map p258 (04-448 5222; www.kidzania.ae; 2nd fl, Dubai Mall; adult/child 4-16yr/child 2-3yr Dh95/140/95; 9am-9pm Sun-Wed, 9am-11pm Thu, 10am-11pm Fri & Sat; M Burj Khalifa/Dubai Mall) For guilt-free shopping without your kids, drop them off in this edutaining miniature city – complete with a school, a fire station, a hospital and a bank – where they get to dress up and slip into adult roles to playfully explore what it's like to be a firefighter, doctor, mechanic, pilot or other professional.

They even earn a salary with which they can buy goods and services, thus learning the value of money. Kids must be at least 120cm tall to be dropped off. There's also a special toddler zone and a baby care centre.

SEGA REPUBLIC AMUSEMENT PARK

Map p258 (04-448 8484; www.segarepublic.com; 2nd fl, Dubai Mall; attractions Dh15-30, day pass from Dh175; 10am-11pm Sun-Wed, 10am-1am Thu-Sat; M Burj Khalifa/Dubai Mall) Bing, boing, beep, zap – this bi-level indoor amusement park with 170 arcade games and 15 tame to (mildly) terrifying thrill rides is a visual and sensory onslaught. Among the adrenaline boosters: race simulators, a small roller coaster, a free-fall tower and a mechanical tornado. Some rides have height restrictions. Pay either per ride or choose from various day passes for unlimited trips.

SPA AT THE PALACE DOWNTOWN DUBAI SPA

Map p258 (☎04-428 7805; www.theaddress.com; Palace – The Old Town, Sheikh Mohammed bin Rashid Blvd; ⏲9am-10pm; Ⓜ Burj Khalifa/Dubai Mall) Give in to your inner sloth in this intimate, sensuously lit spa where treatments incorporate Asian products and techniques. A favourite is the One Desert Journey (Dh825), which involves a rose-petal footbath, a revitalising sand and salt scrub and an oil masque before culminating in a massage using an 'oussada' cushion filled with Moroccan mint.

Once all that's done, you get to drift into semiconscious bliss with a cup of tea in the relaxation room.

TALISE SPA SPA

Map p258 (☎04-319 8181; www.jumeirah.com; Jumeirah Emirates Towers, Sheikh Zayed Rd; ⏲9am-10pm; Ⓜ Emirates Towers) Finally, a spa squarely aimed at jet-lagged executives in bad need of revitalisation. There's the usual range of massages and spa treatments, plus a few esoteric ones. How about bellying up to Oxygen Bar or turbo-recharging your body in a flotation pool? Botox without the needles? Margy's Collagen facial gets rid of those frown lines in no time (temporarily at least).

Jumeirah & Around

Neighbourhood Top Five

❶ Stepping into a modern Arabian souq at **Madinat Jumeirah** (p103) with its sumptuous architecture and surrounding network of Venetian-style canals, subtropical vegetation and Burj Al Arab backdrop. Plan to stay a while to browse, explore, snap selfies, enjoy a drink or meal or catch an *abra* (traditional water taxi).

❷ Sipping cocktails at the **Burj Al Arab** (p103) while debating if it's kitsch or class.

❸ Learning about Islamic architecture and religion on a tour of the intricately detailed **Jumeirah Mosque** (p104).

❹ Earning power shopper status while getting lost in the **Mall of the Emirates** (p104).

❺ Kicking back on **Kite Beach** (p114) and grabbing a Wagyu burger from SALT, Dubai's first gourmet food truck.

For more detail of this area, see Map p254 and p256

Lonely Planet's Top Tip

For the only chance of seeing the inside of a mosque as a non-Muslim in Dubai, show up for the low-cost tours of the Jumeirah Mosque which are operated by the nonprofit Sheikh Mohammed Centre for Cultural Understanding. Aside from admiring the grand architecture, you'll also get the opportunity to ask questions about the Islamic faith and Emirati culture.

Best Places to Eat

- Al Fanar (p106)
- Ravi (p105)
- Pai Thai (p107)
- Samad Al Iraqi (p107)
- Pierchic (p107)

For reviews, see p105.

Best Places to Drink

- 360° (p108)
- Bahri Bar (p108)
- Casa Latina (p108)

For reviews, see p108.

Best Beaches

- Kite Beach (p114)
- Sunset Beach (p114)

For reviews, see p114.

Explore Jumeirah & Around

Hemmed in by the turquoise waters of the Gulf, Jumeirah is practically synonymous with beaches. The neighbourhood extends from just southwest of Port Rashid as far as the Burj Al Arab and the romantically evocative Madinat Jumeirah, a modern take on an Arabian city complete with a souq, high-end resorts and fancy restaurants and bars.

An older part of town, Jumeirah is largely a residential area, dominated by low-rise apartment buildings and handsome villas. The most interesting stretch of its main thoroughfare – Jumeirah Rd – begins just southwest of the Jumeirah Mosque. This is where you'll find designer boutiques, galleries, luxury spas, posh cafes and a smattering of smaller malls like the handsome Mercato Mall. The mosque, incidentally, is the only one in town open to non-Muslims on guided tours.

Jumeirah is poised to undergo major changes in the coming years with the construction of the Dubai Canal, which will link the Dubai Creek with the Gulf. Both Jumeirah Open Beach and Jumeirah Beach Park are closed for the time being as a result, so you'll have to spread your towel further south on Kite Beach and Sunset Beach (which have the added benefit of the Burj Al Arab as a backdrop).

As it stretches for many kilometres, Jumeirah has been officially subdivided into sections Jumeirah 1, 2 and 3 and Umm Suqeim 1, 2, 3. For logistical reasons, we've also included the inland area around the Mall of the Emirates in this chapter.

Local Life

- **Brunch time** Indulge in the time-honoured Dubai tradition of partaking in an opulent brunch at one of the top hotels in Madinat Jumeirah, perhaps paired with free-flowing bubbly.
- **Beaching** Head to Kite Beach to swim in the Gulf, get some exercise at the volleyball net, watch the kite surfers and scarf a burger from the SALT food truck.
- **Designer shopping** Check out what's humming on local and regional sewing machines on an indie boutique hop along Jumeirah Rd.

Getting There & Away

- **Metro** The closest stop to the Burj Al Arab and Madinat Jumeirah is Mall of the Emirates. For the Jumeirah Mosque, get off at World Trade Centre; for Kite Beach, get off at Noor Bank. You'll still need to catch a taxi to reach your final destination.

SYLVAIN SONNET/ GETTY IMAGES ©

TOP SIGHT
BURJ AL ARAB & MADINAT JUMEIRAH

One of Dubai's most attractive recent developments, Madinat Jumeirah is a contemporary interpretation of a traditional Arab village, complete with a souq, palm-fringed waterways and desert-coloured hotels and villas festooned with wind towers. It's especially enchanting at night when the gardens and grounds are romantically lit and the Burj Al Arab gleams in the background. The Burj's graceful silhouette, which is meant to evoke the sail of a dhow (traditional sailing vessel), is as iconic to Dubai as the Eiffel Tower is to Paris.

Completed in 1999, this symbol of modern Dubai sits on an artificial island and comes with its own helipad and a fleet of chauffeur-driven Rolls Royce limousines. Alas, the interior is every bit as over-the-top as the exterior is simple and elegant. The mood is set in the 180m-high lobby, which is sheathed in a red, blue and green colour scheme and accented with pillars draped in gold leaf. If you're not staying, you need to make a reservation for cocktails, afternoon tea or a meal to get past lobby security (a minimum spend applies).

The three hotels that are part of the Madinat Jumeirah complex are almost as exclusive. Wander around to admire their Arabian-style architecture or to enjoy a drink or a meal here or at an alfresco table along the waterfront promenade. This is also the place to hop aboard an *abra* (traditional water taxi) for a cruise around the 4km-long network of canals meandering around the resort.

At the heart of the complex lies Souk Madinat Jumeirah, a maze-like bazaar with shops lining wood-framed walkways. Although the ambience is too contrived to feel like an authentic Arabian market, the quality of some of the crafts, art and souvenirs is actually quite high. If you're in need of a bit of Western culture, see what's playing at the Madinat Theatre.

DON'T MISS

- ➡ Drinks or a meal with a view of the Burj Al Arab
- ➡ A spin around Souk Madinat Jumeirah
- ➡ An *abra* cruise along the resort's canal

PRACTICALITIES

- ➡ Map p256
- ➡ www.jumeirah.com
- ➡ Al Sufouh Rd, Umm Suqeim
- ➡ Ⓜ Mall of the Emirates

SIGHTS

MADINAT JUMEIRAH NEIGHBOURHOOD
See p103.

★JUMEIRAH MOSQUE MOSQUE
Map p254 (04-353 6666; www.cultures.ae; Jumeirah Rd; tours Dh10; tours 10-11.15am Sat-Thu; Emirates Towers, World Trade Centre) Snowy-white and intricately detailed, Jumeirah is not only one of Dubai's most beautiful mosques, but also the only one open to non-Muslims during one-hour guided tours operated by the Sheikh Mohammed Centre for Cultural Understanding (p68). All tours conclude with a Q&A session where you are free to ask any question about Islamic religion and culture. There's no need to prebook. Modest dress is preferred but traditional clothing may be borrowed for free before entering the mosque. Cameras are allowed.

AL SAFA PARK PARK
Map p254 (Sheikh Zayed Rd, 55th St, Al Hadiqa St & Al Wasl St, Jumeirah 2; admission Dh3; 8am-11pm; ; Business Bay) Large sections of this pretty park have been closed due to the construction of the Dubai Water Canal, the epic project that will link the Dubai Creek with the Gulf at Jumeirah Beach.

MAJLIS GHORFAT UM AL SHEEF HISTORIC BUILDING
Map p254 (04-852 1374; near Al Mehemal & Al Bagaara Sts, Jumeirah 3; admission Dh1; 8.30am-8.30pm Sat-Thu, 3.30-8.30pm Fri; Business Bay, Noor Bank) This rare vestige of pre-oil times away from Dubai Creek was built in 1955. Sheikh Rashid bin Saeed al Maktoum, the mastermind of modern Dubai, spent summer afternoons here in rooms cooled by the sea breezes. It's a traditional two-storey structure made of gypsum and coral with a palm frond roof, a wind tower and window shutters carved from East African timber. The palm garden features a traditional *falaj* irrigation system.

MALL OF THE EMIRATES MALL
Map p256 (04-409 9000; www.malloftheemirates.com; Sheikh Zayed Rd, Interchange No 4, Al Barsha; 10am-10pm Sat-Wed, to midnight Thu & Fri; Mall of the Emirates) Home to Ski Dubai, a community theatre, an ultraluxe 24-screen multiplex cinema and – let's not forget – 560 stores...and counting (an expansion should be completed in 2015), MoE is one of Dubai's most popular malls. With narrow walkways and no daylight, it can feel a tad claustrophobic at peak times except in the Italian-arcade-style Galeria lidded by a vaulted glass ceiling.

STREET ART GALLERY GALLERY
Map p254 (055-888 8247; www.streetartdubai.ae; Villa 23, 10B St, Jumeirah 1; 1-7pm Sat-Thu; World Trade Centre) The first Dubai gallery dedicated to promoting street art in the Middle East is the brainchild of art aficionados Thomas Perreaux-Forest and Stephane Valici. Together they show rebel art by international talent, including Denial, Nadib Bandi, Kazilla and Waroox, each distinguished by their own strong style and aesthetic. It's behind the Lime Tree Cafe.

PRO ART GALLERY GALLERY
Map p254 (04-345 0900; www.proartuae.com; 1st fl, Palm Strip Mall, Jumeirah Rd; 10am-9pm Sat-Thu, 1-8pm Fri; World Trade Centre) Based on a donated private collection, this gallery is more like an art museum with original paintings, lithographs and sculptures. The roster includes such smock-and-beret masters as Chagall, Dufy, Damien Hirst, Arman, Le Corbusier and Picasso as

DUBAI WATER CANAL

One of Dubai's latest mega-projects is the construction of the Dubai Canal, a 3km extension of the Dubai Creek all the way to the Gulf. The broad waterway originally ran 15km from its mouth in Deira/Bur Dubai down to the Ras Al Khor Wildlife Sanctuary, but was first extended by 2.2km to the new Business Bay district in 2007.

In December 2013, construction kicked off on the Dubai Canal which will meander from Business Bay below Sheikh Zayed Road, through Al Safa Park and spill into the sea at Jumeirah Beach. As envisioned, it will add 6km of waterfront lined by a shopping mall, hotels, restaurants, cafes, residences, marinas, a public beach, a jogging track and other public spaces. Several bridges will link the banks. The projected completion date is 2017. Until then, there will be numerous traffic diversions, plus the closing of Jumeirah Beach Park and sections of Al Safa Park to contend with.

well as street art phenom Banksy. It's opposite Jumeirah Mosque.

EATING

Jumeirah has an eclectic mix of restaurants, mostly in the midrange to high-end categories. There are many top-end contenders in the hotels, of course, along with some worthwhile indie operations, especially along Jumeirah Rd and in sections of Al Wasl Rd. Although tourist-geared, restaurants at Madinat Jumeirah are incredibly scenic and generally of high quality. Several stage exquisite Friday brunches. Al Dhiyafah Rd in Satwa is a pleasant walking street and tops for a late-night shwarma.

RAVI
PAKISTANI $

Map p254 (04-331 5353; Al Satwa Rd, Satwa; mains Dh8-25; 5-2.30am; World Trade Centre) Everyone from cabbies to five-star chefs flock to this original branch of the legendary Pakistani eatery (dating from 1978) where you eat like a prince and pay like a pauper. Possibly home to the best butter chicken in town, it's also worth loosening that belt for heaping helpings of spicy curries, succulent grilled meats, creamy *dal* and fresh naan.

MAMA TANI
EMIRATI $

Map p254 (04-385 4437; www.mamatani.com; upstairs, Town Centre mall, Jumeirah Rd, Jumeirah 1; khameer Dh11-26; 8am-10pm; ; Burj Khalifa/Dubai Mall) Khameer is a traditional Emirati bread normally eaten at breakfast but served all day at this cheerful cafe decorated with woven-reed discs called *sarrouds*. You can have it plain or like a sandwich stuffed with your choice of sweet or savoury ingredients such as feta, avocado, saffron cream, figs, mint or rose petals.

AL MALLAH
LEBANESE $

Map p254 (04-398 4723; Al Dhiyafah St, Satwa; sandwiches Dh6-12, mains Dh14-60; 6-4am Sat-Thu, noon-4am Fri; World Trade Centre, Al Jafiliya) Serving some of the most delicious shawarmas around, along with excellent other Lebanese staples, this funky eatery with shaded outdoor seating is a great choice for a quick snack and a fresh juice (served in three sizes). It's on Al Diyafah, one of Dubai's most pleasant and liveliest walking streets.

LOCAL KNOWLEDGE

DID YOU KNOW?

The white metal crosspieces at the top of the Burj Al Arab form what is said to be the largest cross in the Middle East – but it's only visible from the sea. Some say the Western architect did it on purpose. Regardless, by the time it was discovered, it was too late to redesign the tower, even if its owner Sheikh Mohammed had wanted to – the hotel has already put Dubai on the map and become the icon for the city. Go see it on a boat charter and decide for yourself. The scale is amazing.

PARS
IRANIAN $

Map p254 (04-398 8444; Al Dhiyafah St, Satwa; mains Dh35-68; 6pm-1am; ; Al Jafiliya, World Trade Centre) Enjoy hot wheels of bread made daily in the outside brick oven along with such classics as creamy *muttabal* (eggplant dip), hummus, and juicy Iranian-style spicy kebabs paired with buttery saffron rice. Opt for a table or feel like a pasha lounging amid the fat pillows on a carpeted platform surrounded by twinkle-lit hedges. It's near Satwa Roundabout.

CHICKEN TIKKA INN
INDIAN $

Map p256 (050-454 1025; www.chickentikkainn.com; Barsha 1; mains Dh18-25; 1-11pm; Mall of the Emirates) This multi-outlet outfit hasn't lost a step since first firing up that charcoal grill in 1972. The chicken tikka has plenty of fans, as do the kebabs, curries and biryanis. They do a brisk takeaway and delivery business, which is why the handful of beige booths amid saffron-and-chilli-coloured walls are rarely full. It's behind Mall of the Emirates.

LIME TREE CAFE
CAFE $

Map p254 (04-325 6325; www.thelimetreecafe.com; Jumeirah Rd, Jumeirah 1; mains Dh20-55; 8am-6pm; ; World Trade Centre) This comfy Euro-style cafe is an expat favourite famous for its luscious cakes (especially the carrot cake), delicious sandwiches (stuffed into their homemade Turkish pide), roast chicken and pastas. It's located next to Spinney's.

THE ONE DELI
INTERNATIONAL $

Map p254 (04-345 6687; www.theone.com; Jumeirah Rd, Jumeirah 1; meals Dh29-54; 10am-10pm; ; World Trade Centre) Deli dabblers will be in heaven at this stylish outpost

LOCAL KNOWLEDGE

MEALS ON WHEELS HIT DUBAI

Gourmet food trucks, the export hits from the US and the UK, finally started rolling into Dubai and Abu Dhabi in 2014. And now that local municipality laws have been somewhat loosened, the trend is bound to take off with a vengeance.

The first mobile kitchen to hit the streets was **SALT** (@findsalt, #findsalt), a classic silver Airstream whose chicken and Wagyu burgers quickly garnered a cult following. It was two Emirati entrepreneurs – avowed foodies Amal Al Marri and Deem Albassam – who came up with the concept and then relied entirely on the power of social media and word of mouth to attract customers (dubbed 'Salters'). Though still a roving business, the truck now seems to have taken up semi-residency at Kite Beach.

Usually popping up at parties, markets, concerts and other special events is catering service spin-off **Ghaf Kitchen** (@ghafkitchen). Brit-owned, it sells upgraded British comfort food from a 1962 Citroen H van found rusting in a field in Normandy, France, refurbished in the UK, outfitted with a kitchen and brought to Dubai.

Gourmet bagel burgers are the stock in trade of jazzily painted **Jake's Food Truck** (@thefoodtruckdubai) whose owners are planning on sending more trucks out on the streets in 2015.

Even hotels have been getting on the food truck wagon. Downtown Dubai's Vida Hotel serves international comfort food like mac 'n' cheese or smoked-brisket sandwiches from its own 1960s Airstream **Vida Food Truck**, usually found outside the Pavilion Downtown Dubai near the hotel. And the Sofitel Dubai Downtown lines up half a dozen trucks around its infinity pool during its Street Food Festival (p121) Friday brunch.

Abu Dhabi is also sending a contender into the running. Called **Meylas** (@meylas), it was founded by Abu Dhabi-born Shaika Al Kaabi and specialises in traditional Emirati cuisine. Dishes on offer include *legimat* (sweet fried dumplings), *batheetha* (a date-based dessert) and sandwiches made with khameer and rgaag breads.

upstairs at THE One home design store. All food is freshly prepared and calibrated to health- and waist-watchers without sacrificing a lick to the taste gods. Reliable choices include the tuna sandwich, the roasted Moroccan chicken and the crayfish salad. Breakfast too. It's near Jumeirah Mosque.

NOODLE BOWL — CHINESE $

Map p254 (04-345 3382; Dune Center, Al Dhiyafa St, Satwa; mains Dh18-35; 9am-midnight; ; World Trade Centre, Al Jafiliya) Noodles are prepared here in every style imaginable – braised, tossed, fried, added to soups and paired with seafood, beef, chicken, duck or tofu. Service is a little lackadaisical and the ambience zero, but if you're just up for a quick and heaping helping of comfort food, you've come to the right place.

BOOKMUNCH CAFE — CAFE $

Map p254 (04-388 4006; www.bookmunchcafe.com; Al Wasl Sq, Al Wasl Rd; mains Dh34-54; 7.30am-10pm Sun-Thu, 8am-10.30pm Fri & Sat; Business Bay) Little literati love this adorable bookstore-cafe combo geared for families. It not only has a fabulous selection of children's books in several languages but also a play corner, reading sessions and a kid-friendly menu. Breakfast is served all day. It's near Al Safa Park.

AL FANAR — EMIRATI $$

Map p254 (04-344 2141; www.alfanarrestaurant.com; Town Centre mall, Jumeirah Rd, Jumeirah 1; mains Dh45-75; 8.30am-11.30pm; Burj Khalifa/Dubai Mall) Al Fanar lays on the old-timey Emirati theme pretty thick with a Land Rover parked outside, a reed ceiling and waitstaff dressed in traditional garb. Make your selection with the help of a picture menu depicting such dishes as *biryani laham* (rice with lamb), *maleh nashef* (salted fish in tomato sauce) and *thereed deyay* (chicken stew with Arabic bread).

PANTRY CAFE — INTERNATIONAL $$

Map p254 (04-388 3868; www.pantrycafe.me; Al Wasl Sq, Al Hadeeqa St, Jumeirah; mains Dh32-100; 7.30am-10pm; ; Business Bay) With its loft-like ceilings, concrete floors, red-brick walls and eco-aware attitude, the Pantry may scream 'Soho transplant' but is actually a laid-back neighbourhood lair serving the best of global comfort food (fish and chips, curry, risotto, pizza, burgers, etc) plus eye-opening breakfasts. Only organic eggs, top quality meats and local herbs and produce make it onto the plates.

SAMAD AL IRAQI IRAQI $$

Map p254 (☎04-342 7887; http://samadaliraqirestaurant.com; Jumeirah Beach Park Plaza, Jumeirah 2; mains Dh50-85; ⏰9-12.30am Sat-Thu, 1pm-1.30am Fri; Ⓜ Business Bay) In a mall packed with restaurants, this huge restaurant with decor evocative of ancient Iraq enjoys an especially loyal local following because of its excellent *masgouf* – wood-fire grilled fish that's considered Iraq's national dish. There's lots of other tempting stews and grills, many served with hot *tanour* bread or biryani rice.

BU QTAIR FISH $$

Map p256 (4D St, Umm Suqeim 1; meals Dh40-70; ⏰6.30-11.30pm; Ⓜ Noor Bank) Always packed to the gills, this seaside shack is a Dubai institution, famous for serving some of the freshest fish in town, marinated in a fragrant masala (curry) sauce and prepared to order. There's no menu, so just point to what you'd like (preferably avoiding unsustainable species like hammour), then lug your cooked-up loot to a rickety plastic table and chow down.

TURATH AL MANDI YEMENI $$

Map p254 (☎04-395 3555; www.turath-almandi.ae; Villa 503, Jumeirah Rd, Jumeirah 3; mains Dh42-84; ⏰noon-midnight; 📶; Ⓜ Noor Bank) An aroma of the daily feast wafts from the kitchen of this authentic Arabian restaurant specialising in traditional food from Yemen. A must-try is *mandi* – the national dish – which stars chicken or mutton slow-cooked in a special oven and served over flavoured rice. Other swoon-worthy picks: *saltah* (meat stew cooked in clay pot) and *syadiah* (fish in a chili tomato sauce).

AL FAYROOZ LOUNGE CAFE $$

Map p256 (☎04-366 6730; www.jumeirah.com; Al Qasr Hotel, Madinat Jumeirah; Emirati breakfast Dh110; ⏰8-12.30am; Ⓜ Mall of the Emirates) We rarely get excited about lobby lounges but this one got our attention for including an Emirati breakfast in its greet-the-day line-up. Aside from Arabic bread and a cold mezze platter, the selection includes such exotic morsels as braised fava beans, cumin-laced chickpeas and *balalit* with egg (rosewater and cardamom vermicelli wrapped in an omelette).

COMPTOIR 102 MACROBIOTIC $$

Map p254 (☎04-385 4555; www.comptoir102.com; Jumeirah Rd 102, Jumeirah 1; mains Dh55-65, 3-course meal Dh90; ⏰8am-11pm; Ⓜ Emirates Towers) In a pretty villa with a quiet patio in back, this concept cafe comes attached to a concept boutique selling beautiful things for home and hearth. The daily changing menu rides the local-organic-seasonal wave and eschews gluten, sugar and dairy. There's also a big selection of super-healthy juices, smoothies and desserts. It's opposite Beach Centre mall.

★ PIERCHIC SEAFOOD $$$

Map p256 (☎04-366 6730; www.madinatjumeirah.com; Al Qasr, Madinat Jumeirah, Al Sufouh Rd, Umm Suqeim 3; mains Dh100-240; ⏰noon-3pm & 6.30-11pm; Ⓜ Mall of the Emirates) Looking for a place to drop an engagement ring into a glass of champagne? Make reservations (far in advance) at this impossibly romantic seafood house capping a long pier with front-row views of the Burj Al Arab and Madinat Jumeirah. The menu is a foodie's daydream, from the champagne ceviche to the poached lobster, all prepared with passion and panache.

★ PAI THAI THAI $$$

Map p256 (☎04-366 6730; www.jumeirah.com; Dar Al Masyaf Hotel, Madinat Jumeirah, Umm Suqeim 3; mains Dh60-195; ⏰6.30-11.30pm; Ⓜ Mall of the Emirates) An *abra* ride, a canal-side table and candlelight are the hallmarks of a romantic night out and this enchanting spot sparks on all cylinders. If your date doesn't make you swoon, then the beautifully crafted Thai dishes should still ensure an unforgettable evening. Or come for Friday brunch (with/without alcohol Dh240/190). Book weeks ahead.

AL MAHARA SEAFOOD $$$

Map p256 (☎04-301 7600; www.jumeirah.com; lower fl, Burj Al Arab; mains Dh320-655; ⏰lunch & dinner; Ⓜ Mall of the Emirates) A lift posing as a submarine deposits you at a gold-leaf-clad tunnel spilling into Dubai's most extravagant restaurant whose name translates as 'oyster shell'. Tables orbit a circular floor-to-ceiling aquarium where clownfish flit and baby sharks dart as their sea bass and halibut cousins are being...devoured. Pretty surreal. Dress code and no children under 12 years old for dinner.

ZHENG HE'S CHINESE $$$

Map p256 (04-366 6730; www.jumeirah.com; Mina A'Salam, Madinat Jumeirah, Al Sufouh Rd, Umm Suqeim 3; mains Dh100-300; lunch & dinner; Mall of the Emirates) A kitchen staff of 20 clatters pans and fires woks behind the glass of the open kitchen at this Sino-chic dining room centred on a pagoda-style ceiling. Many diners go for the live fish tank but there's also a beautiful and inventive dim sum selection and lots of exotic mains like braised foie gras abalone.

THE MEAT CO STEAKHOUSE $$$

Map p256 (04-368 6040; www.themeat.com; Souk Madinat Jumeirah, Al Sufouh Rd; burgers Dh75-135, mains Dh155-385; noon-11.30pm; Mall of the Emirates) Surrender helplessly to your inner carnivore at this canalside hang-out where yummy cuts of steak range from Australian grain-fed Angus to a Brazilian grass-fed beast, all available in small (200g) and large (300g) portions. Other options include a hanging skewer of marinated lamb that goes nicely with delicious veggie side dishes such as wild mushrooms.

DRINKING & NIGHTLIFE

★360° BAR, CLUB

Map p256 (04-406 8741; www.jumeirah.com; Jumeirah Beach Hotel, Jumeirah Rd, Umm Suqeim; 5pm-2am Sun-Wed, 5pm-1.30am Thu-Sat; ; Mall of the Emirates) Capping a long curved pier, this alfresco playground still hasn't lost its grip on the crowd after many years of music, mingling and magical views of the Burj Al Arab, especially when the sun slips seaward. On weekends (guest list) there are top-notch DJs spinning house for shiny happy hotties; other nights are mellower.

BAHRI BAR BAR

Map p256 (04-366 6730; Mina A'Salam Hotel, Madinat Jumeirah; 4pm-2am Sat-Mon, to 3am Tue-Fri; Mall of the Emirates) This chic bar drips with rich Arabian decor and has a fabulous verandah laid with Persian carpets and big cane sofas where you can take in gorgeous views of the Burj Al Arab. The vibe is very grown-up – just the kind of place you take your parents for sunset drinks.

CASA LATINA BAR, CLUB

Map p262 (04-399 6699; Ibis Hotel Al Barsha, Sheikh Zayed Rd; 6pm-2am; ; Sharaf DG) This Cuban-themed bar has much more to offer than salsa and cigars. With its unpretentious vibe and inexpensive drinks, it attracts a laid-back, non-poser crowd of people who are more into the music (drum and bass, funk, techno) than looking good. Happy hour from 6pm to 8pm. Live DJ sets on Thursdays.

SKYVIEW BAR BAR

Map p256 (04-301 7600; www.burjalarab.com; Burj Al Arab, off Jumeirah Rd, Umm Suqeim 3; 1pm-2am Sat-Thu, from 7pm Fri; Mall of the Emirates) Despite the stratospheric tab, cocktails (Dh320 minimum spend) or afternoon tea (Dh565) on the 27th floor of the Burj Al Arab ranks high on tourists' must-do lists. The minimum age is 21 and booking (far) ahead is essential. As for the outlandish Liberace-meets-*Star Trek* interiors, all we can say is: 'Welcome to the Burj'.

PACHA IBIZA DUBAI RESTAURANT, CLUB

Map p256 (04-567 0000; www.pacha.ae; main entrance, Souk Madinat Jumeirah; 8pm-3am Tue-Sat; Mall of the Emirates) The legendary Ibiza nightclub now brings its Balearic sound to a dramatic three-level space at Madinat. Evenings start with dinner and a live show of singers, dancers and acrobats in the main room, which is later heated up by local and international house DJs. Alternative sounds rule the upstairs Red Room while the rooftop is a dedicated *sheesha* (water pipe) and chill zone.

MAZOLOGY MOCKTAILS

Map p256 (04-394 4441; Bait Al Bahar, waterfront; 6-2am; Noor Bank) This uber-cool beach hang-out is popular with local hipsters crouched in lively conversation on white sofas, puffing on a *sheesha* and swilling exotic-looking drinks while being showered by high-octane sounds. Sounds just like your ordinary Dubai nightspot? Not exactly, for there's absolutely no booze in those drinks.

The lounge is part of the Bait Al Bahar, a three-storey venue that also includes an Emirati restaurant and a beachfront diner.

AGENCY WINE BAR

Map p256 (04-366 6730; www.jumeirah.com; Souk Madinat Jumeirah, Umm Suqeim 3; 1pm-1am Sun-Wed, to 2am Thu, 4pm-2am Fri, 5pm-1am

LOCAL KNOWLEDGE

KHANJARS

Visit the Al Ain camel market or the bullfights at Fujairah and you'll see old Emirati men wearing *khanjars* (traditional curved daggers) over their *dishdashas* (men's traditional long robes). Traditionally, *khanjar* handles were made from rhino horn; today, they are often made of wood. Regular *khanjars* have two rings where the belt is attached and their scabbards are decorated with thin silver wire. The intricacy of the wire-thread pattern and its workmanship determine value. Sayidi *khanjars* have five rings and are often covered entirely in silver sheet, with little or no wire, and their quality is assessed by weight and craftsmanship. A *khanjar* ought to feel heavy when you pick it up. Don't believe anyone who tells you a specific *khanjar* is 'very old' – few will be more than 30 to 40 years old. If you're in the market for one, there's an especially good selection at Lata's at Madinat Jumeirah.

Sat; Ⓜ Mall of the Emirates) Madinat's Agency is a civilised spot for pre-dinner drinks with a romantic terrace overlooking the Madinat canals and glimpses of the Burj Al Arab. Happy hour runs from 5pm to 8pm Saturday to Thursday.

LEFT BANK BAR

Map p256 (04-368 6171; Waterfront Promenade, Souk Madinat Jumeirah; 10.30-2am Sat-Thu, to 3am Wed-Fri; ; Ⓜ Mall of the Emirates) The waterside tables next to the *abra* station are great for tête-à-têtes, but the real party is inside where a backlit bar, giant mirrors, leather club chairs and chill beats create a dynamic lounge scene. Ladies scores three free vodka drinks on Wednesdays between 8pm and 10pm.

SHO CHO BAR, CLUB

Map p254 (04-346 1111; www.sho-cho.com; Dubai Marine Beach Resort & Spa, Jumeirah Rd, Jumeirah 1; 7pm-3am Sun-Fri; Ⓜ World Trade Centre, Emirates Towers) The cool minimalist interior, with its blue lights and wall-mounted fish tanks, may draw you in, but the beachside deck is the place to be. Take in the laid-back vibe as the cool ocean breezes blow and the DJ's soundtrack competes with the crashing waves.

BOUDOIR CLUB

Map p254 (050-375 7377; www.boudoirdubai.com; Dubai Marine Beach Resort & Spa, Jumeirah Rd; 9pm-3am; Ⓜ World Trade Centre) High on the glam-o-meter, Boudoir has been around the block once or twice but isn't actually showing its age – and neither are its fashionable patrons. Sounds run the gamut from house to hip-hop to *desi* (Bollywood) nights.

Tufted red-velvet booths, beaded curtains and tasselled draperies lend a super-model vibe – indeed, you may spot one among the wannabes. Free drinks for women from 10pm to 1am on Tuesdays.

KOUBBA BAR, LOUNGE

Map p256 (04-366 6730; www.madinatjumeirah.com; Al Qasr Hotel, Madinat Jumeirah, Umm Suqeim 3; 5pm-2am Sat-Wed, to 3am Thu & Fri; Ⓜ Mall of the Emirates) Score a candlelit table on the terrace overlooking the Madinat canals and illuminated Burj, and you'll instantly know you've found one of the most tranquil and romantic spots in Dubai. With sunset-themed cocktails served from a mixology trolley and a wide selection of *sheesha*, it's a great place for pre- or post-dinner chilling. No reservations.

NAR SHEESHA

Map p254 (04-344 3749; City Walk, Al Safa & Al Wasl Rds; sheesha Dh48-75; 9-1.30am; Ⓜ Burj Khalifa/Dubai Mall) With a prime position facing City Walk's shallow pond, Nar is a popular cool kid hang-out in the cooler months. Aside from a large *sheesha* selection, they make some mean mocktails and also have a full menu featuring mezze, *mishtah* (topped flatbread), *saroukh* (stuffed bread pockets) and other Lebanese munchables.

☆ ENTERTAINMENT

VOX MALL OF THE EMIRATES CINEMA

Map p256 (04-341 4222; www.voxcinemas.com; Mall of the Emirates, Al Barsha; tickets Dh35, 3D films Dh47; Ⓜ Mall of the Emirates) Vox would be just another multiplex were it not for its Gold Class screening rooms, where seats are enormous recliners and servers bring you blankets, popcorn in silver bowls and drinks in glass goblets. Anyone under 18 must be accompanied by an adult. Skip the queue by buying tickets online.

DUBAI COMMUNITY THEATRE & ARTS CENTRE — THEATRE

Map p256 (DUCTAC; ☎04-341 4777; www.ductac.org; top fl, Mall of the Emirates; Ⓜ Mall of the Emirates) This thriving performance venue at the Mall of the Emirates puts on all sorts of diversions, from classical concerts to Bollywood retrospectives, Arabic folklore to large-scale mural projects. Much support is given to Emirati talent, making this a good place to plug into the local scene.

Drivers should take the Ski Dubai car park entrance and park between rows S and T.

MADINAT THEATRE — THEATRE

Map p256 (☎04-366 6546; www.madinattheatre.com; Souk Madinat Jumeirah, Umm Suqeim 3; Ⓜ Mall of the Emirates) The program at this handsome 442-seat theatre at Souk Madinat is largely calibrated to the cultural cravings of British expats. Expect plenty of crowd-pleasing entertainment ranging from popular West End imports to standup comedy and Russian ballet.

SHOPPING

★MALL OF THE EMIRATES — MALL

Map p256 (☎04-409 9000; www.malloftheemirates.com; Sheikh Zayed Rd, Interchange 4, Al Barsha; ⏰10am-10pm Sat-Wed, to midnight Thu & Fri; Ⓜ Mall of the Emirates) With 560 stores (more after an extension in 2015), MoE is (another) one of Dubai's megamalls with retail options ranging from high street to haute couture, but with precious few local or regional contenders. Anchor stores include Harvey Nichols and a vast Carrefour supermarket.

CITY WALK — MALL

Map p254 (Al Safa Rd; Ⓜ Burj Khalifa/Dubai Mall) With only Phase 1 of this low-rise, Euro-style open-air mall completed, there's not much to draw you here in terms of shopping, although the cafes wrapped around a pool – some with a view of the Burj Khalifa – make for an inviting pit stop. Meanwhile, the much larger Phase 2 expansion is taking shape next door. It's located between Al Wasl and Al Satwa Rds.

RECTANGLE JAUNE — FASHION

Map p256 (☎04-341 0288; Mall of the Emirates; ⏰10am-10pm Sat-Wed, to midnight Thu & Fri; Ⓜ Mall of the Emirates) A great store for men, with a terrific selection of dress shirts in snappy stripes and bold patterns by a team of fashion-savvy Lebanese designers. There's another branch in Deira City Centre.

MIKYAJY — COSMETICS

Map p256 (☎04-341 4277; www.mikyajy.com; Mall of the Emirates; ⏰10am-midnight Sat-Wed, to 1am Thu & Fri; Ⓜ Mall of the Emirates) Mikyajy is Arabic for 'my make-up' and that's just what this popular Middle Eastern franchise specialises in. Bestsellers include smokey black mascaras and eyeliners and big beauty cases with a colourful palette of products bound to unleash the princess in every girl.

JUMBO ELECTRONICS — ELECTRONICS

Map p256 (www.jumbo.ae; Mall of the Emirates; ⏰10am-midnight; Ⓜ Mall of the Emirates) The mother of Dubai's electronics stores, this place stocks all the latest computers, cameras, mobile phones, games and gadgets under one giant roof. There are seven more outlets located across town, including one in Deira City Centre and another in the Dubai Mall.

AIZONE — FASHION

Map p256 (☎04-347 9333; Mall of the Emirates; ⏰10am-midnight; Ⓜ Mall of the Emirates) Lose yourself for hours in this enormous Lebanese fashion emporium with hard-to-find trendy labels and snappy fashions for twirling on the dance floor. Look for the latest threads from Bibelot, Juicy Couture, Spy and Lotus.

MERCATO MALL — MALL

Map p254 (☎04-344 4161; www.mercatoshoppingmall.com; Jumeirah Rd, Jumeirah 1; ⏰10am-10pm; Ⓜ Financial Centre, Burj Khalifa/Dubai Mall) With 140 stores, Mercato may be small by Dubai standards but it's distinguished by attractive architecture that's a fantasy blend of a European train station and an Italian Renaissance village. Think vaulted glass roof, brick arches, a giant clock and a cafe-lined central 'square' called Piazza Grande. Retail-wise, you'll find upscale international brands and a Spinney's supermarket.

CARPET BUYING 101

Due diligence is essential for prospective carpet buyers. Though you may only want a piece to match your curtains, you'll save a lot of time and money if you do a little homework. Your first order of business: read *Oriental Rugs Today* by Emmett Eiland, an excellent primer on buying new Oriental rugs.

A rug's quality depends entirely on how the wool was processed. It doesn't matter if the rug was hand-knotted if the wool is lousy. The best comes from sheep at high altitudes, which produce impenetrably thick, long-staple fleece, heavy with lanolin. No acids should ever be applied, otherwise the lanolin washes away. Lanolin yields naturally stain-resistant, lustrous fibre that doesn't shed. The dye should be vegetable-based pigment. This guarantees saturated, rich colour tones with a depth and vibrancy unattainable with chemicals.

The dyed wool is hand-spun into thread, which by nature has occasional lumps and challenges the craftsmanship of the weavers, forcing them to compensate for the lumps by occasionally changing the shape, size or position of a knot. These subtle variations in a finished carpet's pattern – visible only upon close inspection – give the carpet its character, and actually make the rug more valuable.

Dealers will hype knot density, weave quality and country of origin, but really, they don't matter. The crucial thing to find out is how the wool was treated. A rug made with acid-treated wool will never look as good as it did the day you bought it. Conversely, a properly made rug will grow more lustrous in colour over time and will last centuries.

Here's a quick test. Stand on top of the rug with rubber-soled shoes and do the twist. Grind the fibres underfoot. If they shed, it's lousy wool. You can also spill water onto the rug. See how fast it absorbs. Ideally it should puddle for an instant, indicating a high presence of lanolin. Best of all, red wine will not stain lanolin-rich wool.

We've endeavoured to list good dealers, but you'll be taking your chances in Dubai if you're looking for an investment piece. However, if you just want a gorgeous pattern that will look great in your living room, pack a few fabric swatches from your sofa and curtains and go for it. Patterns range from simple four-colour tribal designs in wool to wildly ornate, lustrous, multicoloured silk carpets that shimmer under the light. Look through books before you leave home to get a sense of what you like. Once in the stores, plan to linger a long time with dealers, slowly sipping tea while they unfurl dozens of carpets. The process is great fun. Just don't get too enthusiastic or the dealer won't bargain as readily.

If you're serious about becoming a collector, hold off. Read Emmett Eiland's book; Google 'DOBAG', a Turkish-rug-making cultural-survival project; and check out www.yayla.com for other reliable background info. Follow links to nonprofit organisations (such as DOBAG) that not only help reconstruct rug-making cultures threatened by modernisation, but also help to educate, house and feed the people of these cultures, giving them a voice in an age of industrial domination. And you'll get a fantastic carpet to boot.

O-CONCEPT FASHION, ACCESSORIES

Map p254 (☎04-345 5557; www.oconcept.ae; Al Hudheiba Rd; ⏰10am-10pm; Ⓜ World Trade Center)
This Emirati-owned urban boutique-cum-cafe with shiny concrete floors and ducts wrapped in gold foil is a routine stop for fashionistas in search of up-to-the-second T-shirts, dresses, jeans and other fashions by a changing roster of young international labels like Australia's Deadly Companions or Finland's Shine by Sophia. It's near Jumeirah Mosque.

S*UCE FASHION

Map p254 (☎04-344 7270; http://shopatsauce.com; Village Mall, Jumeirah Beach Rd; ⏰10am-10pm Sat-Thu, 4-10pm Fri; Ⓜ Emirates Towers)
Plain and simple they are not, the clothes and accessories at S*uce (pronounced 'sauce'), a pioneer in Dubai's growing lifestyle fashion scene. Join fashionistas picking through international designers you probably won't find on your high street back home (eg India's Anouk Grewal, Lebanon's Vanina). Pieces can be rather 'out

there', mixing feathers and leather, gold pleats and denim. Also in the Dubai Mall.

HOUSE OF PROSE BOOKS

Map p254 (☎04-344 9021; www.houseofprose.com; Jumeirah Plaza, Jumeirah Rd, Jumeirah 1; ⌚9am-8pm daily; Ⓜ Emirates Towers) This is the original branch of the beloved local lit parlour founded by American bibliophile Mike McGinley. Since 1993, he has supplied readers with new and secondhand English-language books, from classic tomes to obscure biographies and children's books. After you're done, you can return your purchase for a 50% refund.

SUNSET MALL MALL

Map p254 (☎04-330 7333; www.sunsetmall.ae; Jumeirah Rd, Jumeirah 3; ⌚10am-10pm Sun-Thu, to midnight Fri & Sat; Ⓜ Noor Bank) Behind a coated glass facade designed to reflect the heat sits this two-level mall that's popular with fashion-forward locals. Cool stores include Socialista, Rivaage and West LA. Alas, it's often deserted.

★ WEST LA BOUTIQUE FASHION, ACCESSORIES

Map p254 (☎04-394 4248; www.westlaboutique.com; ground fl, Sunset Mall, Jumeirah Rd, Jumeirah 3; ⌚10am-10pm Sat-Thu, 1.30-10pm Fri; Ⓜ Business Bay) Dubai's hipster crowd circles for the latest garb, cosmetics, jewellery, shoes, bags and other trendy must-haves actually sourced by savvy buyers around the globe, not just in West Los Angeles. The selection is huge, the vibe electric and prices surprisingly reasonable. Sunset Mall itself has plenty of other fashion-forward boutiques, including Socialista and Rivaage.

THE GALLERIA MALL MALL

Map p254 (www.thegalleria.ae; Al Wasl Rd, near 13th St; ⌚10am-10pm Sat-Wed, to midnight Thu & Fri; Ⓜ Burj Khalifa/Dubai Mail) This chic concept minimall is a laid-back alternative to the big mall craziness. Pick up outdoor gear at Adventure HQ, 24-carat-gold shower gel at Stenders or a stylish outfit for your preteen at local designer Saucette, then wrap up with a healthy meal at South African cafe Tashas or gooey cakes at Home Bakery. It's next to Jumeirah post office.

SOUK MADINAT JUMEIRAH MALL

Map p256 (☎04-366 8888; www.jumeirah.com; Madinat Jumeirah, Al Sufouh Rd, Umm Suqeim 3; ⌚10am-11pm; Ⓜ Mall of the Emirates) More a tourist-geared shopping mall than a traditional Arabian market, this handsomely designed souq is not a bad place for picking up souvenirs, although bargains are rare and bargaining is a no-no. Plenty of charming cafes, bars and restaurants line the waterfront, while on Saturday mornings an organic farmer's market displays farm-fresh bounty in one of its courtyards (December to May).

YASMINE FASHION, ACCESSORIES

Map p256 (☎04-368 6115; www.jalabiatyasmine.com; Souk Madinat Jumeirah, Al Sufouh Rd, Umm Suqeim 3; ⌚10am-11pm; Ⓜ Mall of the Emirates) This small boutique specialises in elegantly patterned shawls and *jalabiyas* (traditional kaftans native to the Gulf). The finest are handmade by weavers in Kashmir from genuine pashmina (cashmere) or shahtoosh (the down hair of a Tibetan antelope). Machine-made shawls start at Dh150.

CAMEL COMPANY SOUVENIRS

Map p256 (☎04-368 6048; www.camelcompany.ae; Souk Madinat Jumeirah; ⌚10am-11pm; Ⓜ Mall of the Emirates) If you can slap a camel on it, Camel Company has it. This is hands-down the best spot for camel souvenirs: plush stuffed camels that sing when you squeeze them, camels in Hawaiian shirts, on T-shirts, coffee cups, mouse-pads, notebooks, greeting cards and fridge magnets.

LATA'S SOUVENIRS

Map p256 (☎04-368 6216; Souk Madinat Jumeirah; ⌚10am-11pm; Ⓜ Mall of the Emirates) Ignore the kitsch and look for quality Arabian and Middle Eastern souvenirs, such as Moroccan lamps, brass coffee tables, *khanjars*, silver prayer holders and Bedouin jewellery. Browse around or tell the staff what you're after, and they'll steer you right to it.

IF BOUTIQUE FASHION

Map p256 (☎04-394 7260; Villa 26, Umm Al Sheif St, Umm Suqeim 1; ⌚10am-10pm Sat-Thu, 3-10pm Fri; Ⓜ Noor Bank) If you need to steal the show at your next party, you might just find the right outfit at this high-end designer boutique specialising in international fashionista label faves such as Comme des Garcons, Tsumori Chisato and Kolor.

GARDEROBE VINTAGE

Map p256 (☎04-394 2753; www.garderobe.ae; Jumeirah Rd, Umm Suqeim 1; Ⓜ Noor Bank) This is the place to come to snag a one-off vintage item at an affordable price. The pre-loved designer labels and accessories are in tip-top condition and often include items by Chanel, Hermès, and Gucci. It's a concept that has proven to be a big hit here, particularly among the expatriate community.

O' DE ROSE FASHION, ACCESSORIES

Map p256 (☎04-348 7990; www.o-derose.com; 999 Al Wasl Rd, Umm Suqeim 2; ⏰10am-8pm) It helps if you love bold colours and patterns when shopping at this delightful boutique ensconced in a residential villa and run by a trio of free-spirited cousins from Beirut. Their passion for unusual things is reflected in the selection of postmodern ethnic-chic clothing, accessories, art and home decor created mostly by indie designers from around the region.

SPORTS & ACTIVITIES

WILD WADI WATERPARK WATER PARK

Map p256 (☎04-348 4444; www.wildwadi.com; Jumeirah Rd; admission over/under 110cm Dh245/185; ⏰10am-6pm Nov-Feb, to 7pm Mar-May & Sep-Oct, to 8pm Jun-Aug; 👪; Ⓜ Mall of the Emirates) When the kids grow weary of the beach and hotel pool, you'll score big-time by bringing them to Wild Wadi. Over a dozen ingeniously interconnected rides follow a vague theme about Arabian adventurer Juha and his friend Sinbad the Sailor who get shipwrecked together. There are plenty of gentle rides for tots, plus a big-wave pool and a white-water rapids 'river'.

On the 33m-high Jumeirah Sceirah slide you can reach speeds of 80km/h. Kids must be at least 110cm tall for some of the more wicked rides. It's near Jumeirah Beach Hotel.

MADINAT JUMEIRAH ABRA RIDES BOAT TOUR

Map p256 (☎04-366 8888; www.jumeirah.com; Souk Madinat Jumeirah; adult/child Dh75/40; ⏰10am-11pm Nov-Apr, 11am-11pm May-Oct; Ⓜ Mall of the Emirates) Even if you're not staying at Madinat Jumeirah, you can explore its network of winding waterways and stunning architecture and gardens on a leisurely 20-minute tour on a traditional *abra*. Tours leave from the Souk Madinat waterfront (near the Left Bank bar). No reservations are necessary.

TALISE SPA SPA

Map p256 (☎04-366 6818; www.jumeirah.com; Madinat Jumeirah; ⏰9am-10pm; Ⓜ Mall of the Emirates) This world-class Arabian-themed spa has 26 gorgeous temple-like outdoor treatment rooms where you can detox with a green tea salt therapy, get baby soft skin

SKI DUBAI

Picture this: it's 45 degrees outside and you're wearing gloves and a hat and riding a chairlift through a faux alpine winter wonderland. Skiing in the desert? No problem. In Dubai, that is. Right in the gargantuan Mall of the Emirates, **Ski Dubai** (Map p256; ☎04-409 4000; www.skidxb.com; Mall of the Emirates, Al Barsha; Snow Park admission adult/child Dh150/140, 2hr ski pass Dh200/170, penguin encounters from Dh150; ⏰10am-11pm Sun-Wed, 10am-midnight Thu, 9am-midnight Fri, 9am-11pm Sat; 👪; Ⓜ Mall of the Emirates) has delighted everyone from slope-starved expats to curious tourists and snow virgins since opening in 2005 as the first indoor ski park in the Middle East.

Of course the 60m (196ft) vertical drop is an ant hill when compared with an actual ski mountain, but it's challenging enough for beginners, fun for intermediate skiers and a novelty for more advanced skiers. They get to tackle five ski runs (the longest being 400m) and a Freestyle Zone with jumps and rails, both accessed by chairlift.

Pretty much everything is provided, including socks and skis, although gloves and hats must be purchased (unless you happen to have your own), starting at Dh55 and Dh20, respectively.

The slope is embedded in an enchanting ice sculpture–festooned Snow Park where snow bunnies of all ages can have fun tobogganing, tubing or having a snowball fight. For an extra fee they can even get close and personal with the resident gentoo and king penguins.

For the best views of the 'resort' from the mall, head to the 1st-floor viewing gallery near the food court. There's also a full-on view of the slopes from the Après restaurant on the same floor.

LOCAL KNOWLEDGE

LIFE'S A BEACH

If you're not staying at a beachfront five-star hotel but want to swim in the Gulf without forking over big money for a day at a beach club, there are plenty of free (or nearly free) public beaches for dipping into the Gulf. Most are nearly deserted during the week but packed on weekends (Friday and Saturday).

Facilities range from nonexistent to full beach infrastructure and have improved considerably over the years, especially with the opening of the 14km-long Jumeirah Corniche in late 2014. Stretching from Dubai Marine Beach Resort to the Burj Al Arab, it features a boardwalk, a spongy jogging track, kiosks and benches. Some sections though, most notably **Jumeirah Open Beach** (Map p254; south of Dubai Marine Beach Resort & Spa; M WorldTrade Centre) FREE and **Jumeirah Beach Park** (Map p254; ☎04-349 2555; Jumeirah Beach Rd; per person/car Dh5/20; ⌚7am-11pm Sun-Wed, to 11.30pm Thu & Fri; M Business Bay), are actually closed for the foreseeable future, the former because of a private development, the latter because of construction of the Dubai Canal.

But don't worry, there's still plenty of wide open sandy beach for tanning and frolicking. The following beaches are listed northeast to southwest.

Al Mamzar Beach Park (☎04-296 6201; Al Mamzar Creek, Deira; per person/car Dh5/30, pool adult/child Dh10/5; ⌚9am-9pm Sun-Wed, to 10pm Thu-Sat; M Al Quiadah) This lushly landscaped beach park consists of a string of five lovely sandy sweeps and comes with plenty of infrastructure, including a swimming pool, playgrounds, water sports rentals, barbecues, grassy areas and air-conditioned cabanas (per day Dh160 to Dh210, on Beach 4). There are also sun lounges and umbrellas for rent but food outlets are minimal so you might want to bring a picnic. Mondays and Wednesdays are for women and children only. It's about 6.5km from the nearest metro station.

Kite Beach (Sheikh Hamdan Beach; Map p256; 2D St, Umm Suqeim 1; M Noor Bank) FREE Also known as Sheikh Hamdan Beach, this long pristine stretch of white sand is super clean and jam-packed with sporty types keen on kite surfing, soap football, beach tennis, beach volleyball, kayaking and other sports to show off those toned abs. There are showers, toilets, kiosks and changing facilities, plus great views of the Burj Al Arab. Weekends are busy. Turn off Jumeirah Rd opposite Saga World mall.

Sunset Beach (Map p256; Umm Suqeim 3; M First Gulf Bank) FREE Right next to the Jumeirah Beach Hotel and with dreamy views of the Burj Al Arab, Sunset is Dubai's last surfing beach, although waves may soon be blocked because of an expansion of the Jumeirah Beach Hotel marina. For now facilities are limited to a few changing cubicles and a playground. It's north of Jumeirah Beach Hotel.

Black Palace Beach (Map p262; off Al Sufouh Rd, btwn Madinat Jumeirah & Palm Jumeirah; M Dubai Internet City) FREE This small strip of beach is tucked between the royal palaces facing the Palm Jumeirah.

JBR Open Beach (p127) Paralleling The Beach at JBR outdoor mall and The Walk at JBR promenade, with their myriad of food outlets, this beach may not be the widest but it has fabulous, state-of-the-art public infrastructure, including changing rooms, showers and toilets, a soft jogging trail, an outdoor gym and benches. Admission is charged for the kiddie splash playground, an offshore waterpark and a beach club with sun lounges and umbrellas. Watch out for rip currents. It's quieter further down towards the Sheraton, where the public beach ends.

covered in a gold clay body mask or soothe muscle aches with a sea shell massage. Afterwards, you're free to relax in the gender-separated sauna, steam room and pool.

AL BOOM DIVING DIVING

Map p254 (☎04-342 2993; www.alboomdiving.com; cnr Al Wasl Rd & 33 St, Jumeirah 1; guided dives from Dh250; ⌚10am-8pm Sun-Thu, to 6pm Fri & Sat; 👪; M World Trade Centre) Al Boom is the largest dive centre in the country and offers the gamut of PADI certification courses as well as guided wreck dives and night dives off the coast of Dubai, shark dives at the Dubai Aquarium and reef dives off the East Coast and the Musandam Peninsula.

Their training hub is in Jumeirah, but they also operate the dive centre at the Atlantis The Palm resort.

SURF HOUSE DUBAI SURFING

Map p256 (☎050-504 3020; www.surfingdubai.com; Villa 110, 41A St, Sunset Beach; surfing & SUP lessons from Dh110, rental per hr Dh75; ⏰7am-6.30pm; Ⓜ First Gulf Bank) 'Hang 10' central in Dubai is the Surf House, which not only stocks all the latest surf and stand-up paddle (SUP) boards but also offers lessons in both sports. The venue doubles as a community hang-out and includes a cafe and yoga studio.

DUBAI KITE SCHOOL KITE SURFING

Map p256 (☎050-455 9098; www.dubaikiteschool.com; Kite Beach, 2D St, Umm Suqeim 1; lessons private/group per hr Dh250/300; Ⓜ Noor Bank) Located on Kite Beach, one of Dubai's most beautiful beaches, this outfit offers lessons and also rents kites, boards and harnesses to get you up and out on the water. It's located behind Saga Mall.

DUBAI ROAD RUNNERS RUNNING

(www.dubairoadrunners.com; 👪) Founded in 1989, DRR is Dubai's oldest running club and welcomes runners of all ages and fitness levels. It meets up several times weekly for runs in Al Barsha Park and Jumeirah Beach Park. Check the website for the latest schedule and just show up.

Dubai Marina & Palm Jumeirah

DUBAI MARINA | PALM JUMEIRAH

Neighbourhood Top Five

❶ Strolling down **The Walk at JBR** (p118), a pleasant strip chockablock with family-oriented indie cafes, restaurants and shops, and combining this with a spin around The Beach, a chic, new low-rise outdoor mall flanking a beautiful stretch of sandy beach.

❷ Partying from day to night at a sizzling beach club like **Zero Gravity** (p128).

❸ Catching the boat shuttle to the sleek **101 Lounge & Bar** (p123) for cocktails with a million-dollar view of the Dubai Marina skyline.

❹ Enjoying a canalside dinner or drink with gorgeous views of the glittering marina skyscrapers, for instance at **Asia Asia** (p120).

❺ Cruising around the marina by **water bus** (p118), preferably at dusk or early evening.

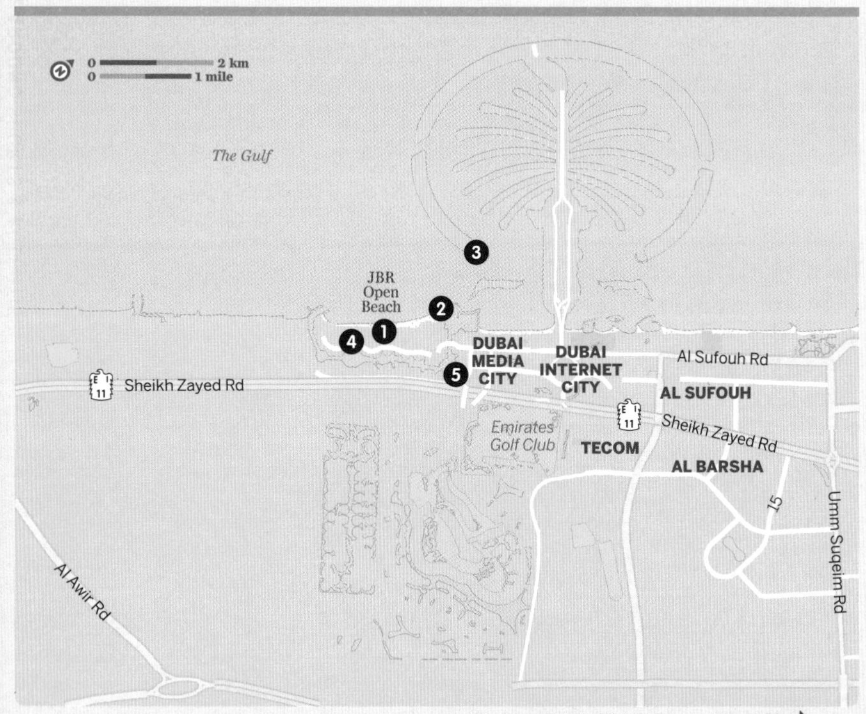

For more detail of this area, see Map p262

Explore Dubai Marina & Palm Jumeirah

Dubai Marina has become one of the most popular places to live in town and, though primarily residential, its pedestrian-friendly areas hold plenty of appeal for visitors. Carved from the desert, this is one of the world's largest man-made marinas, centred on a 3km-long canal flanked by a thicket of futuristic high-rises, including the eye-catching Cayan Tower. A stroll along the Marina Walk promenade is delightful, especially after dusk when you can gaze out at the glittering towers and bobbing yachts, stop by the dancing fountains and find your favourite dinner, drink or *sheesha* (water pipe) spot.

Just as pedestrian-friendly is nearby The Walk at JBR, a 1.7km-long strip of shops and family-oriented eateries paralleling a lovely sandy beach. JBR stands for Jumeirah Beach Residence, a vast cluster of 40 buttercream-yellow apartment and hotel towers overlooking the Gulf. Some sections of the beach are public and there's a jogging path, changing facilities, a small offshore waterpark and a handsome low-rise cluster of, yes, more shops and cafes with alfresco terraces called The Beach.

North of here are some of the most exclusive hotels in town, the tech enclaves of Dubai Internet City and Dubai Media City, where CNN, BBC World, Bloomberg and other outlets are based.

Jutting into the Gulf is the Palm Jumeirah, an artificial island in the shape of a palm tree with a 2km-long trunk, 16-frond crown and 11km-long crescent-shaped breakwater. Built to increase Dubai's beachfront, it's home to luxury apartments, villas and hotels and punctuated by the garish Atlantis The Palm resort with its crowd-pleasing waterpark and aquarium.

Local Life

- **Strolling** Evenings are perfect for people-watching and chilling on The Walk at JBR and Marina Walk.
- **Dinner with a view** Be dazzled by the glittering jewel box that is the Dubai Marina at night from a lofty terrace table.
- **Beach it** Grab a towel and get working on your tan, then wrap up the day with a movie under the stars.

Getting There & Away

- **Metro** The Red Line stops at Damac for the Dubai Marina. For the Walk at JBR, the Jumeirah Lakes Towers station is a bit more convenient.
- **Tram** Dubai Tram links Dubai Media City, JBR and Dubai Marina on an 11km loop.

Lonely Planet's Top Tip

The Dubai Marina is one of the most pedestrian-friendly areas in town and also has some convenient public transport. One way to get from A to B is aboard the brand-new air-conditioned Dubai Tram that trundles between Dubai Internet City and the Jumeirah Beach Residences. For a bargain cruise, explore the Dubai Marina aboard a water bus, preferably after dark.

Best Places to Eat

- Stay (p123)
- Tagine (p120)
- Rhodes W1 (p120)
- Fümé (p119)
- Toro Toro (p119)

For reviews, see p119.

Best Places to Drink

- Jetty Lounge (p123)
- Barasti (p123)
- Atelier M (p124)
- Siddharta (p124)

For reviews, see p123.

Best Views

- Atelier M (p124)
- Observatory (p125)
- 101 Lounge & Bar (p123)

For reviews, see p123.

THE WALK AT JBR
NEIGHBOURHOOD

Map p262 (Jumeirah Beach Residence; Ⓜ Jumeirah Lakes Towers, Damac, Jumeirah Beach Residence 1, Jumeirah Beach Residence 2) In a city of air-conditioned malls, this attractive outdoor shopping and dining promenade was an immediate hit when it opened in 2008. Join locals and expats in strolling the 1.7km stretch, watching the world on parade from a pavement cafe, browsing the fashionable boutiques or ogling the shiny Ferraris and other fancy cars cruising by on weekends.

THE BEACH AT JBR
SHOPPING MALL

Map p262 (www.thebeach.ae; The Walk at JBR; Ⓜ Jumeirah Lakes Towers, Damac, Jumeirah Beach Residence 1, Jumeirah Beach Residence 2) Paralleling the beachfront for about 1km, The Beach is an open-plan cluster of low-lying buildings with an edgy, contemporary aesthetic wrapped around breezy squares and plazas. Restaurants with alfresco terraces dominate, although there are also a few shops thrown into the mix. Facing the ocean are a spongy running track, an outdoor gym, grassy areas and an open-air cinema. It's between the Hilton and Sheraton hotels.

LOST CHAMBERS
AQUARIUM

Map p262 (☎04-426 1040; Atlantis The Palm, Palm Jumeirah; general entry adult/child 6-11yr Dh100/70; ⏲10am-10pm; monorail Aquaventure) This labyrinth of underwater halls, passageways and fish tanks re-creates the legend of the lost city of Atlantis. Some 65,000 exotic marine creatures inhabit 20 aquariums, where rays flutter and jellyfish dance, moray eels lurk and pretty-but-poisonous lionfish float. For an extra fee you can snorkel or dive with the fishes in this 11.5-million-litre tank.

IBN BATTUTA MALL
SHOPPING MALL

Map p262 (☎04-368 5543; www.ibnbattutamall.com; Sheikh Zayed Rd, btwn interchanges 5 & 6; ⏲10am-10pm Sun-Wed, 10am-midnight Thu-Sat; Ⓜ Ibn Battuta) The shopping here is so-so, but this mall is still well worth a visit for its stunning architecture which follows the journeys of 14th-century Arab explorer Ibn Battuta. It's built around six country-themed courts, the most stunning of which is the Persian Court, crowned by a beautiful handpainted dome. China Court centres on a full-size Chinese junk, while in the India Court you can pose with an 8m-high elephant. Surprisingly, there's nothing kitsch or 'Disney' about this place as the craftsmanship and attention to detail are truly impressive.

DUBAI MARINA CRUISING

Dubai Ferry (Map p262; ☎04-800 9090; www.rta.ae; gold/silver ticket Dh75/50; Ⓜ Damac)Dubai Ferry runs several mini-cruises from its landing docks near the Dubai Marina Mall. There are daily departures at 11am, 1pm and 6.30pm up the coast all the way to the Al Ghubaiba docks on Dubai Creek, passing by Madinat Jumeirah, the Burj Al Arab, the World islands and the port in a 90-minute, one-way trip.

Other options are 70-minute afternoon tea (3pm) and sunset cruises (5pm) that travel as far as the Burj Al Arab and back. The boats are quite comfortable with an air-conditioned interior and an open deck in case you want to stick your nose into the breeze. Soft drinks and snacks are available. Children between two and ten pay half price.

Dubai Marina Water Bus (Dubai Marina; tickets Dh3-5, 1-day pass Dh25; ⏲10am-10pm Sat-Wed, to midnight Thu, noon-midnight Fri) For a scenic spin around the Dubai Marina itself, hop aboard the Water Bus, which shuttles between the Marina Walk, Marina Terrace, Marina Mall and the Promenade every 15 minutes. It's especially lovely at sunset or after dark as boats float past the show-stopping parade of shimmering towers.

Tour Dubai (Map p262; ☎04-336 8407; www.tour-dubai.com; Marina Walk, near bridge; tours adult/child Dh130/90, dinner cruises Dh225/125; Ⓜ Damac) This local company runs guided one-hour boat tours with prerecorded English commentary aboard nostalgic dhows outfitted with colourful upholstered benches. There are five tours daily between 10.30am and 5.30pm. In the evening, the dhows set sail for a two-hour dinner buffet with taped music. Alcohol is available.

EATING

Dubai Marina is dominated by sprawling beach resorts, each flaunting several top-end restaurants, bars and nightclubs. But you'll also find excellent eats away from the hotels, especially along the Marina Walk, the Walk at JBR and The Beach. Because of its compact nature, the area is even conducive to hopping from one place to the next on foot.

Dubai Marina

THE COUNTER AMERICAN $

Map p262 (04-2052-640 8814; The Beach at JBR; burgers Dh29-59; 10am-midnight; Jumeirah Beach Residence 2) Let your creativity fly at this postmodern patty-and-bun joint where you build your own gourmet burger by mixing and matching your favourite bun, meat, cheese, toppings and sauce. Apparently, this adds up to 312,120 burger combinations. Ponder that while munching on a bucket of tasty fries. The beef is all natural Angus.

SIMSIM ARABIC $

Map p262 (04-454 2319; www.simsimdubai.com; ground fl, Sadaf block, The Walk at JBR; mezze Dh18-42, mains Dh30-72; 8.30-12.30am; Damac, Jumeirah Beach Residence 1) Sparingly accented with folkloric crafts, this breezy dining room is a suitable setting for the contemporary Arabic cuisine served at this indie outlet. The kitchen turns out all the expected favourites but the perennial bestseller is a Palestinian version of baked chicken called *muskhan dajaj*. On Fridays and Saturdays, insiders order the off-menu *mansaf* (lamb stew).

KCAL INTERNATIONAL $

Map p262 (04-276 6181; www.kcalhealthyfastfood.com; Plaza level, Amwaj 1, The Walk at JBR; mains Dh40-49; 11am-11.30pm Sun-Thu, noon-11.30pm Fri & Sat; Jumeirah Lakes Towers) UAE-founded Kcal is all about making fast food healthy. Fortify yourself without an iota of guilt while noshing on quinoa salad with avocado and sweet potato, pasta-free lasagne, cranberry salsa chicken or yummy wraps and sandwiches.

SALADICIOUS DELI DELI $

Map p262 (04-423 0855; www.saladicious.com; ground fl, Sadaf block, The Walk at JBR; mains Dh40-81; 7.30am-11.30pm; Damac, Jumeirah Lake Towers, Jumeirah Beach Residence 1) They've got salads at this upbeat cafe, sure, and creative ones at that, all served with a choice of 10 dressings, including the intriguing amaretto mandarin vinaigrette. If you're in the mood for something more substantial, go for the robust risottos, velvety soups or perky pastas. Everything's prepared fresh and attractively presented.

FÜMÉ INTERNATIONAL $$

Map p262 (04-421 5669; www.fume-eatery.com; Pier 7; mains Dh55-95; noon-2am; Damac, Dubai Marina Mall) With its funky design elements, relaxed crew and crowd, and rustic comfort food, Fümé brings more than a touch of urban cool to the Marina. The menu is casual enough not to intimidate yet endowed with plenty of creative dishes to keep foodies happy. Bestseller: the super-juicy beef chuck ribs roasted for six hours in a closed charcoal oven. No reservations. It's next to Dubai Marina Mall.

MASSAAD LEBANESE $$

Map p262 (04-362 9002; www.massaadfarmtotable.com; ground fl, Amwaj block, The Walk at JBR; mains Dh36-70; 10-4am; Jumeirah Lakes Towers, Jumeirah Beach Residence 2) All the usual Lebanese mezze and grills are accounted for at this teensy country-style eatery, but what really sets the place apart is that most of the fresh ingredients – from lemons to chickens – are sourced from growers based in nearby Al Ain. Specialities include the rolled pita chicken sandwiches and fingerlickin' *shish tawooq* (marinated chicken grilled on skewers) served on a traditional wooden board called *tablieh*.

SUSHI ART JAPANESE $$

Map p262 (04-800 220; www.sushiart.ae; The Beach at JBR; nigiri Dh25-42, maki per piece Dh7-22; 11am-midnight; Jumeirah Lakes Towers, Jumeirah Beach Residence 2) Sushi purist or not, you're sure to find your favourite among the huge, attractive selection at this minimalist cafe. The most enticing morsels are those designed by French Michelin chef Joël Robuchon and include a swoon-worthy crispy lobster roll that goes well with a crunchy, sesame-infused seaweed salad.

TORO TORO SOUTH AMERICAN $$

Map p262 (04-317 6000; www.torotoro-dubai.com; ground fl, Tower Two, Grosvenor House; small plates Dh60-130; 7.30pm-2am Sat-Wed, to 3am Thu & Fri; Damac, Jumeirah Beach

Residence 1) The decor packs as much pizazz as the food at this pan-Latin outpost conceived by star chef Richard Sandoval. Opt for the *rodizio* menu (a free-flow of grilled meats carved at your table) or put together a meal from small-plate dishes: lamb shank in adobo sauce, salmon ceviche or grilled octopus are among top picks. Great rum and cachaça selections.

TAGINE MOROCCAN $$

Map p262 (☎04-399 9999; http://royalmirage.oneandonlyresorts.com; The Palace, One&Only Royal Mirage, Al Sufouh Rd; tagine Dh105; ⏰7-11.30pm Tue-Sun; Ⓜ Dubai Internet City, 🚊Media City) Get cosy between throw pillows at a low-slung table in the seductively lit dining room, then treat your taste buds while tapping your toes to the live Moroccan duo. Fez-capped waitstaff serve big platters of couscous and tagines with all the extras, including a vegetarian choice. The cumin-laced roast lamb shoulder is another fine menu pick.

ZERO GRAVITY INTERNATIONAL $$

Map p262 (☎04-399 0009; www.0-gravity.ae; Al Seyahi St, Skydive Dubai Drop Zone; mains Dh65-165; ⏰8-2am; Ⓜ Damac) Next to the Skydive Dubai drop zone, this stylish outpost with attached beach club checks off all the culinary boxes from breakfast to late-night snacks. Pizza, pasta, sandwiches, grills and salads are all fresh, healthy and perfectly pitched to mainstream tastes. The upstairs alfresco wrap-around terraces invite post-meal chilling. Ladies' night on Tuesdays.

FRANKIE'S ITALIAN BAR & GRILL ITALIAN $$

Map p262 (☎04-399 3411; www.frankiesdubai.com; Oasis Beach Tower, The Walk at JBR; pasta & pizza Dh60-135, mains Dh135-300; ⏰noon-4pm Fri & Sat, 5.30pm-2am daily; Ⓜ Damac, Jumeirah Lakes Towers, 🚊Jumeirah Beach Residence 1) Super-chef Marco Pierre White and horse-racing legend Frankie Dettori teamed up to create this always-buzzing Italian port of call decked out in cosy russet tones. An aroma of the daily feast wafts from the kitchen, be it pizza or pasta or innovative mains like eggplant roulade or halibut with artichoke cream and foie gras.

RHODES W1 MODERN BRITISH $$$

Map p262 (☎04-317 6000; www.rw1-dubai.com; Grosvenor House, Al Sufouh Rd; mains Dh95-190; ⏰7-11pm; Ⓜ Damac, 🚊Jumeirah Beach Residence 1) Michelin-decorated chef Gary Rhodes is famous for bringing British cuisine into the 21st century. At this revamped Dubai outpost, his dedication to revolutionising humble classics like shepherd's pie, rack of lamb and roast cod into sophisticated, zeitgeist-capturing dishes shines brightly. The breezy decor is as sharp as the flavours and accented with eye-catching butterfly chandeliers.

ASIA ASIA FUSION $$$

Map p262 (☎04-276 5900; 6th fl, Pier 7; mains Dh70-180; ⏰4pm-midnight; Ⓜ Damac) Prepare for a culinary journey along the ancient Spice Route as you enter this gorgeous restaurant via a candle-lit corridor that spills into an exotic booth-lined lounge with dangling birdcage lamps. The menu blends Asian and Middle Eastern flavours, usually with finesse and success. The sambal chicken tagine, Persian black cod and Peking duck are signature dishes. Full bar. It's next to Dubai Marina Mall.

MAYA MEXICAN $$$

Map p262 (☎04-316 5550; www.maya-dubai.com; Le Royal Meridien Beach Resort & Spa, Al Sufouh Rd; mains Dh80-230; ⏰dinner Mon-Sat; Ⓜ Damac, 🚊Jumeirah Beach Residence 1) Richard Sandoval, the man who introduced modern Mexican food to the US, is behind the menu at this sophisticated restaurant where you'll be treated to a piñata of flavours. Start out with creamy guacamole, prepared tableside of course, before moving on to such succulent mains as *mole poblano,* tequila chipotle prawns or sizzling chicken fajitas. Lovely rooftop lounge as well.

INDEGO BY VINEET INDIAN $$$

Map p262 (☎04-317 6000; www.indegobyvineet.com; ground fl, Tower One, Grosvenor House, Al Sufouh Rd; mains Dh125-310, brunch with/without alcohol Dh350/250; ⏰lunch & dinner; Ⓜ Damac, 🚊Jumeirah Beach Residence 1) India's first Michelin-starred chef, Vineet Bhatia, is the man behind the menu at what many consider Dubai's top Indian restaurant. Though gorgeous, the intimate dining room – lorded over by big brass Natraj sculptures – is still eclipsed by such exquisite dishes as house-smoked salmon, wild mushroom biryani and chocolate samosas. Great brunch, too.

BARRACUDA FISH $$$

Map p262 (☎04-452 2278; www.barracudarestaurant.net; Marina Walk; mains Dh85-205; ⏰noon-11.30pm; 📶; Ⓜ Jumeirah Lakes Tower)

LET'S DO BRUNCH...

Friday brunch is a major element of the Dubai social scene and just about every hotel-restaurant in town sets up an all-you-can-eat buffet with an option for unlimited wine or bubbly. Some indie eateries also do brunch but without alcohol. Here are our top pig-out picks in town. Bookings are essential at any of them.

Al Qasr Friday Brunch (Map p256; ☎04-366 6730; Al Qasr Hotel, Madinat Jumeirah, Jumeirah; brunch with soft drinks/alcohol/champagne Dh475/575/795; ⊙12.30-4pm Fri; Ⓜ Mall of the Emirates) Expect to loosen your belt after enjoying this unbelievable cornucopia of delectables – roast lamb, sushi, cooked-to-order seafood, foie gras, beautiful salads, mezze, all sorts of hot dishes, plus an entire cheese room.

Brunch under the Stars (☎04-362 7900; Aquara, Dubai Marina Yacht Club, Dubai Marina; brunch with soft/house/premium drinks Dh220/350/400; ⊙7.30-10.30pm Fri; Ⓜ Jumeirah Lakes Towers) If guzzling free-flowing champagne midday isn't your thing, hit Aquara's (p122) evening buffet to expand your waistline while chilling with a view of the sparkling Dubai Marina. Put your tummy into a state of contentment with a beautifully presented smorgasbord of seafood, sushi, mezze, salads, wok dishes and dim sum.

Bubbalicious, Westin Dubai Mina Seyahi (Map p262; Al Sufouh Rd, Dubai Marina; brunch with soft drinks/house drinks/sparkling wine Dh390/490/650; ⊙1-4pm Fri; Ⓜ Nakheel) This culinary bonanza is orchestrated by three of the Westin's restaurants: the family-friendly Blue Orange, the Hunters Room & Grill steakhouse and the Asian-flavoured Spice Emporium. Look on as your food is prepared in front of you, indulge in sushi and sashimi, and don't miss out on a trip to the cheese section.

Jazz@PizzaExpress (Map p262; ☎04-441 6342; www.pizzaexpressuae.com; Cluster A, Jumeirah Lakes Towers, Dubai Marina; brunch with/without alcohol Dh189/99; ⊙noon-4pm Fri; Ⓜ Jumeirah Lakes Towers) This cheap and cheerful brunch has you filling up on Italian faves – antipasti to pasta to thin-crust pizza – ordered à la carte and brought to your table. Live jazz sets the mood. The venue (p126) is next to the Mövenpick Hotel.

Grand Friday Brunch, Mina A' Salam (Map p256; ☎04-366 6730; Mina A' Salam Hotel, Madinat Jumeirah, Jumeirah; brunch with/without alcohol Dh525/425; ⊙12.30-4pm Fri; 👪; Ⓜ Mall of the Emirates) Three restaurants – Tortuga (Mexican), Al Muna (Arabic) and Zheng He's (Chinese) – pull out all the stops at this epic brunch with dreamy views of the Burj Al Arab from coveted waterfront tables. Pace yourself while sampling everything from roast lamb to fat shrimp and shucked oysters while a band belts out popular hits.

Street Food Festival (Map p258; ☎04-503 6666; Sheikh Zayed Rd, Downtown Dubai; brunch with soft drinks/house drinks/champagne Dh220/300/450; ⊙12.30-4pm; Ⓜ Burj Khalifa/Dubai Mall) The Sofitel has jumped on the street food trend with this family-friendly brunch. Six food trucks offering Thai, Lebanese, Mexican, Indian, Chinese and Italian orbit the hotel's infinity pool, and there's also cheese, barbecue and dessert stations. Little ones can frolic in the pool and the kids' club while grown-ups enjoy the food and Burj Khalifa views.

Spice Island (Map p244; Crowne Plaza Dubai, Deira; brunch with soft/house/premium drinks Dh199/259/329; ⊙noon-4pm Fri; 📶 👪; Ⓜ Salah Al Din, Abu Baker Al Siddique) The oldest brunch buffet in town, Spice Island offers seven cuisines and six live cooking stations, including grilled food, dim sum, kebabs and biryani. Great value and popular with families.

Traiteur Brunch (www.restaurants.dubai.hyatt.com; Park Hyatt Dubai, Deira; brunch with soft drinks/house drinks/champagne Dh465/570/690; ⊙12.30-4pm; Ⓜ Deira City Centre) The Friday brunch at this French restaurant (p60) at the Park Hyatt in Deira is a study in understated opulence with a huge array of appetisers and live cooking stations. Get your protein kick from freshly shucked oysters, spit-roast lamb and grilled salmon so you won't have to feel bad about loading up on the carbs at the dessert buffet.

Yalumba (Map p246; ☎04-217 0000; Le Meridien Dubai, Airport Rd, Deira; champagne brunch Dh499; ⊙12.30-3.30pm Fri; Ⓜ GGICO, Airport Terminal 1) Free-flowing champagne fuels the raucous fun at this long-running party brunch. Breakfast is ordered à la carte so you won't have to schlep plates, although there's also a smallish but choice buffet featuring international delicacies.

The original Jumeirah branch of this Egyptian seafood restaurant has an intensely loyal following and the Marina location looks set to become another crowd favourite. Pick your *poisson* (mullet, sea bream, pomfret) from the ice display and have it prepared the way you like it. The classic is oven-grilled and doused with olive oil and lemon. It's next to Dubai Ferry station.

AQUARA SEAFOOD **$$$**

Map p262 (☎04-362 7900; www.dubaimarinayachtclub.com; Dubai Marina Yacht Club, Marina Walk; mains Dh95-200; ⏰6.30pm-midnight; Ⓜ Jumeirah Lakes Towers) The views of fancy yachts and a forest of sleek high-rises impress almost as much as the Asian-infused fare at this chic seafood shrine serving dock-fresh ingredients and flawlessly crafted plates. There's lots of special events, like a Caribbean barbecue on Saturday afternoons, a British roast on Saturday nights and a Friday evening brunch.

BUDDHA BAR ASIAN **$$$**

Map p262 (☎04-317 6000; Tower 1, Grosvenor House, Al Sufouh Rd; mains Dh90-500; ⏰8pm-2am Sat-Wed, to 3am Thu & Fri; Ⓜ Damac, 🚊Jumeirah Beach Residence 1) So what if the pounding music requires you to shout over the table? You're in the shadow of a giant Buddha, rubbing shoulders with Dubai's pretty people and you look fabulous in that new outfit. Oh, the food? It's a pan-Asian spread that hopscotches from Japan to China with excursions to Thailand and Indonesia, often with convincing results.

SPLENDIDO ITALIAN **$$$**

Map p262 (☎04-399 4000; Ritz-Carlton Hotel, The Walk at JBR; pastas Dh70-130, mains Dh185-250; ⏰6-11pm; 📶; Ⓜ Damac, 🚊Jumeirah Beach Residence 1) Tall palms sway in the breeze around the outdoor patio at the Ritz-Carlton's Italian restaurant, creating the perfect vibe for romantics. The cooking captures all the soulful flavours from around the boot in such dishes as lamb in clementine sauce or seafood gnocchi. It's not as formal as one might expect, given the setting and pricing.

EAUZONE INTERNATIONAL **$$$**

Map p262 (☎04-399 9999; http://royalmirage.oneandonlyresorts.com; Arabian Court, One&Only Royal Mirage, Al Sufouh Rd; mains lunch Dh65-170, dinner Dh135-250; ⏰lunch & dinner; 📶; Ⓜ Nakheel, 🚊Media City) This jewel of a restaurant is an inspired port of call drawing friends, romancing couples and fashionable families to a sublime setting with shaded decks jutting out over illuminated pools. The Asian focus of the lunch menu is supplemented by European accents at dinnertime. Try the seared scallops, herb-crusted sea bass or twice-cooked duck.

AL KHAIMA MIDDLE EASTERN **$$$**

Map p262 (☎04-316 5550; www.alkhaima-dubai.com; Le Royal Meridien Beach Resort & Spa, Al Sufouh Rd; mains Dh135-275; ⏰dinner; Ⓜ Nakheel, 🚊Jumeirah Beach Residence 1) In the cooler months there are few places more romantic than the *majlis*-style tents in the garden of the relaxed Meridien resort. Classic mezze such as *baba ghanoog* (purée of grilled aubergines), hummus and *fattoosh* (salad of toasted bread, tomatoes, onions and mint leaves) are orchestrated into culinary symphonies, and the enormous platters of charcoal-grilled kebabs are just as delicious. Wind down the evening languidly puffing on a *sheesha*.

BICE ITALIAN **$$$**

Map p262 (☎04-318 2520; Hilton Dubai Jumeirah, The Walk at JBR; pasta Dh80-125, mains Dh170-245; ⏰12.30-11.30pm Sat-Thu, 1-11.30pm Fri; Ⓜ Jumeirah Lakes Towers, 🚊Jumeirah Beach Residence 1, Jumeirah Beach Residence 2) This restaurant has a pedigree going back to 1930s Milan. That was when Beatrice 'Bice' Ruggeri first opened her trattoria, which by the 1970s had become one of the city's most fashionable. Today, Dubai's BiCE carries on the tradition with chef Cosimo adding his creative touch to such traditional dishes as oven-baked sea bass and veal tenderloin with foie gras sauce.

Palm Jumeirah

AL NAFOORAH LEBANESE **$$**

Map p262 (☎04-453 0444; www.jumeirah.com; Jumeirah Zabeel Saray, West Crescent; mains Dh50-180; ⏰2pm-midnight) With its bold archways, dark-wood carvings and elegant tables, Al Nafoorah is no slouch in the looks department, especially when sitting outside with a view of the pool and the Gulf. Nibble on a three-tier platter of olives, nuts and carrots while anticipating soulful menu picks like hummus, *arayees* (minced lamb with tomato and spices) and grilled fish.

PALM JUMEIRAH: PITFALLS IN PARADISE

Even in a city known for its audacious megaprojects, the Palm Jumeirah pushes the limits of innovation: a huge artificial island in the shape of a palm tree. It is an extraordinary feat of engineering, especially when considering that only natural materials – rock and sand – were used in its construction.

Built to almost double Dubai's existing 72km of coastline, it consists of a 2km trunk and 16-frond crown protected by an 11km-long crescent-shaped breakwater. An elevated driverless monorail whisks passengers from the bottom of the trunk (where it links with the Dubai Tram) to the Atlantis The Palm hotel, the first of several giant resorts to be completed. In recent years, it has been joined by a few others, including the One&Only The Palm, the Waldorf Astoria, the Jumeirah Zabeel Saray, the Kempinksi and Rixos The Palm.

Perhaps not surprisingly, the daring and unprecedented construction of a vast island has resulted in a number of problems and challenges. Delayed completion and residents disgruntled by the increased construction density and lower building quality were only the beginning. A bigger problem turned out to be the breakwater. The original continuous crescent prevented natural tidal movement, leading to stagnant seawater, excessive algae growth and smelly beaches. Now that two 100m-wide gaps have been cut out of the crescent the problem appears to have been solved.

An ongoing issue, though, is the erosion of Dubai's sandy mainland beaches. Building the giant island so close to the shoreline changed the wave movement and diverted the natural current, which is affecting the outline of the shore. In some areas sand is deposited, in others the beach is eroded by up to 10m per year, threatening roads and resorts if left unchecked. Experts expect that over time the coastline will settle down, but, in the meantime, replacing the eroded sand is a costly and Sisyphean process.

Another study reported that the Palm is actually sinking by a clip of 5mm per year, but the developer Nakheel has categorically refuted the claim.

STAY FRENCH $$$

Map p262 (☎04-440 1030; http://thepalm.oneandonlyresorts.com; Western Crescent, One&Only The Palm; mains Dh190-300; ⊙dinner) Triple-Michein-starred Yannick Alléno introduces his culinary magic to Dubai in this subtly theatrical, vaulted dining room accented with black crystal chandeliers. His creations seem deceptively simple (the beef tenderloin with fries and black pepper sauce is a best-seller), letting the superb ingredients shine brightly. An unexpected stunner is the Pastry Library, an entire wall of sweet treats.

101 LOUNGE & BAR MEDITERRANEAN $$$

Map p262 (☎04-440 1030; thepalm.oneandonlyresorts.com; West Crescent, One&Only The Palm; mains Dh85-220, tapas selection of 3/6/9 Dh90/160/220; ⊙11-1am) With to-die-for views of the Marina high-rises, it may be hard to concentrate on the food at this buzzy marina-adjacent pavilion at the ultraswish One&Only The Palm resort. Come for nibbles and cocktails in the bar or go for the full dinner experience (paella, grills, pastas). Ask about the free boat shuttle when making reservations.

DRINKING & NIGHTLIFE

★JETTY LOUNGE BAR, LOUNGE

Map p262 (☎04-399 9999; www.royalmirage.oneandonlyresorts.com; The Palace, One&Only Royal Mirage, Al Sufouh Rd; ⊙2pm-late; 📶; Ⓜ Nakheel) From the moment you start following the meandering path through the One&Only's luxuriant gardens, you'll sense that you're heading for a pretty special place. Classy without the pretence, Jetty Lounge is all about unwinding (preferably at sunset) on plush white sofas scattered right in the sand. There's a full bar menu and snacks for nibbling.

BARASTI BAR

Map p262 (☎04-399 3333; www.barastibeach.com; Le Meridien Mina Seyahi Beach Resort, Dubai Marina, Al Sufouh Rd; ⊙11am-1.30am Sat-Wed, to 3am Thu & Fri; Ⓜ Nakheel) Beachside Barasti is primarily a Brit-expat favourite for lazy days on the beach and is often jampacked with shiny happy party people knocking back the brewskis. There's soccer and rugby on the big screen, a deck with pool tables, occasional bands and drinks specials on Monday nights.

★BASEMENT CLUB

Map p262 (☎04-434 5555; www.boutique7.ae; Boutique 7 Hotel & Suites, Tecom; ⏲10pm-3am; Ⓜ Dubai Internet City) The antithesis of the see-and-be-seen glamour vibe, Basement is about as underground as things get in Dubai. It draws dedicated clubbers to parties hosted by different promoters and featuring both local and visiting DJ talent playing a soundscape from house and funk to dancehall.

BLISS LOUNGE BAR

Map p262 (☎04-315 3886; www.blissloungedubai.com; Sheraton Jumeirah Beach Resort, Al Sufouh Rd; ⏲noon-3am; 📶; Ⓜ Jumeirah Lakes Towers) Feel the breeze in your hair as you stake out your turf at the circular bar or on a cushiony sofa at this beachfront bar just off The Walk at JBR. Resident DJs play deep house for dedicated chilling with cocktails and eye-candy. Sushi and tapas dominate the menu.

SIDDHARTA BAR, LOUNGE

Map p262 (☎04-399 8888; Tower 2, Grosvenor House, Al Sufouh Rd; ⏲10am-1pm Sat-Wed, to 2am Thu & Fri; Ⓜ Damac) Part of Buddha Bar in the same hotel, Siddharta is an urban oasis and great spot to join Dubai's glam crowd in taking the party from daytime by the pool to basking in the glow of the Marina high-rises. Nice music, expertly mixed cocktails and swift service make up for the rather steep price tab.

BLUE MARLIN IBIZA UAE CLUB

(☎056-113 3400; www.bluemarlinibiza-uae.com; Golden Tulip Al Jazira Hotel, Ghantoot; ⏲1-11pm Fri & Sat; 📶) This Ibiza-style beachside 'meet' market is one of Dubai's top day-to-night dance clubs and worth the trek out of town, especially when big-time house DJs like Finnebassen and Los Suruba fuel the party. Expect lots of wrinkle-free, hormone-happy hotties showing off their tan. A taxi from Dubai Marina needs about 20 minutes and should cost around Dh50.

ATELIER M BAR, CLUB

Map p262 (☎04-450 7766; www.atelierm.ae; Pier 7; Ⓜ Damac) Atelier M is a three-floor treat atop the circular Pier 7 building. The lift drops you at the restaurant which serves inspired French-Asian dinners best enjoyed on the wraparound terrace with views of the twinkling Dubai Marina. A spiralling staircase leads up to the bar looking splendid in futuristic art deco. The rooftop lounge is the place to be for drinks and dancing on weekends. It's next to Dubai Marina Mall.

ROOFTOP TERRACE & SPORTS LOUNGE BAR

Map p262 (☎04-399 9999; http://royalmirage.oneandonlyresorts.com; Arabian Court, One&Only Royal Mirage, Al Sufouh Rd; ⏲5pm-1am; 📶; Ⓜ Nakheel) With its fabric-draped nooks, cushioned banquettes, Moroccan lanterns and Oriental carpets, this lounge is one of Dubai's classiest sports bars. Catch live games in the circular bar, then report to the rooftop for chilling under the stars. There's also a good menu of mezze, in case you're feeling peckish.

TAMANYA TERRACE BAR, SHEESHA

Map p262 (☎04-366 9111; www.radissonblu.com/hotel-mediacitydubai; Radisson Blu Hotel, Dubai Media City; ⏲5pm-2am Sun-Thu, 6pm-2am Fri & Sat; 📶; Ⓜ Nakheel) On the 8th floor of the Radisson, this is a fab spot for kicking off a long night of partying with sundowners against a backdrop of the forest of sparkling Marina skyscrapers. Mod furnishings, sassy lighting and international DJs fuel the vibe.

REEM AL BAWADI SHEESHA

Map p262 (☎04-452 2525; www.reemalbawadi.com; Marina Walk; sheesha Dh40; ⏲9-3am; Ⓜ Damac) This is the prettiest branch of a local mini-chain serving regional faves in a dimly lit, endearingly over-the-top *Arabian Nights* setting complete with costumed waitstaff. The spacious terrace is ideal for kicking back with a *sheesha* while keeping tabs on the marina action. It's near Spinney's.

PURE SKY LOUNGE BAR

Map p262 (☎04-399 1111; Hilton Dubai Jumeirah Resort, The Walk at JBR; ⏲5pm-2am; Ⓜ Damac) When it comes to glorious views over the beach and Palm Jumeirah, this chic indoor-outdoor lounge is in a lofty league on the 35th floor of the beachfront Hilton. White wicker chairs and lounges accented with turquoise pillows channel a chill, maritime mood. Half-price cocktails during happy hour (5pm to 7pm).

BUDDHA BAR BAR

Map p262 (☎04-317 6000; Grosvenor House, Al Sufouh Rd; ⏰7.30pm-2am Sat-Wed, to 3am Thu & Fri; Ⓜ Damac) If there are celebs in town, they'll show up at Buddha Bar, where the dramatic Asian-inspired interiors are decked out with gorgeous chandeliers, a wall of reflective sheer glass and an enormous Buddha lording over the heathens. The bartenders put on quite a show with their impressive shakes. Arrive early or prepare to queue; otherwise book dinner for guaranteed admission.

OBSERVATORY BAR

Map p262 (☎04-319 4000; Dubai Marriott Harbour Hotel & Suites, Al Sufouh; ⏰5pm-1am; 📶; Ⓜ Damac) Home of the guilt-free ladies' night where drinks have no more than 150 calories, the Observatory also scores with skyline lovers thanks to its eye-popping 360-degree views on the 52nd floor of the Marriott. Happy hour runs from 5pm to 10pm Saturday to Tuesday and to 8pm on Friday.

DEK ON 8 BAR

Map p262 (☎04-427 1000; www.mediaone-hotel.com; Media One Hotel; ⏰noon-midnight; Ⓜ Nakheel) Mingle with media types beside the pool at this alfresco chill zone on the 8th floor of the Media One Hotel. On weekends, beat junkies press flesh on the dance floor, then refuel with bar bites while reclined on leather sofas and lounge beds.

The Thursday happy hour (5pm to 8pm) is perfect for ringing in the weekend with Dh33 drinks.

MAYA LOUNGE BAR

Map p262 (☎04-316 5550; www.maya-dubai.com; Le Royal Meridien Beach Resort & Spa, Al Sufouh Rd; ⏰6pm-2am Mon-Sat; Ⓜ Damac) Arrive an hour before sunset to snag one of the Gulf-view tables on the rooftop bar of this upmarket Mexican restaurant and swill top-shelf margaritas as the sun slowly slips into the sea. On Señorita Sunday ladies can score three free drinks between 7pm and 1am.

NASIMI BEACH BEACH CLUB

Map p262 (☎04-426 2626; www.atlantistheplan.com; West Beach, Atlantis The Palm; minimum spend weekday/weekend Dh150/250; ⏰11am-midnight Sun-Thu, to 1am Fri & Sat; monorail Aquaventure) This beach club at the Atlantis caters to hip and libidinous party animals (no kids allowed) working on their tan sprawled on a double sunbed while being showered with house, funk and electro. The vibe picks up in the afternoon, especially on weekends when happy hour runs from 5pm to 7pm.

THE COURTYARDS SHEESHA

Map p262 (☎04-399 9999; http://royalmirage.oneandonlyresorts.com; One&Only Royal Mirage, Al Sufouh Rd; ⏰7pm-1am; Ⓜ Nakheel) Reclining on beaded cushions and thick carpets and puffing on a *sheesha* will make you feel as if you're in the *majlis* (living room) of a local home. Choose from two locations: one in the Palace wing, the other in the Arabian Courtyard wing. Mezze for noshing and a live Arabic band complete the exotic experience.

BLENDS BAR

Map p262 (☎04-423 8888; The Address Dubai Marina; ⏰6pm-2am Sat-Wed, to 3am Thu & Fri; Ⓜ Damac) Blends folds three distinct libation stations into its 4th-floor space. Channel Ernest Hemingway in the clubby dark wood-panelled cigar room or let the meister-mixologists whip up a potent concoction in the cocktail bar. For date night, the candlelit champagne bar, with its floor-to-ceiling windows, provides a suitably sultry setting for a quiet tête-à-tête.

LIBRARY BAR BAR

Map p262 (☎04-399 4000; Ritz-Carlton Hotel, The Walk at JBR; ⏰noon-1.30am; Ⓜ Damac) Polished wood, muted lighting, leather sofas and rich carpets combine to create a timeless colonial-style atmosphere in this hushed and classic bar that feels like a retreat from Dubai's in-your-face modernity. Just the kind of place to steer your luxury sedan for a post-dinner Glenfiddich or port.

N'DULGE CLUB

Map p262 (☎04-426 0561; www.atlantisthepalm.com; Atlantis The Palm; ⏰9.30pm-3am; monorail Aquaventure) Headlining DJs rock the Arena, the centrepiece dance floor of this sexy nightclub where magicians, mimes, dancers and stilt walkers perform on a circular suspended catwalk. For a chill interlude, head to the Lounge for drinks, a bite and deep house or to the Terrace for sushi, *sheesha* and house with an Arabic twist.

ENTERTAINMENT

MUSIC HALL LIVE MUSIC

Map p262 (☎056-270 8670; www.jumeirah.com; Jumeirah Zabeel Saray; mains Dh180-290; ⊙9pm-3am Thu & Fri) It's not a theatre, not a club, not a bar and not a restaurant – Music Hall is all those things. The concept hails from Beirut where it's had audiences clapping since 2003 with an eclectic line-up of live music – from Indian to country, and rock to Russian ballads. The food, however, is an afterthought (minimum spend).

JAZZ@PIZZAEXPRESS LIVE MUSIC

Map p262 (☎04-441 6342; www.pizzaexpressuae.com; Cluster A, Jumeirah Lakes Towers; MJumeirah Lakes Towers) It's really a pizza joint tucked amid residential high-rises, but this pretense-free place gets hopping almost nightly with open-mic jam sessions, swing nights, acoustic songwriter nights and happening bands. It's next to Mövenpick Hotel.

SHOPPING

DUBAI MARINA MALL MALL

Map p262 (☎04-436 1020; www.dubaimarinamall.com; Dubai Marina; ⊙10am-10pm Sun-Wed, 10am-midnight Thu-Sat; MDamac) This mall has around 160 stores, so you won't get lost quite so readily as in its mega-size cousins, yet the shops are just as good. You'll find great options like H&M, Reebok, Mango, Boots, Mothercare, Monsoon, Miss Sixty, the Early Learning Centre and the upmarket UK supermarket chain Waitrose, as well as a good number of restaurants and cafes.

MARINA MARKET MARKET

Map p262 (www.marinamarket.ae; Promenade behind Dubai Marina Mall; ⊙10am-10pm Wed, to 11pm Thu-Sat; MDamac) This lively market sets up behind the Dubai Marina Mall and delivers clothing, handicrafts, jewellery and unusual gift items galore. Look for Turkish hammam towels, upcycled handbags and handmade necklaces.

IBN BATTUTA MALL MALL

Map p262 (☎04-368 5543; www.ibnbattutamall.com; Sheikh Zayed Rd, btwn Interchanges No 5 & No 6; ⊙10am-10pm Sun-Wed, 10am-midnight Thu-Sat; MIbn Battuta) The shopping is good if nothing extraordinary, but it's the lavish and exotic design and architecture that steal the show in this mall, which traces the way stations of 14th-century Arab explorer Ibn Battuta in six themed courts (China, Persia, Egypt, India, Tunisia, Andalusia). Highlights include the lifestyle boutique Bauhaus and whimsical fashion at Ginger & Lace.

GINGER & LACE FASHION

Map p262 (☎04-368 5543; http://gingerandlace.blogspot.de; Ibn Battuta Mall, Sheikh Zayed Rd; ⊙10am-10pm Sun-Wed, to midnight Thu-Sat; MIbn Battuta) Ginger & Lace stocks an eclectic selection of colourful, whimsical fashion by high-spirited New York designers Anna Sui and Betsey Johnson, London-based bag maven Zufi Alexander and Spanish illustrator-turned–fashion designer Jordi Labanda.

BAUHAUS FASHION

Map p262 (☎04-368 5551; India Court, Ibn Battuta Mall, Sheikh Zayed Rd; ⊙10am-10pm Sun-Wed, to midnight Thu-Sat; MIbn Battuta) High-energy tunes keep girls and boys flipping fast through Evisu denim, Bulzeye tees and Drifter hoodies at this hip lifestyle boutique

THE ROYAL TREATMENT

In a city built on facsimiles and gimmicks, the not-to-be-missed Oriental Hammam at the One&Only Spa stands out as the hands-down best re-creation of another country's cultural institution: a Moroccan bathhouse. Moroccan-born attendants walk you into a giant, echoey, steamy marble room lit by stained-glass lanterns, where they wrap you in muslin, bathe you on a marble bench from a running hot-water fountain, then lay you down on an enormous, heated marble cube – head-to-toe with three other men or women (depending on the day) – and scrub your entire body with exfoliating coarse gloves. Next, they bathe you again, then lead you to a steam room where you relax before receiving an invigorating mud body mask and honey facial, a brief massage and your final rinse. Afterwards, you're wrapped in dry muslin and escorted to a meditative relaxation room, where you drift to sleep beneath a blanket and awaken to hot mint tea and dates – just like in Morocco. Pure bliss!

specialising in nonmainstream fashion, art and music. The store design was inspired by the revolutionary 1920s Bauhaus design movement and mixes all sorts of materials, from acrylic to wood, and leather to metal and bricks.

BOUTIQUE 1 FASHION

Map p262 (☎04-425 7888; www.boutique1.com; The Walk at JBR; ⏰10am-11pm; Ⓜ Jumeirah Lakes Towers) Ground zero for prêt-à-porter straight off the runways of Paris and Milan, Boutique 1 feeds Dubai's fashion cravings with the latest from classic and avant-garde designers from around the globe. Its gorgeous three-storey store on The Walk stocks not only fashionable frocks but also home accessories, beauty products, furniture and books.

GALLERY ONE ART, STATIONERY

Map p262 (☎04-423 1987; www.g-1.com; The Walk at JBR; ⏰10am-10pm; Ⓜ Jumeirah Lakes Towers) If you love art but can't afford an original, pick up a highly decorative print by well-known Middle Eastern artists without breaking the bank. Some motifs are also available as greetings cards, posters, notebooks and calendars. The latest collection includes works by Syrian graphic artist Helen Abbas, British photographer James Domine and Iraqi calligrapher Malik Anas.

SPORTS & ACTIVITIES

AQUAVENTURE WATERPARK WATER PARK

Map p262 (☎04-426 0000; www.atlantisthepalm.com; Atlantis The Palm; admission over/under 120cm Dh250/205; ⏰10am-sunset; 👪; monorail Aquaventure) Adrenalin rushes are guaranteed at this waterpark at the Atlantis The Palm resort. A 1.6km-long 'river' with rapids, wave surges and waterfalls meanders through the vast grounds that are anchored by two towers. The ziggurat-shaped Tower of Neptune is the launchpad for three slides, including the aptly named Leap of Faith, a near-vertical plunge into a shark-infested lagoon.

The 37m-high Tower of Poseidon boasts four terrifying slides, including the world's longest. Little ones can keep cool with tamer rides, a wave pool and an enormous water playground. Tickets also include same-day access to a private beach.

DOLPHIN BAY DOLPHIN PARK

Map p262 (☎04-426 1030; www.atlantisthepalm.com; Atlantis The Palm; shallow-/deep-water interaction Dh795/960; ⏰10am-6pm, varies seasonally; 👪; monorail Aquaventure) Dolphin Bay offers a range of interactive experiences with bottlenose dolphins. Animal welfare groups say that keeping marine life in captivity is harmful and stressful, exacerbated further by human interaction.

JBR OPEN BEACH BEACH

Map p262 (Jumeirah Beach Residence; Ⓜ Jumeirah Lakes Towers) FREE This clean and wonderful outdoor playground comes with plenty of facilities, including showers, toilets and changing rooms housed in distinctive panelled pods. Kids can keep cool in a splash zone or an offshore waterpark. Since it's right next to The Beach at JBR and The Walk at JBR, there's no shortage of food and drink outlets, although alcohol is only available in the hotels.

BEACH WATER PARK WATER PARK

Map p262 (www.arabianwaterparks.com; JBR Open Beach; per hr adult/child 6-11yr Dh60/50, day pass Dh195; ⏰8am-6pm; Ⓜ Jumeirah Lakes Towers) This colourful, bouncy playground floats in the Gulf 150m off The Beach outdoor mall and consists of inflatable slides, jumping platforms, climbing walls, trampolines, balance beams and other fun features.

SKYDIVE DUBAI SKYDIVING

Map p262 (☎04-377 8888; www.skydivedubai.ae; Skydive Dr, Dubai Marina; tandem jump, video & photos Dh2000; ⏰8am-4pm Mon-Sat; Ⓜ Damac) Daredevils can experience the rush of jumping out of a plane and soaring above the Dubai skyline by signing up for these tandem parachute flights. The minimum age is 18; weight and height restrictions apply as well.

ONE&ONLY SPA SPA

Map p262 (☎04-315 2140; http://royalmirage.oneandonlyresorts.com; One&Only Royal Mirage, Al Sufouh Rd; ⏰9.30am-9pm (women only until 1pm); Ⓜ Nakheel) Do you want to unwind, restore or elevate? These are the magic words at this exclusive spa with a dozen treatment rooms where massages, wraps, scrubs and facials are calibrated to achieve your chosen goal. Staff can help find the perfect massage or wrap for whatever ails you, although you can never go wrong with a session in the Oriental Hammam.

LIVING IT UP IN A BEACH CLUB

If you're not staying in a five-star resort, you can still get the full luxury beach 'day-cation' experience by snagging a day pass, as many hotels set aside a limited number for visitors. Reservations are required year-round. Generally speaking, chances of getting one are much greater during the week than during busy weekends. Rates often include a few dirham towards food and drinks. Butler service, cabanas, cold towels and so on, cost extra.

Club Mina (Map p262; ☎04-318 1420; www.lermeridien-minaseyahi.com; Le Meridien Mina Seyahi Beach Resort, Al Sufouh Rd; day pass weekday/weekend Dh225/350; Ⓜ Nahkeel) Set along 500m of private beach, this club is a joint venue of the Westin and Le Meridien Mina Seyahi beach resorts and gets a big thumbs up from families for its five pools (two covered ones for kids), a kids' club and a water sports centre. Nice touch for grown-ups: cocktails in the swim-up bar.

Meydan Beach Club (Map p262; ☎04-433 3777; www.meydanbeach.com; The Walk at JBR; day pass weekday/weekend Dh150/250; ⏲10-1am; Ⓜ Damac) Teeming with buff and bronzed bods, this stylish shoreline retreat near Dubai Marina has you stretching out on comfy white lounges surrounding a deep-blue infinity pool with floating sunbeds. There's a lounge for chilling with a cocktail and a spa for being pummeled into a state of blissfulness.

Zero Gravity (Map p262; ☎04-399 0009; www.0-gravity.ae; Al Seyahi St, Skydive Dubai Drop Zone; day pass weekday/weekend Dh150/250, incl food & beverage Dh50/100; ⏲9-12.30am Sat-Wed, to 3am Thu & Fri ; Ⓜ Damac) Keep an eye on the Dubai Marina skyline and the daredevils jumping out of planes at this sleek beach club–bar next to the Drop Zone of SkyDubai, then cap a day of chilling and swimming with a night of drinks, snacks and international DJs. Fridays bring the Onshore Social, a late brunch running from 3pm to 6pm.

25' Beach Club (Map p262; ☎04-457 3388; www.fairmont.com/palm-dubai; Fairmont The Palm, Palm Jumeirah; day pass weekday/weekend adult Dh200/250, child Dh150; Ⓜ Nakheel) Views back at the mainland are one of the most memorable aspects of a day at this family-oriented club at the swish Fairmont Hotel. Parents get to wiggle their toes in the sand or by the pool while the little ones let off steam in the Fairmont Faclon Juniors' Club with activities and playstations for toddlers to teens.

FAVOURITE THINGS — ACTIVITY CENTRE

Map p262 (☎04-434 1984; www.favouritethings.com; 2nd fl, Dubai Marina Mall; ⏲9am-9pm; 👪; Ⓜ Damac) This is one of the best and most popular indoor playgrounds in town for children up to age seven. It has a wide variety of stimulating environments to get busy, learn, role play and make new friends, including an art studio, a race track and a fancy dress room.

Parents can join in or hit the mall and leave their kids in the hands of the professional staff.

JUMEIRAH GOLF ESTATES — GOLF

(☎04-818 2000; www.jumeirahgolfestates.com; near Jebel Ali, off Sheikh Zayed Hwy; Fire/Earth Sun-Thu Dh655/795, Fri & Sat Dh875/995) Part of a fancy residential development, Jumeirah Golf Estates has two par 72 Greg Norman-designed courses called Fire and Earth that measure 7480 yards and 7706 yards, respectively. Both are nicely embedded into the desert landscape and host the DP World Tour Championship. Take Interchange No 7 towards Abu Dhabi; the club is near the intersection with Emirates Rd.

EMIRATES GOLF CLUB — GOLF

Map p262 (☎04-380 1555; www.dubaigolf.com; Interchange No 5, Sheikh Zayed Rd; Majlis/Faldo Sun-Thu Dh995/595, Fri & Sat Dh1100/695; Ⓜ Nakheel) This prestigious club has two courses: the flagship international championship Majlis course, which hosts the annual Dubai Desert Classic, and the Faldo course, which is the only floodlit 18-hole course in the country. Beginners can go wild on the par-three nine-hole course (peak/off-peak Dh130/95).

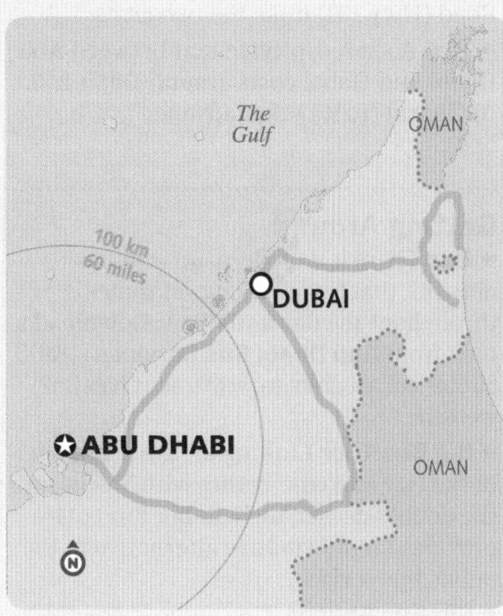

Abu Dhabi

Explore

The world's largest hand-loomed carpet, the fastest roller coaster, the highest high tea, the tower with the greatest lean, the largest cluster of cultural buildings of the 21st century – Abu Dhabi is not afraid to challenge world records. Welcome to an exciting city where nothing stands still... except perhaps the herons in the capital's protected mangroves.

For those looking to engage with Gulf culture, Abu Dhabi, the capital of the United Arab Emirates (UAE), offers opportunities to understand this desert nation's human and natural heritage through museums, exhibitions and tours. But thankfully Emirati heritage here isn't boxed and mothballed, it is also experienced through strolls around the dhow harbour, haggling in markets and absorbing the atmosphere at *sheesha* (water pipe) cafes and family picnics in the city's many parks.

The Best...

➡ **Sights** Sheikh Zayed Grand Mosque (p151), Emirates Palace (p137), Abu Dhabi Heritage Village (p137)

➡ **Places to Eat** Al Arish Restaurant (p158), Café Arabia (p134), Vasco's (p141)

➡ **Activities** Cycling the Corniche (p145), kayaking through mangroves (p166), Ferrari World (p165)

Top Tips

➡ **Safety** Walkable day and night.

➡ **Key areas** Breakwater, the Corniche and two blocks inland.

➡ **Navigation** Easy grid system despite confusing road names.

➡ **Bus** Big Bus Tour links main sights in suburbs and islands.

Getting There & Away

➡ **Air** Abu Dhabi International Airport is one of the biggest and best airports in the world and the national carrier, Etihad, is a multiple-award-winning airline.

➡ **Bus** Buses between Abu Dhabi's main bus terminal and Dubai's Al Ghubaiba station leave every 40 minutes (single/return Dh20/40, two hours). Intercity buses connect the capital with most Emirati destinations.

➡ **Car** Abu Dhabi is approximately two hours' drive from Dubai. Sheikh Zayed Road (Hwy E11) links the two cities.

➡ **Taxi** A shared/private taxi between Abu Dhabi and Dubai costs around Dh50/250. Al Ghazal (p216) takes advance bookings.

Getting Around

➡ **Bus** There is a modern, air-con bus network that travels along set routes throughout the day and night. Download a map from **Abu Dhabi Bus Services** (☎800 55 555; dot.abudhabi.ae; within Abu Dhabi Dh2) website.

➡ **Big Bus Tour** Linking all the major sites in the city and connecting with Yas Island, the double-decker, air-con Big Bus (p144) provides an informative alternative to the public bus service.

➡ **Big Bus Shuttle** This audio-guided **shuttle service** (☎toll free 800 244 287; www.bigbustours.com; ⏲9am-5.30pm) takes in the main points of interest on Yas Island and connects with Masdar City. It intersects with the main Big Bus Tour outside Manarat Al Saadiyat on Saadiyat Island.

➡ **Bicycle** Funride (p145) cycle-hire stations are scattered about the city.

➡ **Yas Express** This complimentary shuttle bus links all the main attractions and amenities on Yas Island. The **Yas Express** (☎02-496 8110; www.yasisland.ae; ⏲9am-9pm) FREE also links Yas with Saadiyat Island.

➡ **Water Taxi** Traditional water taxis (p156), called *abras*, ply the waters of Khor al Maqta and link to the Eastern Mangroves Hotel & Spa.

Need to Know

➡ **Area Code** ☎02

➡ **Tourist Office** ☎02-444 0444

➡ **Police/Ambulance** ☎999

➡ **Tourist Police** ☎02-699 9999

Al Markaziyah

Although Abu Dhabi has many vibrant districts, if you had to put your finger on the one that represents the city centre then the area around the city's oldest building, Qasr Al Hosn, is surely it. At the beating heart of this central district, and built on the former site of the city's original souq, is the World Trade Centre. The district is busy by day and by night with city traders, office workers, shoppers and visitors, and the foundations of the fine contemporary buildings in this area are rooted in the soil of ancient settlement, signified perhaps by the large number of mosques in this area.

SIGHTS

A conscious effort by modern town planners to make the city green has resulted in numerous attractive parks and gardens, many of which are arranged along the inland side of the Corniche. A walk or cycle along the seaboard side of the Corniche is a good a way to view the main buildings of this district before plunging into the teeming city centre in and around Hamdan and Zayed the First Sts.

★QASR AL HOSN FORT

Map p136 (White Fort; Sheikh Zayed the First St) Featured on the back of the Dh1000 note, and built on the site of a watchtower dating back to 1761 that safeguarded a precious fresh-water well, this fort became the ancestral home of the ruling Al Nahyan family in 1793. The stone building seen today was constructed in the 20th century and served as the family's residence until 1966. After a brief spell as an administrative centre, the palace was closed in 1990 and has been undergoing long-term restoration ever since.

The fort has been on the point of reopening as a memorial to Sheikh Zayed for several years now and it's rumoured that, when eventually complete, it will include exhibits about the Al Nahyan family and the political and social history of Abu Dhabi. In February 2015, a major cultural event, the Qasr Al Hosn Festival, took place with a temporary reopening of the fort and the adjoining Cultural Foundation Building. It is hoped that the festival will become an annual event.

BURJ MOHAMMED BIN RASHID BUILDING

Map p136 (World Trade Centre, 2nd St) This 92-floor giant (382m) among tower blocks forms part of the World Trade Centre and is an important landmark in this mixed-use development marking the middle of Downtown. Not only is this Abu Dhabi's tallest building (at least for now) but it may just be unique in having an indoor terraced garden on the 90th floor. The tower is the tallest of two matching towers with distinctive sloping, elliptical roofs that look remarkable when lit at night.

ETISALAT HEADQUARTERS BUILDING

Map p136 (cnr 7th & 2nd Sts) This iconic 27-floor building, with a 'golf ball' as its crowning glory, makes an excellent landmark for navigating the city's grid system. Built in 2001, it houses the headquarters of the local telephone service provider.

KHALIFA MOSQUE MOSQUE

Map p136 (Khalid bin Al Walid St) In common with all mosques in the city, this beautiful mosque stands in non-alignment with the grid system, honouring the direction of Mecca instead. It is closed to non-Muslims.

STREET SCULPTURE MONUMENTS

Map p136 (2nd & Khalifa Sts) There was a time when no self-respecting Gulf city would be seen without a giant concrete coffee pot. Those days have gone, but a little reminder of the pioneering days of oil riches and the city development they brought can be seen in the traffic island between the World Trade Centre and Etisalat buildings.

The five concrete monuments show a date cover, incense burner, rosewater shaker, coffee pot and fort, symbolising the traditions of hospitality and Bedouin culture at the heart of Emirati life, together with the impulse to safeguard the land from marauding seafaring invaders.

LAKE PARK & FORMAL PARK PARKS

Map p136 (Corniche Rd (East); ⌚24hr) These two shady parks straddling 4th St and spread along the Corniche provide a welcome respite to the intense traffic and crowds of Downtown. The centrepiece of Lake Park is the 15m-high fountain; there is also a popular *sheesha* cafe beside the lake. Formal Park has a maze, barbecue pits and an exercise track.

CAPITAL GARDENS PARK

Map p136 (Muroor Rd, near Khalifa St; adult/child under 10yr Dh1/free; ⌚8am-10pm Sun-Wed, to 11pm Thu-Sat) This park in the heart of Downtown offers swings and a mini climbing wall, and there's an erupting fountain giving a bit of lively respite to the stifling heat of summer.

AL MARKAZIYAH GARDENS PARK

Map p136 (Corniche Rd (West); ⌚24hr) Spread over three distinct areas, Al Nahyan Park, Family Park and Urban Park, Al Markaziyah

Greater Abu Dhabi

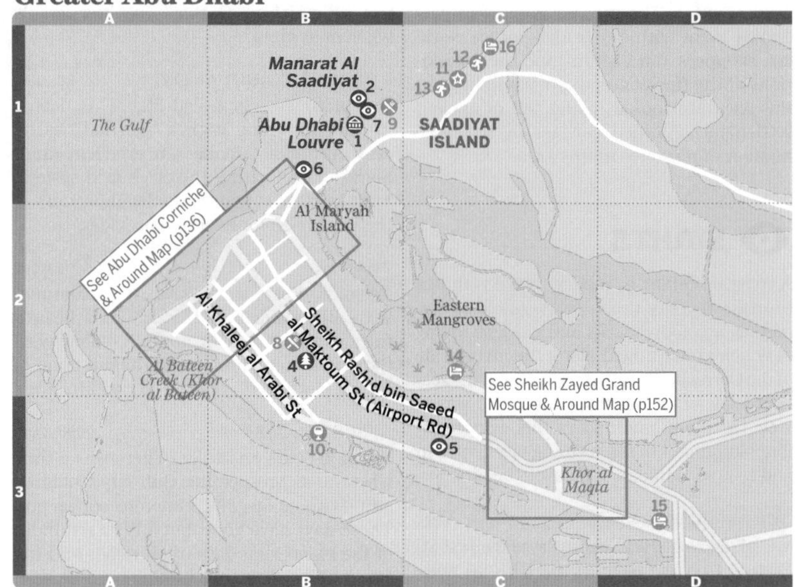

Gardens forms a broad band of recreational lawns parallel to the Corniche. The facilities offer toddlers' and children's play areas, fountains and shaded seating.

EATING

Al Markaziyah is the quarter of cafes and coffeeshops, curry houses and chop shops, kebab corners and shwarma stands. Strike out south of Zayed the First St and explore the teeming eateries to the north of Al Manhal district. Wedged into this area are dozens of places bearing names like 'Syrian Palace', 'Lebanese Flower' and 'Turkish Sheep'. They're all local, authentic options so you can't go too wrong, but a good rule of thumb is to pick the busiest.

★LEBANESE FLOWER — LEBANESE $

Map p136 (☎02-665 8700; near Zayed the First St; mains Dh25-50; ⏰7-3am) Amid a cluster of Middle Eastern snack, grill and pastry outlets, a short walk from Al Husn Fort, this Lebanese restaurant is a local legend, attracting a multinational clientele of city residents. The generous plates of mezze include traditional favourites such as chicken livers, fried halloumi and tabouli and are excellent value. There's a pleasant family section upstairs. It's one block southeast of Zayed the First St.

AL IBRAHIMI RESTAURANT — INDIAN $

Map p136 (☎02-632 1100; www.ibrahimigroup.com; opposite Madinat Zayed Shopping & Gold Centre; biryani Dh30; ⏰11.30-12.30am) This restaurant isn't going to win any prizes for decor but it does muster up delicious, authentic Indian and Pakistani dishes (particularly biryanis) and there is an outside seating area where life chaotically passes by.

AUTOMATIC RESTAURANT — LEBANESE $

Map p136 (☎02-676 9677; cnr Hamdan & 6th Sts; sandwiches Dh4-7, mains Dh18-65; ⏰11-1am) Fresh shwarma, perfect hummus and whole heads of lettuce, raddish, rucola and pickles make this no-nonsense chain one of the most popular in the Gulf.

LA BRIOCHE CAFÉ — FRENCH $

Map p136 (☎02-626 9300; www.labriocheuae.com; Khalifa St; mains Dh22-70) A slice of Paris in the UAE, this mini-chain charmer makes healthy salads, bulging sandwiches and some of the best bread, croissants and pastries (baked fresh and local) in town. Service is swift and smiling, making this ideal for a takeaway to eat at Capital Gardens, which are almost opposite.

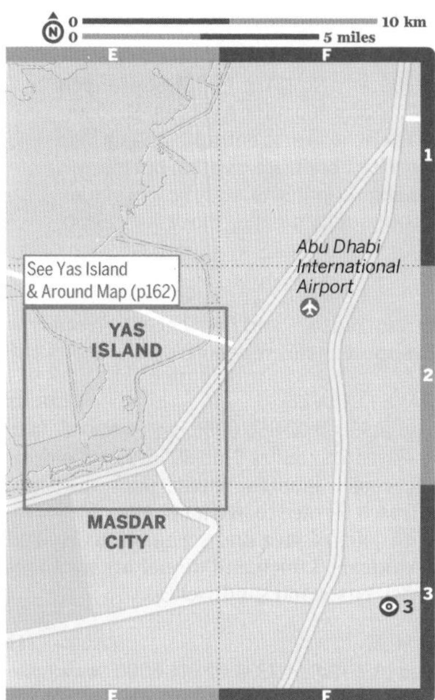

Greater Abu Dhabi

Top Sights

1 Abu Dhabi Louvre B1
2 Manarat Al Saadiyat B1

Sights

3 Abu Dhabi Falcon Hospital F3
4 Al Mushrif Children's Garden B2
5 Capital Gate C3
6 Fruit & Vegetable Market B1
7 UAE Pavilion B1

Eating

18° .... (see 5)
Beach House .... (see 16)
8 Café Arabia B2
9 Fanr Restaurant B1
Turquoiz .... (see 11)

Drinking & Nightlife

De La Costa .... (see 12)
10 Relax@12 .... B3

Entertainment

11 People by Crystal Abu Dhabi C1

Sports & Activities

Abu Dhabi Pearl Journey .... (see 14)
Anantara Spa .... (see 14)
12 Saadiyat Beach Club C1
13 Saadiyat Public Beach C1

Sleeping

14 Eastern Mangroves Hotel & Spa C2
15 Ibis Hotel Abu Dhabi Gate D3
16 Park Hyatt Abu Dhabi C1

IDIOMS INTERNATIONAL $

Map p136 (☎02-681 0808; off Corniche Rd (West); mains Dh20-40; ⏰lunch & dinner) Despite being around for a few years, this hip eatery (around the corner from Roi's and opposite TcheTche), with its minimalist design, is a breath of fresh air. It does delicious soups, pizzas, pastas and espresso cocktails that pack a punch.

CAFÉ DU ROI FRENCH $

Map p136 (☎02-681 5096; Corniche Rd (West); mains Dh15-35; ⏰7am-midnight; 📶) With professional coffee and delicious pastries, croissants and sandwiches, plus seven choices of fluffy filled omelettes, this French-style cafe is the perfect spot for some leisurely lingering. Also at Abu Dhabi Mall.

BUTT SWEETS SHOP BAKERY $

Map p136 (☎02-633 8058; Hamdan St, opposite Tawash Bldg; candied fruit from Dh2) Beloved as much for its name as for its goods, this shop sells interesting local confections with candied fruit, sesame and nuts featuring heavily.

TCHETCHE MIDDLE EASTERN $

Map p136 (☎02-681 1994; Corniche Towers, off Corniche Rd (West); mains from Dh25; ⏰9am-midnight) This Jordanian import is a vaunted haunt of both locals and expats who come to pick their favourite smoke from the long *sheesha* menu, while Arabic music videos play in the background. You don't need to participate in the smoking to get a sense of the vibe – the Arabic food alone is reason enough for a visit.

★ **ZYARA CAFÉ** LEBANESE $$

Map p136 (☎02-627 5006; Al Jazeera Tower, Corniche Rd (East); mains Dh50; ⏰8am-midnight) Red is the overwhelming impression of this fun and eccentric little eatery. Scarlet cushions, ruby drapes, carmine tablecloths and a whole medley of Eastern-patterned fabrics make the interior a riot of colour – a relief in a city of predominantly modern monotones. The mezze and home-baked cakes are delicious and the Corniche views lovely, but avoid the lunchtime crush.

CAFÉ ARABIA

The homely **Café Arabia** (Map p132; ☎02-643 9699; Villa No 224/1, 15th St, btwn Airport (2nd) Rd & Al Karamah (24th) St; lunch around Dh 90; ⌚8am-10pm Thu & Fri, 8am-11.30pm Sat-Wed), housed in a three-floor villa, is run by a Lebanese arts enthusiast, Aida Mansour. Tasty pastries, wholesome lunches and Turkish coffee are on offer, but many come for the Arabian ambience, photographs, hanging lanterns, eclectic mix of furniture and book-swap service. Something of a community meeting place, arts exhibitions and literary groups are hosted here.

KABABS & KURRIES INDIAN **$$**

Map p136 (☎02-628 2522; Ground Level, Souq Central Market, off Hamdan St; mains from Dh35) On the site of Abu Dhabi's original market, and located in the heart of Foster's attractive modern-day equivalent, you can imagine that Indian food (or at least food using Indian spices) has been served up on or near this spot for centuries. An extensive menu and outside terrace make this a refined and popular venue for a curry.

CHO GAO ASIAN **$$**

Map p136 (☎02-616 6101; www.ichotelsgroup.com; Crowne Plaza Abu Dhabi, Hamdan St; mains Dh70; ⌚noon-4pm & 7pm-1am) This is a highly recommended restaurant, not so much for the tasty pan-Asian fusion food as for the highly sociable ambience of this Downtown favourite. There's always something happening, a work anniversary, a birthday or a girls' night out among the Emirati, Arab, Western and Asian clientele, making the restaurant, with its prominent bar, feel more club than pub.

JONES THE GROCER INTERNATIONAL **$$**

Map p136 (☎02-639 5883; www.jonesthegrocer.com; ground fl, Pearl Plaza Tower, 32nd St; mains Dh50-60; ⌚8am-11pm Sun-Thu, 9am-11pm Fri & Sat) Catering to an urban-chic clientele, this local outpost of the Australian chain has open kitchens overlooking the dining area decked out in stainless steel and earthy wood colours. Talking points include a chilled cheese room with samples to taste, and an eclectic menu with plenty of organic goodies.

SHAKESPEARE & CO INTERNATIONAL **$$**

Map p136 (☎02-639 9626; www.shakespeare-and-co.com; ground fl, Souq Central Market; English breakfast from Dh54; ⌚7am-1pm) The decor in this chintzy, Edwardian-style diner may not give you much indication of the Gulf location, but its popularity with Arab diners certainly will. Renowned as a favourite breakfast venue, there's a full English (with turkey sausage and beef bacon) on offer, or Lebanese-style crêpes.

CAFÉ FIRENZE CAFE **$$**

Map p136 (☎02-666 0955; cnr Al Nasr & Tariq ibn Ziyad Sts; dishes Dh15-35; ⌚9am-10pm) In the cooler months, expats pack the large alfresco terrace to live it up *dolce vita*–style with jolts of java and scrumptious cooked breakfasts. Lunch and dinner are all about pizza, pasta and sandwiches.

MARAKESH MOROCCAN **$$$**

Map p136 (☎ext 7334 02-614 6000; www.milleniumhotels.ae; Millennium Hotel, Khalifa St; meals from Dh190; ⌚7pm-3am) If the exotic Moroccan decor and the bona fide cuisine, including delicious *tajines* and couscous, aren't enough to bring you here, there's an excellent Moroccan band, belly dancer and singer. Evenings here are memorable and go late.

DRINKING & NIGHTLIFE

In Al Markaziyah, the drinking is either licenced and rooftop, or it is strictly non-alcoholic and ground floor. Either way, it's lively until the small hours.

CAFÉ LAYALI ZAMAN SHEESHA CAFE

Map p136 (☎02-627 7745; Lake Park, Corniche Rd (West); ⌚9-2am) This family-friendly *sheesha* cafe serves snacks (Dh50) as well as coffee, though some may find the strong smell of *sheesha* over-pervasive. It is ever-popular with locals, particularly later at night.

TIARA RESTO CAFÉ SHEESHA CAFE

Map p136 (Urban Park, Al Markaziyah Gardens, Corniche Rd (West); ⌚noon-midnight) This smart little cafe in Urban Park, just across from the Corniche, offers seating 'in the round' – or at least arranged in a crescent. An outside terrace looks onto the park's fountains – a perfect spot for a late-night coffee and a chat with a friend in family-friendly company. *Sheesha* smoking is common here.

COLOMBIANO COFFEE HOUSE COFFEE

Map p136 (☎02-633 7765; www.cchuae.com; Urban Park, Corniche Rd (West); ⏰8am-midnight) Sitting in the cafe part of this establishment, beside the pond in comfortable armchairs, makes for a pleasant and sociable experience, especially on warm nights before the full heat of summer.

LEVEL LOUNGE BAR

Map p136 (☎02-616 6101; www.crowneplaza.com; Crowne Plaza Abu Dhabi, Hamdan St; cocktails from Dh40; ⏰6pm-2am) This relaxing poolside rooftop lounge is open to the stars and offers a piece of tower-top calm in the middle of the hectic city. It makes a good local haunt for *sheesha* and a chat with 'chill-out' music.

SAX CLUB

Map p136 (☎02-674 2020; www.leroyalmeridienabudhabi.com; Le Royal Méridien Abu Dhabi, 6th St; ⏰9pm-3.30am) In the early evening Sax lures chatty jet-setters huddled in intense tête-à-têtes, then cranks up the superb sound system to pack the dance floor with a glam-tastic, international crowd. Different promotions – Ladies' Night, Cabin Crew Night, Lebanese Weekend – keep things dynamic.

STRATOS LOUNGE

Map p136 (☎toll free 800-101 101; www.stratosabudhabi.com; Le Royal Méridien Abu Dhabi, 6th St; afternoon tea Dh149; ⏰3pm-2am Mon-Wed, to 3am Thu-Sat) This impressive revolving lounge gives a panoramic view of the city, although it can no longer command an uninterrupted vista. Has a good cocktail menu and Ladies' Night on Tuesdays, and there's also a fine high tea (or tippling tea with champagne) if you wanted to keep the night for Sax – the nightclub downstairs.

☆ ENTERTAINMENT

There's usually something going on in one or other of the many business hotels in Al Markaziyah. The Crowne Plaza is a good bet for a live band or for watching a big game in their sports bar. *Time Out Abu Dhabi* (www.timeoutabudhabi.com) has a full listing of area hot spots.

CRISTAL LIVE MUSIC

Map p136 (☎02-614 6000; www.milleniumhotels.ae; Millennium Hotel, Khalifa St; ⏰5pm-2am) A resident pianist provides genteel entertainment in the dapper Cristal. Dressed in polished oak and illuminated by candlelight and a fireplace, this is a haven of old-world charm in the heart of a frenetic city. Whisky and cigars are *de rigueur* for men, while the ladies sip on champagne. For style on the cheap, come during happy hour (5pm to 8pm).

SHOPPING

You may have seen it all before at a gold souq in other parts of the region, but don't miss seeing it all again at Abu Dhabi's collection of jewellers in Madinat Zayed Shopping Centre. By contrast, the Souq Central Market and World Trade Centre mall provide an altogether more global shopping experience.

★SOUQ CENTRAL MARKET MARKET

Map p136 (☎02-810 7810; www.centralmarket.ae/souk; Khalifa St; ⏰10am-10pm Sun-Thu, to 11pm Fri & Sat) Norman Foster's reinterpretation of the traditional souq is a stylish composition of warm lattice woodwork, stained glass, walkways and balconies on the site of Abu Dhabi's historic central market. There are plenty of enticing stores here, including the Persian Carpet House & Antiques, Kashmir Cottage and the Chocolate Factory, and many boutiques selling perfumes and handicrafts.

WORLD TRADE CENTRE MALL MALL

Map p136 (☎02-508 2400; www.wtcad.ae; Hamdan St; ⏰10am-10pm Sun-Thu, 10am-11pm Fri & Sat) One of Abu Dhabi's newest malls, with lots of inaugural high-street and designer outlets.

SHOPPING FOR GOLD

Gold is bought by weight while the cost of the fine handicraft of each piece of jewellery is usually free. Some visitors are dismissive of the **gold souq** (Madinat Zayed Shopping & Gold Centre) as just a place to visit but not to shop: a missed opportunity when something beautifully crafted with local pearls can be bought for a fraction of what it would cost back home. Besides, there can't be a more local way to spend an hour or two than deciding on a gold purchase.

MADINAT ZAYED SHOPPING & GOLD CENTRE GOLD MARKET

Map p136 (☎02-633 3311; www.madinatzayed-mall.com; 4th St; ⏰9am-11pm) For first-time visitors to a gold souq, the window displays of bridal necklaces, earrings and belts, the trays of precious stones and the tiers of gold bangles are an attraction in their own right. For those familiar with dazzling arrays of jewellery, Madinat Zayed Shopping & Gold Centre offers another reason to visit – affordable pearls set in gold necklaces and rings.

SPORTS & ACTIVITIES

Activities in Al Markaziyah are centred around the beach at the Corniche and in various low-key exercise stations and children's playgrounds in the city parks.

FUNRIDE – CHAMBER OF COMMERCE BICYCLE RENTAL

Map p136 (☎02-556 6113; www.funridesports.com; Corniche Rd (West); per hr from Dh20; ⏰4pm-midnight) One of several stations for bike hire along the Corniche. If this is unstaffed, head for the main terminus outside the Hiltonia Beach Club at the far west end of the Corniche.

Breakwater & Around

For at least a decade, visitors have been attracted to this part of town because of the Emirates Palace, one of the most opulent hotels in the Middle East. Still a big draw, the Emirates Palace holds its own but it has been joined by other attractions. These

Abu Dhabi Corniche & Around

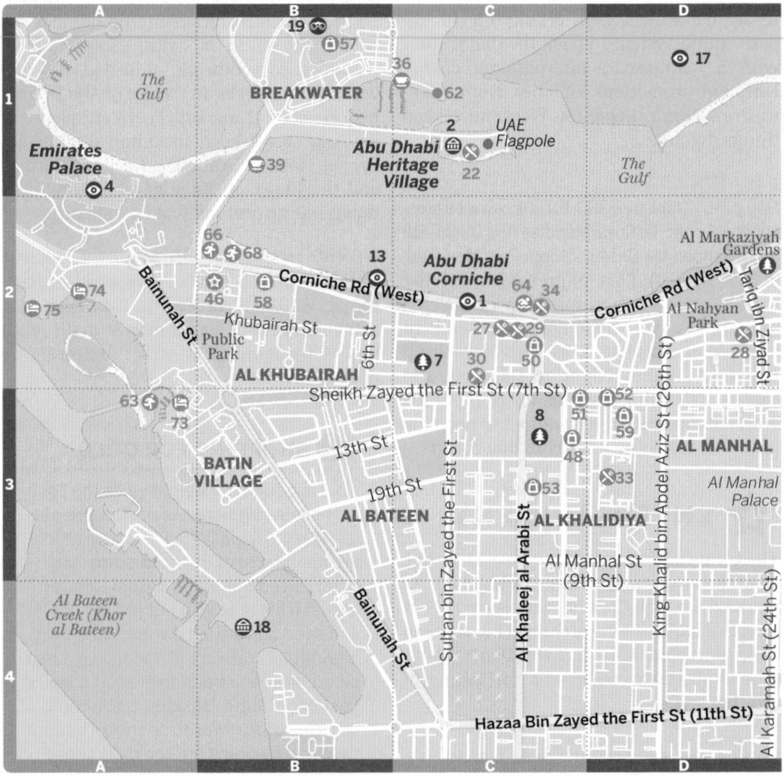

include the clustered Etihad Towers and the lofty St Regis. Back down to earth, the landscaped Western Corniche is helping transform Abu Dhabi into an urban beach destination while the Heritage Village is a reminder of the city's Bedouin roots.

SIGHTS

★EMIRATES PALACE BUILDING

Map p136 (☎02-690 9000; www.emiratespalace.com; Corniche Rd (West)) What the Burj Khalifa in Dubai is to the vertical, the Emirates Palace is to the horizontal, with audacious domed gatehouses and flying ramps to the foyer, 114 domes and a 1.3km private beach. Built at a cost of US$6 billion, this is the *big* hotel in the Gulf, with 1002 crystal chandeliers and 400 luxury rooms and suites. You don't have to check in to check out the Emirates Palace, as it doubles as a cultural hub of the city.

Hosting opera and renowned orchestras during the Abu Dhabi Classics concert season, and showing screenings during the Abu Dhabi Film Festival, the Emirates Palace has played its part in the cultural expansion of the capital. Other reasons to visit include the Barakat Gallery, which offers exquisite fine art from ancient China, Egypt, Africa, Greece and Rome; ever-popular afternoon high tea in the foyer (Dh225); and a unique ATM that dispenses solid gold bars.

★ABU DHABI HERITAGE VILLAGE MUSEUM

Map p136 (☎02-681 4455; near Marina Mall, Breakwater; ⏲9am-5pm Sat-Thu, 3.30-9pm Fri) FREE This reconstructed village gives an insight into pre-oil life in the UAE – a life that is still in evidence in many parts of the Arabian Peninsula to this day. The walled complex includes all the main elements of

Abu Dhabi Corniche & Around

Top Sights

1 Abu Dhabi Corniche C2
2 Abu Dhabi Heritage Village C1
3 Dhow Harbour H1
4 Emirates Palace A1
5 Qasr Al Hosn E2
6 Sowwah Square H3

Sights

7 Al Khalidiyah Kid's Park C2
8 Al Khalidiyah Public Park C3
9 Al Maryah Island Promenade H3
10 Al Mina Fish Market H1
Barakat Gallery .... (see 4)
11 Burj Mohammed bin Rashid E2
12 Capital Gardens G2
13 Corniche – Al Khalidiyah B2
14 Etisalat Headquarters E2
15 Heritage Park H2
16 Lake Park & Formal Park F2
17 Lulu Island D1
18 Sheikh Zayed Centre for Studies & Research B4
19 Sky Tower B1
20 Street Sculpture E2

Eating

Abu Dhabi Co-op Hypermarket .... (see 47)
21 Al Arish Restaurant H1
22 Al Asala Heritage Restaurant C1
Al Dhafra .... (see 61)
Al Ibrahimi Restaurant .... (see 70)
23 Al Mina Modern Cuisine & Restaurant H1
24 Automatic Restaurant G3
25 Automatic Restaurant F2
Brasserie Angélique .... (see 74)
26 Butt Sweets Shop F2
27 Café Du Roi C2
28 Café Firenze D2
Cho Gao .... (see 72)
Finz .... (see 71)
Godiva Chocolate Café .... (see 6)
29 Idioms C2
30 Jones the Grocer C2
Kababs & Kurries .... (see 60)
31 La Brioche Café F2
32 Lebanese Flower E3
33 Living Room Café D3
Marakesh .... (see 45)
Matam Fiyroom .... (see 10)
Mezlai .... (see 4)
34 Nova Beach Café C2
Saudi Cuisine VIP .... (see 50)
Sayad .... (see 4)
Scott's .... (see 74)
Shakespeare & Co .... (see 60)
TcheTche .... (see 50)
Vasco's .... (see 68)
35 Zyara Café F2

Drinking & Nightlife

36 Al Bateen Resort Yacht Club C1
Arabic Café .... (see 68)
Belgian Beer Café .... (see 73)
Bentley Bistro & Bar .... (see 6)
37 Café Layali Zaman F2
38 Colombiano Coffee House E2
Etoiles .... (see 4)
Havana Café & Restaurant .... (see 36)
Hemingway's .... (see 46)
39 Le Boulanger Marina Café B1

traditional Gulf life: a fort to repel invaders from the sea, a souq to trade goats for dates with friendly neighbours, and a mosque as a reminder of the central part that Islam plays in daily Arab life.

Take a look at the *barasti* house, designed to catch the breeze through the palm frond uprights, an ox-drawn well without which settled life was impossible, and the ancient *falaj* (irrigation) system, which still waters the crops (note the stones for diverting the water) in the plantations of Al Ain and Liwa Oasis today.

Most Emiratis proudly claim desert descent and while the nomadic life has largely disappeared from the UAE, many locals still like to return to their roots by camping in goat-hair tents similar to the ones on display in the Bedouin part of the village. Camels continue to play their role in the country's identity with many families owning a few in desert farms and attending regular races. Little surprise, then, that this is the section that always attracts the biggest interest from visiting Emiratis.

Spare some time to watch artisans at work in various labours at the tannery, pottery and glass-blowing workshop. At the swordsmiths, you can see artisans honing the *khanjar* blades. These traditional curved daggers remain an important part of ceremonial costume across the region.

Finally pop into the museum in the old fort with its traditional wind tower for cooling the interior. There are good displays of jewellery here and the paraphernalia of

Le Café ......(see 4)
Level Lounge ......(see 72)
40 Navona Restaurant & Coffeeshop......H1
Observation Deck at 300......(see 74)
41 Planet Café G2
Ray's Bar......(see 74)
42 Sax......F2
Stratos......(see 42)
43 Tiara Resto Café E2

Entertainment
44 49er's The Gold Rush......G3
Abu Dhabi Classics......(see 4)
45 Cristal F2
Grand Cinemas Abu Dhabi......(see 47)
46 Jazz Bar & Dining......B2
Vox Cinemas......(see 57)

Shopping
47 Abu Dhabi Mall H3
48 Abu Dhabi Pottery Establishment......C3
Avenue at Etihad Towers......(see 74)
49 Carpet Souq H2
50 Centre of Original Iranian Carpets C2
51 Eclectic......C3
52 Folklore Gallery D3
Galleria ......(see 6)
53 Ghaf Gallery......C3
Grand Stores......(see 47)
54 Iranian Souq H1
Jashanmal......(see 47)
55 Khalifa Centre G3
56 Madinat Zayed Shopping & Gold Centre......F3
57 Marina Mall B1
58 Nation Galleria......B2
59 Paris Avenue D3
Souq Central Market......(see 60)
60 World Trade Centre Mall E2

Sports & Activities
61 Abu Dhabi Dhow Cruise......H1
62 Abu Dhabi Helicopter Tour C1
Beach Club ......(see 71)
63 Belevari Catamarans A3
64 Corniche Beach......C2
Emirates Palace Spa......(see 4)
Fun City......(see 57)
65 Funride - Chamber of Commerce......E2
66 Funride - Hiltonia Beach Club......B2
67 Funride - Sheraton G1
68 Hiltonia Health Club & Spa......B2
Lulu Boats ......(see 36)
Nation Riviera Beach Club ......(see 58)
Sense ......(see 6)
Shuja Yacht......(see 36)

Sleeping
69 Al Diar Regency Hotel......G2
70 Al Jazeera Royal Hotel......E3
71 Beach Rotana Hotel & Towers......H3
72 Crowne Plaza Abu Dhabi......F2
Emirates Palace......(see 4)
73 InterContinental Abu Dhabi......A3
74 Jumeirah at Etihad Towers......A2
75 Khalidiya Palace Rayhaan by Rotana......A2
76 Sheraton Abu Dhabi Hotel & Resort G2

the pearl-diving industry, upon which Abu Dhabi was founded before cultured pearls from Japan and the discovery of oil made pearling redundant.

★SHEIKH ZAYED CENTRE FOR STUDIES & RESEARCH — MUSEUM

Map p136 (Baba Zayed's House; off Bainunah St, Al Bateen; ⏲8am-3pm Sun-Thu) FREE This eclectic collection of artefacts and personal memorabilia documents the life of Sheikh Zayed, the founding father of the Emirates. The collection is housed in a rare assembly of old villas sporting traditional wind towers, on the coast near the new Al Bateen developments. The museum complex, complete with 'Baba' (Father) Zayed's favourite blue Mercedes and beat-up Land Rover, is looking unloved, perhaps in anticipation of the new national museum on Saadiyat Island.

The main hall of the museum has an interesting set of black-and-white photographs that capture pre–Arab Spring veterans, Hosni Mubarak and Colonel Gaddafi. Also on display are various gifts from visiting dignitaries, including a stuffed leopard and anaconda skins, but the most poignant exhibits are the intimate pieces, such as a used cologne bottle, a rifle that guests can handle to feel closer to Sheikh Zayed, and his legendary falcon clock that signals his legendary respect for time. Visit before the historical buildings comprising the research centre, which look particularly magical in the late afternoon, are swallowed up in the surrounding high-rise development.

THE BEDOUIN

Visit the Abu Dhabi Heritage Village (p137) in Breakwater and you'll be sure to find Emirati visitors clustered around the camel enclosure and the Bedouin tent. They may belong to an urbane and urban generation but the capital's citizens are quick to claim Bedouin roots.

Today's Modern Bedouin

There are few Bedouin in the UAE who live up to their name as true desert nomads these days, but there are still communities who live a semi-traditional life on the fringes of the Empty Quarter. Their survival skills in the harsh terrain and their ability to adapt to changing circumstances are part of their enduring success. Most of today's Bedouin have modernised their existence with 4WDs (it's not unusual to find the camel travelling by truck these days), fodder from town and purified water from bowsers. All these features have limited the need to keep moving. Some have mobile phones and satellite TV and most listen to the radio. Many no longer move at all.

Mutual Benefit

Part of the ancient Bedouin creed is that no traveller in need of rest or food should be turned away. Likewise, a traveller assumes the assured protection of his hosts for a period of three days and is guaranteed a safe passage through tribal territory. Such a code of conduct traditionally ensured the survival of all in a difficult environment with scant resources. Even today a city host will walk a guest to the front gate, symbolic of this ancient custom.

BARAKAT GALLERY GALLERY

Map p136 (☎02-690 8950; www.barakatgallery-uae.com) This exclusive private gallery, with branches in Beverly Hills, Los Angeles and Mayfair, London, houses some exquisite artefacts. With a heritage of over 100 years as art dealers, the family-run business has contributed pieces to museums, corporations and private collections around the world.

CORNICHE – AL KHALIDIYAH PROMENADE

Map p136 (Corniche Rd (West), opposite Nation Towers; 24hr) It's hard to believe, while sitting on a municipal sunbed, swimming in the sea or strolling under the flowering trees, that this was a dhow loading bay for cargo and passengers in the 1970s. In 2004 land was reclaimed to form the 8km Corniche and a decade later a major landscaping project transformed the seafront into this first-class public amenity. The western end of the Corniche, at Al Khalidiyah, offers the most facilities and is on the bus route.

A complex of parks, fountains, cycle tracks, walking paths and beaches snake along the waterside. Lots of benches, shady spots and exercise stations make this a popular destination for strollers and joggers and there's a growing number of cafes. Parking is at the far southwestern end of the Corniche and at various points on the opposite side of the dual carriageway, accessible by pedestrian underpass.

UAE FLAGPOLE LANDMARK

Map p136 At 122m this giant flagpole was the tallest free-standing flagpole in the world when it was constructed in 2001. It lost its title to the Raghadan Flagpole in Jordan in 2004 and is now a long way short of the world's tallest. That said, the Emirati flag makes a fine landmark and the small promenade beneath the pole offers one of the best photo opportunities in the city for an uninterrupted view of the skyline. It's near the Abu Dhabi Heritage Village.

SKY TOWER VIEWPOINT

Map p136 (☎02-681 9009; Marina Mall, Breakwater; 10am-10pm) FREE You may pay a bit extra for a burger, sandwich or salad in the aerial Colombiano Coffee House at the top of this observation tower but there's no charge for the panoramic view from 360-degrees' worth of windows. If you'd rather not walk round the view yourself, head for Tiara, the revolving restaurant upstairs.

LULU ISLAND ISLAND

Map p136 (daylight hours) This idyllic-looking island of sandy beaches, date palms and dunes, visible from the Corniche and a short boat ride away from the marina on

Breakwater, has risen like a mirage from the sea as one of the city's many ambitious tourism projects. Not yet officially open to the public, many pitch up for an ad hoc picnic on the reclaimed land. Check with Lulu Boats (p146) for a ride over.

AL KHALIDIYAH PUBLIC PARK PARK
Map p136 (Khalidiyah Garden; between 16th & 30th (Al Khaleej al Arabi) Sts; adult/child Dh1/free; 24hr) One of many popular, shady parks in Abu Dhabi, this park offers a respite from the heat of the Corniche in the summer months. There's a jogging track (20-minute circuit) and a variety of climbing frames and other attractions for youngsters.

AL KHALIDIYAH KID'S PARK PARK
Map p136 (Sheikh Zayed the First (7th) St; 6am-midnight) With a few fruit-shaped climbing frames, this is a popular spot at weekends for local women and children (no boys over 10 years old allowed).

EATING

When it comes to dining in and around Breakwater, the sky's the limit – literally, if you head for the Observation Deck at the Etihad Towers. That said, some of the best eating experiences are down to earth in the cheap and cheerful cafes dotted along the Corniche where there's a chance to join the city at rest.

LIVING ROOM CAFÉ CAFE $
Map p136 (02-639 6654; www.thelivingroom-cafeabudhabi.com; Khalifa bin Shakhbout (28th) St; light meals around Dh10; 7.30am-11.30pm Sun-Thu, 8am-11.30pm Fri & Sat) This award-winning, family-run venue started life as a coffee-and-cake experience and has grown by word of mouth into a much-beloved restaurant. With an emphasis on family-friendly fare (including a VIP children's menu and kid's corner), the home-baked cakes, all-day breakfasts, toasted sandwiches and healthy salads will especially please those with a craving for something out of mum's kitchen. It's inside the Sarouh Compound.

NOVA BEACH CAFÉ CAFE $
Map p136 (02-658 1879; Corniche Rd (West); snacks around Dh40; noon-10.30pm) One of the few public places to have a coffee and light bite overlooking the sea, this cafe has a devoted local following. If you're walking or cycling the Corniche, or looking for a snack between swims, this is a sociable venue where you can catch the sea breeze.

AL ASALA HERITAGE RESTAURANT EMIRATI $$
Map p136 (02-681 2188; www.alasalahrestaurants.com; mains Dh60, buffet Dh75; noon-4pm daily, buffet 1-5pm & 6.30-9pm Fri) Offering traditional *jasheed* (minced shark), *harees* (meat and wheat 'porridge') and *umm ali* (Arab bread pudding) in the Heritage Village, this restaurant, with its fine view of the Abu Dhabi skyline, caters mainly for tour groups sampling the buffet as part of their cultural tour. If unaccompanied by a tour guide you'll be attentively looked after.

SAUDI CUISINE VIP ARABIAN $$
Map p136 (02-665 5355; behind Corniche Towers; meals Dh100; 11am-11pm) A snug little den of an eatery decked out with sheepskins and partitioned tables, this restaurant is the perfect place to try lamb dishes from the heart of the Peninsula. Roasted slowly for many hours and served with rice and chilli sauce, the lamb falls easily off the bone. Hands are the best utensils in this local favourite.

★**VASCO'S** SEAFOOD $$$
Map p136 (02-692 4247; www.placeshilton.com/abu-dhabi; Corniche Rd (West); mains around Dh120; noon-3.30pm & 7-11pm) This is the perfect place to enjoy a lazy lunch. With a patio overlooking the Arabian Sea, accommodating and hospitable staff and a delicious fine-dining menu offering an interesting blend of regional and international cuisine, it's not surprising reservations are recommended. The Vasco twist to the menu is a good reminder of the early Portuguese influence in the region. Adjacent to Hiltonia Health Club & Spa.

MEZLAI EMIRATI $$$
Map p136 (02-690 7999; www.kempinski.com; 1st fl, Emirates Palace; mains Dh110-205; 1-10.30pm) Meaning 'old door lock', Mezlai delivers a rare chance to enter the world of local flavours. The Emirati food is prepared from organic and locally sourced ingredients. A popular dish is the lamb *medfoun* (shoulder of lamb, slow-cooked in a banana leaf). The potato mashed with camel's milk makes for an interesting side dish.

SAYAD SEAFOOD $$$

Map p136 (☎02-690 7999; www.emiratespalace.com; Emirates Palace, Ras Al Akhdar; mains Dh150-200; ⏲6.30-11.30pm) Serving the city's finest seafood in a striking aquamarine setting (quite a contrast to the traditional marble and silk of the surrounding Emirates Palace), Sayad has earned a reputation as a top choice for a special occasion. Dishes are imaginative, such as the lobster salad with watermelon and mango. Reservations are essential.

SCOTT'S SEAFOOD $$$

Map p136 (☎02-811 5666; Jumeirah at Etihad Towers; mains around Dh120; ⏲noon-3.30pm & 6.30-11pm) Although related to the famous London restaurant of the same name and carrying many of the London signature dishes, the chargrilled kingfish and the salt-baked Sultan Ibrahim is caught locally from the Gulf. The blue-lit, oyster-shaped architecture is appropriate to the gems served up from this award-winning restaurant. It has a romantic outdoor terrace and extravagant sea views.

BRASSERIE ANGÉLIQUE FRENCH $$$

Map p136 (☎02-811 5666; www.jumeirah.com; Jumeirah at Ethihad Towers; mains Dh150; ⏲noon-3.30pm & 7-11.30pm) It may seem perverse to recommend French food in the capital city of the Emirates but this awarding-winning, fine-dining restaurant, which only opened in 2013, has taken the city by storm. The chandeliers are thoroughly Gulf but the food is thoroughly Gallic with foie gras, escargots and bouillabaisse headlining the chef's menu.

DRINKING & NIGHTLIFE

Drinking and nightlife in Abu Dhabi centres around coffee, a percolated smoke and lively conversation. Join the locals in their nightly pursuits in Breakwater's favourite *sheesha* cafes or for a more international experience, glam up for the many hotel bars and clubs that have a liquor licence and expect a minimum of 'smart casual' from their guests.

★**OBSERVATION DECK AT 300** CAFE

Map p136 (☎02-811 5666; www.jumeirah.com; Level 74, Tower 2, Jumeirah at Etihad Towers; entry Dh75, incl Dh50 for food or drink, high tea Dh175; ⏲10am-6pm) This chic coffee shop on the 74th floor of the iconic Jumeirah at Etihad Towers hotel serves the highest high tea in Abu Dhabi with a sublime panorama of city, sea and surrounds. The '300' refers to the metres above ground.

LE CAFÉ HIGH TEA

Map p136 (☎02-690 7999; www.emiratespalace.com; Emirates Palace, Corniche Rd (West); high tea from Dh278; ⏲high tea 2-6pm) Try an Arabic twist on the classic English high tea with

ℹ ROAD NAMES

Whether you're looking for Sheikh Zayed the First, 7th or Electra St will largely depend on what map you're using. The initiative to rename the city's roads (a term used interchangeably with 'streets') from the former numbering system has resulted in confusion, especially as some districts have been renamed too (including Tourist Club Area, now known as Al Zahiyah).

Currently main roads are named after prominent Emirati figures while smaller roads reflect places. As former and current names are still common currency, here's a list of the main roads and their alternative names (without the suffix):

Al Khaleej al Arabi 30th

Sheikh Rashid bin Saeed al Maktoom 2nd, Airport

Sultan bin Zayed the First 4th, East, Muroor, New Airport

Fatima bint Mubarak 6th, Umm al Nar, Bani Yas, Baniyas

Sheikh Zayed bin Sultan 8th, Al Salam, East Coast, Eastern Ring, New Corniche

Khalifa bin Zayed the First 3rd, Khalifa, Sheikh Khalifa bin Zayed, Al Istiqalal

Sheikh Hamdan bin Mohammed 5th, Hamdan, Al Nasr, Al Khubairah

Sheikh Zayed the First 7th, Electra

Al Falah 9th, Old Passport Rd

mezze, Arabic savoury pastry and baklava with a camelccino made with camel's milk or a cappuccino sprinkled in 24kt gold flakes. High tea of both the classic and Arab variety is practically an institution at the Emirates Palace so book in advance to avoid the minimum spend fee of Dh100 per person.

ARABIC CAFÉ SHEESHA CAFE

Map p136 (☎02-681 1900; Hilton Abu Dhabi, Corniche Rd (West); ⊙8am-10pm Thu & Fri, to 11.30pm Sat-Wed) If you are tempted to while away the evening the local way with a puff of *sheesha*, a sip of coffee, a fresh fruit juice and good conversation with a friend, then this is a sheltered venue to try it out for size before hitting the real thing on pavements across town.

ETOILES BAR

Map p136 (☎02-690 8960; www.etoilesuae.com; Emirates Palace Hotel, Corniche Rd (West), Ras Al Akhdar; ⊙11pm-4am Mon-Fri) Don those killer heels, gals, slick back the hair, chaps, and join the super-chic crowd at this achingly stylish late-night bar. It's perfect for post-dinner drinks.

BELGIAN BEER CAFÉ BAR

Map p136 (☎02-666 6888; www.belgianbeercafe.com; InterContinental Hotel, Bainunah St, Khor al Bateen; ⊙5pm-1am) Not convinced there's more to beer than a canned lager? Head to the Belgian Beer Café, overlooking the marina at the InterContinental, and the 18 specialist draughts and bottles behind the bar may just convince you otherwise. Follow the expat lead and order *frites* (fries) with a very Belgian pot of mussels – reputedly the best in town.

HEMINGWAY'S BAR

Map p136 (☎02-681 1900; www.abudhabi.hilton.com; Hilton Abu Dhabi, Corniche Rd (West); ⊙noon-1am) A cantina popular with long-term expats, Hemingway's is the place to lounge in front of the big screen for beer, chips (albeit nacho chips) and football. There's a live band from Monday to Saturday, Ladies' Night is on Tuesday and Sunday is Quiz Night.

RAY'S BAR BAR

Map p136 (☎02-811-5555; www.jumeirah.com; Jumeirah at Etihad Towers; ⊙5pm-2am) For a sense of the sheer audacity of Abu Dhabi's architectural vision, a visit to the Etihad Towers is a must. Arrive at sunset and be dazzled by the light bouncing off the outside of these spectacular towers. The elegant and intimate bar on the lofty 62nd floor is currently the 'top' spot in town – measured in metres!

LE BOULANGER MARINA CAFÉ SHEESHA CAFE

Map p136 (☎02-681 8194; 18th St, Breakwater; mains from Dh90; ⊙8-1am) With a prime location on the Breakwater seafront, this sociable restaurant is always buzzing with life. There is a menu of vaguely Middle Eastern pedigree with tasty savoury pastries but most people turn up for coffee and a *sheesha*.

AL BATEEN RESORT YACHT CLUB SHEESHA CAFE

Map p136 (☎02-222 2886; near Marina Mall; fresh fruit juice Dh20; ⊙24hr) Serving a variety of tasty fruit juices and basic Lebanese dishes, this is a popular place to enjoy an evening of alfresco *sheesha* in the company of locals.

HAVANA CAFÉ & RESTAURANT SHEESHA CAFE

Map p136 (☎02-681 0044; Marina, Breakwater; sheesha from Dh35; ⊙7am-2pm) With one of the very best views of night-time Abu Dhabi, the outside terrace at this highly popular *sheesha* cafe is always teeming with appreciative puffers, smokers and gurglers. The service is attentive despite the crowds.

☆ ENTERTAINMENT

JAZZ BAR & DINING LIVE MUSIC

Map p136 (☎02-681 1900; www.abudhabi.hilton.com; Hilton Abu Dhabi, Corniche Rd (West); mains Dh50-200; ⊙7pm-12.30am Sat-Mon, to 1.30am Tue-Fri) Cool cats flock to this sophisticated supper club that serves contemporary fusion cuisine in a modern art deco–inspired setting. But the venue is less about the food and more about the music – jazz bands play on a stage to an audience of sagely nodding aficionados.

ABU DHABI CLASSICS CLASSICAL MUSIC

Map p136 (☎toll free 800-555; www.abudhabiclassics.com; Emirates Palace; tickets Dh30-400) This concert series brings top classical performances – including international soloists and famous orchestras – to the city throughout a season lasting from October to the end of May. Venues include the Emirates Palace Auditorium, Manarat Al Saadiyat, a floating stage off the Breakwater during the Volvo Ocean Race and some historical sites in Al Ain.

VOX CINEMAS CINEMA

Map p136 (☎02-681 8464; www.voxcinemas.com; Marina Mall; tickets from Dh47) Showing 3D and 4D films as well as a full repertory of new releases, Vox Cinemas can be booked online.

SHOPPING

Breakwater and the western end of the Corniche run the gamut of enticing shopping opportunities, from the enormous Marina Mall to the craft-oriented boutiques of Al Khalidiyah.

MARINA MALL MALL

Map p136 (☎02-681 2310; www.marinamall.ae; Breakwater; ⏰10am-10pm Sat-Wed, to 11pm Thu, 2-11pm Fri) For locals, the main draw of this big mall on the Breakwater seems to be IKEA, but fortunately there are over 400 other stores in case you don't need yet another Billy bookcase. Entertainment options include a multiplex cinema, tiny ice-skating rink and Fun City (p146), a huge activity centre for children that includes a (relatively tame) roller coaster and dodgem cars.

AVENUE AT ETIHAD TOWERS FASHION

Map p136 (☎toll free 800 384 4238; www.aveneatetihadtowers.ae; Etihad Towers, Corniche Rd (West)) Designer-led, luxury fashion items in an exclusive, opulent venue; this is boutique shopping at its finest.

NATION GALLERIA MALL

Map p136 (☎02-681 8824; Nation Towers, Corniche Rd (West)) This new shopping experience is not just your average mall – it houses many unique stores, extravagent eateries and a huge Wafi Gourmet, the celebrated Lebanese restaurant chain.

CENTRE OF ORIGINAL IRANIAN CARPETS CARPETS

Map p136 (☎02-681 1156; www.coicco.com; off Al Khaleej al Arabi St; ⏰9.30am-1.30pm & 5-9.30pm Sat-Thu) For many the carpet galleries of the Gulf cities are likely to represent the best opportunities for buying a Persian carpet. At this gallery, spread over three floors, there are over 4000 carpets to choose from – it's one of the largest collections of carpets in the Middle East. On the shop's detailed website there's a useful buyer's guide and glossary.

ABU DHABI POTTERY ESTABLISHMENT CERAMICS

Map p136 (☎02-666 7079; www.abudhabipottery.com; 16th St; ⏰9am-1pm & 4.30-9pm Sat-Thu) A showcase for the collectable ceramics of Homa Vafaie-Farley, the venue also doubles as a pottery workshop with classes on offer.

ECLECTIC ANTIQUES

Map p136 (☎02-666 5158; Zayed the First St; ⏰10.30am-1.30pm & 5-9pm Sat-Thu) A delightful browsing experience with old furniture and textiles hobnobbing with new paintings, ceramics and sculpture by local Gulf artists.

FOLKLORE GALLERY PAINTINGS

Map p136 (☎02-666 0361; www.folkloregallery.net; Zayed the First St) An opportunity to invest in a piece by up-and-coming local resident artists from a shop that started life mainly as a framing service in 1995.

PARIS AVENUE FASHION

Map p136 (☎02-653 4030; www.parisavenue.ae/; off Zayed the First St, near Al Khalidiyah Mall; ⏰10am-8pm) A favourite boutique that trends with the latest fashionable accessories from young graduate designers from Europe.

GHAF GALLERY ART GALLERY

Map p136 (☎02-665 5332; ghafgallery@gmail.com; Al Khaleej al Arabi St; ⏰10am-9pm Sat-Thu) FREE One of only two private galleries devoted to modern art in Abu Dhabi, the Ghaf Gallery is a beautiful little exhibition space in the heart of Al Khalidiyah. The gallery, which is the brainchild of Mohammed Kanoo, a Bahraini artist and patron, and local Emirati artist, Jalal Luqman, comes into its own during the Abu Dhabi Festival when it showcases the work of artists in residence.

SPORTS & ACTIVITIES

The water is the focus of most of the activities in this area – on it, over it, beside it, and on all manner of craft and vehicles. The public beaches are free (or there's a nominal fee for family-only areas) or for full spa experiences, the beach clubs offer attractive packages.

★BIG BUS ABU DHABI BUS TOUR

(☎02-449 0026; www.bigbustours.com; 24hr adult/child Dh200/100, 48hr Dh260/130; ⏰9am-7pm) For an informative introduction to the

ANNUAL SPORTS EVENTS

Abu Dhabi has stolen the march on its more extroverted neighbour, Dubai, in bringing the following world-class sporting events to the capital:

Abu Dhabi Grand Prix (02-659 9800; www.yasmarinacircuit.ae; Nov) The Formula One Abu Dhabi Grand Prix is the last race of the Formula One season and a major event. Offering one of the most spectacular circuits on the race calendar since its inauguration in 2009, this day-night race includes a marina setting and a section of track that passes through the Viceroy Yas Hotel.

XCAT World Series Powerboat Race (www.xcatracing.com; Corniche; Dec) These 6000cc powerboats reach speeds of more than 190km/h along the Breakwater in front of the Abu Dhabi Corniche, making for an exhilarating spectacle. Lots of street entertainment springs up along the beachfront as well, making for an enjoyable day out.

Mubadala World Tennis Championship (www.mubadalawtc.com; Sheikh Zayed Sports City; Jan) Featuring the world's best players, including Djokovic, Nadal, Wawrinka and Murray, this is a key event at the start of the tennis year.

Red Bull Air Race (www.redbullairrace.com; Corniche Breakwater; Feb) This spectacular, low-altitude air race virtually skims the water at 370km/h, flying only 20m above the water's surface. Pilots have to navigate a pylon obstacle course – thrilling viewing from the Corniche.

World Triathlon (www.abudhabi.triathlon.org; Mar) If you thought you were fit, watch the world's best competitors swim, cycle and run and you may feel it's time to get back in the gym. There's good viewing from the Corniche.

Desert Master Trek (www.liwachallenge.com; Feb) Spread over the high dunes of the Empty Quarter near Liwa, this gruelling sand race covers two distances (100km and 200km), with a finale on the ridge of the highest dune.

city, this hop-on, hop-off service is hard to beat. The route lasts 90 minutes and passes all the major sights, including Sheikh Zayed Grand Mosque, the Corniche, the Heritage Village and Emirates Palace Hotel. Tickets, which include free headphones, are available online, from hotels and from kiosks next to the Big Bus stops.

A separate shuttle, leaving every 90 minutes, covers Yas Island and Masdar City between 9am and 5.30pm daily. There is also a night bus (adult/child Dh115/75) that leaves from the Marina Mall at 7.15pm every evening and takes two hours. You can board the bus at any stop but the nominal starting point is the Marina Mall (Breakwater).

★FUNRIDE – HILTONIA BEACH CLUB — CYCLING

Map p136 (02-441 3264; www.funridesports.com; Corniche Rd (West); per hr adult/child Dh30/20; 6.30am-midnight) A great way to appreciate the modern skyline of Abu Dhabi's western shore is to cycle the dedicated bike path along the Corniche. Bicycles (men's, women's and children's) are available for rent at four stations along the road, with the most reliably staffed station at the far western end of the road, near the Hilton Beach Club.

It is 8km from here to the Dhow Harbour and there is a Dh10 surcharge for collecting the bike at one station and dropping it off at another.

CORNICHE BEACH — SWIMMING

Map p136 (Bake UAE; www.bakeuae.com; Corniche Rd (West); adult/child under 10yr Dh10/5; 8am-8pm) There are several gates to this spotlessly maintained, blue-flagged public beach. The turquoise sea, view of Lulu Island, palm trees and gardens make it an unexpected pleasure in the heart of a capital city. A lifeguard is on duty until sunset.

HILTONIA HEALTH CLUB & SPA — BEACH

Map p136 (02-692 4247; Corniche Rd (West); adult/child Fri & Sat Dh195/90, Sun-Thu Dh150/70; 8am-8pm) This recommended beach club occupies prime position at the western end of the Corniche. Set in beautifully landscaped gardens alongside a white-sand beach shaded by palm trees, the club offers a variety of water sports, three swimming pools, a gym and cafe. Punctuate a lazy day with a seafood salad and glass of wine at the excellent restaurant, Vasco's (p141). The admission charge includes towel, locker, shower facilities and access to the swimming pools.

NATION RIVIERA BEACH CLUB BEACH

Map p136 (☎02-694 4444; www.nationrivierabeachclub.com; Corniche Rd (West); day use Sun-Thu Dh300, Fri & Sat Dh400) The white pavilions and choice of subtropical planting make this new club owned by St Regis Hotel instantly attractive. With steam room, sauna, Jacuzzi, water sports and a gym, there's plenty for those who just can't keep still. For those who can, the perfect beach, with its private, 200m unruffled shoreline, offers a peaceful view of Breakwater and beyond.

EMIRATES PALACE SPA SPA

Map p136 (☎02-690 7978; www.kempinski.com; Emirates Palace) For the ultimate indulgence, enquire about their three-hour gold ritual. This includes a 24kt-gold facial, an application of gold from head to toe and a massage using gold shea butter. If you don't come out feeling like Tutankhamun's mummy, it won't be for want of trying. Prices on request (sit down first).

BELEVARI CATAMARANS CRUISE

Map p136 (☎02-643 1494; http://belevari.com; InterContinental, Bainunah St, Al Bateen; adult /child Dh350/250; ⏲5pm Thu) A chance to board Abu Dhabi's largest catamaran, a 22.5m-long, 11m-wide luxury boat, on a 2½-hour cruise with soft drinks, snacks and music included.

ABU DHABI HELICOPTER TOUR SCENIC FLIGHTS

Map p136 (☎04-294 6060; http://abudhabihelicoptertour.com; Marina Mall Terminal; 20/30min flight Dh3350/5000 for 6 passengers; ⏲by appointment) Abu Dhabi, with its many spectacular buildings, islands and expanses of mangrove may look inspiring from the Big Bus tour but it takes on a whole different perspective from the air. Rising vertically above the Marina but finding yourself at eye-level with a middle floor of a tower block is one way to gauge the full height of the city's achievements.

LULU BOATS CRUISE

Map p136 (☎050-642 9777; www.luluboats.com; Marina, Breakwater; from around Dh150) Arranges daily harbour cruises and fishing trips. Call the office at the harbour to make a booking and negotiate a price.

SHUJA YACHT CRUISE

Map p136 (☎02-674 2020; Marina, Breakwater; brunch Dh350-500) Operated through Le Royal Méridien Abu Dhabi, the elegant luxury yacht *Shuja* plies the placid seas on a number of bay cruises, including the popular brunch cruise. There's a sunset cruise (5.30pm to 6.30pm), and the dinner cruise (8pm to 11pm) includes a fresh seafood buffet.

FUN CITY RIDES

Map p136 (☎02-681 5527; funcity.ae; Marina Mall, Breakwater; various packages available from around Dh50; ⏲10am-10pm) Offering games and rides for pre-teens, the Fun City brand is a favourite with children across Gulf countries.

Al Zahiyah & Al Maryah Island

Welcome to the mall quarter of the capital, where old and new shopping districts straddle Al Zahiyah and the new developments of Al Maryah Island. This is the neighbourhood where shopping remains one of the principle activities, whether you've come looking for camel kebabs for dinner, a pot to cook them in or designer plates to serve them on.

SIGHTS

The sights of Al Zahiyah, a district formerly known as 'Tourist Club Area' and still referred to by many as such today, now spill across to Al Maryah Island.

★SOWWAH SQUARE BUILDINGS

Map p136 (www.sowwahsquare.ae; Al Maryah Island) In the heart of the new urban development taking place on Al Maryah Island, Sowwah Sq is at the leading edge of modern town planning. Home to some of the city's most exciting buildings, it encompasses the sophisticated Rosewood Abu Dhabi hotel and glamorous Galleria mall. From the square's adjacent promenade there are striking views across the water while various feats of engineering vie for attention, including the Cleveland Clinic with its catwalk podium, and the island's new suspension bridge.

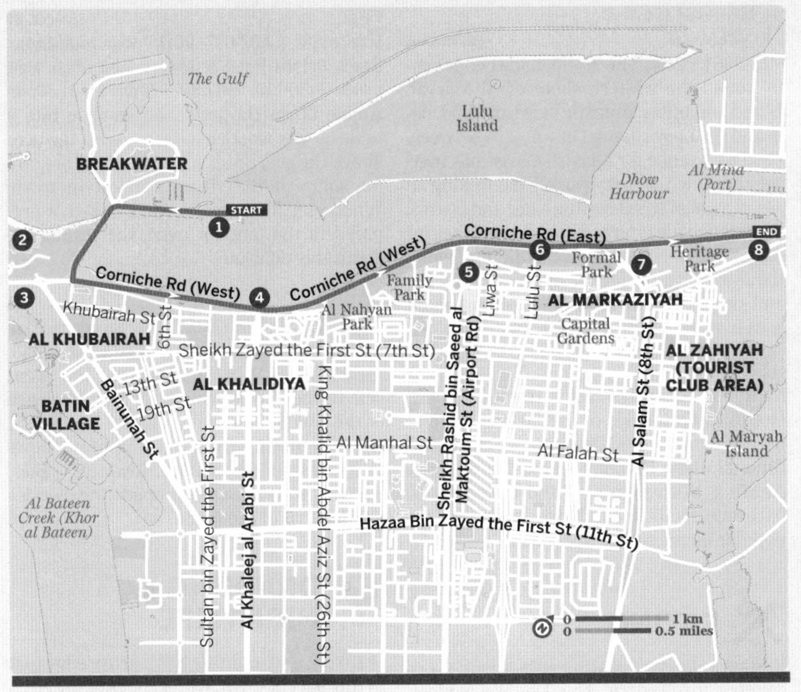

Neighbourhood Walk
A Stroll Downtown

START ABU DHABI FLAG
END HERITAGE PARK
LENGTH 10.5KM; FOUR HOURS

From the giant flag, the symbol of unity in this capital city, it's a brief walk to ❶ **Abu Dhabi Heritage Village** (p137). Here you can enjoy a glimpse of Emirati life before oil revenues transformed the country forever.

Follow the Breakwater, which comes alive during the powerboat racing championships. Across the road, there's an oyster statue, a reminder of the city's former pearling industry. The view beyond is dominated by the ❷ **Emirates Palace** (p137) – hotel, spa, cultural centre and general city icon.

Joining the Corniche, you'll notice a billboard-sized poster of Sheikh Zayed, father of the nation. His 'benign dictatorship' brought development to Abu Dhabi and the country as a whole, as demonstrated by the architectural optimism of buildings like ❸ **Etihad Towers**, clustered opposite.

Along the Corniche, you'll see similar expressions of confidence, such as Nation Towers, home to the St Regis. The Hiltonia and the Nation Riviera Beach Clubs offer luxurious swimming, and the public ❹ **Corniche Beach** (p145) is blue-flagged for cleanliness. Take a break at the Nova Beach Café here.

Pause next at Rashid bin Saeed al Maktoum St. The inland procession of fine buildings includes the ❺ **Burj Mohammed bin Rashid** (p131), the city's tallest tower, home to the World Trade Centre, and the Etisalat building.

Think you've been walking west to east? In fact the orientation is southwest to northeast but this tends to be overlooked on maps. This stretch is beautifully landscaped and parallels attractive ❻ **Lake Park** (p131), connected by an underpass.

In a city where the shoreline has been dredged and reshaped, it's endearing to see that the *khor* (creek) beside the ❼ **Sheraton Hotel** (p168) has not been filled in. The Corniche passes over it, leaving this venerable hotel with its treasured beach.

Continue on to ❽ **Heritage Park** (p148) and a romantic view of the dhows floating two-abreast in the harbour opposite.

AL MARYAH ISLAND PROMENADE — PROMENADE

Map p136 (⌚24hr) This promenade bends gently round the western shore of Al Maryah Island and offers fantastic views of Abu Dhabi and the busy channel of water in between. Used as a venue for a lavish Christmas market and New Year's fireworks, and linking an assortment of trend-setting cafes and bistros, the promenade is already a meeting place for Abu Dhabi's elite. Notable buildings along the 2km route include the upmarket Galleria, and the Cleveland Clinic that almost manages to make healthcare look inviting.

HERITAGE PARK — PARK

Map p136 (⌚24hr) This attractive family park straddles both sides of the far eastern end of the Corniche, with great views of the traditional dhow harbour across the water in Al Mina. With fountains and faux grottos, barbecue facilities and play areas, it is a popular picnic site at weekends.

EATING

Restaurants representing just about every country involved in Abu Dhabi's modern development are represented in the malls and back streets of Al Zahiyah, from British fish and chips, Baluchi mutton biryani, Indian vegetarian set lunches and Filipino chicken *adobo*. A government publication called 'Where to Eat' lists all these restaurants by type.

AUTOMATIC RESTAURANT — LEBANESE $

Map p136 (☎02-677 9782; Hamdan St, Al Zahiyah; mains around Dh30; ⌚8am-3pm) No one has really got to the bottom of the name of this chain of unlicenced restaurants selling the local equivalent of fast food. But the name matters not, as the food (dips, grills and rocket salads) is automatically trustworthy and delicious. As Automatic Restaurants represent something of an institution across the Gulf, don't leave Abu Dhabi without at least one visit.

ABU DHABI CO-OP HYPERMARKET — SUPERMARKET $

Map p136 (☎02-645 9777; www.abudhabicoop.com/english; ground fl, Abu Dhabi Mall, 10th St; ⌚8am-midnight) Pick up the wherewithal for a barbecue here and head off to the Eastern Corniche or one of the city parks to cook it up.

FINZ — SEAFOOD $$

Map p136 (☎02-697 9011; www.rotana.com; Beach Rotana Hotel & Towers, Abu Dhabi Mall; mains Dh50-100; ⌚12.30-3.30pm & 7-11.30pm) Amble down the jetty and snuggle into a table at this wooden A-frame with terraces above the sea, order a cocktail and prepare for some of the finest seafood in town. Whether grilled, wok-cooked, baked or prepared in the tandoor oven, the results are invariably delicious.

GODIVA CHOCOLATE CAFÉ — CAFE $$

Map p136 (☎02-667 0717; www.galleria.ae; Galleria Mall, Al Maryah Island; coffee & cake Dh80; ⌚11am-10pm) What makes this indulgent cafe in the new Marina Mall an experience is the exceptional view of Abu Dhabi's Al Zahiyah district from the wall of windows in its mezzanine location. Beautiful cakes, pastries and chocolate-dipped strawberries are delights of the menu.

DRINKING & NIGHTLIFE

Drinking and nightlife has a gritty edge to it in this part of town, with echoes of the city's expat, oil-pioneering past ingrained in the carpets of many a faded hotel. The new developments around Al Maryah Island have begun to change all that, however, attracting a new generation of city wheelers and dealers with cash to spend.

★BENTLEY BISTRO & BAR — COCKTAIL BAR

Map p136 (☎02-626 2131; www.bentleybistro.com; Galleria Mall; mocktails/cocktails Dh30/40; ⌚8-2am) With a wicked assortment of carefully crafted mocktails and cocktails, this classy bar attracts a well-dressed clientele. Balance the drinks with upper-crust snacks, such as wagu-beef burgers and hand-cut chips. The bistro offers a classic European menu with a suitably first-class view of Abu Dhabi's skyline.

ALLY PALLY CORNER — PUB

(☎02-679 4777; www.alainpalacehotel.com; Al Ain Hotel; ⌚noon-1am) For something low-key in a city of high-brow, the Ally Pally's infamous pub is a good place for a retro vibe – or at least reminiscent of a bygone expat era. Quiet during the week, it metamorphoses at the weekend into the kind of venue that only solo men (or broad-minded couples) would appreciate.

LOCAL KNOWLEDGE

SHEESHA CAFES

The scent of apple and vanilla commonly fills the midnight air, accompanied by the low rumbling and mumbled conversations of assembled puffers and gurglers, dragging on velvet hoses. This is not a psychedelic dream, it's a *sheesha* (water pipe) cafe.

Sheesha cafes are spread across the sea rim from the inland parks of the Corniche to the terraces of Breakwater and offer a wonderful, non-alcoholic opportunity to engage with local people. Before you puff on a peach hubble-bubble, however, be aware that although they are not narcotic, *sheesha* pipes are just as nicotine-laden as cigarettes. In fact, the habit is regularly banned by local governments for being harmful to health, but is quickly returned to the streets by the will of the people.

If you're tempted to sniff out this redolent activity, here are some lively venues in the middle of the city:

- Planet Café
- Café Layali Zaman (p134)
- Level Lounge (p135)
- Tiara Resto Café (p134)
- Arabic Café (p143)
- Al Bateen Resort Yacht Club (p143)
- Havana Café & Restaurant (p143)
- Le Boulanger Marina Café (p143)

PLANET CAFÉ SHEESHA CAFE

Map p136 (02-676 7962; Hamdan St; mains Dh150; 8-1.30am Sat-Thu, noon-1.30am Fri) A hugely popular, independent cafe (women-friendly) that has nothing especially to write home about other than the sense of participating in a beloved local ritual. If you're keen on board games, then you'll have to be quick off the mark to reserve one.

ENTERTAINMENT

Head to any of the established four-star hotels in the area and you can rely on a DJ at the very least for entertainment.

49ER'S THE GOLD RUSH LIVE MUSIC

Map p136 (02-645 8000; www.aldiarhotels.com; Al Diar Dana Hotel, cnr Zayed the First & Al Firdous Sts; noon-3am) This long-running nightclub has earned its spurs over the years, with its Wild West theme, Stetsons, bucking bronco decorations, and built-in barbecue kitchen serving up Texas-sized steaks and fries. There's a resident band and a DJ.

GRAND CINEMAS ABU DHABI CINEMA

Map p136 (02-645 8988; www.grandcinemas.com; Level 3, Abu Dhabi Mall; tickets Dh35) This multiplex shows the latest Hollywood films, some of which are shown in 3D.

SHOPPING

With two of the city's main malls, the Galleria and the old favourite, Abu Dhabi Mall, most brands are covered if you're looking for fashion and interior design. The area has more to offer than marble aisles and shop windows, however, as an exploration of the area around Le Meridien shows: independent carpet, souvenir and craft shops here provide a refreshing break from the more uniform mall experience.

ABU DHABI MALL MALL

Map p136 (02-645 4858; www.abudhabi-mall.com; 10th St; 10am-10pm Sat-Wed, to 11pm Thu, 4-10pm Fri) This elegant mall has the expected 200 stores, cinemas and children's amusements, but it also has shops with a local twist. On Level 3, head for Arabesq sweets (from Syria, Oman, Lebanon, Jordan, and honey from Yemen) and the Al Rifai nut shop. On Level 1, Bateel dates make good gifts.

The discerning Emirati browser will buy *ouds* (perfumes) from Cambodia and India in the celebrated store called Yas – The Royal Name of Perfumes (Level 1). Also on Level 1, *abeyyas* (full-length black robes worn by women) cost around Dh1700 from Khunji, while men's delicate *bishts* (outer garment worn on ceremonial occasions) cost anything from Dh300 to Dh2000.

GRAND STORES SILVER

Map p136 (Abu Dhabi Mall; ⌚10am-10pm Sat-Wed, to 11pm Thu, 4-10pm Fri) To buy a gift for someone who has everything, you may like to hunt down a miniature silver oil rig complete with helicopter (Dh2315). More modest oil platforms go for half the price. This is also the place to buy a giant silver-plated falcon or dhow.

JASHANMAL DEPARTMENT STORE

Map p136 (☎02-644 3869; Abu Dhabi Mall; ⌚10am-10pm Sat-Wed, 10am-11pm Thu, 4-10pm Fri) Set up by an Indian businessman in 1919 in Basra, Iraq, this wholesale and retail enterprise has become the Gulf's answer to Debenhams or Macy's.

KHALIFA CENTRE SOUVENIRS, HANDICRAFTS

Map p136 (10th St; ⌚10am-1pm & 4-10pm Sat-Thu, 4-10pm Fri) For a wide range of souvenirs (*sheesha* pipes, camel-bone boxes, stuffed leather camels, carpets and cushion covers) head to the Khalifa Centre, across the road from the Abu Dhabi Mall, where you'll find a dozen independent stores, mostly run by the expat Indian community, selling handicrafts and carpets.

Most of the goods on sale are from India, Turkey and Syria and many are made in China, but it's a fun place to root around and try your bargaining skills.

GALLERIA MALL

Map p136 (☎02-616 6999; www.thegalleria.ae; Al Maryah Island; ⌚10am-10pm Sat-Wed, 10am-midnight Thu, noon-midnight Fri) One of the newest and most elegant shopping malls is being promoted as 'Abu Dhabi's foremost lifestyle destination' with valet parking, big-name designers and highly fashionable, internationally branded restaurants.

SPORTS & ACTIVITIES

SENSE SPA

Map p136 (☎02-813 5537; www.rosewoodhotels.com; Rosewood Hotel; 30min milk bath Dh280; ⌚10am-11pm) With nine treatment rooms, white leather lounges, and traditional hammams this is a temple of relaxation and therapy. It offers a master class in decadent design showcasing a marble soaking tub, bronze tiles, mist rooms, fibre-optic features, and an infra-red stone wall. Soak in a Cleopatra bath with goats' milk and the tub back home will never be the same again.

FUNRIDE – SHERATON CYCLING

Map p136 (☎02-556 6113; www.funridesports.com; Corniche Rd (East); per hr child/adult Dh15/20) One of the four stations along the Corniche where bikes may be hired. If this station is closed, the one outside the Hiltonia Health Club at the far southwestern end of the Corniche is more reliably staffed.

BEACH CLUB SWIMMING

Map p136 (☎02-697 9302; www.rotana.com; Beach Rotana Hotel & Towers, 10th St; ⌚6am-11pm, pool 8am-10pm) With a small but pleasant beach, swimming pools and a wet bar/cafe, this club welcomes day visitors. There's an increasingly impressive view of the Al Maryah Island developments opposite.

Sheikh Zayed Grand Mosque & Around

Three bridges straddle the approach from the mainland to Abu Dhabi Island, and from each there is one sight that dominates the view, namely Sheikh Zayed Grand Mosque. This exquisite building is not just an exceptional piece of architecture, it also represents the living soul of this heritage-minded emirate by providing a place of worship for thousands of the capital's residents and a memorial to the nation's founding father.

While the mosque is undoubtedly the key focus of the district from a visitor's perspective, there are other attractions in and around the southeastern end of the island, including the new developments of Bain al Jessrain.

SIGHTS

In addition to the Sheikh Zayed Grand Mosque, there are sights scattered across the lower end of Abu Dhabi Island but mostly they are not within walking distance. The Big Bus tour links the exhibition centre with the mosque and the Eastern Corniche but doesn't stray across to the mainland so taxis or car hire may offer the best way to visit this area.

★SHEIKH ZAYED GRAND MOSQUE
MOSQUE

Map p152 (☎02-441 6444; www.szgmc.ae; 2nd Sheikh Rashid bin Saeed al Maktoum St; ⊙9am-10pm Sat-Thu, 4.30-11pm Fri) FREE Rising majestically from beautifully manicured gardens and visible from each of the bridges joining Abu Dhabi Island to the mainland, the Shiekh Zayed Grand Mosque represents an impressive welcome to the city. Conceived by the first president of the UAE, Sheikh Zayed, and marking his final resting place, the mosque accommodates 40,000 worshippers and is one of the few regional mosques open to visitors.

With more than 80 marble domes dancing on a roofline held aloft by over 1000 pillars and punctuated by four 107m-high minarets, Sheikh Zayed Grand Mosque is a masterpiece of modern Islamic architecture and design. Over 100,000 tons of pure white Greek and Macedonian marble were used in the mosque's construction. Delicate modern floral designs inlaid with semi-precious stones, such as lapis lazuli, red agate, amethyst, abalone, jasper and mother-of-pearl, decorate a variety of marbles and contrast with the more traditional geometric ceramic details.

While including references to traditional Mamluk, Ottoman and Fatimid styles, the overwhelming impression of the breathtaking interior is contemporary and innovative, with three steel, gold, brass and crystal chandeliers filling the interior of the main prayer hall with shafts of primary coloured light. The chandeliers, the largest of which weighs approximately 12 tons, sparkle with Swarovski crystals and shine with 40kg of 24kt galvanised gold.

One of the prayer hall's most impressive features is the world's largest loomed carpet. The medallion design with elaborate arabesque motifs took 1200 artisans two years to complete, half of which was spent on hand knotting the 5700 sq metres of woollen thread on a cotton base. That translates as two billion, 268 million knots.

Visitors are welcome to enter the mosque except during prayer times. A worthwhile free 45-to-60-minute guided tour (in English and Arabic) helps explain some fundamentals of the Islamic religion while pointing out some of the stylistic highlights of the interior. These walk-in tours begin at 10am, 11am and 5pm from Sunday to Thursday, with an extra tour at 2pm on Saturday, and at 5pm and 7pm on Friday. Check the website for prayer timings, which change daily. Mosque etiquette requires all visitors to wear long, loose-fitting, ankle-length trousers or skirts, long sleeves and a headscarf for women. Alternatively, women can head for the basement where *abeyyas* with hoods are loaned for free.

Sheikh Zayed's mausoleum is on the approach to the mosque entrance. Prayers are continually recited by attendants here. While photographs are not permitted of the mausoleum, visitors are free to photograph all other parts of the mosque, but sensitivity should be shown towards those in prayer.

ℹ TOURIST INFORMATION

The **Abu Dhabi Tourism Authority** (ADTA; ☎toll free 800 555; www.visitabudhabi.ae) maintains information desks in the airport arrivals hall, Emirates Palace, Ferrari World and Souq Central Market. In addition, the following official websites give comprehensive tourist information:

Visit Abu Dhabi (www.visitabudhabi.ae) The city's main tourist-oriented website.

Abu Dhabi Tourism (www.abudhabitourism.ae) The website of the Abu Dhabi Tourism & Culture Authority.

Yas Island Information (www.yasisland.ae) A good online overview of what's on, when and where on Yas Island.

SHEIKH ZAYED GRAND MOSQUE CENTRE LIBRARY
LIBRARY

Map p152 (☎02-441 6444; www.szgmc.ae; 4th fl, North Minaret, Sheikh Zayed Grand Mosque; ⊙9.30am-4.30pm Sat, 9am-8pm Sun-Wed, to 4pm Thu) FREE With rare collections of Arabic calligraphy and copies of the Holy Quran dating back to the 16th century, this priceless collection of manuscripts is intended primarily as a research centre but is also open to public view. Part of the magic of the collection is its location in the mosque's minaret, giving an aerial perspective on the mosque's magnificent multiple domes and the city and outlying islands beyond.

Sheikh Zayed Grand Mosque & Around

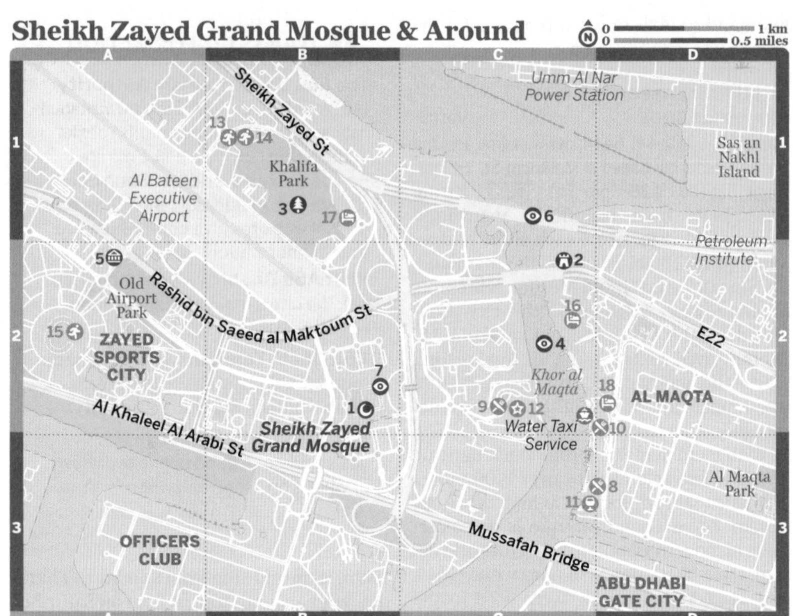

MIRAJ ISLAMIC CENTRE MUSEUM

Map p152 (☎02-650 5830; www.mirajabudhabi.com; ground fl, Hilton Abu Dhabi Capital Grand, Rashid bin Saeed al Maktoum St; ⏲9am-7pm) FREE Showcasing beautiful objects, including Persian carpets, calligraphy, ceramics and textiles, this private, museum-quality collection is open for view, with some pieces also for sale. There is a second showroom in the south-facing villas (Villa 14b) on the Breakwater, near Marina Mall.

KHOR AL MAQTA WATERFRONT

Map p152 (Bain al Jessrain) This historic waterway separates Abu Dhabi from the mainland, guarded by the now-somewhat hidden Al Maqta Fort and a small watchtower, on a rocky promontory in the middle of the *khor* (creek). Referred to by some as the 'Grand Canal', both sides of the *khor* have been developed as a luxury resort destination and the charming Souq Quriyat al Beri. Walking paths and *abras* (traditional water taxis) help visitors move between one attraction and the next. On the immediate horizon, Sheikh Zayed Grand Mosque graces the view, a beacon toward the city beyond.

AL MAQTA FORT & WATCHTOWER FORT

Map p152 (Al Maqta Bridge; ⏲24hr; interior closed) FREE Despite being one of the oldest sights in Abu Dhabi, this 200-year-old guardian of the city was restored and then more or less abandoned. The tourist information centre once housed there is also now closed. Although neglected, this old relic, with its companion watchtower on a rocky island in Khor al Maqta (the so-called Abu Dhabi Grand Canal), is worth an up-close view – if you can find it!

There are lots of brown signs leading to the fort, but it is frustratingly difficult to get to. Take the road into Al Maqta district, turn right at the first roundabout and follow the road leading under Al Maqta Bridge (an icon of the 1960s) to the fort, which is marooned in the middle of highways and building sites.

SHEIKH ZAYED BRIDGE BRIDGE

Map p152 Said to symbolise the flow of energy into the capital, this stunning modern bridge designed by Zaha Hadid is reputedly the most intricate bridge in the world. Its curvilinear form is reminiscent of sand dunes and at night the lighting scheme gives a sense that the dunes are on the move.

CAPITAL GATE BUILDING

Map p132 (☎02-596 1234; http://abudhabi.capitalgate.hyatt.com; Al Khaleej al Arabi St, ADNEC) Look out of the window from many points

Sheikh Zayed Grand Mosque & Around

Top Sights
1 Sheikh Zayed Grand Mosque B2

Sights
2 Al Maqta Fort & Watchtower C2
3 Khalifa Park B1
4 Khor al Maqta C2
5 Miraj Islamic Centre A2
6 Sheikh Zayed Bridge C1
7 Sheikh Zayed Grand Mosque Centre Library B2

Eating
8 Bord Eau D3
Marco Pierre White Steakhouse & Grill .... (see 16)
9 Mijana C2
Sho Cho .... (see 18)
10 Ushna D2

Drinking & Nightlife
Cooper's .... (see 17)
11 Eight C3

Entertainment
Chameleon .... (see 16)
12 Giornotte C2

Shopping
Souq Qaryat al Beri .... (see 18)

Sports & Activities
13 Byky Bike B1
Eton Institute .... (see 17)
14 Murjan Splash Park B1
15 Zayed Sports City A2

Sleeping
16 Fairmont Bab Al Bahr C2
17 Park Rotana Abu Dhabi B1
18 Traders Qaryat al Beri D2

in Abu Dhabi at night and you could be forgiven for thinking you've had one too many at the bar: the city's southeastern skyline is dominated by the odd sight of a dramatically listing skyscraper, all 35 floors of it. It is in the *Guinness Book of Records* as the world's most leaning building (at 18-degree westwards, it's over four times more wayward than the leaning tower of Pisa).

EASTERN CORNICHE PROMENADE
(New Corniche; Sheikh Zayed St) The seaward side of Sheikh Zayed St has been developed into a promenade to rival the main Corniche, with a series of landscaped gardens, parking bays, picnic areas and pathways. Offering excellent views of the mangroves, this is a good place to watch birds or dangle a line in the water. It gets busy on winter nights.

KHALIFA PARK PARK
Map p152 (www.adm.gov.ae; Al Salam St; adult/child under 10yr Dh1/free; ⏲8am-10pm Sun-Wed, to 11pm Thu-Sat) This large and leafy park, not far from the Sheikh Zayed Grand Mosque, has a number of attractions including a football playing area, fountains, ponds and waterfalls, lots of shaded seating, a children's amusement park and a small train that trundles around the site.

EATING

The hotels around Bain al Jessrain offer a cornucopia of exotic cuisines in fine dining venues, many of which feature spectacular views of Sheikh Zayed Grand Mosque. On the menu, locally caught seafood or the rich flavours of the Middle East predominate. It's advisable to book tables for many of these restaurants, particularly in high seasons (around the Western New Year and school holidays), during Islamic Eid festivals and during the Grand Prix weekend. Without a reservation, you won't go hungry as there are cafes at most places of interest, with the notable exception of Sheikh Zayed Grand Mosque, which discourages eating and drinking in the mosque's vicinity.

★**MIJANA** LEBANESE $$
Map p152 (☎02-818 8282; www.ritzcarlton.com; Ritz Carlton, Abu Dhabi Grand Canal; mains from Dh80; ⏲4pm-1am) Offering contemporary Lebanese cuisine with interesting twists on favourite themes, such as beetroot *moutabel* (smoked aubergine dip), six varieties of hummus and *habra niyah* – a raw mince lamb 'cooked' in fresh mint and garlic. Leave space for a camel's-milk smoothie or a signature-flavoured *sheesha* on the terrace with live Arabic music.

MARCO PIERRE WHITE STEAKHOUSE & GRILL STEAK $$$

Map p152 (☎02-654 3333; Fairmont Bab Al Bhar; meals around Dh250; ⏰7.30pm-midnight) Strictly carnivore in emphasis, this restaurant is the creation of British celebrity chef Marco Pierre White. A dramatic 'flame wall' gives the dining area a Dante-esque quality, but fortunately the culinary pyrotechnics produce heavenly results. The focus is squarely on quality cuts, prepared in both classic English style and innovative grilled variations.

USHNA INDIAN $$$

Map p152 (☎02-558 1769; Souq Qaryat al Beri, Bain al Jessrain; meals Dh250) The large Indian expat community helped to construct the modern shape of Abu Dhabi and they brought with them a cuisine that is now firmly established as a local favourite. There are many local curry houses across town but this restaurant offers some of the most refined flavours, with beautiful views across the capital's 'Grand Canal' to the Sheikh Zayed Grand Mosque.

SHO CHO JAPANESE $$$

Map p152 (☎02-558 1117; www.sho-cho.com; Souq Qaryat al Beri, Bain al Jessrain; mains Dh100-210; ✍) A stylish Japanese restaurant with appropriate minimalist decor. Dishes are delicious, if a tad minimalist, too. Don't miss the red snapper crisps starter or the delicate and decorative *maki* sushi rolls. There's a DJ at weekends. Reservations are essential. The Souq Qaryat al Beri is located 15km from the centre via the Airport Rd.

ℹ CAPITAL HEALTH CARE

The standard of health care in Abu Dhabi is generally high and emergency treatment is free. For locations of 24-hour pharmacies, call ☎777 929.

Pharmacies The **Dawn Pharmacy** (☎02-622 8295; www.dawnpharmacy.com; Hamdan & Liwa Sts, opposite Baroda Bank; ⏰24hr) in Al Markaziyah is one of many open 24 hours.

Hospitals The vast Sheikh Khalifa Medical City (p222) is one of numerous well-equipped hospitals in the city with 24-hour emergency service.

Clinics The Gulf Diagnostic Centre (p222) is a well-regarded private health centre.

BORD EAU FRENCH $$$

Map p152 (☎02-509 8888; www.shangri-la.com; Shangri-La Hotel, Qaryat al Beri; mains Dh90-150, 5-course blind tasting menu with wine Dh500; ⏰6.30-11.30pm) Bord Eau is *le* restaurant for French fine dining in Abu Dhabi. The classic French fare (onion soup, foie gras, chateaubriand) is flawlessly executed with a modern twist and the flavours are calibrated to perfection. With simple elegance (including reproduction Degas ballerinas gracing the walls), the ambience matches the refined quality of the food in this award-winning restaurant.

18° MEDITERRANEAN $$$

Map p132 (☎02-596 1440; www.abudhabi.capitalgate.hyatt.com; Hyatt Capital Gate, ADNEC, Al Khaleej al Arabi St; mains from Dh120; ⏰7-11.30pm, Fri brunch noon-3pm) Named after the degree of 'lean' in Abu Dhabi's famous Capital Gate (p152) skyscraper, and after the 18th floor on which it's situated, this Mediterranean-style restaurant offers many Levantine favourites. Watch your dinner being cooked at the three show kitchens or sit outside on the terrace and wonder how it is that food stays on the plate in this apparently leaning tower.

DRINKING & NIGHTLIFE

There are numerous lounge and bar options, serving mocktails and cocktails, scattered around the hotels on the eastern side of Khor al Maqta. Most of these nightspots are within ambling distance of each other along the paths that follow the water's edge. Souq Qaryat al Beri is at the heart of Bain al Jessrain, offering coffeeshops and cafes in a tasteful, modern rendition of an ancient souq.

COOPER'S BAR

Map p152 (☎02-657 3333; www.rotana.com; Park Rotana Abu Dhabi; ⏰noon-2.30am) A well-established bar, with an old-fashioned, wood-panelled, brass-trimmed ambience, this watering hole is renowned for its popular Ladies' Nights (Mondays to Fridays) with complimentary spirits.

RELAX@12 BAR

Map p132 (☎02-654 5183; www.relaxat12.com; Khaleej al Arabi St, near ADNEC, Aloft Abu Dhabi; ⏰5pm-2am Sun-Wed, to 3am Thu-Sat) This stylish rooftop bar indeed puts you in a mood for relaxing with mellow sounds, comfy seating and an extensive drinks menu that won't eviscerate your wallet. Sushi and tapas are available to help you stay stable and dancing is in the attached Club So-HI (Mondays to Fridays).

EIGHT BAR, CLUB

Map p152 (☎02-558 1988; Shangri-La Hotel, Souq Qaryat al Beri; ⌚8pm-4am) Popular with cabin crews, this libation station at the Shangri-La delivers a potent cocktail of style. At night it morphs into a hot-stepping club that on occasion gets some really peppery DJs from the international circuit to hit the turntables. Great views.

ENTERTAINMENT

Most entertainment in this part of the city takes the form of music designed to accompany dining or drinking. There are times, however, when the dining or drinking is an entertainment in its own right...

GIORNOTTE LIVE MUSIC

Map p152 (☎02-818 8282; www.ritzcarlton.com; Ritz-Carlton Grand Canal; Fri brunch with/without drinks Dh375/275; ⌚12.30-4pm Fri) Live piano music provides the entertainment for one of the city's best brunches. If that isn't entertainment enough, there are 27 live stations (chefs preparing food at counters in the restaurant), wagyu beef carving, a noodle-making show and oyster-opening, not to mention trips to a dedicated dessert room. For those who can resist the desire to sleep, a DJ takes the party into the Sorso Bar until the small hours.

CHAMELEON MIXOLOGY

Map p152 (☎02-654 3333; www.fairmont.com; Fairmont Bab al Bahr, Bain al Jessrain; cocktails around Dh50; ⌚6pm-1am) Cool cucumber mojitos, flaming Rosemary gimlets, and Smitten Watermelon Ritas are just some of the signature cocktails shaken but not stirred by the entertaining mixologists in this sophisticated lounge bar. A resident DJ adds to the fun from 10pm onwards.

SHOPPING

For those with an interest in local shopping, the streets of Al Maqta, inland from the tourist facilities of Bain al Jessrain, offer an interesting insight into local life. There are *abeyya* shops selling the latest diamanté-encrusted fashions, highly colourful frock shops selling the long dresses favoured by many local women, tailors selling men's *kandura* (men's long robes) and dozens of outlets selling traditional perfumes and water pipes. For a more visitor-oriented shopping experience head for Souq Qaryat al Beri.

★SOUQ QARYAT AL BERI MARKET

Map p152 (☎02-558 1670; ⌚10am-10pm) This 21st-century take on the classic souq gets thumbs up for its appealing Arabian architecture and waterfront location. The shops cater to a very different clientele than found at an authentic souq but many of the items on sale have their roots in Arabia, including exotic perfumes, chocolate-covered dates and hand-crafted jewellery. Some small stalls sell souvenirs and craft items. Next to the Shangri-La Hotel, between Maqta and Mussafah Bridges.

SPORTS & ACTIVITIES

It's probably fair to say that activities are not the main focus of a visit to this district, unless, that is, you are a dedicated sports fan. In that case, Zayed Sports City with its tournament-quality tennis courts and bowling alleys may be your kind of heaven. For family fun, head to Khalifa Park (p153) or explore the local mangroves by dhow.

ZAYED SPORTS CITY BOWLING

Map p152 (☎02-403 4648; www.zsc.ae; Al Khaleej al Arabi St; per game from Dh15; ⌚9-1am) Housing the Khalifa International Bowling Centre, this huge complex is open to the public; there are a somewhat intimidating 40 lanes of play. Also on site is an ice rink and professional tennis courts, venue of the Mubadala World Tennis Championship (p145), where you can play on the same court as your idol – though, sadly, not at the same time.

BYKY BIKE CYCLING

Map p152 (☎50-844 0556; www.q8byky.com; Khalifa Park, Sheikh Zayed St; per 30 mins Dh20) If you fancy a day in the saddle, Byky offers a selection of different people-powered vehicles from go-karts and bikes for four, to single-seater, Ferrari-licenced, pedal-powered karts. They have a popular station in Khalifa Park and also three outlets on the Corniche; the most reliably staffed is next to the Hiltonia Beach Club. Open October to April.

MURJAN SPLASH PARK WATER PARK
Map p152 (☎050-878 1009; www.murjansplash-park.weebly.com; Khalifa Park, Al Salam St; under/over 75cm free/Dh40; ⌚2-6pm & 7-11pm) Offering a range of children's activities including water slides, water guns, 'lazy river ride', trampolines and a 'surf wrangler' for learning surfing with an instructor present.

ABU DHABI PEARL JOURNEY CRUISE
Map p132 (☎02-641 9914; www.adpearljourney.com; Eastern Mangroves Hotel & Spa, Sheikh Zayed Rd; 90-min cruise adult/child under 12yr Dh500/400; ⌚cruises 9am-8pm) These walk-in tours, which leave when the boat reaches its maximum capacity of 18 passengers, tour the mangrove channels on a traditional dhow, *Jalboot*. Cruises include informative descriptions about Abu Dhabi's former heritage as a pearling village, demonstrate traditional seafaring songs and offer coffee and dates. Tours end with oyster-opening and the chance to keep the pearl.

ANANTARA SPA SPA
Map p132 (☎02-656 1146; www.abu-dhabi.anantara.com; Eastern Mangroves Hotel; 90min signature massage Dh765; ⌚10am-10pm) With 15 treatment rooms and facilities for couples, the best part of this spa is the traditional Turkish hammam. A celebration of marble, and mirrors, the spa feels fit for royalty.

WATER TAXI SERVICES

Traditional **water taxis** (Map p152; to Eastern Mangroves one way/return adult Dh50/80, child Dh30/50; ⌚6pm-midnight), called *abras*, ply the waters of Khor al Maqta, ferrying passengers for free from one five-star hotel to another. They also connect the hotels with Souq Qaryat al Beri.

A new service also links Khor al Maqta with the Eastern Mangroves Hotel & Spa (p169), stopping at the Eastern Corniche on the way. This service, which runs once an hour and takes 25 minutes one way, offers some of the best night-time views of Abu Dhabi.

Al Mina & Saadiyat Island

This neighbourhood casts an interesting light on Abu Dhabi's cultural inheritance, past and present, and affords a glimpse of the city's future as cultural capital of the Gulf with the Louvre, due to open in 2015. The port is home to the old dhow harbour and interesting souqs, while Saadiyat Island's sandy beaches and protected coastal environment offer a world removed from city life.

SIGHTS

The main sights of Saadiyat Island will be clustered within walking distance of Manarat Al Saadiyat, the equivalent of a visitors centre for the slowly evolving Abu Dhabi Cultural District. For now, this centre and the neighbouring UAE Pavilion, at the far western point of Saadiyat Island, are the only cultural sights, but that will change with the opening of the Louvre. Beaches and hotels are strung along the western shore beyond this area. The Yas Express links Saadiyat with Yas Island via the impressive Sheikh Khalifa bin Zayed Hwy.

★**MANARAT AL SAADIYAT** VISITOR CENTRE
Map p132 (☎02-657 5800; www.saadiyat.ae; Cultural District, Saadiyat Island; ⌚9am-8pm) FREE For a glimpse of Abu Dhabi's expansive ambitions of the future, a visit to Manarat Al Saadiyat (place of enlightenment) is an excellent way to understand the breadth of vision involved in creating a cultural hub from scratch. The visitor centre, housed in a piece of postmodern architecture with a honeycomb mantel, houses a permanent display of architectural models showcasing the key destinations planned for the Cultural District, and a contemporary gallery showing international exhibitions.

The permanent exhibition space charts the history of Abu Dhabi from the small pearling village of *barasti* houses of the 1970s to the cosmopolitan metropolis of today. The highlight of the exhibition, however, is undoubtedly the 'Saadiyat Experience' exhibition, which displays models of the Abu Dhabi Louvre (due to open in 2015), Sheikh Zayed

National Museum (2016) and the Guggenheim Abu Dhabi (2017). Also worth reading are the monographs of the international architects who won the contracts to build the densest cluster of world-class cultural destinations of the 21st century. Norman Foster's five-tower museum, for example, takes inspiration from the wing tips of falcons, while Frank Gehry's Guggenheim hints at ancient Emirati wind towers.

UAE PAVILION BUILDING

Map p132 (☎02-406 1501; www.saadiyatculturaldistrict.ae/; Cultural District, Saadiyat Island) FREE Shaped like two parallel sand dunes, smooth and curvaceous on the windward side, steep and rippled on the eroded side, this award-winning building by Sir Norman Foster and partners was designed for the 2010 Shanghai Expo. Now used as an exhibition space for touring cultural shows, this striking building is worth a visit in its own right. It particularly comes into its own in November when it hosts the Abu Dhabi contemporary art fair. It's next to Manarat Al Saadiyat.

ABU DHABI LOUVRE GALLERY

Map p132 (www.saadiyat.ae; Cultural District, Saadiyat Island) The Louvre, designed by Jean Nouvel, is well on the way to completion. Already the theme of palm-tree shading is detectable in the elaborate filigree domed roof, which seems to hover over the structure, and which will create a rain of light in the interior. Set to open at the end of 2015, the Louvre will form one of the leading collections of fine art (objects and paintings) in the world with loans from French museums.

If you want to know more about the concept of the collection, visit the website for a good explanation of the unique approach to displays that will transcend geographical boundaries and focus on cultural interconnectivity. While the gallery is still under construction, it's worth calling into the Saadiyat Experience in Manarat Al Saadiyat where you can see a full-scale model of the Louvre and interesting accounts of the inspiration behind its unique design.

AL MINA FISH MARKET MARKET

Map p136 (Dhow Harbour, Al Mina; ⏲5am-11pm) Never mind the prospect of lots of tasty seafood, the fish market is a visual feast of colour, texture and design. Rhythmical arrangements of prawns, orange-spotted trevally, blue-shelled crabs, red snappers, pink Sultan Ibrahims and a host of unlikely edibles from the sea straddle the ice bars of this large fish market.

FRUIT & VEGETABLE MARKET MARKET

Map p132 (Al Mina; ⏲24hr, shops 7am-midnight) This vast wholesale market, part of which is open-air, is the exchange point for melons from Jordan, potatoes from Turkey and onions from just about everywhere. The best part of a visit is cruising along dates alleyway where shops sell around 45 different varieties (from Dh25 per kilogram). Giant *majdool* dates from Saudi cost Dh65 per kilogram, while medicinal *ajwa* dates fetch Dh110 per kilo. Try the plump, yellow *sucri* dates, which are prized for their sweetness.

The friendly vendors (from India mostly) are happy to let you sample but it's polite to leave with a small purchase. If you buy fresh dates, choose half-ripe ones for the bittersweet contrast, and eat within a couple of days. Dried dates last a lifetime (well almost).

DHOW HARBOUR HARBOUR

Map p136 (Al Mina) There's nothing quite so fascinating as sitting by the harbourside watching these beautiful old wooden boats slip off to sea. At any time of day there's work going on as fishermen mend their nets, pile up lobster pots, hang out colourful sarongs to dry, unload fish and congregate for communal chats about the weather. Surveying the resting dhows strung together, five abreast, Abu Dhabi's modern backdrop can be almost forgotten and it's ancient past as a pearling village is revealed.

EATING

With limited residential areas on the island so far, eating is pretty much restricted to the hotels and the beach clubs. This is no hardship, however, as there are plenty of options to fit all budgets.

AL MINA MODERN CUISINE & RESTAURANT SEAFOOD $

Map p136 (☎02-673 3390; Al Mina; mains Dh45; ⏲noon-midnight) Most visitors steam on past this wonderful little restaurant in the hunt for its more famous neighbour, Al Arish Restaurant. That's a pity because the ambience in here is every bit as authentic, with lots of old photographs on the wall, pet fish in the aquarium and the catch of the day delivered virtually from dhow to dinner plate.

MATAM FIYROOM SEAFOOD $

Map p136 (Fish Market, Al Mina; set lunch from Dh6; ⏲5am-11pm) If you really want a flavour of how seafood is most enjoyed locally, nose round the back of the fish market, near the dry fish section. This tiny Indian restaurant (name in Arabic only) serves as a canteen for harbour hands and traders but they are accommodating to those looking to sample their delicious set platters of rice, fish, sambal and dhal.

★AL ARISH RESTAURANT MIDDLE EASTERN $$

Map p136 (☎673 2266; Al Mina; lunch & dinner buffet Dh175; ⏲noon-4.30pm & 7pm-midnight) This aged, flamboyant gem, with its fading Arabian decor, *barasti* ceiling and hand-carved furniture, sports a sumptuous *majlis* (lounge) that has entertained princes and sheikhs over the decades despite the unlikely harbourside venue. The lunch buffet offers one of the best opportunities in Abu Dhabi to sample local dishes, including *ouzi* (baked lamb) and *majboos* (chicken baked in rice). Al Arish supplies the buffet for the popular Al Dhafra evening dinner cruise.

BEACH HOUSE MEDITERRANEAN $$

Map p132 (☎02-407 1138; http://abudhabi.park.hyatt.com; Park Hyatt Abu Dhabi; mains from Dh60; ⏲9am-midnight) Open for breakfast, lunch and dinner this restaurant, with its emphasis on homely cooked Mediterranean fare, has an enviable location amid the sand dunes on the Saadiyat Island coast. In the cooler months, go up to the Beach House Rooftop (5pm to 1am) for arguably Abu Dhabi's best views of the sunset.

FANR RESTAURANT INTERNATIONAL $$

Map p132 (☎02-657 5888; www.fanrrestaurant.ae; Manarat Al Saadiyat, Saadiyat Island; mains Dh55; ⏲10am-11pm) This sophisticated casual dining restaurant, with floor-to-ceiling windows and dressed in shades of white like the exhibition space that surrounds it, offers some imaginative salads, smoothies, and regional and international favourites.

TURQUOIZ SEAFOOD $$

Map p132 (☎02-498 8888; www.turquoizabudhabi.com/; St Regis Saadiyat Island Resort; mains from Dh50; ⏲noon-3pm & 6.30-11pm) It would be hard to find a more romantic venue for a sunset drink, a bowl of mussels and an ambient waft of *sheesha*. Housed in a set of wooden pavilions with decked terraces overlooking the sea, this lovely restaurant feels a world away from the pseudo-Mediterranean hotel to which it belongs, let alone the city beyond.

A DAY IN THE DESERT

The great desert explorer, Wilfred Thesiger, claimed that no one could live like the Bedouin in the desert and remain unchanged. To get an inkling of what he meant, a day in the sand dunes, with their rhythm and their song (some whistle when it is windy), is a wonderful way to understand both Abu Dhabi's rich Bedouin heritage and also the city's remarkable growth against the physical odds.

Many tour companies offer exciting excursions into dunes and the oases of the Abu Dhabi Emirate. They offer an opportunity to learn about Bedouin traditions, to ride a camel, and appreciate the beauty of the desert and the surprisingly abundant life it harbours. Try to avoid companies that promote 'dune bashing': 4WD trips are a legitimate way of exploring the desert but tearing up the dunes with speed as the only objective is not the healthiest engagement with this fragile environment. The following companies are recommended:

Emirates Tours & Safari (☎02-491 2929; www.eatours.ae; half-day desert safari adult/child Dh290/200) Offering a half-day desert experience with barbecue.

Abu Dhabi Adventure Tours (☎055-484 2001; www.abudhabiadventure.com; evening desert safari per person Dh250) If time allows, take their overnight tour to Liwa, home to the largest sand dune in the UAE.

Arabian Adventures (☎02-691 1711; www.arabian-adventures.com; per person from Dh315) Sundowner tours leave late afternoon and return after dinner in the desert.

AL DHAFRA BUFFET, EMIRATI $$$

Map p136 (☎02-673 2266; Dhow Harbour, Al Mina; dinner cruise per person Dh180; ⏰cruise 8-10pm) This floating restaurant is on board a traditional dhow. The popular Al Arish Restaurant supplies the buffet for the nightly dinner cruise from Al Mina to the Breakwater and back. Al Dhafra offers a fun setting for sampling Emirati dishes while sitting cross-legged on sedans and cushions and enjoying stunning views of Abu Dhabi's night-time skyline.

DRINKING & NIGHTLIFE

DE LA COSTA LOUNGE

Map p132 (☎02-656 3572; Saadiyat Beach Club; ⏰4pm-midnight Sat-Wed, to 2am Thu & Fri) With a beautiful vista, comfortable armchairs and sophisticated tipples, this is a delightful place to watch the sun go down across the water.

NAVONA RESTAURANT & COFFEESHOP CAFE

Map p136 (Area 5, Dhow Harbour, Al Mina; coffee & cake from Dh20; ⏰9-3am Sat-Thu, from 11am Fri) After a dusty morning slipping in and out of hot aisles of merchandise, haggling with stall-holders and photographing life along the harbour, you may just fancy somewhere shady for a cold drink and a sandwich. Together with neighbouring Morka Restaurant, this unassuming cafe has indoor and outdoor seating and a chance to chat with expats from across the region.

ENTERTAINMENT

PEOPLE BY CRYSTAL ABU DHABI LIVE PERFORMANCE

Map p132 (☎050-297 2097; St Regis Saadiyat Island Resort; ⏰11pm-4am Thu & Fri) Offering what the promoters describe as a 'mash-up of house and urban music', this super-chic nightclub has international artists, theatrical and musical extravaganzas and high-tech projections on the sophisticated LED screens. Needless to say, given its location, it attracts Abu Dhabi's elite and delivers on its promise of a serious night out.

LOCAL KNOWLEDGE

DIY FISH SUPPER

For a memorable lunch or dinner for under Dh20, buy your fish at the market from the men in blue, and take it to the men in red in the gutting and filleting station. Take the fillets next door (alongside the dry fish section) and jostle with seafarers for your favourite spices. At the back of the spice area, give your purchases to the cooks, who will make it into a firey hot Kerralite fish curry or simply grill it rubbed in salt and dried chillies. Take the finished dish onto the dhow harbour outside, and sit on a lobster pot to eat it. It doesn't get fresher than that.

SHOPPING

CARPET SOUQ CARPETS

Map p136 (Al Mina; ⏰9am-11pm) Forget notions of bazaars selling fine Persian silk carpets, the carpet souq in Al Mina is far more authentic. This is where the average Gulf family comes to buy a carpet for the *majlis*, a new prayer rug or a set of cushions and floor-level settees upholstered in traditional Bedouin geometric patterns of red, black and green.

The garrulous traders from Baluchistan are very friendly but don't expect to leave without at least a cushion cover. There are a few tribal carpets rolled up at the back of various shops in the hope of attracting a Western buyer but most locals are looking for the wool-and-nylon pile numbers that are more easily washable. If you fancy a look at the tribal rugs (mostly from northern Pakistan and Afghanistan), be prepared to bargain hard.

IRANIAN SOUQ HOMEWARES

Map p136 (Al Mina; ⏰7am-midnight) If you've never been to a regional wholesale hardware market before, then this cramped collection of stalls huddled around the harbour edge is a fun destination. Aluminium cooking pots large enough to cook for a family of 14, melamine trays sporting European floral designs, Chinese plastic decorations, wickerware, thermoses and copper coffeepots are just some of the assorted imports in this lively souq. Look out for a few local crafts like rice mats (around Dh40).

SPORTS & ACTIVITIES

With sandy beaches and shallow seas, Saadiyat Island is ideal for water sports with both the hotels and the beach clubs offering a variety of waterborne craft and of course swimming. There's also a popular golf course open to the public.

ABU DHABI DHOW CRUISE CRUISE

Map p136 (☎052-214 4369; http://www.abudhabidhowcruise.com; Dhow Harbour, Al Mina; adult/child Dh200/100) This company offers lunch (1.30pm to 3pm), sunset (5.45pm to 6.45pm) and dinner cruises (8pm to 10pm). The food is simple fare but includes fresh fish. There is a minimum of 15 required for the lunch and sunset trips, which cruise along from the harbour. For an extra fee the company operates a pick-up service from major hotels.

SAADIYAT PUBLIC BEACH WATER SPORTS

Map p132 (BAKE Beach; www.bakeuae.com; Saadiyat Island; adult/child Dh25/15; ⏲8am-sunset) A boardwalk leads through a protected zone of coastal vegetation to this beautiful powdery white beach, home to nesting turtles, on the northwest coast of Saadiyat Island (near Park Hyatt Abu Dhabi). There's a lifeguard during daylight hours and towels are available for Dh10. Also for rent are kayaks (Dh80 per hour), skimboards (Dh50), paddle boats (Dh120) and body boards (Dh50). The club is unlicenced.

SAADIYAT BEACH CLUB SPA

Map p132 (☎02-656 3500; www.saadiyatbeachclub.ae; Saadiyat Island; weekend day rate adult/child/teen/couple Dh315/free/155/525; ⏲beach 9am-sunset, other facilities to 8pm) This luxurious and exclusive beach club, spa and fitness centre is open to day visitors and offers a full spa experience, beautiful pools and an expanse of pristine beach. Protected hawksbill turtles nest along the coast and the occasional school of dolphins is spotted in the turquoise waters.

Yas Island & Around

Helping to define Abu Dhabi as a dynamic destination, Yas Island has blossomed into the activities hub of the capital. While the Grand Prix attracts a global audience in November each year, there's much more to Yas Island than Formula One. Enjoy engineering wizzardry in Ferrari World rides and simulations, in the wave makers of Waterworld and in a restaurant where the burgers arrive by rollercoaster. As a rewarding contrast, explore the beautiful natural environment of the mangroves dotted along the edge of the Gulf in a number of ecofriendly adventures.

SIGHTS

Yas Island has been developed entirely with the visitor in mind, so there's a wealth of information on what to see and do. That said,

WORTH A DETOUR

ABU DHABI FALCON HOSPITAL

Standing by the front door of the hospital watching anxious owners from across the region delivering their hooded 'patients' in person, you will quickly realise that this is a much-needed and much-loved facility. Falcons are an integral part of traditional Gulf culture and no expense is spared in restoring these magnificent birds to full health, as a visit to this fascinating falcon hospital (the largest of its kind) shows. Tour reservations (bookable on line) are mandatory.

Guided tours include a visit to the falcon museum, the examination room and the free-flight aviary. If you're willing to brave an arm, these well-behaved raptors will perch for a photograph.

Abu Dhabi Falcon Hospital (☎02-575 5155; www.falconhospital.com; Al Raha; 90min tour adult/child Dh170/60; ⏲tours 2pm Sat, 10am & 2pm Sun-Thu) is about 6km southeast of Abu Dhabi airport. Coming from central Abu Dhabi, follow Airport Rd (E20) to Sweihan Rd in the direction of Falah City; about 3km past the junction with Hwy E11 turn right after the water tank (before exit 30A) and follow the signs to the hospital.

WORTH A DETOUR

AL WATHBA RACE TRACK

Sporting colourful nose bags and matching blankets, the camels are the stars of the show at the **Al Wathba Race Track** (02-583 9200; Al Wathba; 7.30am & 2.30pm Thu-Sat Oct-Apr) FREE, 45km southeast of Abu Dhabi. Races are great fun, even just to watch the enthusiasm of the owners who drive alongside the track cheering their beloved animals along. Arrive 30 minutes ahead of the starting block to absorb the pre-race excitement.

the emphasis is less on sights than on activities, and a half-day tour by bike, on the Big Bus or the free Yas Express, is enough for a good flavour of the main points of interest if you haven't the time or inclination to get more involved.

★YAS MARINA CIRCUIT — RACING CIRCUIT

Map p162 (02-659 9800; www.yasmarinacircuit.ae; tours Dh120; tours 10am-noon & 2-4pm Tue-Sat) While this circuit explodes into life during the Abu Dhabi Grand Prix every November, it's an interesting place to explore at any time of year. Visitors can go behind the scenes of this marina-side track, with stops at the support pit garages, the media centre and the paddock area included in the tour.

Tours are arranged through Yas Central (p165), the gateway to the Yas Marina Circuit. You can also drive and cycle on the track in various guided and solo experiences, and jogging enthusiasts can trot along the circuit from 6pm to 9pm on Tuesdays.

★MASDAR CITY — GREEN COMMUNITY

Map p162 (toll free 800 627 327; www.masdar.ae; btwn Hwys E10 & E20, just west of airport; 8.30am-4.30pm Sun-Thu) As part of a pioneering, environmentally friendly community, Masdar City residents pride themselves on their green credentials. The city is open to formal visits, arranged through the Masdar City website, as well as to the casually curious who need to see it to believe it. Download the excellent City Tour Map for a 90-minute walking route, and also see the website for info about healthy lunches at the Organic Foods & Café and rides on the driverless Personal Rapid Transit (PRT) system.

With cities occupying around 2% of the world's land mass but demanding 80% of the world's resources and being responsible for 75% of its carbon emissions, this eco-project is exploring ways of minimising the negative environmental impact of increasing urbanisation through solar and other green technologies. The community, which is one day expected to house 40,000 residents and attract an additional 50,000 commuters, is built around a research hub, the Masdar Institute of Science and Technology. This graduate university pioneers various innovative projects that explore sustainable technologies for energy production, desalination and water conservation, electricity-driven transport, energy-saving building techniques and greener building materials.

MUSICAL FOUNTAINS — FOUNTAINS

Map p162 (Yas Marina) These fountains are fun for kids during the day and spectacular when set to music at night. Enjoy them on a promenade around the marina.

YAS BEACH — BEACH

Map p162 (07-534 8729; www.yasbeach.ae; Yas Island; adult/child under 8yr/child 9-16yr Dh100/free/50, half price Sun-Wed; 10am-7pm Sun-Wed, to 10pm Fri & Sat) A surprisingly low-key corner of this high-tech island, Yas Beach is a lovely place to relax and enjoy the sea views, dabble in some water sports or generally chill with a cool beer. The kitchen rustles up grilled local fish and other tasty light bites. A DJ plays soothing sounds on Fridays. Day admission includes towel, sunbed, parasol and showers.

ALDAR HQ — BUILDING

Map p162 (Al Bandar) This remarkable building dubbed 'The Coin' has become a landmark of the Abu Dhabi suburbs, visible from afar and highly distinctive given its giant penny-shaped architecture. The world's first circular skyscraper, this slender-width monument to modern design houses Aldar, one of the largest property developers in the Emirates.

EATING

There are some truly memorable restaurants on Yas Island, serving the signature dishes of various famous international

Yas Island & Around

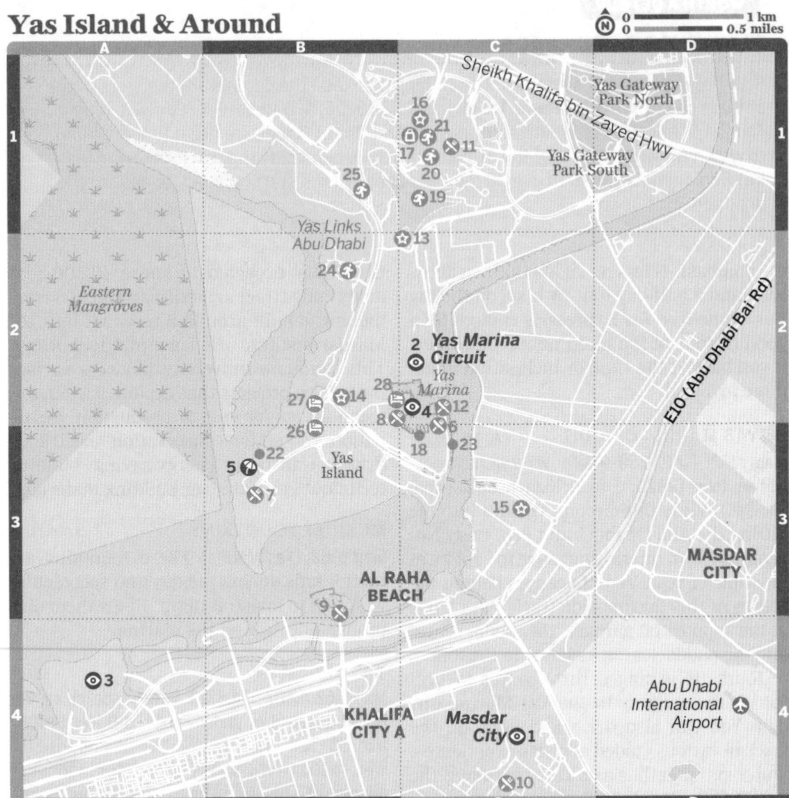

kitchens. Just as memorable, for those with an interest in nature, is a deli sandwich eaten in the company of herons and lurking dugongs on a sandspit out at sea.

C.DELI SANDWICHES $

Map p162 (☎02-656 4444; Centro Yas Island; sandwiches around Dh35; ⏲24hr) If you don't fancy a full dinner at a restaurant but would still like something tasty, then the all-day deli concept at the Rotana gives you the flexibility of a gourmet snack that you can take to your own favourite Yas Island haunt.

ORGANIC FOODS & CAFÉ SANDWICHES $

Map p162 (☎02-557 1406; www.organicfoodsandcafe.com; Masdar City; sandwiches from Dh30; ⏲9.30am-7pm Sat-Thu) This deli and organic store makes an ideal place to grab a sandwich for a picnic in the courtyards of Masdar Institute's campus, or you can sit in for friendly service.

★AQUARIUM SEAFOOD $$

Map p162 (☎02-917 5605; Yas Marina; dishes Dh60; ⏲noon-midnight) With stunning floor-to-ceiling aquariums gracing the interior of this casual-dining restaurant, there's no doubting its speciality. With indoor and outdoor seating, it makes a lovely lunchtime venue for Arabian-caught, Asian-prepared seafood, including sushi and sashimi on Sundays. Themed nights (including classic English fish and chips) are about to broaden the menu further.

ROGO'S BURGERS $$

Map p162 (☎02-565 0888; www.rollercoaster-restaurant.com; Level 1, Yas Mall, Yas Island West; meals around Dh55; ⏲noon-11pm) If you haven't got the stomach for Ferrari World, you may muster more of an appetite for this novel rollercoaster restaurant. Two conveyor belts deliver your meal from the kitchen via a pair of 12m-high tornado (spiral), double-loops, lifts and other engineering wizardry.

Yas Island & Around

Top Sights
1 Masdar City C4
2 Yas Marina Circuit C2

Sights
3 Aldar HQ A4
4 Musical Fountains C2
5 Yas Beach B3

Eating
6 Aquarium C3
7 C.Deli B3
8 Cipriani B2
9 Nolu's Café B3
10 Organic Foods & Café C4
11 Rogo's C1
12 Rozanah C2

Drinking & Nightlife
Iris .... (see 12)
Stills Bar & Brasserie .... (see 27)

Entertainment
Burlesque Restaurant & Lounge .... (see 28)
13 Du Arena C2
14 Du Forum B2
15 O1NE C3
16 Vox Cinemas C1

Shopping
Saturday Market .... (see 28)
17 Yas Mall C1

Sports & Activities
18 Captain Tony's C3
19 Ferrari World Abu Dhabi C1
20 Fun Works C1
Funride - Yas Island .... (see 27)
21 iPILOT C1
22 Noukhada Adventure Company B3
23 Seawings C3
Snow City .... (see 21)
Watercooled .... (see 12)
Yas Central .... (see 2)
24 Yas Links Abu Dhabi B2
25 Yas Waterworld B1

Sleeping
26 Centro Yas Island B3
27 Crowne Plaza Abu Dhabi Yas Island B2
28 Viceroy Yas Abu Dhabi B2

Food of indifferent flavour is delivered in metal pots on plastic trays, and ordered via tablet.

NOLU'S CAFÉ FUSION $$

Map p162 (☎02-557 9500; www.noluscafe.com; Al Bandar; meals Dh100; ⏰8am-10pm Sat-Wed, to 11pm Thu & Fri) Those in the know have been extolling the virtues of this trendy, modern cafe ever since it opened. With its starburst abstract panels and its lime green decor, it feels more California than Abu Dhabi, but the secret recipes of the owner's Afghani mother shine a delightfully regional light on little-known Afghani specialities such as *aushak*, *bolani* and *korma challow*. Next to Spinney's.

ROZANAH LEBANESE $$$

Map p162 (☎02-496 3411; www.rozanah.ae; Yas Marina; meal Dh300; ⏰noon-2am) This restaurant is in a perfect spot for watching the sun set, and its panoramic views are accompanied by delicious hot and cold mezze and a post-supper *sheesha*. Movable walls and ceilings allow for alfresco dining in the winter and air-con in the summer.

CIPRIANI ITALIAN $$$

Map p162 (☎02-657 5400; www.cipriani.com; Yas Marina; mains around Dh150; ⏰6pm-midnight) The cuisine at this renowned restaurant may be Italian (including a lot of signature dishes from world-famous Harry's Bar in Venice) but the view is distinctly Emirates. The terrace looks out over the grandstands of the Yas Marina Circuit, designer yachts moored alongside and the Yas Viceroy, with its mantel of amethyst and diamond lights.

DRINKING & NIGHTLIFE

Yas Island is a party place, lit up with lasers and innovative, ambient light shows, and with licenced bars offering themed nights in all the hotels. If you like your nights early, though, you may have come to the wrong place!

IRIS BAR

Map p162 (☎55-160 5636; www.irisabudhabi.com; Yas Marina; ⏰6pm-3am) The wooden outdoor furniture gives a rustic angle to

WORTH A DETOUR

ARABIAN SALUKI CENTRE

You'll probably hear them before you see them as a howl goes up when a visitor approaches this hound pound. A visit to the **Arabian Saluki Centre** (☎02-575 5330; www.arabiansaluki.ae) FREE involves entering the kennels, meeting the affectionate and well-looked-after residents, picking up a puppy or two and perhaps watching bath-time. The Centre is in the Falcon Hospital Complex; prebook an appointment.

Prized for their hunting skills and their speed over long distances, salukis have for centuries been man's best friend to the Bedu, and after a visit to this breeding and training centre it's easy to see why.

Originating in China, the saluki is thought to be one of the first breeds of dog to be domesticated and their speed, tolerance to high temperatures and intelligence made them the perfect companions for nomadic communities who used them to catch rabbits and other small game. While there's not much call for their skills in the desert these days, they remain a beloved part of the Arabian Peninsula heritage with pure-bred, well-behaved dogs fetching thousands of dirhams.

Many are bred to race and, according to the *Guinness Book of Records*, a saluki holds the record for four-legged speed at 68.8km/h, clocked up in 1996. Their beauty is also prized and dogs are paraded before judges for their pride, stride and condition of coat. To see these wonderful, shaggy eared dogs in action, visit the 10-day Al Dhafra Festival, in the deserts of Madinat Zayed in the Western Region of the Abu Dhabi Emirate.

this relaxed bar in the middle of a high-tech destination at the heart of Yas Island. With occasional live jazz adding to the mellow atmosphere, this a companionable venue for sundowners.

STILLS BAR & BRASSERIE BAR

Map p162 (☎02-656 3053; www.ichotelsgroup.com; Crowne Plaza, Yas Island; ⊙noon-1am, Ladies' Nights 8-11pm Thu) Boasting the longest bar in Abu Dhabi and with live entertainment, this is a lively spot for a cocktail.

ENTERTAINMENT

Yas Island's middle name is entertainment and, in addition to the Grand Prix, it attracts some of the biggest names in music at two purpose-built arenas.

DU ARENA CONCERT VENUE

Map p162 (☎02-509 8000; www.live.du.ae; www.ticketmaster.ae; Yas Island) This exceptional outdoor entertainment venue (formerly known as Yas Arena) regularly hosts the big names of the regional and Western music world. With excellent acoustics and a unique cooling system, this venue has become one of the must-do stops on international tours. Tickets are available through UAE's Ticketmaster website.

DU FORUM CONCERT VENUE

Map p162 (www.duforum.ae) This striking indoor entertainment venue holds art exhibitions, concerts, comedy shows and sports events. Unlike the other Yas Island entertainment venue, Du Arena, it is fully air conditioned, allowing for big-ticket acts such as Tom Jones and events such as the Oktoberfest to take place year round.

BURLESQUE RESTAURANT & LOUNGE CABARET

Map p162 (☎056-498 7580; www.burlesqueuae.com; Viceroy Yas Abu Dhabi, Yas Island; show/set menu per person Dh400; ⊙7pm-2am Sat & Mon-Wed, to 4am Thu & Fri) The star of the show at this red-velvet venue with scarlet, high-backed sofas and opulent drapes is the Friday cabaret (9.30pm to 11.30pm), with extravagant singing, dancing and live acts. From 11.30pm join centre stage with the After Show party's glamorous DJs.

O1NE DANCE

Map p162 (☎052-788 8111; www.o1neyasisland.com/; Yas Island; ⊙11pm-late Thu & Fri) For clubbers, this is one venue clearly remembered in the morning. A total of 19 international graffiti artists used 6000 cans to spray-paint the 3000-sq-metre exterior walls of the club. Arrive in style in a matching limousine and enjoy world-class artists and six resident DJs doing their thing in a unique interior of 3D projected images.

VOX CINEMAS CINEMA

Map p162 (☎600 599 905; uae.voxcinemas.com; Level 1, Yas Mall, Yas Island West; tickets from around Dh35; ⊙9am-midnight) If you like to smell the rubber on your car chase and feel the earth rumble as screaming tyres race across a 24.5m screen, then the 4D experience at Vox Cinema's XD Theatre won't disappoint. Book online.

SHOPPING

There wasn't much in the way of shopping on Yas Island until recently but the mega Yas Mall changed all that when it opened at the end of 2014. However, mall shopping isn't the only buyer's experience worth having on the island – those in the know head for the local craft market at the marina on Saturdays.

YAS MALL MALL

Map p162 (☎toll free 800 927 6255; www.yasmall.ae; Yas West; ⊙10am-10pm Sat-Wed, to midnight Thu & Fri) Bright and spacious and with 55 trees and a growing plant wall, Yas Mall is the latest addition to the Abu Dhabi megashopping scene. Look out for two 12m-high, tree-themed sculptures by acclaimed South African artist Marco Cianfanelli, with leaves inspired by Arabic calligraphy. There's access to Ferrari World, cinemas, Xtreme Zone entertainment and a Géant hypermarket.

SATURDAY MARKET CRAFTS

Map p162 (info@tinybeanevents.com; Yas Marina; ⊙1-6pm Sat) Tired of the impersonal mall experience? Then you may like to head for this open-air weekly market featuring crafts, printed cottons, watercolour paintings, novelty gifts and souvenirs from stalls arranged along the promenade.

SPORTS & ACTIVITIES

A dedicated activity enthusiast could spend a week or more trying out all the high-octane attractions on Yas Island. For those with less energy or a preference for a more natural pace of life, there are lots of water sports on offer.

★FERRARI WORLD ABU DHABI AMUSEMENT PARK

Map p162 (☎02-496 8000; www.ferrariworldabudhabi.com; Yas Island; adult/child under 1.3m Dh250/205, premium admission Dh450/365; ⊙11am-8pm; seasonal variations) If you want bragging rights to having 'done' Formula Rossa, the world's fastest roller coaster, visit this temple of torque and celebration of all things Ferrari in a spectacular building on Yas Island. Accelerating from zero to 240km/h in 4.9 seconds, this is as close to an F1 experience as most of us are likely to get.

Tamer diversions include a flume ride through a V12 engine, a motion-simulator that lets you ride shotgun with a racecar champion, and an imaginative 4D adventure. There's also a somewhat saner roller coaster that has you 'race' a Ferrari F430 Spider around the track. Between thrills, check out the car exhibitions or live shows.

YAS CENTRAL CAR DRIVING

Map p162 (☎02-659 9800; www.yasmarinacircuit.com; Yas Island; driver/passenger rides from Dh1700/500; ⊙9am-11pm) Outside of the racing calendar, Yas Central (the commercial hub of Yas Marina Circuit) offers several opportunities to experience the Yas Marina Circuit up close – so close in fact, that there seems to be only a friction burn between

WORTH A DETOUR

EMIRATES NATIONAL AUTO MUSEUM

If a spin round the Yas Marina Circuit has whetted your appetite for all things automobile, then a trip out to the **Emirates National Auto Museum** (☎05-749 2155; www.enam.ae; Hwy E65; admission Dh50; ⊙8am-6pm) is recommended. A hangar-sized homage to the car, the museum is some 45km south of Abu Dhabi, on the lonely Hwy E65 that leads to Liwa Oasis. The pyramid-shaped structure holds 250 vehicles – from concept cars to American classics – and includes a steam-powered Mercedes from 1885.

The museum is the private collection of Sheikh Hamad bin Hamdan al Nahyan, aka the 'Rainbow Sheikh'. In 1983 the sheikh bought seven Mercedes 500 SELs, one for each day of the week, painted in the colours of the rainbow, and all seven are on display in the museum. The car park is the resting place of several iconic vehicles, including the sheikh's monster truck, an eight-bedroom motorhome complete with balcony, and the Globe Trailer dubbed the 'earth on wheels'.

you and the race track. Opt to drive a racing car on your own, book three laps in the passenger seat, or bring your own car on a drag night. Bookings need to be made a week in advance either online or by phone.

YAS WATERWORLD WATER PARK

Map p162 (02-414 2000; www.yaswaterworld.com; Yas Island; adult/child Dh240/195, fast pass Dh440/365; 10am-6pm Nov-Feb, to 7pm Mar-May, Sep & Oct, to 8pm Jun-Aug) The UAE's most elaborate waterpark offers opportunities to get soaked on 43 rides, slides and other liquid attractions as you follow Emirati cartoon character, Dana, on her quest for a magical pearl. A wave pool, two lazy rivers and sunbeds offer relaxing alternatives to the rides if you're just looking to beat the Gulf heat.

With four thrill levels, there are rides for the fearful as well as the fearless. Top draws include the Bandit Bomber rollercoaster with water and laser effects; a hair-raising slide called Liwa Loop; and Dawwama, a wild tornado ride through a 20m-high funnel that takes a gravity-defying 1½ minutes. In contrast to other waterparks, Yas Waterworld leaves you in no doubt about your destination: there's even a pearl-diving show, *barasti* shelters and a souq to complement the heritage theme.

SEAWINGS SCENIC FLIGHTS

Map p162 (01-120 0000; www.seawings.ae; Yas Marina; scenic tour per person Dh895) If you like to make a bit of a splash on entry, then consider arriving in Yas Island by seaplane. The scenic tour takes 25 minutes and takes off from the sea at either the Emirates Palace or Yas Marina. Book online.

IPILOT FLIGHT SIMULATOR

Map p162 (50-507 5660; www.flyipilot.ae; Yas Mall, Yas Island West; 15min Dh349) Ever fancied landing an Airbus A380 or a Boeing 737 at Kai Tak Airport in Hong Kong (or 24,000 other airports around the world)? Now it's possible with the help of experienced pilots in the cockpit of these flight simulators – this is one heck of a ride. A fear-of-flying program is also available. Bookings online.

NOUKHADA ADVENTURE COMPANY KAYAKING

Map p162 (02-558 1889; http://noukhada.ae/; Yas Beach, Yas Island; kayaking tours adult/child from Dh220/170 (minimum of 4); 8.30am-5.30pm) Specialising in local exploration by paddle, this tour company runs popular kayaking trips through the local mangrove swamps. A 90-minute tour is a great way to experience this unusual habitat. The two-hour Eco Tour gives an even deeper understanding of this unique environment and there's even a full moon tour once a month (adults only, Dh200).

This company also runs sailing adventures with chances to see water birds such as waders, gulls, herons and flamingos and possible sightings of dolphins. Hobie 16 (Dh300 per hour) and Hobie 18 (Dh400 per hour) boats are available for hire (minimum two hours). Stand-up paddling (SUP), snorkelling and cycling are conducted through Noukhada, and, for a serious workout, they arrange bike rides around the Yas Marina Circuit.

WATERCOOLED WATER SPORTS

Map p162 (02-406 2022; www.watercooled-dubai.com/abu-dhabi/; Yas Marina) Offering wakeboarding, waterskiing, wake-surfing, kite-surfing, knee-boarding and mono-skiing plus SUP yoga, kayaking and towed inflatables, this company (reputedly the best for water sports in the UAE) has its finger on the pulse of the latest idea trending on H_2O. Powerboating instruction is also offered.

YAS LINKS ABU DHABI GOLF

Map p162 (02-810 7777; www.yaslinks.com; Yas Island; visitor rates 18 holes Dh599 Sun-Thu, Dh899 Fri & Sat; practice facilities/clubhouse 24hr) This beautiful 18-hole championship course, the first links course in the Middle East, was designed by Kyle Phillips and is partially set among mangroves.

CAPTAIN TONY'S CRUISE

Map p162 (02-650 7175; http://captaintonys.ae/; Gangway 3, Yas Marina; 90min sunset cruise adult/child Dh250/150; 4.30pm, times vary with season) Offering a wide range of cruises with an ecofriendly approach, this company runs the relaxing and popular sunset tour, ecotours to the mangroves, and a four-hour escape to a natural sand bar with sandwiches, umbrellas, deckchairs, buckets and spades. SUP and fishing is also on offer.

FUNRIDE – YAS ISLAND CYCLING

Map p162 (02-445 5838, 02-441 3264; www.funridesports.com; Crowne Plaza, Yas Island; per hr adult/child Dh30/20; 9am-8pm, tour 6-9pm Tue & Wed) Hire a bike and enjoy the well-crafted cycle track (complete with water stations) running around the main sights of Yas Island. For a good overview of the island's highlights, take the twice-weekly guided cycle tour (around Dh110).

FUN WORKS RIDES

Map p162 (☎02-565 1242; www.funworks.ae; Yas Mall, Yas Island West; ⏰9am-10pm) With bouncy buildings, rides, rooms to reconstruct, play stations and toys, the 6300 sq metres of interative play targeted at fun learning is guaranteed to keep kids amused for hours.

SNOW CITY AMUSEMENT PARK

Map p162 (www.yasmall.ae; Yas Mall, Yas Island West; ⏰10am-10pm Sat-Wed, to midnight Thu & Fri) Build your own igloo, sledge through a snow storm, skate, ski and snowmobile in Abu Dhabi's answer to the famous Ski Dubai.

SLEEPING

Downtown

AL JAZEERA ROYAL HOTEL HOTEL $

Map p136 (☎02-632 1100; www.aljaziraroyal.ae; opposite Madinat Zayed Shopping & Gold Centre; r from Dh280;) With some of the cheapest rates in town, this friendly little hotel opposite the gold souq largely caters for Indian and Asian business clientele and has an excellent, low-key Indian restaurant, Al Ibrahimi (p132), on site. This is a good place to get a feel for local life and, appropriately, it doesn't have a bar.

AL DIAR REGENCY HOTEL HOTEL $

Map p136 (☎02-676 5000; www.aldiarhotels.com; Al Meena St; r from Dh250;) Performing a pretty good sister act with Al Diar Mina over the road, this hotel caters for those on a limited budget. Guests can use the facilities of either hotel, the combined entertainments of which include a gym, a popular karaoke club and bars.

★**CROWNE PLAZA ABU DHABI** HOTEL $$

Map p136 (☎02-616 6166; www.crowneplaza.com; Hamdan St; r from Dh540;) This thoroughly amenable hotel, with its generous rooms and grand views of the city, knows exactly how to please its guests. Emphasis is on providing excellent service and a sociable experience, which is accomplished through the highly popular pan-Asian restaurant and lounge, Cho Gao (p134), Heroes bar and a rooftop cocktail bar.

BEACH ROTANA HOTEL & TOWERS HOTEL $$

Map p136 (☎02-697 9011; www.rotana.com; 10th St; r from Dh600;) Joined at the hip to the ever-popular Abu Dhabi Mall, this hotel has become a firm city favourite despite targeting conference-goers. Staff manage to keep several hundred guests happy when they have just spent a harrowing day with the credit card at the mall next door.

ACCOMMODATION IN ABU DHABI

There are essentially two types of hotel in Abu Dhabi, the five-star luxury beach resort and the midrange city hotel. Respected business chains such as Ibis offer the best-value budget accommodation. There is a growing trend for 'dry' hotels that do not serve alcohol and these are generally good value, too. Generally, spending more on accommodation in Abu Dhabi pays disproportionate dividends.

Promotional discounts are on offer in beach resorts and city hotels throughout the year, especially during the summer months (April to September). Here's a brief outline of the main accommodation districts in Abu Dhabi:

Downtown (Al Markaziyah East & Al Zahiyah) Good-value, midrange favourites are scattered in walking distance of the key Downtown sights.

Western Corniche Top-notch hotels are clustered at the end of the Corniche and promise an exceptional experience in the region's best pleasure domes.

Khor al Maqta Offering great dining, Grand Mosque views and a beach by the *khor* (creek), hotels here are neither 'city' nor 'seaside' and feel a tad raw.

Islands Saadiyat is home to luxury beach resorts, Yas to activity-based hotels good for weekend breaks, and Al Maryah promises new urban chic. Look out, too, for the brand-new Zaya Nurai Island – a luxurious resort complex off Saadiyat Island.

SHERATON ABU DHABI HOTEL & RESORT RESORT $$

Map p136 (☎02-677 3333; www.sheratonabudhabihotel.com; Corniche Rd (East); r from Dh500; P@🛜🏊) A visitor could be forgiven for taking one look at the outside of this particularly pink hotel and running off to the competition. That would be a pity, however, as this old war horse is a city centre icon in which to unwind in the landscaped garden or dip a toe in the private lagoon.

Western Corniche

★**INTERCONTINENTAL ABU DHABI** HOTEL $$

Map p136 (☎02-666 6888; www.intercontinental.com/AbuDhabi; Bainunah St, Al Bateen; r from Dh760; P⊖❄@🛜🏊) The InterContinental hotels in the Gulf region may not be the most 'des res' addresses in town, but they are invariably favourites with local residents. The InterCon in Abu Dhabi is no exception, offering excellent service, large rooms, carefully targeted amenities (such as a private beach and marina), the best fish restaurant in town and lots of quality live entertainment.

KHALIDIYA PALACE RAYHAAN BY ROTANA HOTEL $$

Map p136 (☎02-657 0000; www.rotana.com; Corniche Rd (West); r from Dh670; P@🛜🏊) With a large beach, pools and landscaped gardens, facilities aimed at children (such as 'mini-me' climbing frames, swings and a crèche) and a relaxed atmosphere, this unlicenced hotel has established a following among local families seeking a weekend getaway. There's an authentic Arabic restaurant, Kamoon, equally popular with locals.

★**EMIRATES PALACE** HOTEL $$$

Map p136 (☎02-690 9000; www.emiratespalace.com; Corniche Rd (West); r from Dh1900; @🛜🏊) While this remarkable Abu Dhabi landmark is a destination in its own right, offering excellent entertainment and restaurants, an overnight stay enhances what is already a class act. Features of the experience include 24-hour butler service, daily fresh flowers in the rooms, temperature-controlled swimming pools and resident-only beaches. The concierge can book tickets, order a limousine and, of course, arrange helicopter transfers. A kids' club helps entertain youngsters while ma and pa can spa in peace.

HOTEL BOOKING SITES

Lonely Planet Hotels (www.hotels.lonelyplanet.com) Lonely Planet's online booking service with the lowdown on the best places to stay.

Visit Abu Dhabi (www.visitabudhabi.ae) The city's official tourism website gives useful information including places to stay.

Abu Dhabi Bookings & City Guide (www.abudhabi.com) Covers a wide selection of capital hotels.

Dnata (www.dnatatravel.com) A local listing of hotels in Abu Dhabi.

JUMEIRAH AT ETIHAD TOWERS HOTEL $$$

Map p136 (☎02-811 5555; www.jumeirah.com; Corniche Rd (West); r from Dh1260; P@🛜🏊) This exceptional hotel, occupying one of a group of five landmark towers that rise from the end of the Corniche like polished organ pipes, lives up to the group's tagline: 'Stay Different'. Aimed at top executives, international conference attendees and well-heeled visitors, the hotel has top-class restaurants (including Scott's; p142), an observation deck, luxury spa, private beach and adjacent mall.

Khor al Maqta

IBIS HOTEL ABU DHABI GATE HOTEL $

Map p132 (☎02-509 0999; www.ibis.com; Rd 34, Bain al Jessrain; r from Dh255; P⊖❄🛜) One of the few modern budget hotels in Abu Dhabi, it offers excellent value for money. Midway between town and airport and intended primarily as a business hotel, the Ibis has small but comfortable rooms, a quiet location and a pleasant terrace. Free access is offered to the pool and gym at the Novotel Abu Dhabi Gate next door.

PARK ROTANA ABU DHABI HOTEL $$

Map p152 (☎02-657 3333; www.rotana.com; Salam St, Khalifa Park; r from Dh560; P⊖❄@🛜🏊) One of the more affordable five-star hotels, the Park Rotana is conveniently located for visiting the Grand Mosque and the exhibition centre. Built on the edge of Abu Dhabi's biggest park, a stroll before dinner is *de rigueur*. Dining options range from a British pub to a chef's table at Teatro, a pan-Asian restaurant.

TRADERS QARYAT AL BERI HOTEL **$$**

Map p152 (☎02-510 8880; www.kuoni.co.uk; Qaryat al Beri, Bain al Jessrain; r from Dh550; P@≋) With a pop art vibe and bright colours in the lobby, this offers a funky alternative to the standard marble and crystal of neighbouring hotels. Rooms are subdued but spacious. A private beach is an attractive feature and residents can use the facilities of nearby Shangri-La Qaryat al Beri for free. Some of the city's best restaurants are a stroll away.

FAIRMONT BAB AL BAHR HOTEL **$$**

Map p152 (☎02-654 3000; www.fairmont.com; r from Dh650; P@≋) With stark glass facade and rectilinear night-lighting, this hotel resembles an office complex, but inside the vast atrium, dramatic chandeliers and textured surfaces signal a sophisticated accommodation. Rooms are richly dressed in wood and marble with unparalleled views of Sheikh Zayed Grand Mosque. Special features include a Chocolate Gallery cafe, star chef Marco Pierre White's flagship restaurant (p154) and Friday brunch.

EASTERN MANGROVES HOTEL & SPA HOTEL **$$$**

Map p132 (☎02-656 1000; www.abu-dhabi.anantara.com; Eastern Ring Rd, Salam St; d from Dh1000; P@≋) Stepping into the lobby with its *mashrabiya* patterns and *oud* player, it's clear that Arab hospitality is taken seriously at this luxurious accommodation. Overlooking the eponymous mangroves (kayak tours available), rooms are soothingly furnished in teal green. Work up an appetite in the infinity pool before grazing on Arabic mezze prepared in the Impressions restaurant. Sheikh sightings distinctly possible.

Islands

CENTRO YAS ISLAND HOTEL **$**

Map p162 (☎02-656 4444; www.rotana.com; Golf Plaza, Yas Island; r from Dh360; P@≋) A good-value option in the centre of the hotel district of Yas Island, this contemporary hotel with compact rooms is a decent choice for the budget conscious and attracts a younger crowd. There is no beach access but rates include access to the luxurious facilities at the adjacent Yas Island Rotana.

CROWNE PLAZA ABU DHABI YAS ISLAND HOTEL **$$**

Map p162 (☎02-656 3000; www.ihg.com; Yas Island; r from Dh570; P@≋) This friendly hotel with hospitable staff and comfortable rooms overlooks the Yas Links, the island golf course, and the Gulf beyond in a complex of hotels near the Yas Marina Circuit. Home to a popular night spot, Stills (p164), and a Lebanese restaurant, Barouk, the hotel also hosts a bike rental – the perfect way of getting around the island attractions.

VICEROY YAS ABU DHABI HOTEL **$$**

Map p162 (☎02-656 0000; www.viceroyhotelsandresorts.com; Yas Island; from Dh850; P@≋) Appealing especially to race-goers, this dramatic hotel sits in pole position on Yas Island, literally straddling the Yas Marina Circuit. The avant-garde, steel-and-glass structure with its corrugated mantel flung over the race track is dramatically studded with lights at night, and the blue-white interior, reminiscent of an ice hotel, is a haven of cool in the Gulf heat.

Prices go through the roof at this hotel during the Grand Prix and rooms are booked months in advance.

PARK HYATT ABU DHABI RESORT **$$$**

Map p132 (☎02-407 1234; abudhabi.park.hyatt.com; Saadiyat Island; r from Dh1300; P@≋) Encompassing a long stretch of white, sandy beach surrounded by a protected nature reserve, an infinity pool where you feel eye-to-eye with the ripples of the open Gulf, and an 18-hole championship golf course designed by Gary Player, this beautiful low-rise luxury hotel offers a perfect retreat from the city.

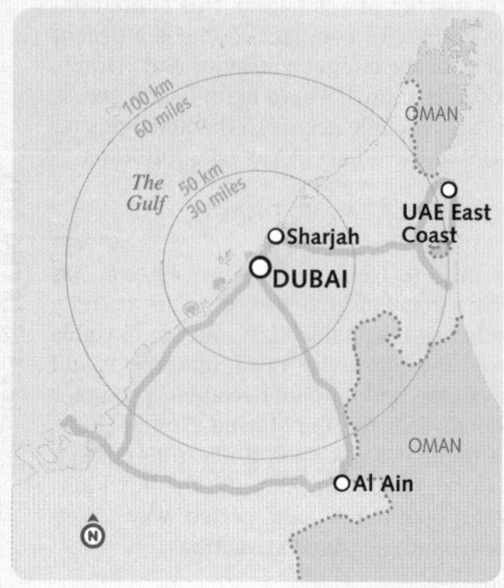

Day Trips from Dubai & Abu Dhabi

Sharjah p171
Dubai's northern neighbour, the emirate of Sharjah, is almost joined at the hip to Dubai's suburbs. Once there, however, particularly around the restored central Heritage and Arts Area, this cultured and heritage-oriented emirate feels like a world apart.

Al Ain p173
The famous Al Ain oasis, with wonderful forts, museums and even ancient Bronze Age burial sites, offers a rural retreat after the frantic pace of Dubai.

UAE East Coast p176
Sleepy fishing villages, rugged mountains, desert dunes, museums and the oldest mosque in the United Arab Emirates (UAE) bring the rest of the Arabian Peninsula within a day trip of the Gulf cities.

Sharjah

Explore

Long before Abu Dhabi began improving its cultural credentials, Sharjah was declared the Unesco Cultural Capital of the Arab World – and deservedly so. Once you have penetrated the confusing outskirts of town, the historic old town, located north across Sharjah Bridge, is easy to navigate on foot. Plan on setting aside several hours to explore its Heritage and Arts Area, as well as the souqs and excellent museums.

One caveat: Sharjah takes its decency laws very seriously, so do dress modestly. That means no exposed knees, backs or bellies – and that goes for both men and women. It's also the only emirate that is 'dry' (ie no alcohol is available anywhere).

The Best...

- **Sight** Sharjah Museum of Islamic Civilisation
- **Place to Eat** Shababeek (p172)
- **Place to Shop** Central Souq (p172)

Top Tip

If you're visiting more than one museum in Sharjah, a 'Multi-Museum Ticket' will save you some dirhams. These cost Dh15 for individuals and Dh20 for families and are good for admission to several museums, as well as a few smaller venues. You can pick them up at any of the museums or the tourist office.

Getting There & Away

- **Bus** Buses to Sharjah's Al Jubail station near the Central Souq and Heritage and Arts Area depart every 10 minutes from Al Ittihad station in Deira and from Al Ghubaiba station in Bur Dubai. The ride takes about 40 to 60 minutes and costs Dh10. From Abu Dhabi there's a bus from the main bus station every 30 minutes from 5am to 11pm (Dh30, minimum three hours).
- **Car** From the World Trade Centre roundabout in Dubai, take the E11 (Sheikh Zayed Rd) north to Sharjah where it's called Al Ittihad Rd. Traffic can be horrible, especially during rush hours, so it's best to travel in the late morning and late evening. The drive can take from 30 minutes to two hours, depending on traffic. Add another one hour 50 minutes if coming from Abu Dhabi along the E11.
- **Taxi** A taxi from Dubai starts at about Dh60, Dh20 of which is a tax that the taxi driver has to pay to the Sharjah authorities.

Need to Know

- **Area Code** ☎06
- **Location** 15km north of Dubai; 166km north east of Abu Dhabi.
- **Tourist Office** (☎06-556 6777; www.sharjah-welcome.com; 9th fl, Crescent Tower, Buheirah Corniche, Al Majaz; 7.30am-2.30pm Sat-Thu)

SHARJAH MUSEUM OF ISLAMIC CIVILISATION MUSEUM

(☎06-565 5455; www.islamicmuseum.ae; cnr Corniche & Arabian Gulf St; adult/child Dh5/free; ⏲8am-8pm Sat-Thu, 4-8pm Fri) Pretty much everything you always wanted to know about Islam is addressed in this well-curated museum in a converted souq right on the waterfront. The ground-floor galleries zero in on different aspects of the Islamic faith, such as the Five Pillars of Islam, including the ritual and importance of hajj. Other rooms trace Arab scientific accomplishments, especially in mathematics and astronomy, while the upper floor navigates through 1400 years of Islamic art and artefacts with manuscripts, ceramics, armour, woodwork, textiles and jewellery.

BAIT AL NABOODAH HISTORIC SITE

(☎06-568 1738; www.sharjahmuseums.ae; Heritage Area, off Corniche; adult/child Dh5/free; ⏲8am-8pm Sat-Thu, 4-8pm Fri) This 1845 house, a former pearl trader's home with a grand entranceway, elaborately carved decorations and an ample courtyard, is a fine example of early Emirati architecture and daily living. Head upstairs for close ups of the pretty porch.

SHARJAH ART MUSEUM MUSEUM

(☎06-568 8222; www.sharjahmuseums.ae; Arts Area, off Corniche; ⏲8am-8pm Sat-Thu, 4-8pm Fri) FREE Just east of the Heritage Area, the Arts Area is anchored by one of the region's largest and most impressive art museums and the organiser of the Sharjah Biennal. Its galleries are a great place to keep tabs on Arab contemporary art, including works by Biennial winners and such established artists as UAE painter Abdul Qader Al Raes. Watercolours of historic Sharjah by Ali Darwish also get a lot of wall space, as do paintings by 18th- and 19th-century European Orientalists.

A highlight here are the dozen lithographs by Scottish artist David Robert.

Curators keep things dynamic by mounting monthly changing exhibits, and there's a nice cafe to boot. Many of the surrounding historic buildings contain galleries, workshops and studios, including one for disabled artists.

SHARJAH DESERT PARK ZOO

(☎06-531 1999; www.breedingcentresharjah.com; adult/child Dh15/5; ⏱9am-6pm Sun, Mon, Wed, & Thu, 2-6pm Fri, 11am-6pm Sat) About 26km east of central Sharjah towards Al Dhaid, Sharjah Desert Park packs four venues into a 1-sq-km package. The main attraction is the Arabian Wildlife Centre, a zoo and breeding centre showcasing the diversity of critters that call the region home.

AL QASBA & AL MAJAZ CANAL

(Al Khan; ) South of the Khalid Lagoon, popular Al Qasba is an attractively landscaped and lively mix of restaurants, cafes and entertainment venues along a canal. Diversions include a Ferris wheel, *abra* (traditional water taxi) rides on the lagoon, and a superb contemporary art gallery, the Maraya Art Centre, which opened in 2011. Next door is the emirate's latest waterfront project, Al Majaz, another family-friendly development with fountains, playgrounds, jogging paths and green spaces.

SHARJAH AQUARIUM AQUARIUM

(☎06-528 5288; sharjahmuseums.ae; Al Meena St (far west end); adult/child incl Maritime Museum Dh25/15; ⏱8am-8pm Mon-Thu & Sat, 4-10pm Fri) Enter an 'abandoned dhow' for close ups of maritime creatures from the UAE's west and east coast without getting your feet wet. Moray eels lurk, black-tip reef sharks prowl, eagle rays flop and jellyfish dance around tanks that re-create Dibba Rock, mangroves, Shark Island's coral reefs and other local watery habitats. We like the touchscreens, but a few more labels wouldn't hurt.

SHARJAH MARITIME MUSEUM MUSEUM

(☎06-522 2002; http://sharjahmuseums.ae; Al Meena St (far west end); adult/child Dh10/5; ⏱8am-8pm Sat-Thu, 4-8pm Fri) For a salty introduction to the UAE, visit this charming museum that displays enough traditional dhows, exhibits on pearling and fishing equipment to keep your imagination afloat for a half hour or so.

EATING

★SHABABEEK LEBANESE $$

(☎06-554 0444; www.shababeek.ae; Block B, Qanat Al Qasba; mezze Dh18-26, mains Dh35-65; ⏱noon-11.30pm) With its deep-purple walls, black furniture and Arabic design flourishes, this chic Lebanese restaurant channels Dubai swish but without the attitude – or the alcohol. Portions are not huge but flavours are delicately paired and the selection way beyond the usual hummus, tabbouleh and kebabs.

SADAF IRANIAN $$

(☎06-569 3344; www.sadaffood.com; Al Mareija St; mains Dh40-80; ⏱lunch & dinner) The Sharjah branch of this popular mini-chain enjoys cult status among locals for its excellent authentic Iranian cuisine. The spicy, moist kebabs are particularly good and the *zereshk polo meat* (rice with red barberries and chicken or meat) is another solid choice. There are also plenty of other dining options on this street.

SHOPPING

CENTRAL SOUQ MARKET

(Blue Souq; near Al Ittihad Sq, east Khalid Lagoon; ⏱9am-1pm & 4-11pm Sat-Thu, 4-11pm Fri) The beautiful Central Souq occupies two structures designed in an appealing, if flashy, Arabic style. The ground floor has mostly modern jewellery, watches and designer clothing, while the little stores upstairs sell pashminas, rugs and curios from such far-flung places as Afghanistan and Rajasthan. If possible, visit in the evenings – only tourists shop here during the day.

SOUQ AL ARSAH MARKET

(Courtyard Souq; Heritage Area, off Corniche; ⏱9am-9pm Sat-Thu, 4-9pm Fri) One of the oldest souqs in the UAE (which in this case

DUBAI DESERT CONSERVATION RESERVE

On the outskirts of Sharjah, the 225-sq-km **Dubai Desert Conservation Reserve (www.ddcr.org)** accounts for 5% of the emirate's total land. The reserve was established in 1999 and has been involved in projects to reintroduce mountain gazelles, sand gazelles and Arabian oryx.

It's possible to stay inside the reserve at Al Maha Desert Resort & Spa (p188), designed as a model for super-luxury ecotourism. The reserve is divided into four zones, the third of which is only open to resort guests and the fourth to a small number of desert tour operators, including Arabian Adventures (p218), which offers less-costly ways of gaining admission than overnighting at the resort.

means about 50 years), Souq Al Arsah once crawled with traders from Persia and India and local Bedu stocking up on supplies, their camels fastened to posts outside. Despite a thorough facelift, it's still an atmospheric place, though vendors now vie for tourist dirham with pashminas, *dhallahs* (coffee pots), herbs and spices, old *khanjars* (daggers) and traditional jewellery in air-conditioned comfort.

SLEEPING

COPTHORNE HOTEL SHARJA HOTEL
(06-593 0555; www.milleniumhotels.ae; Corniche Rd, Al Buhaira; r from Dh40;) The Copthorne Hotel Sharja, overlooking Khalid Lagoon, is a recommended midrange hotel with comfortable rooms and a convenient location on the Corniche.

Al Ain

Explore

With markets, forts, museums and a famous date-palm oasis, Al Ain is a breath of fresh air after the frantic pace of Dubai. On the border with Oman, about a 90-minute drive out of town, the birthplace of Sheikh Zayed has greatly benefited from his patronage and passion for greening the desert; it's even nicknamed 'Garden City'. But the desert is never far away: simply driving the serpentine road up Jebel Hafeet will treat you to sweeping views of the arid splendour that is the Empty Quarter. Al Ain itself is an increasingly dynamic place with a couple of excellent museums, an archaeological park, a superb zoo and abundance of greenery.

Al Ain is quite tough to navigate due to the many roundabouts. Follow the brown signs.

The Best...

- **Sight** Sheikh Zayed Palace Museum (p174)
- **Place to Eat** Makani (p175)
- **Place to Drink** Trader Vic's (p175)

Top Tip

Plan your trip in time for some of the zoo's top experiences, such as feeding the giraffes, the parrot and bird shows and informative keeper talks. Check the zoo's comprehensive website (www.awpr.ae) for timings.

Getting There & Away

- **Car** Al Ain is a 90-minute drive along the E66 from Dubai or nearly two hours along the E22 from Abu Dhabi.
- **Public transport** Al Ghazal runs minibuses between Al Ain (Dh20, 1½ hours) and the Al Ghubaiba bus station in Dubai every hour from 6.30am to 11.30pm. There are also buses every 30 minutes from Abu Dhabi's main bus station between 4.30am and midnight (Dh25, 2¼ hours). Al Ain's bus station is off the Al Murabba roundabout opposite the Lulu Centre. A taxi to/from Dubai or Abu Dhabi will cost around Dh180.

Need to Know

- **Area Code** 03
- **Location** 160km southeast of Dubai and 175km east of Abu Dhabi.
- **Tourist Office** (03-784 3996; www.visitabudhabi.ae; Al Jahili Fort; 9am-5pm Tue-Thu, Sat & Sun, 3-5pm Fri)

SIGHTS

SHEIKH ZAYED PALACE MUSEUM — MUSEUM

(☎03-751 7755; www.adach.ae; cnr Al Ain & Sultan bin Zayed First Sts; ⊙8.30am-7.30pm Sat, Sun & Tue-Thu, 3-7.30pm Fri) FREE This nicely restored, rambling palace on the edge of Al Ain Oasis was Sheikh Zayed's residence from 1937 until 1966. It is a beautiful cinnamon-coloured building set around several courtyards amid beds of cacti, magnolia trees and lofty palms. You can step inside the *majlis* where the ruler received visitors, see his wife's curtained, canopied bed and snap a photo of the Land Rover he used to visit the desert Bedu.

AL AIN ZOO — ZOO

(☎03-782 8188; www.awpr.ae; off Zayed Al Awwal & Nahyan Al Awwal Sts; adult/child Dh20/10; ⊙9am-8pm Sat-Wed, to 9pm Thu & Fri Oct-May, 4-10pm Jun-Sep) The region's largest and most acclaimed zoo, founded by Sheikh Zayed in 1968, has spacious enclosures inhabited by both indigenous and exotic species. Observe grazing Arabian oryx, big-horned Barbary sheep, lazy crocodiles, tigers and lions and dozens of other species, some of them born at the zoo, which has a well-respected conservation and breeding program. Special treats for tots include the Elezba petting zoo, bird shows and giraffe feedings.

The foot-weary can hire golf-cart-style shuttles to take them around the nicely landscaped grounds, with hop-on and hop-off options at the main enclosures. There's also a reasonably priced cafeteria and lots of nice picnic spots.

THE FRAGILE DESERT

By supporting the Dubai Desert Conservation Reserve (p173) and limiting the area in which desert safari companies can operate to the environs of Al Awir, the government is taking important steps to protect the environment. To do your bit, stick to tracks wherever possible when driving off-road and avoid damaging vegetation. Don't drive in wadis: these are important sources of drinking water and can be polluted by oil and grease from cars. Finally, take your rubbish home with you.

AL AIN CAMEL MARKET — MARKET

(Zayed bin Sultan St, behind Bawadi Mall; ⊙7am-sunset) FREE It's dusty, noisy, pungent and chaotic, but never mind: Al Ain's famous camel market is a wonderful immersion in traditional Arabic culture that's so rare in the UAE today. All sorts of camels are holed up in pens, from wobbly legged babies that might grow up to be racers to imposing studs kept for breeding. The intense haggling is fun to watch. Trading takes place in the morning, but it's usually possible to see the corralled animals all day long.

Some traders may offer to give you a tour (for money) but you're totally free to walk around on your own. If you want to take photographs, ask first and perhaps offer a small tip.

The market is about 7km south of central Al Ain, near the Meyzad border crossing to Oman. Buses 900, 950, 960 and 980 stop at nearby Bawadi Mall.

AL AIN OASIS — OASIS

(☎763 0155; www.adach.ae; off Zayed bin Sultan St) FREE Seven gates lead into the great date plantations of this famous oasis. Try entering at Gate 2 (opposite Al Ain Souq) and follow the signs for the mosques along the paved route. You are free to wander around but there are no tourist facilities in the oasis and the signs don't always lead you to where they promise!

AL AIN NATIONAL MUSEUM — MUSEUM

(☎03-764 1595; www.adach.ae; Zayed bin Sultan St; adult/child Dh3/1; ⊙8.30am-7.30pm Sat, Sun & Tue-Thu, 3-7.30pm Fri) This charmingly old-fashioned museum is perfect for boning up on the ancient past of the Al Ain region. Highlights include ancient weapons, jewellery, pottery and other objects excavated from tombs at nearby Hili and Umm an-Nar, which date to the 3rd millennium BC.

The ethnography galleries zero in on various aspects of the daily life of the Bedu and settled people, including education, marriage and farming.

There's some beautiful silver jewellery, traditional costumes and a harrowing display of simple surgical instruments with lots of sharp points and hooks – ouch!

AL JAHILI FORT — HISTORIC SITE

(☎03-784 3996; Hazah St; 9am-5pm Sat, Sun & Tue-Thu, 3-5pm Fri) FREE Beautifully restored, this massive fort was built in 1890 by Sheikh Zayed I (1836–1909) as a summer residence.

WORTH A DETOUR

JEBEL HAFEET

Don't leave Al Ain without driving up Jebel Hafeet. This jagged, 1240m spine of limestone rears out of the plain south of Al Ain. A zigzag road snakes up to the **Mercure Grand Jebel Hafeet** (www.mercure.com; r Dh450;) and some coffee shops on the summit. The arid crags of the jebel (mountain) are home to red foxes, feral cats and the rock hyrax, which resembles a large rabbit but is improbably related to the elephant.

The virulently green slopes at the bottom of the mountain are fed by natural hot springs emanating from the mountainside. A small resort with a lake and giant fountain has grown up around the springs, with segregated bathing, camping and picnicking opportunities. The **Qemat Jebel Hafeet Restaurant & Cafeteria** (mains Dh30; 7am-midnight.) offers a good perch alongside the wadi with its shaded terrace and tasty snacks.

The top of Jebel Hafeet is about 30km from central Al Ain, including the 12km stretch of mountain road. From the town centre, head west on Khalifa bin Zayed St towards the airport, then follow the brown signs.

His grandson, UAE founding father Sheikh Zayed, may have been born here in this building in 1918. Today it houses a visitor information centre and small exhibits on Zayed I and on British explorer, writer and photographer Sir Wilfred Thesiger.

HILI ARCHAEOLOGICAL PARK ARCHAEOLOGICAL SITE

(www.adach.ae; Hili; 10am-1pm, families only 4-11pm) FREE Honoured as a Unesco World Heritage Site in 2011, this remarkable set of Bronze Age funeral chambers is protected by a peaceful park on the edge of town. Six hundred people were found buried in one of the tombs, interred over a period of 100 years.

EATING

SHAHRYAR IRANIAN $

(Al Ain Mall; dishes from Dh15) Located in the Al Ain Mall, near the camel market and souq (around 35km north of the centre), this simple, spotless eatery serves reliable Iranian staples, including kebabs, rice dishes and a tasty salad combo with tabbouleh, hummus and *fattoosh* (with strips of bread), along with fresh-from-the-oven traditional Iranian bread.

MAKANI LEBANESE $$

(Hilton Al Ain Mall; mains from Dh55; 6pm-1am) Meaning 'my place' in Arabic, the alfresco atmosphere is a delight, with plenty of palms and comfortable rattan-style furniture. Indulge in traditional Lebanese and Arabic specialities, many of which are prepared at your table. Live Arabic music creates a fitting accompaniment, as does the selection of Lebanese wines.

AL DIWAN RESTAURANT INTERNATIONAL $$

(03-764 4445; Khalifa St; mains Dh30-70; 8am-2am) Lebanese *shish tawooq* (marinated chicken grilled on skewers), margarita pizza, Mexican steak, Iranian yoghurt chicken – this big, bright eatery with floor-to-ceiling windows certainly covers all the bases. Judging by what's on the plates of diners, though, the grilled meats are the main reason the place retains its local-fave status.

DRINKING

TRADER VIC'S BAR

(03-754 5111; Al Ain Rotana Hotel, Zayed bin Sultan St; 12.30-3.30pm & 7.30-11.30pm) Sip exotic rum concoctions while taking in the trippy tiki decor and enjoying a wide choice of tasty bar snacks. Still hungry? Then consider booking a table for dinner when a live Cuban band will get your toes tapping between courses.

SLEEPING

DANAT AL AIN RESORT RESORT $$

(03-704 6000; http://alain.danathotels.com; cnr Khalid bin Sultan (147th) & Al Salam Sts; r from Dh700; P) Surrounded by lush gardens, this resort is good for families, with an attractive pool area and dedicated children's activities. Rooms are fairly bland but the restaurant choice is impressive, specialising in cuisines from East to West. The atmospheric Nawafeer Tent Lebanese restaurant has live music every night.

AL AIN ROTANA HOTEL HOTEL $$
(☎03-754 5111; www.rotana.com; Zayed bin Sultan St; d from Dh675; P 📶 🏊) This central, top-end hotel, with its soaring atrium, sunken pool bar and plush, spacious rooms with balconies, is another good choice.

UAE East Coast

Explore

The relentless drive to create the tallest, longest, biggest and best versions of just about everything has made Dubai and Abu Dhabi the star cities of 21st-century urban development. But while the mad developers of the city get ever closer to complete domination of the *Guinness World Records,* some of the villages and towns on the East Coast amble along as if in a completely different country. Tiny roadside mosques, date palms burdened with fruit, camels wandering down the middle of highways and pristine white-sand beaches with barely a hotel in sight are the attractions of this forgotten corner of the UAE.

Plan an early start if you're going just for the day. Catch the bull-butting in Fujairah (Fridays only) on the way home. There's dense traffic at weekends.

The Best...

- **Sight** Badiyah Mosque (p176)
- **Place to Eat** Al Meshwar (p177)
- **Place to Stay** Le Méridien Al Aqah Beach Resort (p177)

Top Tip

Although many of the beaches in the UAE look calm, they often have dangerous rip tides. If you are swimming at any of the beaches on the East Coast, be very careful as most are unpatrolled and there are regular reports of people drowning.

Getting There & Away

From Dubai it takes about 90 minutes to get to the East Coast; it takes three hours from Abu Dhabi.

- **Car** Take the E11 towards Sharjah and then head in the direction of Al Dhaid, on the E88. At Masafi you can take the E89 road heading north to Dibba or south to Fujairah; we recommend going north first to Dibba and then driving south along the coast.
- **Public transport** Minibuses to Fujairah leave from Al Ittihad station (corner of Omar ibn al Khattab & Al Rigga Rds) in Deira every 45 minutes and cost Dh30. It will cost over Dh250 if you go by taxi. A taxi from Fujairah to Al Aqah beach costs around Dh80. Unfortunately there's no public transport from Fujairah to Dubai, so you will have to return by taxi. There's no direct route from Abu Dhabi.

Need to Know

- **Area Code** ☎09
- **Location** 130km east of Dubai; 300km east of Abu Dhabi
- **Tourist Office** (☎09-223 1436; www.fujairah.ae; 9th fl, Fujairah Trade Centre Bldg, Hamad bin Abdullah Rd; ⏰8am-1pm Sat-Wed)

SIGHTS

BADIYAH MOSQUE MOSQUE
Map p244 (Dibba Rd (Hwy E99); ⏰7am-10pm) Badiyah (also spelt Bidyah and Bidiya) is known mainly for its mosque. Thought to be the oldest in the UAE (possibly dating back to the early 15th century), it's a small and simple structure, adorned with four pointed domes and resting on an internal pillar.

DIBBA VILLAGE
From Masafi, point the compass north and cut through the dramatically rugged Hajar Mountains to the sleepy fishing village of Dibba. This is the northernmost point of the 65km scenic East Coast highway to Fujairah, hemmed in by the Hajars, shimmering beaches and the turquoise expanse of the Gulf of Oman. The diving and snorkelling are still good here, despite the damaging effects of a prolonged red tide.

BEATING THE DRUM

Here's an environmentally friendly, social and entertaining way to see the desert: join a drum circle. **Dubai Drums** (www.dubaidrums.com) hosts regular full-moon drum circles (adult/child Dh250/100 including drum hire) in desert camps. Sessions usually last several hours and occasionally until the early hours of the morning. Watch for the near-legendary all-nighter events. Drums and a barbecue dinner are provided.

KHOR FAKKAN CORNICHE BEACH

(Khor Fakkan;) Khor Fakkan is home to a busy container port. Still, the town is not without its charms, especially along the Corniche, which extends for several kilometres and is flanked by palm trees, gardens, kiosks and a playground, making it popular with families for picnics and waterfront strolls.

EATING

IRANIAN PARS RESTAURANT IRANIAN $

(09-238 7787; cnr Corniche Rd & Sheikh Khalid bin Mohammed al Qassimi St, Khor Fakkan; mains Dh30-45; 11am-midnight) Locals give this simple restaurant the thumbs up for its generous portions of Persian cuisine – try the tasty *chelow kebab* (rice topped with a kebab) – served with enormous plates of delicious rice.

AL MESHWAR LEBANESE $$

(09-222 1113; Hamad bin Abdullah Rd, Fujairah; mezze Dh15-30, mains Dh25-80; 9-1am;) Simple fare – hummus, grilled meats, *sambousek* (meat pies) – is available at this highly popular local restaurant. There's a cosy *sheesha* lounge downstairs and more formal family dining upstairs.

SPORTS & ACTIVITIES

The beautiful stretch of beach south of Dibba is increasingly being snapped up by hotels and resorts and is one of the UAE's most popular diving sites.

AL BOOM DIVING DIVING

(04-342 2993; www.alboomdiving.com; Golden Tulip Hotel, Dibba; dives from Dh300, 3pm snorkel trip Dh150;) Covering most of the UAE, Al Boom is an excellent diving operation with several dive sites in the Musandam.

AL MARSA DIVING

(06-544 1232; www.almarsamusandam.com; Dibba; dives from Dh400, sunset cruise Dh150;) Based at Dibba harbour (with their main office in Sharjah), this reliable local diving operator offers a wide range of courses, including scuba diving, advanced courses, rescue and dive-master courses. Al Marsa also offers dhow trips, including a sunset cruise.

ABSOLUTE ADVENTURE OUTDOORS

(04-345 9900; www.adventure.ae; day trips from Dh350; Oct-Apr) Located near the Golden Tulip Hotel, this well-named outfit organises a wide range of activities including kayaking tours, trekking, mountain biking and camping in the Hajar Mountains.

SLEEPING

LE MÉRIDIEN AL AQAH BEACH RESORT RESORT $$

(09-244 9000; www.lemeridien-alaqah.com; Dibba Rd (Hwy E99); d Dh850;) With a beautiful location embracing a private beach, this resort offers top-end quality for midrange prices. The balconied rooms are spacious and overlook the lush gardens and Arabian Sea beyond. Almost a destination in its own right, you can dive, waterski, play volleyball or spend lazy days by the pool and enjoy a range of quality dining options at night.

Sleeping

Butler service, Rolls Royce limousines, champagne baths – only your imagination is the limit when it comes luxe lodging in Dubai. Yet the tiny turbo emirate offers the entire gamut of places to unpack your suitcase (yes, even a youth hostel), including boutique hotels, heritage B&Bs and, of course, just about every international hospitality brand under the sun.

Accommodation Options

Dubai has some 85,000 beds, a number that's expected to double in the run-up to World Expo 2020. With so much competition, standards are generally high and even most budget hotels deliver decent-sized rooms with at least a modicum of style, a private bathroom, cable TV and wi-fi.

Midrange hotels often have superb facilities, including a pool, multiple restaurants, a gym, satellite TV and a bar. Top end hotels boast the full spectrum of international-standard amenities plus perhaps a scenic location, great views and ritzy designer decor.

Beach resorts come with private beaches, fancy spas and an entire village worth of restaurants and bars. City hotels, especially in the Financial District, tend to flaunt corporate flair, with design and amenities to match.

Free wi-fi is commonplace, with only a few hotels charging as much Dh100 per day for access. In some hotels, access may be restricted to the public areas.

Most hotels have at least one snack bar or restaurant, although only the international four- and five-star properties serve alcohol.

By law, unmarried men and women are not permitted to share a room, but in reality most hotels turn a blind eye. Having two different last names is no tip-off, as most married Arab women keep their name.

Hotel Apartments

Although designed for long-term stays, hotel apartments are also a great way for wallet-watching travellers to economise in comfort. There are clusters of them in Bur Dubai behind the BurJuman Mall and in Al Barsha, next to the Mall of the Emirates, with a few scattered around Jumeirah and Dubai Marina. Available in various configurations from studios to two-bedroom apartments, they come with ample space, kitchenettes or full kitchens and daily room cleaning service. Facilities like a gym or pool are fairly standard, but onsite restaurants or bars are not. Rates start at Dh300 per night.

Boutique & Heritage Hotels

In a city where a 'bigger is better' mentality rules, boutique hotels have been slow to catch on but there is a growing number of charismatic heritage hotels. Located in Bur Dubai and Deira, they're essentially B&Bs set up in historic courtyard buildings and offering ample authenticity and sense of place. Travellers in need of buckets of privacy, high comfort levels or the latest tech amenities, however, may not feel as comfortable here.

Room Rates

Accommodation listings in this chapter are organised first by neighbourhood and then by budget. Room rates fluctuate enormously, spiking during festivals, holidays and big events and dropping in the summer months.

The best beds often sell out fast, so make reservations as early as possible if you've got your eye on a particular place. Most properties now have an internet booking function with a best-price guarantee.

Lonely Planet's Top Choices

XVA Hotel (p183) Connect to the magic of a bygone era in this art-filled heritage den.

One&Only Royal Mirage (p189) Sumptuous resort with lavish Arabian-style architecture and expansive gardens.

Pearl Marina Hotel Apartments (p188) All the charms of Dubai Marina at your feet without having to rob a bank.

Al Qasr Hotel (p186) Posh player with A-lister clientele, 2km of private beach and canalside dining.

Palace Downtown Dubai (p184) Romantic inner-city pad with easy access to top shopping and dreamy views of Burj Khalifa.

Best by Budget

$

Barjeel Heritage Guest House (p182) Dream sweetly at this Creekside charmer straight out of *Arabian Nights*.

Grand Midwest Tower (p187) Steps from a metro station, this city hotel offers four-star comforts at two-star prices.

Premier Inn Dubai International Airport (p181) Easy in, easy out at this airport-adjacent budget designer hotel.

$$

Centro Barsha (p186) Near Mall of the Emirates, this is an excellent value-for-money pick beloved by urban adventurers.

Beach Hotel Apartments (p186) Rare bargain in Jumeirah with a killer location and easy access to tanning and shopping.

Radisson Blu Hotel (p181) Oldie but goodie with skyline views across the Creek and some of Deira's best restaurants.

Media One Hotel (p188) High-octane hotspot with mod design, party pedigree and unpretentious attitude.

$$$

Grosvenor House (p189) Art deco–inspired hotel draws local cognoscenti galore to its hip bars and restaurants.

Park Hyatt Dubai (p182) Class act surrounded by lush landscaping with superb facilities and golf course access.

Mina A'Salam (p187) A warm beachfront port of call for blue-sky holiday cravers.

Raffles Dubai (p184) Slick, chic decor with water features and top-rated Japanese rooftop restaurant and lounge.

Best for Shopping

Kempinski Hotel Mall of the Emirates (p190) This alpine-themed city slicker is practically built into the Mall of the Emirates.

Address Dubai Mall (p185) No need to step outside to segue from this urban outpost straight to the Dubai Mall.

Arabian Courtyard Hotel & Spa (p183) Smack dab in bustling Bur Dubai, steps from the charismatic souqs.

Best City Escapes

Desert Palm Per Aquum (p188) Easy retreat from the urban hubbub makes for a perfect desert staycation.

One&Only The Palm (p189) Cocoon of quiet sophistication with kiss-worthy skyline views.

Al Maha Desert Resort (p188) Five-star Bedouin hideaway with sensuous spa.

Jumeirah Zabeel Saray (p189) Feel like royalty at this palace-style retreat.

NEED TO KNOW

Price Ranges

The following room rate breakdown serves only as a guideline. Listed rates refer to one night in a standard double room with private bathroom during high season (October to April) but outside of major events, festivals and Islamic holidays like *eid* (Islamic feast).

$	under Dh500
$$	Dh500–1000
$$$	over Dh1000

Tourism Tax

A 10% room tax and 10% service has long been added to room rates, but in March 2014 an additional tourism tax (ranging from Dh7 to Dh20 per night) was introduced to raise funds for World Expo 2020 projects.

Check-In & Check-Out

Flights arrive in Dubai at all hours, so be sure to confirm your check-in time with the hotel prior to arrival. The earliest check-in is generally at 2pm, although if the room is ready, early access is usually no problem. Checkout is 11am or noon.

Websites

➡ **www.lonelyplanet.com/hotels** Lonely Planet's online booking service.

➡ **www.visitdubai.com** The official tourist authority site also has a room booking function.

Where to Stay

Neighbourhood	For	Against
Deira	Atmospheric area near the Creek and souqs. The nicest places overlook the Creek, those closer to the airport often have excellent rates.	Noisy, chaotic. Budget choices can be brothels, so check carefully. Heavy traffic and nightmare parking during busy times of the day.
Bur Dubai	Value-priced hotel apartments cluster behind BurJuman Mall, international budget and midrange chains hug the main streets, and heritage boutique hotels are near the Creek.	Can be soulless away from Meena Bazaar (the souq area), lacking the atmosphere of Deira and the glitz of modern Dubai.
Downtown Dubai	In the midst of major sightseeing and shopping magnets, superb luxury hotels, excellent restaurants and trendy nightlife.	Horrendous rush-hour traffic, some distance from the sea. Expensive.
Jumeirah & Around	Good for beachfront hotels and Burj Al Arab views. Hotel apartments cluster near Mall of the Emirates.	Many hotels are a taxi ride from the nearest metro station. Shortage of budget options.
Dubai Marina & Palm Jumeirah	Super-ritzy beach hotels around the Marina and on the Palm, midrange places in Dubai Media City and Dubai Internet City. Terrific views, nightlife and gastro scene.	Cookie-cutter international chains can seem anonymous and don't provide a sense of place. Resorts on Palm Jumeirah are a long way from anywhere. Paucity of budget options.

Deira

PREMIER INN DUBAI INTERNATIONAL AIRPORT
HOTEL $

(04-885 0999; www.premierinn.com; 52nd St, opp Terminal 3; r from Dh350; P@; MAirport Terminal 3) If your plane lands late or leaves early, the Dubai airport outpost of this UK-based budget chain is a convenient place to check in. It delivers modern yet pocket-sized digs appealingly accented with the company's trademark purple. Plane-spotters can indulge their obsession while floating in the rooftop pool. Free airport shuttles run every 30 minutes.

DUBAI YOUTH HOSTEL
HOSTEL $

(04-298 8151; www.uaeyha.com; 39 Al Nahda Rd, Al Qusais; dm/s/d/tr incl breakfast HI members Dh110/220/260/330, nonmembers Dh120/230/270/360; reception 24hr; @; MStadium) Dubai's only hostel is north of the airport, far from most Dubai attractions but only a short walk from a metro station and a mall. The range of facilities (pool, tennis court, coffee shop and laundry) is impressive. Private rooms in the newer wing (Hostel A) come with TV, refrigerator and bathrooms. Amenities in the four-bed dorms in the older wings (Hostels B and C) are minimal. It's located between Lulu Hypermarket and Al Bustan Mall.

CORAL DUBAI DEIRA HOTEL
HOTEL $

Map p246 (04-224 8587; www.hmhhotelgroup.com; Al Muraqqabat Rd; d from Dh450; P@; MAl Rigga, Abu Baker Al Siddique) In a handy location near some of Deira's best budget restaurants, the Coral hides considerable comforts behind its business demeanor. The tone is set with the free welcome juice at check-in and continues all the way up to the good-sized rooftop pool. Handy assets include free parking and wi-fi. No alcohol.

LANDMARK HOTEL BANIYAS
HOTEL $

Map p244 (04-228 6666; http://landmarkhotels.net/baniyas; Baniyas Sq; d from Dh400; @; MBaniyas Sq) Just off Baniyas Sq, this is one of the better hotels in a hyper-busy business district near the Gold Souq. Rooms have laminate flooring, warm colours and enough space to feel comfortable, if not to do cartwheels. Instead, get the heart pumping in the well-equipped rooftop gym sitting next to a small pool with an atmospheric panorama of Deira.

AHMEDIA HERITAGE GUEST HOUSE
B&B $$

Map p244 (04-225 0085; www.ahmediaheritageguesthousedubai.com; Al Ras Rd; r incl breakfast Dh500; ; MAl Ras) Rooms outfitted with Persian carpets on tiled floors, rich drapes and cosy beds (some of them four-poster) make you feel like you've dropped into an Arabic fairytale. This charmer sits next to two historic museums, close to the Spice Souq and the metro station and has a nice sauna and steam room for post-sightseeing unwinding.

RADISSON BLU HOTEL
HOTEL $$

Map p244 (04-222 7171; www.radissonblu.com/hotel-dubaideiracreek; Baniyas Rd; r from Dh650; P@; MUnion, Baniyas Sq) This Creekside stalwart was Dubai's first five-star hotel when it opened in 1975 and fits as comfortably as your favourite jeans. Standard rooms won't hold a ton of luggage but boast a good range of amenities, an upbeat contempo colour scheme and small, furnished balconies. The hotels' trump card is its range of excellent restaurants, including China Club for yum cha, Shabestan for Persian and Yum! for noodles.

RIVIERA HOTEL
HOTEL $$

Map p244 (04-222 2131; www.rivierahotel-dubai.com; Baniyas Rd; d incl breakfast from Dh700; @; MUnion) Though updated, this old-timey hotel can't quite compete in the amenity department. However, it gets bonus points for its Creek location, proximity to the Deira souqs and ample breakfast buffet. Rooms feature carpets, patterned wallpaper and bold colour accents and overlook either the Creek or the souqs. No alcohol.

SHERATON DUBAI CREEK HOTEL & TOWERS
HOTEL $$

Map p244 (04-228 1111; www.sheratondubaicreek.com; Baniyas Rd; r from Dh850; P@; MUnion) Make sure you score a Creek-facing room for maximum enjoyment of the sparkling views through floor-to-ceiling windows, the most impressive feature of what otherwise are comfortable but fairly generic rooms. Kudos to the 42-inch TV, the ultra-comfy mattresses and the walk-in shower with bathrobes and slippers for winding down in comfort.

AL BUSTAN ROTANA
HOTEL $$

Map p246 (04-282 0000; www.rotana.com; Casablanca St, Garhoud; r from Dh700; P@;

MAirport Terminal 1, GGICO) Everything works like a well-oiled machine at this business hotel handily situated 1km from the airport. Rooms are dressed in tactile fabrics, thick carpets and soothing earth tones, while wall-mounted TVs, large desks and good mattresses are additional comforts. An oversized pool, tennis courts and a gym are handy for counteracting culinary over-indulgence. Wi-fi is Dh95 per day.

★ **PARK HYATT DUBAI** HOTEL $$$

Map p246 (04-602 1234; www.dubai.park.hyatt.com; near Dubai Golf Creek & Yacht Club; d incl breakfast from Dh1400; P@; MDeira City Centre) The mile-long driveway through a lush date-palm grove is the first hint that the Park Hyatt is no ordinary hotel – an impression quickly confirmed the moment you step into the domed and pillared lobby. Tiptoeing between hip and haute, it has oversized pastel rooms with arabesque flourishes and balconies for counting the dhows plying the Creek. The spa and restaurants are all top-notch and the golf course setting further lends an air of exclusivity.

HILTON DUBAI CREEK HOTEL $$$

Map p244 (04-227 1111; www.hilton.com; Baniyas Rd, Rigga; r from Dh1100; P@; MAl Rigga) In a building designed by Bastille Opera architect Carlos Ott, this glass-and-chrome hotel offers a smart alternative to the usual white-marble opulence so common in Dubai. After a day of turf-pounding you can retreat to rooms with wood-panelled walls, leather-padded headboards, grey-granite baths and fabulous beds with feather-light duvets.

Your flatscreen TV may have a gazillion channels, but you'll probably prefer the Creek views. There's some great eats, including Table 9 helmed by Darren Velvick. Wi-fi costs Dh100 per 24 hours.

Bur Dubai

BARJEEL HERITAGE GUEST HOUSE GUESTHOUSE $

Map p248 (04-354 4424; www.barjeelguesthouse.com; Shindagha Waterfront, near Heritage Village; r incl breakfast from Dh400; ; MAl Ghubaiba) Right on the historic Shindagha waterfront, where Dubai's royal family used to make its home, this charismatic retreat lets you connect with the city's history in a beautifully restored *barjeel* (wind tower) building. In typical local style, rooms wrap around a quiet courtyard and feature romantic four-poster beds; suites have a *majlis*-style sitting area. Rates include English or Arabic breakfast.

FOUR POINTS BY SHERATON BUR DUBAI HOTEL $

Map p248 (04-397 7444; www.fourpointsburdubai.com; Khalid bin Al Waleed Rd, Mankhool; r from Dh400; P@; MAl Fahidi) A long stone's throw from a metro station, this Four Points has spruced up carpeted rooms

THE CALL TO PRAYER

If you're staying in the older areas of Deira or Bur Dubai you might be woken around 4.30am by the inimitable wailing of the *azan* (the Muslim call to prayer) through speakers positioned on the minarets of nearby mosques. There's a haunting beauty to the sound, one that you'll only hear in Islamic countries.

Muslims pray five times a day: at dawn; when the sun is directly overhead; when the sun is in the position that creates shadows the same length as the object shadowed; at the beginning of sunset; and at twilight, when the last light of the sun disappears over the horizon. The exact times are printed in the daily newspapers and on websites. Once the call has been made, Muslims have half an hour to pray. An exception is made at dawn: after the call they have about 80 minutes in which to wake up, wash and pray before the sun has risen.

Muslims needn't be near a mosque to pray; they need only face Mecca. If devotees cannot get to a mosque, they'll stop wherever they are. If you see someone praying, be as unobtrusive as possible, and avoid walking in front of the person. All public buildings, including government departments, libraries, shopping centres and airports, have designated prayer rooms. In every hotel room arrows on the ceiling, desk or bedside table indicate the direction of Mecca. Better hotels provide prayer rugs, sometimes with a built-in compass.

decked out in soothing yellows and anchored by supremely comfortable beds with marshmallow-soft feather pillows. You'll find an adequate gym, a small pool, a hot tub and two superb restaurants, Antique Bazaar (Indian) and Picante (Portuguese).

FOUR POINTS BY SHERATON DOWNTOWN DUBAI — HOTEL $

Map p248 (☎04-354 3333; www.fourpoints-downtowndubai.com; 4C St, off Al Mankhool Rd; r from Dh400; P @ ☎ ≋; M Al Karama, Al Fahidi) An excellent value-for-money pick, this outpost has rooms spacious enough for a small family beyond its chrome-and-marble lobby. The location is a bit nondescript, but extras such as comfy mattresses, big flatscreen TVs, and a rooftop gym and pool compensate.

HOLIDAY INN EXPRESS — HOTEL $

Map p254 (☎04-407 1777; www.hiexpress.com/dubai; Jumeirah Rd, near Al Dhiyafah Rd; r incl breakfast from Dh450; P @ ☎; M Al Jafiliya) This contemporary property would be more attractive if it didn't overlook Port Rashid, but at least you'll be close to the Gulf and the Jumeirah beaches. The overall look is clean and contemporary, starting in the Bauhaus-meets-Arabia lobby and transitioning nicely to the rooms kitted out in chocolate and apricot hues. No pool but free shuttle to the beach.

★ XVA HOTEL — HERITAGE HOTEL $$

Map p248 (☎04-353 5383; www.xvahotel.com; off Al Fahidi St, Al Fahidi Historic District; r incl breakfast from Dh700; ☎; M Al Fahidi) This art-infused heritage hotel occupies a century-old wind-tower house smack dab in the Al Fahidi Historic District. Its 13 rooms open onto a courtyard (making them rather dark) and sport classy decor inspired by local themes, such as the Henna Room and the Dishdash Room. All feature artwork, arabesque flourishes and rich colours. The charming cafe serves breakfast.

ORIENT GUEST HOUSE — B&B $$

Map p248 (☎04-351 9111; www.orientguesthouse.com; off Al Fahidi St, Al Fahidi Historic District; r incl breakfast from Dh700; ☎; M Al Fahidi) This romantic B&B in a former private home in the Al Fahidi Heritage District beautifully captures the feeling of old Dubai. Rooms are entered via heavy wooden doors and surround a central courtyard where breakfast is served. Furnishings exude traditional Arabic flair and feature richly carved wooden armoires, four-poster beds with frilly drapes, and tiled floors.

MAJESTIC HOTEL TOWER — HOTEL $$

Map p248 (☎04-359 8888; www.dubaimajestic.com; Al Mankhool Rd; r from Dh600; P @ ☎ ≋; M Al Fahidi) Despite its ho-hum location on a busy street, this hotel scores high for comfort, design and a 'with it' vibe thanks to a happening Greek restaurant and the best live music club in town. All rooms come with plush beds and heavy drapes in neutral colours but the 'standard' ones are tiny, so book 'deluxe' if you need more elbow room.

RAMADA HOTEL — HOTEL $$

Map p248 (☎04-351 9999; www.ramadadubai.com; Al Mankhool Rd; r from Dh800; P @ ☎ ≋; M Al Fahidi) The most attention-grabbing feature of this longstanding hotel is its cathedral-like stained-glass feature that stretches 10 storeys up in the atrium lobby and, fittingly for Dubai, is among the world's tallest such artworks. Rooms get a thumbs up for their split-level spaciousness and thoughtful layout. There are six restaurants to combat thirst and hunger pangs, including the popular Lucien Belgian Cafe.

ARABIAN COURTYARD HOTEL & SPA — HOTEL $$

Map p248 (☎04-351 9111; www.arabiancourtyard.com; Al Fahidi St, Meena Bazaar; r from Dh650; @ ☎ ≋; M Al Fahidi) Opposite the Dubai Museum, this hotel is an excellent launch pad for city explorers. The Arabian theme extends from the turbaned lobby staff to the design flourishes in the decent-sized rooms, some of which catch glimpses of the Creek across the souq. Facilities include a pub, several restaurants, a swimming pool, spa and gym. One child under 11 stays free.

SAVOY CENTRAL HOTEL APARTMENTS — HOTEL APARTMENTS $$

Map p248 (☎04-393 8000; www.savoydubai.com/savoy-central; Al Rolla Rd, Meena Bazaar; r from Dh700; P @ ☎ ≋; M Al Ghubaiba, Al Fahidi) In the heart of the Meena Bazaar district, these roomy studios with small kitchens and big purple sofa beds put you within steps of fabulous budget eats, the Bur Dubai souqs and major historic sights, including the Dubai Museum. New owners have seriously slicked up the place from the lobby up to the rooftop pool, perfect for splashing under the stars.

MÖVENPICK HOTEL & APARTMENTS BUR DUBAI HOTEL **$$**

Map p252 (☎04-336 6000; www.movenpick-hotels.com; 19th & 12A Sts, Oud Metha; r from Dh800; P@; MOud Metha, Dubai Healthcare City) A lobby decorated in shades of charcoal and cream leads to a sweeping *Gone with the Wind* staircase and from there to 255 good-sized and well-lit rooms dressed in sumptuous chocolate, cherry and vanilla. There's half a dozen restaurants, including the excellent Chutney for Indian fare. It's opposite the American Hospital, close to the airport; plane spotters especially will love the rooftop pool.

ROSE GARDEN HOTEL APARTMENTS HOTEL APARTMENTS **$$**

Map p248 (www.rosegardenuae.com; 26A & 3B Sts; studio from Dh700; P; MBurJuman) This traditionally run hotel is a hop, skip and jump from the BurJuman Mall and metro station and has well-kept, modern studios and one- or two-bedroom apartments with at least a pantry kitchen. A rooftop pool and nicely equipped gym beckon sporty types, but party animals should go elsewhere since no alcohol or visitors (except close family members) are allowed in the rooms.

GOLDEN SANDS HOTEL APARTMENTS HOTEL APARTMENTS **$$**

Map p248 (☎04-355 5553; www.goldensands-dubai.com; off Al Mankhool Rd; studio apt from Dh500; @; MBurJuman) This Dubai hotel apartment pioneer has 750 studios and one- or two-bedroom serviced apartments with kitchenettes and balconies spread over a dozen boxy mid-rises behind the BurJuman Mall. All have ample space but some units could use a sprucing up, especially the bathrooms. It's in a residential area with lots of other hotel apartments around.

★**RAFFLES DUBAI** HOTEL **$$$**

Map p252 (☎04-324 8888; www.raffles.com/dubai; Sheikh Rashid Rd, Wafi City, Oud Metha; r from Dh1400; P@; MDubai Healthcare City) Built in the shape of a pyramid, Raffles is a stylish hotspot with magnificent oversized rooms (with balconies) blending Asian and Middle Eastern design accents and bathrooms dressed in natural Egyptian stone and boasting whirlpool tubs and walk-in showers. Zeitgeist-capturing in-room touches include Lavazza espresso machines, lighting controlled from a bedside console, iPod docking stations and free superfast wi-fi.

Downtown Dubai

IBIS WORLD TRADE CENTRE HOTEL **$**

Map p258 (☎04-332 4444; www.ibishotel.com; Sheikh Zayed Rd, Financial District; r Dh450; P@; MWorld Trade Centre) Of the several Dubai branches of this good-value chain, this one behind the World Trade Centre is the most central (the cheapest is in Deira). After the airy feel and modern design in the public areas, the ship's-cabin-sized rooms are a bit of a let down, but it's hard to find a hotel that's cleaner or more comfortable at this price.

WARWICK DUBAI HOTEL **$$**

Map p258 (☎04-506 9999; http://warwickhotels.com/dubai; Sheikh Zayed Rd; r from Dh 650; P@; MFinancial Centre) Close to good eats, sights and a metro station, the Warwick is an affordable crash pad for urban explorers. Distinctive features include a rooftop pool with killer views and a reasonably priced attached spa. Rooms are too generic to win design awards but the comfort level is high and the decor pleasing. Special kudos to the friendly staff.

NOVOTEL WORLD TRADE CENTRE HOTEL **$$**

Map p258 (☎04-332 0000; www.novotel.com; 2nd Za'abeel Rd; r from Dh750; P; MWorld Trade Centre) The no-nonsense Novotel adjoins the convention centre and comes with smallish but well-thought-out rooms with lots of desk space and a sofa. The rectangular swimming pool is sufficient for laps, and there's a pretty good gym with circuit-training equipment. The Blue Bar is one of the best places for jazz in town. It's behind the World Trade Centre.

DUSIT THANI DUBAI HOTEL **$$**

Map p258 (☎04-343 3333; www.dusit.com; Sheikh Zayed Rd, next to Interchange No 1; r from Dh900; P@; MFinancial Centre) Shaped like an upside-down tuning fork, one of Dubai's most architecturally dramatic towers hides traditional Thai decor behind its futuristic facade. Although geared towards the business brigade, urban nomads will also appreciate the lovely interplay of warm woods, earth tones and rich fabrics in the oversized rooms or the stellar views from the rooftop pool.

★**PALACE DOWNTOWN DUBAI** HOTEL **$$$**

Map p258 (☎04-428 7888; www.theaddress.com; Sheikh Mohammed bin Rashid Blvd, Old

Town Island; r from Dh1700; P@; MBurj Khalifa/Dubai Mall) City explorers with a romantic streak will be utterly enchanted by this luxe lakefront contender with its winning alchemy of Old World class and Arabic aesthetics. Rooms are chic and understated, styled in easy-on-the-eye natural tones and boast balconies overlooking Dubai Fountain. With Burj Khalifa and the Dubai Mall steps away, it's a perfect launch pad for shopaholics. Personal attention is key, from the check-in desk to the world-class spa and restaurants.

ADDRESS DOWNTOWN DUBAI — HOTEL $$$

Map p258 (04-436 8888; www.theaddress.com; Sheikh Mohammed bin Rashid Blvd; r from Dh1800; P@; MBurj Khalifa/Dubai Mall) This hotel embodies everything Dubai has to offer: beauty, style, glamour and ambition. Since its opening, it has drawn the cognoscenti in droves, not only to its rooms but also to its edgy restaurants and bars. If you do stay, you'll find XL-sized rooms dressed in rich woods and tactile fabrics, endowed with killer views and the latest communication devices. If that's not enough, the 24-hour gym and five-tiered infinity pool beckon.

VIDA DOWNTOWN DUBAI — BOUTIQUE HOTEL $$$

Map p258 (04-428 6888; www.vida-hotels.com; Sheikh Mohammed bin Rashid Blvd; r from Dh1200; P@; MBurj Khalifa/Dubai Mall) A revamp has transformed the former Qamardeen into Vida, a crash pad for next-gen creatives and entrepreneurs. No need to run with this crowd to appreciate the upbeat public areas with cool lamps and other design accents that smoothly segue to white, bright rooms and huge open bathrooms with a tub and enclosed walk-in shower. All electronics are controlled by the TV.

MANZIL DOWNTOWN DUBAI — HOTEL $$$

Map p258 (04-428 5888; www.vida-hotels.com; Sheikh Mohammed bin Rashid Blvd; r from Dh1200; P@; MBurj Khalifa/Dubai Mall) Arabesque meets mid-century modern at this lifestyle hotel that draws global hipsters with high-tech touches, design cachet and thoughtful services. The open-plan rooms whip vanilla, chocolate and orange hues into a sophisticated style sorbet and feature giant rain showers and free-standing tubs. If you're jetting in on a late flight, the 24-hour gym might help you loosen up.

ADDRESS DUBAI MALL — HOTEL $$$

Map p258 (04-438 8888; www.theaddress.com; Sheikh Mohammed bin Rashid Blvd; r from Dh1600; P@; MBurj Khalifa/Dubai Mall) A mod interpretation of Arabic design traditions, this fashionable hotel is directly connected to the Dubai Mall. Lug your bags back to spacious rooms where sensuous materials – leather, wood and velvet – provide a soothing antidote to shopping exhaustion. Besides ultracomfy beds you'll find the gamut of lifestyle essentials, including iPod docking stations and Nespresso machines.

The gym and business lounge are both open around the clock.

JW MARRIOTT MARQUIS HOTEL DUBAI — HOTEL $$$

Map p258 (04-414 0000; www.marriott.com; Sheikh Zayed Rd, Business Bay; r from Dh1100; P@; MBusiness Bay) Standing 355m tall, the mammoth Marriott is the world's tallest hotel with 1600 rooms split across two jagged towers inspired by the trunk of a date palm. Cathedral-like loftiness also dominates much of the public areas, while rooms have floor-to-ceiling windows to better appreciate the stunning views.

FAIRMONT DUBAI — HOTEL $$$

Map p258 (04-332 5555; www.fairmont.com/dubai; Sheikh Zayed Rd, Financial District; r from Dh1200; P@; MWorld Trade Centre) This city slicker wows especially at night when its four-poster towers are dipped in coloured lights. With a direct link to the Financial Centre, it courts high-powered execs and even has rooms with an extra-large desk to help you ink that deal. The two rooftop pools are lovely indulgence zones as are the Exchange Grill steakhouse and Cavalli Club glamour pit. Internet access is charged at Dh100 per day.

SHANGRI-LA — HOTEL $$$

Map p258 (04-343 8888; www.shangri-la.com/dubai; Sheikh Zayed Rd, Financial District; r from Dh1200; P@; MFinancial Centre) Shangri-La is the mythical paradise first described in James Hilton's 1933 novel *Lost Horizon*. In Dubai, it's a business hotel imbued with an understatedly sexy vibe. Rooms are a winner in the looks department, with their blond wood, soft leather headboards and free-standing tubs. The range of first-rate restaurants is superb, as is the sizzling cabaret-club The Act.

JUMEIRAH EMIRATES TOWERS HOTEL $$$

Map p258 (☎04-330 0000; www.jumeirah.com; Sheikh Zayed Rd, Financial District; d from Dh1150; P@; MEmirates Towers) An eye-catching steel-and-glass high-rise harbours one of the top-ranked business hotels in the Middle East. Glide up in the panoramic lift to sumptuous, high-tech rooms with power views, a black-and-grey aesthetic and a sleek, exec-oriented layout. Women might prefer the Chopard ladies' floor, where pink replaces grey and in-bath fridges let you chill your caviar face cream. Rates include shuttle and admission to the Wild Wadi Waterpark.

Jumeirah & Around

CHELSEA PLAZA HOTEL HOTEL $

Map p254 (☎04-398 2222; http://crimsonhotels.com/chelseaplaza; Al Dhiyafah Rd, Satwa; r from Dh450; P@; MAl Jafiliya, World Trade Centre) In the heart of polyethnic Satwa, the Chelsea has clubby, English-style decor with patterned wallpaper, plush carpeting and shiny dark-wood furniture. Bathrooms come with both tubs and big showers. The sports bar is justifiably popular and the health club has great circuit-training machines while the pool is big enough for laps.

★**BEACH HOTEL APARTMENT** HOTEL APARTMENTS $$

Map p254 (http://beachhotelapartment.ae; Al Hudhaiba Rd & 10B St; apt from Dh900; P; MWorld Trade Centre) Terrific service-minded staff, nice architecture, a sunny rooftop pool and a fantastic location give this place a considerable edge. You'll be steps from the beach, Jumeirah Mosque, trendy cafes and boutiques as well as a Spinney's supermarket in case you want to make use of your kitchen. No alcohol, but you'll find plenty of diversions at the Dubai Marine hotel across the street.

AL KHOORY EXECUTIVE HOTEL HOTEL $$

Map p254 (☎04-354 6555; http://corp-executive-al-khoory-hotel.dubaihoteluae.com; Al Wasl & Al Hudhaiba Rds; r from Dh500; P@; MWorld Trade Centre) Although the lobby exudes buttoned-up business flair, this mid-size hotel actually has plenty in store for leisure travellers, including a superb location a mere 10-minute walk from the beach, the Jumeirah Mosque and fun boutiques along Jumeirah Rd. Other assets include a better-than-average gym. Rooms are smallish but comfy. It's opposite the Iranian Hospital.

CENTRO BARSHA HOTEL $$

Map p256 (☎04-704 0000; www.rotana.com/centrobarsha; Rd 329, Al Barsha 1; d from Dh700; P@; MSharaf DG) An easy 10-minute walk from the Mall of the Emirates, this is the Rotana brand's entry into the budget design hotel category. Rooms are compact but stylish and outfitted with all the key lifestyle and tech touches, including satellite TV and IP phones. Kick back in the comfy cocktail bar, the 24-hour gym or by the pleasant outdoor pool. Wi-fi is charged at Dh70 per 24 hours. It's behind the Mall of the Emirates.

DONATELLO HOTEL APARTMENTS HOTEL APARTMENTS $$

Map p256 (☎04-340 9040; www.donatello-hotel-dubai.com; cnr 21st & 2nd Sts, Al Barsha; apt from Dh600; P; MSharaf DG) A 10-minute walk from the Mall of the Emirates, this modern hotel is a great base for power shoppers. You'll have plenty of space to stow away your loot in stylish apartments equipped with classic furniture, tiled floors, natural stone bathrooms and a kitchenette with microwave. Reflect upon the day's adventures while splashing around the rooftop pool.

IBIS MALL OF THE EMIRATES HOTEL $$

Map p256 (☎04-382 3000; www.ibis.com; 2A St, Al Barsha; r from Dh500; P@; MMall of the Emirates) Classic Ibis: a good deal with low-frill but sparkling clean rooms. If you'd rather drop your cash in the adjacent mall than loll by the pool or nosh on pillow treats, this is not a bad place to hang your hat. Just remember that you can't hang much more than that in the shoebox-sized rooms. It's near the Mall of the Emirates.

LA VILLA NAJD HOTEL APARTMENTS HOTEL APARTMENTS $$

Map p256 (☎04-361 9007; www.lavillahospitality.com/Najd; btwn 6A & 15 Sts, Al Barsha; apt from Dh615; P@; MMall of the Emirates) One of the nicer of the hotel apartments mushrooming around the Mall of the Emirates, Najd is a welcoming host. The tiled-floor apartments make maximum use of space, packing a living room, bedroom, kitchen, full bathroom and guest bathroom into a relatively compact frame. Ask for a unit overlooking Ski Dubai. Basic gym, nice rooftop pool. It's behind the mall.

★**AL QASR HOTEL** HOTEL $$$

Map p256 (☎04-366 8888; www.jumeirah.com; Madinat Jumeirah, Al Sufouh Rd, Umm Suqeim 3; r from Dh2200; P @ ; M Mall of the Emirates) If cookie-cutter hotels don't cut it, try this polished pad styled after an Arabian summer palace. Details are extraordinary, from the lobby's Austrian-crystal chandeliers to mirror-polished inlaid-marble floors. Rooms sport arabesque flourishes, rich colours and cushy furnishings, while balconies overlook the grand display of Madinat Jumeirah. Excellent service, 2km of private beach, and one of the biggest pools in town.

MINA A'SALAM HOTEL RESORT **$$$**

Map p256 (04-366 8888; www.jumeirah.com; Madinat Jumeirah, Al Sufouh Rd, Umm Suqeim 3; r from Dh2500; P @ ; M Mall of the Emirates) The striking lobby is a mere overture to the full symphony of relaxed luxury awaiting in huge, amenity-laden rooms. Each comes with a balcony overlooking the romantic Arabesque jumble that is Madinat Jumeirah or the striking Burj Al Arab. Guests have the entire run of the place and adjacent sister property Al Qasr, including the pools, the 2km-long private beach and the kids club. Rates include free admission to Wild Wadi Waterpark.

JUMEIRAH BEACH HOTEL RESORT **$$$**

Map p256 (04-348 0000; www.jumeirah.com; Jumeirah Rd, Umm Suqeim 3; r from Dh1900; P @ ; M Mall of the Emirates) Shaped like a giant wave, this family-oriented resort on a 1km-long private beach is tailor-made for active types, with plenty of water sports, a superb health club, a climbing wall and tennis and squash courts. Little ones can make new friends in Sinbad's Kids Club or get their kicks at the adjoining Wild Wadi Waterpark (free admission for hotel guests).

Many rooms face the Burj Al Arab.

DUBAI MARINE BEACH RESORT & SPA RESORT **$$$**

Map p254 (04-346 1111; www.dxbmarine.com; Jumeirah Rd, Jumeirah 1; r from Dh1000; P @ ; M World Trade Centre) You'll sleep well at this compact beachside resort, with villas set among pools and tropical gardens; it's within earshot of the waves and the Jumeirah Mosque. The beach is rather small, but there's a kids' club for little ones to romp around and an entire village worth of restaurants, bars and nightclubs for grown-ups, including Boudoir and Sho Cho.

Rooms are comfy enough, but it's the facilities that stand out.

TAXI, SIR? TAXI, MA'AM?

Many four- and five-star hotels in Dubai offer guests a dedicated taxi service in chauffeur-driven sedans under contract with the hotel. These 'limos' have no signage, though they do have meters (if not, don't get in) and slightly higher rates than a regular taxi. When you're stuck in heavy traffic, the meter ticks fast and you may end up paying nearly double the fee of a regular cab. If you don't want to use this service, tell the bell captain you want a regular taxi (you might have to insist). But if you are pressed for time – and there are no other cabs available – you'll be grateful for the wheels.

BURJ AL ARAB HOTEL **$$$**

Map p256 (04-301 7777; www.burj-al-arab.com; Jumeirah Rd, Umm Suqeim 3; ste from Dh8000; P @ ; M Mall of the Emirates) This sail-shaped hotel is an iconic Dubai landmark and regularly beds pop stars, royalty, billionaire Russians and the merely moneyed. Beyond the striking lobby with its attention-grabbing fountain lie 202 suites with more trimmings than a Christmas turkey. Even the smallest measure 170 sq metres and spread over two floors, making them bigger than most apartments.

The decor is l-u-s-h, with moiré silk walls, mirrored ceilings over the beds, curlicue high-backed velvet chairs and inlaid bathroom tiles displaying scenes of Venice. And all that gold? Yes, it's the real 24-carat thing.

Dubai Marina & Palm Jumeirah

GRAND MIDWEST TOWER HOTEL **$**

Map p262 (04-436 2000; www.grandmidwest.com; Sheikh Zayed Rd; r from Dh425; P @ ; M Dubai Internet City) This is a top value pick thanks to fall-over-backwards friendly staff and generously sized studios and apartments. All are sheathed in warm hues and outfitted with well-stocked and stylish kitchens, ultra-comfy beds, fast internet and balconies. Sitting right next to a metro station doesn't hurt either and neither do the multiple pools, one with a distant view of the Burj Al Arab.

DESERT DREAMS

Just a short drive from the traffic jams, construction sites and megamalls are three stellar desert resorts. If you crave a little peace and quiet and are prepared to spend some serious money, these hotels will show you a calmer, less-hurried side of Dubai.

Desert Palm Per Aquum Retreat (04-602 9333; http://desertpalm.peraquum.com; Al Awir Rd; r incl breakfast from Dh1100, villa from Dh3600; P) Feel the stress nibbling at your psyche evaporate the moment you step inside this luxe boutique retreat, just a short drive outside Dubai and set on a private polo estate. You can opt either for a palm suite with floor-to-ceiling windows overlooking the polo field (plus plasma TV, Bang & Olufsen surround sound, Nespresso machine and iPod) or go for total privacy in one of the villas with private pool. Either way, you'll feel quite blissed out amid copper-toned decor, fancy linens and vast green landscapes. There's also an infinity pool, an on-site spa and a gourmet deli for picking up tasty treats to enjoy on the terrace or as a desert picnic.

Bab Al Shams Desert Resort & Spa (04-381 3231; www.meydanhotels.com/babalshams; near Endurance Village, off E611; r incl breakfast from Dh1200; P @) Resembling a fort and effortlessly blending into the desertscape, Bab Al Shams is a tonic for escapists seeking to indulge their *Arabian Nights* fantasies. Its labyrinthine layout displays both Arabic and Moorish influences; rooms are gorgeous, spacious and evocatively earthy, with pillars, lanterns, paintings of desert landscapes and prettily patterned Bedouin-style pillows. While this is the perfect place to curl up with a book or meditate in the dunes, the stimuli-deprived will also find plenty to do. A wonderful infinity pool beckons, as do the luscious Satori Spa and an archery range. Children under 12 years of age can let off steam in Sinbad's Club. Off-site activities include desert tours and horse and camel rides. Bab Al Shams is about 45 minutes south of Dubai.

Al Maha Desert Resort & Spa (04-832 9900; www.al-maha.com; Dubai Desert Conservation Reserve, Al Ain Rd; full board from Dh5500;) It may only be 65km southeast of Dubai (on the Dubai to Al Ain Rd), but Al Maha feels like an entirely different universe. Gone are the skyscrapers, traffic and the go-go attitude. At this remote desert ecoresort it's all about getting back to some elemental discoveries about yourself and where you fit into nature's grand design. Part of the Dubai Desert Conservation Reserve (DDCR), Al Maha is one of the most exclusive hotels in the Emirates and named for the endangered Arabian oryx, which is bred as part of DDCR's conservation program. The resort's 42 luxurious suites are all standalone, canvas-roofed bungalows with private plunge pools. Each one has its own patio with stunning vistas of the beautiful desert landscape and peach-coloured dunes, punctuated by mountains and grazing white oryx and gazelles. Rates include two daily activities such as a desert wildlife drive or a camel trek. Private vehicles, visitors and children under 12 are not allowed.

★PEARL MARINA HOTEL APARTMENTS — HOTEL APARTMENTS $$

Map p262 (04-447 1717; w ww.pearlmarina-hotel.com; Marina Waterfront; apt from Dh700; P; M Jumeirah Lakes Towers) Tucked into the far end of the Dubai Marina, the Pearl may not be as flashy as its high-rise neighbours, but who cares if the price tag is only a fraction compared to the big boys, giving you more dirham to spend on fun, food and fashion. The fabulous beach and The Walk at JBR are only a hop, skip and jump away.

MEDIA ONE HOTEL — HOTEL $$

Map p262 (04-427 1000; www.mediaonehotel.com; Al Falak St, Dubai Media City; r from Dh800; P @; M Nakheel, Marina Tower) Match your mood to the room: Hip, Cool, Calm or Chill-Out. This lifestyle hotel loads up on all the Zeitgeist essentials global nomads crave, like IP phones, iPod docking stations and satellite TV. On Thursdays and Fridays you get to mingle poolside with Dubai party people and international DJs. It's behind the American University.

GLORIA HOTEL HOTEL $$

Map p262 (☎04-399 6666; www.gloriahotel-dubai.com; Sheikh Zayed Rd; studio from Dh550; P@📶≋; M Dubai Internet City) Handily located next to a metro station, the popular Gloria actually flaunts numerous assets that'll make you want to stay put, including a top-notch gym, a 25m outdoor pool (with a separate one for kiddies), and roomy, well-proportioned apartments with kitchen. The decor varies depending on whether you go for a Californian, Classic, Modern or Mediterranean design theme.

★**ONE&ONLY ROYAL MIRAGE** RESORT $$$

Map p262 (☎04-399 9999; http://royalmirage.oneandonlyresorts.com; Al Sufouh Rd; r from Dh1800; P@📶≋; M Nakheel, 🚊Media City) A class act all around, the Royal Mirage consists of the Moorish-style Palace, the romantic Arabian Court, and the ultra-discreet Residence & Spa hideaway. The latter harbours the posh Health & Beauty Institute whose stunning hammam and spa are open to nonguests. All resort rooms are sea-facing, luxuriously furnished and teem with thoughtful feel-at-home touches.

No less impressive are the gardens that channel both Granada's Alhambra and an English garden, with bubbling fountains and croquet-quality lawns. Loll around the giant lagoon-style pools or kick back on the 1km private beach. The bars and restaurants here are among Dubai's best. A boat shuttle departs hourly to the even more luxe sister hotel One&Only The Palm.

ONE&ONLY THE PALM BOUTIQUE HOTEL $$$

Map p262 (☎04-444 1180; http://thepalm.oneandonlyresorts.com; West Crescent, Palm Jumeirah; r from Dh3400; P📶≋; M Nakheel) The stunning Dubai skyline looms across the Gulf, yet this romantic and megaposh gem offers a complete retreat from the city. Exuding the feel of an exclusive private estate, it has rambling gardens, several pools and Moorish-influenced suites daubed with turquoise and purple colour accents and outfitted with all requisite 21st-century tech touches. Privacy is key throughout. When you're ready to get back to the real world, there's a free boat shuttle to the sister property One&Only Royal Mirage on the mainland.

JUMEIRAH ZABEEL SARAY HOTEL $$$

Map p262 (☎04-453 0000; www.jumeirah.com; West Crescent, Palm Jumeirah; r from Dh1800; P@📶≋; M Nakheel) With its domed ceiling, golden pillars and jewel-like lamps, Zabeel Saray's lobby is as lavish and majestic as an Ottoman palace. The rich decor transfers in more subtle ways to the rooms, where everything is calibrated to take the edge off travel, including balconies to let in the ocean breeze and admire the sparkling Dubai skyline. The Talise Spa, too, is a supreme relaxation station, complete with a Turkish hammam and a saltwater lap pool. A great selection of restaurants makes for content tummies. The hotel is about a 15-minute taxi ride from the nearest metro station (Dh40).

LE ROYAL MERIDIEN BEACH RESORT & SPA RESORT $$$

Map p262 (☎04-399 5555; www.leroyalmeridien-dubai.com; off Murjan Ave, northern end of The Walk at JBR; r from Dh1000; P@📶≋; M Damac) An urge to splurge is well directed towards this 500-room resort flanking a gorgeous beach and extensive gardens. The main building has family-friendly rooms with connecting doors, but couples may be more charmed by the elegant, classically furnished retreats in the Tower Building. All have sea-view balconies. Boredom is banished thanks to three pools, a top-notch gym, lots of water sports and kids' activities.

GROSVENOR HOUSE HOTEL $$$

Map p262 (☎04-399 8888; www.grosvenor-house-dubai.com; Al Sufouh Rd, Dubai Marina; r from Dh1050; P@📶≋; M Damac) Grosvenor House was the first hotel to open among the jumble of the Marina's sky-punching towers. The public areas are sleek, grown-up and angular in a vague art deco aesthetic, but rooms feel warm and homey with their cream and brown hues brightened by red accents. The hotel's Buddha Bar and Siddharta Lounge are destinations for Dubai's 'it' crowd. Grosvenor guests also get full access to the pool and beach facilities at the nearby sister hotel, Le Royal Meridien.

WESTIN DUBAI MINA SEYAHI BEACH RESORT & MARINA RESORT $$$

Map p262 (☎04-399 4141; www.westinminaseyahi.com; Al Sufouh Rd; r from Dh1500; P@📶≋; M Nakheel, 🚊Mina Al Seyahi) A top choice for water sports enthusiasts, this sophisticated beach resort feels like a cross between an Arabian summer palace and an Italian palazzo. With classic furniture and vanilla and cocoa hues, the oversized rooms look sharp yet homey. The three pools include a

150m-long lagoon-like pool for lazing (the others are for kiddies and for swimming laps). The hotel shares facilities, including a water sports centre, with the neighbouring Le Meridien Mina Seyahi.

LE MERIDIEN MINA SEYAHI BEACH RESORT & MARINA RESORT $$$

Map p262 (04-399 3333; www.lemeridien-minaseyahi.com; Al Sufouh Rd; r from Dh1300; P @ ; M Nakheel, Mina Al Seyahi) Twinned with the Westin, this beachfront hotel is nirvana for active types, offering a plethora of water sports (from waterskiing to kayaking), tennis courts and an enormous gym with state-of-the-art equipment and courses in everything from Thai boxing to Pilates. The giant free-form pool is as lovely as the meandering palm-tree-lined gardens and calm beach.

ADDRESS DUBAI MARINA HOTEL $$$

Map p262 (04-436 7777; www.theaddress.com; Dubai Marina; r from Dh1100; P @ ; M Dubai Marina, Dubai Marina Mall) This place has the sophistication of a city hotel, but its location close to the beach, the Marina Mall, and the Marina Walk and Walk at JBR pulls a healthy crowd of leisure lovers. You'll sleep well in modern rooms dressed in homey natural tones and equipped with the gamut of mod cons. The huge infinity pool on the 4th floor has head-spinning views of the yachts and high-rises.

RITZ-CARLTON DUBAI HOTEL $$$

Map p262 (04-399 4000; www.ritzcarlton.com/dubai; The Walk at JBR; r Dh1250; P @ ; M Dubai Marina, Jumeirah Lakes Towers, Jumeirah Beach Residence 1) The Ritz-Carlton exudes an aura of timeless elegance. When it first opened in 1998, Dubai Marina was still the middle of nowhere. Now the Mediterranean-villa-style resort is dwarfed by high-rises, but the mature gardens and tall palms create a visual berm. Despite a 2013 expansion that added 148 rooms, a spa and another pool to the existing four, it still feels intimate.

KEMPINSKI HOTEL MALL OF THE EMIRATES HOTEL $$$

Map p256 (04-341 0000; www.kempinski-dubai.com; Sheikh Zayed Rd, Mall of the Emirates, Al Barsha; r from Dh1200; P @ ; M Mall of the Emirates) Linked to the Mall of the Emirates, the Kempinski exudes alpine coolness and is a perfect launch pad for a shopping immersion. The monumental marble lobby contrasts with the rooms, which are drenched in warm silver, burgundy and snowy white and decorated with Arabic design accents. Some of the bathrooms sport enormous tubs and marble rain showers. A big hit, especially with Arabian guests, are the alpine-style 'Ski Chalet' apartments overlooking Ski Dubai.

Understand Dubai & Abu Dhabi

Dubai & Abu Dhabi Today

Dubai and Abu Dhabi are at an exciting juncture: behind them lie the bad old days of regional unrest, global recession and economic vulnerability. Ahead lies the prospect of enhanced stability, stronger regional ties and closer integration with the international community. With prestigious cultural and infrastructure projects underway, this is an excellent time to visit two cities that are at the heart of Arabia while being a world away from neighbouring troubles.

Best on Film

Mission: Impossible – Ghost Protocol (2011) Tom Cruise scales the Burj Khalifa in this 'Mission' thriller.
Syriana (2005) This political thriller starring George Clooney and Matt Damon was partly shot in Dubai.
Duplicity (2009) Spy-themed comedy features exterior shots of Dubai.
Naqaab (2007) Bollywood suspense thriller largely shot in and around Jumeirah Beach.

Best in Print

Arabia through the Looking Glass (Jonathan Raban; 1979) One of the first Western travel accounts of modern Arabia.
Dubai: the Story of the World's Fastest City (Jim Krane; 2009) Balanced review of Dubai's rags-to-riches story.
Dubai: Gilded Cage (Syed Ali; 2010) Scholarly and critical examination of Dubai's rapid transformation.
From Rags to Riches: A Story of Abu Dhabi (Mohammed Al-Fahim; 2011) A memoir of the city written by an Emirati.

Regional Union

Arab Gulf states (except Iraq) already collaborate through a forum called the Gulf Cooperation Council (GCC), established in Abu Dhabi in 1981. There is now a growing appetite for closer union.

The practicalities of union, however, are problematic. When locating the central bank needed for currency union, Oman and the United Arab Emirates (UAE) pulled out. No one can decide whether to admit new members… and so it goes on. Where the cooperation between Arab states has met with success is in the customs union, implemented in 2015, and a common market whereby GCC citizens can gain education and health care, work, own property and retire in all member states.

Global Integration

The GCC has also successfully cooperated on shared water and power projects and integration hopes are now pinned on a US$15.5 billion railway. The project, linking six member states, will create a regional transport corridor from Iraq to Oman designed to boost trade, carry freight and tighten regional ties. The first leg of the 1940km track, between UAE and Oman, is due to be completed by 2018.

The railway is axiomatic of a desire for international integration. Dubai and Abu Dhabi have led the charge, bringing collaborations with foreign institutions, providing an exchange of peoples through the world's largest transport hubs, giving a platform for global sporting events and providing a forum for international arts.

Diversification

To be an international player, you have to have the funds, and to date oil and gas have ensured a healthy bank balance. This financial security is not guaranteed, however, as the recent 'sheikhs versus shale' battle has shown. The

OPEC response to US fracking has been to continue supplying oil, resulting in tumbling oil prices – where hundred-dollar oil seemed here to stay, now the price of a barrel is half this value. The latest spat in a volatile industry has highlighted that, with just 33% of the market share (down from 53% in 1970), OPEC's domination of the world's energy supply is diminishing, forcing all countries in the region to diversify.

Thankfully for the UAE, Abu Dhabi has banked billions (over US$900 billion in assets are retained in the Abu Dhabi Investment Authority) and Dubai has successfully invested in trade and tourism, with oil and gas contributing to just 2% of its GDP. This is good news for the visitor who can expect more showstopping projects, such as the Frame (a 150m by 93m picture frame capturing Dubai's cityscape), in the run up to Expo 2020.

Environmental Awareness

Modifying the taste for iconic projects is an awareness that the future must be sustainable. For decades the natural environment of the UAE has been subjected to indiscriminate exploitation for human economic advantage. Oil extraction in the Empty Quarter is a brutal business, not just in terms of drilling but also the apparatus of dispersal – trucks, pipelines, labour camps, dumping of waste. The UAE's marine environment has undergone a similar assault, with thousands of tonnes of seabed scalped for the purpose of shaping new islands for human amusement.

But the tide is turning; there is a genuine desire, showcased by Masdar City, to lessen the impact on the environment and to find a more sustainable approach to future development.

Education & Emiratisation

Sustainability also applies to the human composition of the UAE. It's easy to forget that 70 years ago education was virtually nonexistent. Today, Emiratis pilot planes, teach at universities, perform surgery and engage at an ever-increasing level in global sports and arts. This rapid transformation from fishing, pearling and farming communities to full participation in the world's professions is outstanding. But there's a hidden challenge.

You can't train people and then expect them to watch others do the job: expats have played an indisputable role in building human resources but they now have to be willing to step aside and let the local population assume responsibility for themselves. This process of 'Emiratisation' is not easy when expats have made the country of their labours their home, naturally seeking jobs for their own families. Finding a way to accommodate a multicultural population, where the same rights and opportunities are shared by all, is therefore likely to be one of the defining challenges for the government in the future.

if UAE were 100 people

19 would be Emirati
23 would be other Arabs and Iranians
8 would be Western European
50 would be South Asian

belief systems

(% of population)

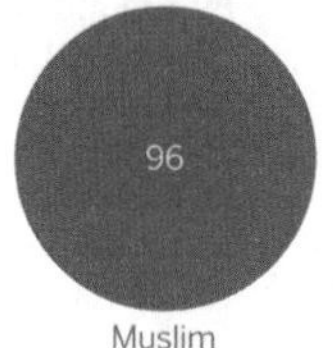

population per sq km

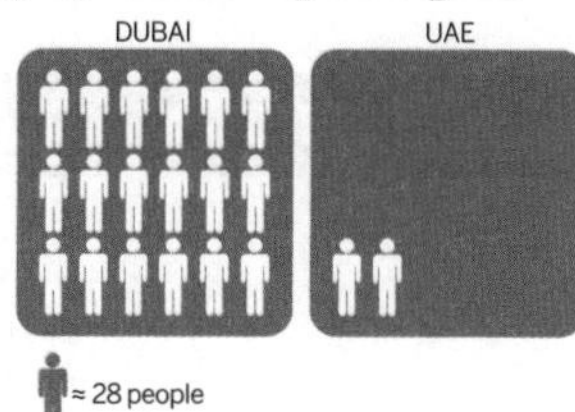

History

Travel along the main arteries of Dubai and Abu Dhabi and it's hard to picture these cities before their modern incarnations. The term 'rags to riches' is used widely to describe their rapid development but there's very little evidence now of the pre-oil days except in pockets of largely reconstructed heritage sites. History here has not been laid down in buildings and monuments but in customs and manners – these take longer to fathom, perhaps, but their foundations run just as deep.

Historical Reads

Arabia and the Arabs: From the Bronze Age to the Coming of Islam by Robert G Hoyland

The Arabs by Peter Mansfield

Arabian Sands by Wilfred Thesiger

Trade Roots

They may not be the most obvious attractions in Abu Dhabi but small enclosed areas on the outskirts of town show the modest relics of ancient civilisations dating back to the Bronze Age. Spearheads and other archaeological evidence suggest that human settlement in the region has an even older lineage, with Homo sapiens arriving in the region by around 100,000 BC, attracted by the savannah-like grasslands that dominated much of the Arabian Peninsula. These hunter-gatherer groups burned fires and reared livestock, forming the first organised communities in the region.

Inevitably, when organised communities innovate to survive they produce items desirable to other communities: in other words, they trade. As early as 6000 BC loose groups of Stone Age and Bronze Age individuals set up intricate trade routes between Arabia, Mesopotamia and the Indus Valley. They traded largely in copper mined in Magan (the ancient name of Oman) and exchanged goods with the Dilmun Empire (centred around modern-day Bahrain). It's easy to simplify the lives of the ancients, but the early seafaring traders of the Gulf were no barbarians: they spent their mineral wealth on fine glass, ate too many dates and suffered bad teeth. They took the time to thread beads, enjoyed complex legends, and expressed their interest in life through their administrations of death.

All trace of the great Magan civilisation ceased after the 2nd millennium BC, with some historians speculating that the desertification of the area hastened its demise. But the die was cast: this was to be a

TIMELINE

3000 BC

Dilmun, the first great civilisation in the Arabian Peninsula, is founded off the coast of Bahrain. It extends across today's UAE to the hills of Oman and facilitates regional trading.

AD 570

Prophet Mohammed is born in the same year that the Ma'rib dam in Yemen burst its banks. These twin events lead to the great Arab diaspora.

700–850

The Umayyads introduce Arabic and Islam to the Gulf region. Mecca and Medina lose their earlier political importance but grow as the spiritual homes of Islam.

land of trading routes, where frankincense from the south, transported by camel caravan across the great deserts of the interior, was swapped for spices and textiles from India, silk and porcelain from China, and bitumen from the Dead Sea. Visit any souq in Dubai or Abu Dhabi today and the pots and pans, electronic gadgetry, gold necklaces, plastic buckets and inlaid boxes, none of which are produced locally, are evidence of how trade continues to run through the blood of the region.

Foreign Influence

Given that today one out of every four people are Muslim, there can be no greater moment of historical importance on the Arabian Peninsula than the birth of the Prophet Mohammed in the year AD 570. And if you are in any doubt as to the lasting legacy of the religion he founded, just listen to these two Emirati cities at dawn and dusk when they reverberate with the call to prayer. Mammon may have a foothold in today's malls but a deep respect for Islam is at the heart of daily life, as evidenced by the innumerable mosques built in the last decade and, more to the point, the number of people frequenting them.

Pearl diving sounds romantic, however, it was an industry founded on suffering. A diver's life was one of hardship and the rewards no match for the dangers involved. Most divers were East African slaves and profits went into the pockets of the boat owner.

In historical terms, the arrival of Islam to the Gulf was significant for two reasons. The ports of the Gulf helped facilitate the outward flow of Islam, transporting Prophet Mohammed's teachings across the waters of the Arabian Sea by dhow (sailing vessel), uniting people in worship of the 'one true god' and the condemnation of idols. Equally, the same ports welcomed an inward flow of pilgrims in search of spiritual renewal during the annual hajj to Mecca and Medina. The ebb and flow of pilgrims brought a different kind of exchange, a cultural interaction with a succession of powerful dynasties such as the Umayyads and the Abbasids from the north. Their influence helped define the early nature of Gulf settlements and encouraged trade to flourish.

Given the lively trade of the region, it's not surprising that the Peninsula attracted the attention of European powers too. In 1498, a great Omani seafarer, Ahmed bin Majid, unwittingly helped a Portuguese explorer, Vasco da Gama, to navigate the Strait of Hormuz. The Portuguese took advantage of this knowledge by annexing Yemen's Socotra Island, occupying Oman and colonising Bahrain. Travel along the Gulf today and Portuguese forts appear with regularity: cut inland and there's no trace of them. The Portuguese were only interested in protecting their trade routes and made no impact on the interior of Peninsula countries at all. When they were eventually ousted by the mid-17th century, they left not much more than a legacy of military architecture and the Maria Theresa dollar – an important local currency.

850–1300

Arabia's old trade routes collapse and the Peninsula declines in wealth and importance. Petty sheikhdoms bicker over limited resources, under the control of Tartar moguls, Persian and Ottoman Turks.

1580

Gasparo Balbi, a Venetian jeweller, investigates the region's potential for the pearling trade and visits a town in the Gulf called 'Dibei'. Pearling eventually becomes the region's economic mainstay.

1793

The Bani Yas, the main power among the Gulf's Bedouin tribes and the ancestors of today's Emirati ruling families, move their capital to Abu Dhabi.

1805–92

The British engage in a number of skirmishes along the 'Pirate Coast' of Abu Dhabi and Dubai. The local sheikhdoms capitulate to become British protectorates, known collectively as the 'Trucial States'.

The Portuguese were followed in the 17th and 18th centuries by the French and the Dutch, who understood the strategic significance of the Gulf coast in terms of protecting their own trade routes to the east. Other powerful entities, such as the Wahhabi tribes (of what is now Saudi Arabia), the Ottoman Empire and the Persians were also attracted by the Gulf's strategic importance. But it was the British who most successfully staked a claim in the region's future.

The Trucial Coast

There were around 350 shops in Deira, Dubai by 1908, and another 50 in Bur Dubai, where the Indian community was concentrated. To this day, the Bur Dubai Souq shows a strong Indian influence, and Bur Dubai is home to the only Hindu temple in the city.

On the one hand, the various treaties and 'exclusive agreements' that Britain signed with the emirs of the region kept the French at bay and thereby safeguarded British trading routes with India. On the other hand, the British helped maintain the claims to sovereignty of the emerging Gulf emirates against Turkish and Persian interests, and from the ambitions of the eventual founder of Saudi Arabia, Ibn Saud. In exchange for British protection, the local sheikhs relinquished all jurisdiction over their foreign affairs. As a result of these treaties, or truces, Europeans called the area 'the Trucial Coast', a name the territory retained until the 1971 federation that created the United Arab Emirates (UAE).

So what had become of these two Gulf cities during these international machinations? Fresh water was discovered in Abu Dhabi Island in 1793, encouraging the powerful Al Nahyan family out of the desert oasis of Liwa to the coast. Until then, the ruling Al Nahyan tribe, part of the Bani Yas tribal confederation, had lived a Bedouin lifestyle, looking after camels and goats, tending small plantations in the oasis and generally living a frugal life in a desert environment. The story goes that, during their nomadic peregrinations, they were led by a gazelle to Abu Dhabi ('father of the gazelle', in Arabic), an island blessed with fresh water. This made life by the coast sustainable and the family put down roots by the coast, building the foundations of what was destined to become today's great city.

Dubai meanwhile was little more than a small fishing and pearling hamlet, perched on a disputed border between two local powers – the seafaring Qawassim of present-day Ras al-Khaimah and Sharjah, to the north, and the Bani Yas tribal confederation to the south. In 1833, under the leadership of Maktoum bin Butti (r 1833–52), a tribe from Abu Dhabi overthrew the town of Dubai, thereby establishing the Al Maktoum dynasty, which still rules the emirate of Dubai today. For Maktoum bin Butti, good relations with the British authorities in the Gulf were essential to safeguard his small sheikhdom against attack from the larger and more powerful surrounding sheikhdoms. In 1841 the Bur Dubai settlement extended to Deira on the northern side of the

1930

Sheikh Rashid identifies the collapse of the pearling industry caused by the Great Depression of 1929–34 and the introduction of Japanese cultured pearls.

1951

The British establish the Trucial States Council, which brings together the leaders of the sheikhdoms that would later form the UAE.

1958

After almost 20 years of de facto leadership, Sheikh Rashid officially becomes ruler of Dubai after his father's death, a position he holds until almost the end of the century.

1960

The first commercial oil field is discovered at Babi in Abu Dhabi. Six years later, oil is discovered in Dubai, spurring a period of rapid economic growth for both emirates.

Creek, although throughout the 19th century it largely remained a tiny enclave of fishermen, pearl divers, Bedouin, and Indian and Persian merchants. Interestingly, the Indians and Persians (now Iranians) are still largely the custodians of the area, providing the Creek with much of its modern character.

Throughout the 19th century, both towns developed significantly, largely thanks to the income from the pearl industry. Sheikh Zayed bin Mohammed (Zayed the Great) helped Abu Dhabi become the most significant of the Gulf emirates, assisted in this regard by his relationship with the British. But Dubai was soon to catch up under the visionary ruler, Sheikh Maktoum bin Hasher al Maktoum (r 1894–1906). It was he who gave foreign traders tax-exempt status, leading to the establishment of Dubai as a duty-free port, a move that catapulted the emirate ahead of its rivals. Disillusioned traders from Persia crossed the Strait of Hormuz to take advantage of tax-free trade, becoming permanent residents in the area known as the Bastakia Quarter.

Sheikh Rashid, the driving force behind Dubai's phenomenal growth and 'father of (modern) Dubai', died in 1990 after a long illness and was succeeded as emir by his son, Sheikh Maktoum bin Rashid al Maktoum. Maktoum had already been regent for his sick father for several years and continued Dubai's expansion.

From Protectorate to Federation

By the beginning of the 20th century both Abu Dhabi and Dubai were well-established towns, with populations approaching 10,000. Both towns were hit hard by the collapse of the pearling trade, the mainstay of the Gulf economy for decades. The trade had fallen victim to the Great Depression of 1929–34 and to the Japanese discovery in 1930 of a method of artificial pearl cultivation.

Sheikh Saeed al Maktoum (r 1912–58) of Dubai realised that alternative sources of revenue were necessary, so while Abu Dhabi threw in its lot with the exploration for oil, Dubai embraced the concept of re-export. This exporting involved the importing of goods (particularly gold), which entered and exited Dubai legally but which were sold on to other ports abroad tax free – a dubious practice akin to smuggling according to some but highly lucrative for Dubai.

The wealth generated from trade in yellow gold in Dubai was quickly trumped by the riches earned from black gold in Abu Dhabi. The first commercial oil field was discovered at Babi in Abu Dhabi in 1960 and six years later, Dubai struck it lucky, too. The discovery of oil greatly accelerated the modernisation of the region and was a major factor in the formation of the UAE. In 1951 the Trucial States Council was founded, for the first time bringing together the rulers of the sheikhdoms of what would eventually become a federation.

When Britain announced its departure from the region in 1968, Sheikh Zayed bin Sultan al Nahyan took the lead in forming alliances among the seven emirates that made up the Trucial States. Unification

Visitors to Dubai and Abu Dhabi will no doubt notice enormous posters of a smiling Arab. This is Sheikh Zayed bin Sultan al Nahyan, the first president of the UAE. Revered by his people, and often called 'father' by Emiratis, his compassion, modesty and wisdom commanded huge respect across the Middle East.

1968

The British announce their intention to withdraw from the Trucial States by 1971 leaving local leaders to discuss the shape of a future nation.

1971

After negotiating a federation with neighbouring emirates, Sheikh Zayed becomes the founding president of a united UAE. Sheikh Rashid of Dubai is declared prime minister.

1990

Sheikh Rashid dies during the first Gulf War and his son, Sheikh Maktoum, takes over as Dubai's ruler. His brother Mohammed succeeds the flamboyant sheikh in 2006.

1996

Two major annual events, the Dubai Shopping Festival and the Dubai World Cup are launched, thereby establishing Dubai's reputation as a tourist destination.

MODERNISING RULERS

Overseeing Dubai's transformation into a 21st-century metropolis is the third son of the dynasty, Sheikh Mohammed bin Rashid al Maktoum, who was the face of modern Dubai even before he succeeded his older brother as ruler in 2006. Having ruled Dubai as a de facto leader since the mid-1990s, Sheikh Mohammed has brought consistency and continuity to Dubai in a period of tremendous social, cultural and economic change.

In Abu Dhabi, Sheikh Khalifa bin Zayed al Nahyan, a highly regarded philanthropist, was elected to the role of UAE president when his esteemed father died in 2004. He has spent more than a decade continuing the great man's work, quietly transforming the city into an international metropolis and the assured capital of the UAE.

talks that extended to Bahrain and Qatar collapsed but Sheikh Zayed was successful in persuading his counterpart in Dubai, Sheikh Rashid bin Saeed al Maktoum, and the other emirs to create a single state.

On 2 December 1971, thanks to Sheikh Zayed's persistence, the United Arab Emirates was created. It consisted of the emirates of Dubai, Abu Dhabi, Ajman, Fujairah, Sharjah and Umm al-Quwain; Ras al-Khaimah joined in 1972. Impressively, given the volatility in the region, the UAE remains to this day the only federation of Arab states in the Middle East.

In February 2008 Sheikh Mohammed named his son Hamdan bin Mohammed bin Rashid al Maktoum, aka 'Fazza 3', as the emirate's crown prince and his likely successor. The young prince, a Sandhurst graduate who publishes romantic poetry, is already popular – check out his YouTube fan videos or friend him on Facebook.

Establishing a Stable State

Abu Dhabi, the largest of the emirates, and Dubai carried the most weight in the new federation, but each emir remained largely autonomous. Sheikh Zayed became the supreme ruler (president) of the UAE, and Sheikh Rashid of Dubai assumed the role of vice-president.

The fledgling nation had its share of teething problems, with border disputes between the emirates continuing throughout the 1970s and '80s together with negotiations about the levels of influence and independence enjoyed by each emirate. The relationship between the two leading emirates has not been without its troubles either. Achieving an equitable balance of power, as well as refining a unified vision for the country, was much debated until 1979 when Sheikh Zayed and Sheikh Rashid finally compromised to reach an agreement.

The result was a much stronger federation in which Dubai remained a bastion of free trade while Abu Dhabi imposed a tighter federal structure on the other emirates. Zayed remained as president and Rashid became prime minister; together they remained commited to the federation throughout their respective lives.

2004

Sheikh Zayed dies. The father of the nation is deeply mourned across the UAE and celebrated for steering the country towards stability and success.

2008

The world financial crisis severely affects Dubai's economy. Abu Dhabi extends a helping hand in a gesture that demonstrates the bond between the two emirates.

2010

The extraordinary Burj Khalifa opens. At 828m it's the world's tallest building. It has more than 160 floors and the highest outdoor observation deck in the world.

2015

The final phase of a customs union, originally launched in 2003, is implemented, making the objectives of a common market between GCC member states ever more tangible.

Politics & Economy

The United Arab Emirates (UAE) is a federation of small autonomous states, governed by individual absolute monarchs. The seven states of the federation have made a success of rubbing along together, showing that there's greater strength in union than in the sum of their constituent parts. Among the emirates, Dubai has the highest profile abroad but Abu Dhabi is the indisputable capital, with the greatest wealth and the largest territory. A certain tribal rivalry between them has helped spur the union on.

Federal Politics

Despite Dubai becoming so strong over the last few years, it has had to fight to preserve as much of its independence as possible and to minimise the power of the country's federal institutions. As in Ras al-Khaimah, it maintains a legal system that is separate from the federal judiciary.

Politically, the relative interests of the seven emirates are fairly clear. Abu Dhabi is the largest and wealthiest emirate and has the biggest population. As such it is the naturally dominant member of the federation. Dubai is the second-largest emirate by population, with both an interest in upholding its free-trade policies and a pronounced independent streak. The relationship between the two emirates was redefined during the financial turmoil of 2008–9 when the capital came to Dubai's rescue on several occasions. The other emirates are dependent on subsidies from Abu Dhabi, though the extent of this dependence varies widely.

The president of the UAE is traditionally drawn from the Al Nahyan tribe, the ruling family of Abu Dhabi, while the prime minister is of the Al Maktoum ruling family, from Dubai.

The Decision-Makers

The seven rulers, or emirs, of the UAE form the Supreme Council, the highest body in the land. The Council ratifies federal laws and sets general policy. New laws can be passed with the consent of five of the seven rulers. The Supreme Council also elects one of the emirs to a five-year term as the country's president. After the death in late 2004 of Sheikh Zayed, the founder and first president of the country, power passed peacefully to his son, Sheikh Khalifa bin Zayed al Nahyan.

There is also a Council of Ministers, or cabinet, headed by the prime minister (the Emir of Dubai). The prime minister appoints ministers from across the emirates. Naturally, the more populous and wealthier emirates such as Abu Dhabi and Dubai have greater representation. The cabinet and Supreme Council are advised, but can't be overruled, by a parliamentary body called the Federal National Council (FNC).

Dubai's current emir, 'Sheikh Mo,' is a keen fan of falconry and equestrianism and runs the Godolphin Stables; he is estimated to be worth US$10 billion. Abu Dhabi's current emir, Sheikh Khalifa, is a highly regarded philanthropist who has spent over US$460 million of his personal fortune on various charitable causes.

Benign Dictatorsip

During the 2011 uprisings across the region there was much talk about democracy but not much appetite to see it implemented. It may go against the grain of Western assumptions, but democracy is not as universally desired in the region as the media would have us believe. Perceived as promoting the interests of the individual over those of the community, democracy is considered by many in this part of the world to run contrary to tribal traditions, where respect for elders is

CENSORSHIP

Gone are the days when certain clothing labels had to be snipped from your underwear if you wanted to get through customs, and when international papers looked as though they'd been mauled by the dog before reaching the newsstand. But that's not to say that the censor has given up the fight entirely. According to a report issued by the OpenNet Initiative (ONI), 'The government of the United Arab Emirates (UAE) censors political and religious content and pervasively filters websites that contain pornography or content relating to alcohol or drug use, gay and lesbian issues, or online dating or gambling.'

Local journalists working in Dubai know that some topics, such as criticism of the UAE's rulers or anything that could be perceived as negative towards Islam, are off limits. Alcohol remains a taboo also: you'll have to read between the lines to pick up which bars serve alcohol in publications like *Time Out*, but you don't have to be Sherlock Holmes to detect that 'hoppy beverages' are unlikely to refer to lemonade.

paramount. In common with other parts of the Middle East, the people of the UAE tend to favour strong, centralised government under an autocratic leader – what has been dubbed 'benign dictatorship'. Of course, benign dictatorship is only as good as the person in charge and both Dubai and Abu Dhabi have been lucky in this respect, enjoying a half century of visionary and dynamic leadership.

Sheikh Mohammed bin Rashid al Maktoum of Dubai is a case in point. When he was named one of the world's 100 most influential people by *Time* magazine, it came as no surprise. Having spent several years as a de facto ruler while he was crown prince, Sheikh Mohammed was the only candidate for the top job when his brother, Sheikh Maktoum, died in early 2006. Although he is surrounded by some of the greatest minds in the Gulf, as well as political and economic experts imported from all over the world, there's no uncertainty about where executive power lies. 'Sheikh Mo', as he is affectionately called, has a flair for generating publicity for the city and was deeply involved in the planning and construction of landmark projects such as the Burj Al Arab, Palm Jumeirah and Burj Khalifa.

Economics on the Web

- *www.kippreport.com*
- *www.uaeinteract.com*
- *www.abudhabi.ae*
- *www.emirateseconomist.blogspot.com*

Visitors from Western countries may feel uncomfortable with the large-scale portraits of the ruler on billboards and buildings around town. Yet these are not simply the propaganda tools of an autocratic regime; many people in Abu Dhabi and Dubai revere their rulers. Few world leaders are able to drive themselves around town, as Sheikh Mohammed does, without a bodyguard and without any fear of being attacked. Although dissenting voices aren't tolerated and the local media is uncritical, most people admire the emirs for creating a haven of peace and prosperity in a troubled part of the world.

Taking the Public Pulse

A vital part of becoming a successful autocratic leader is finding ways of listening to the people. Since 2006, half of the country's FNC (the 40-person body established to review and debate legislation) has been elected; the other 20 are appointed by each emirate.

At present the FNC can only advise the government, and less than 1% of Emiratis (a tiny fraction of the UAE's total population) are able to vote for candidates from a list approved by the government. There are future plans, however, to grant the FNC some legislative powers and eventually to give the vote to all UAE citizens.

A Diversified Economy

The UAE as a whole has the world's seventh-largest oil reserves (after Saudi Arabia, Iran, Iraq, Canada, Kuwait and Venezuela), with the vast majority of it concentrated in the emirate of Abu Dhabi. It is thought that at current levels of extraction, reserves will last for another century but, as the dramatic drop in oil prices in 2015 has shown, the country cannot afford to be complacent about its continuing wealth.

In common with Gulf neighbours, therefore, the UAE is looking at alternative sources of energy and ways of diversifying the economy. Dubai's strategy for diversification has shown particular foresight, largely thanks to the vision and ambition of Sheikh Mohammed bin Rashid al Maktoum. Dubai's reserves of oil and gas were never that large, but the resources were used wisely to finance a modern and efficient infrastructure for trade, manufacturing and tourism. Today, revenues for oil and gas account for less than 2% of Dubai's GDP. Inflation slowed down significantly in 2011 and by 2015 hovered around 1.3%.

Economic Challenges

Until September 2008 it looked as though Dubai had the Midas touch. But then the world financial crisis struck and the emirate's economy collapsed like the proverbial house of cards. Real estate was particularly hard hit, with prices plummeting by as much as 50%, and Dubai was left

ABU DHABI'S BLACK GOLD

You only have to sniff the air during F1 race weekend at Yas Marina Circuit to recognise that Abu Dhabi is a capital city that celebrates its fuel!

Abu Dhabi's Oil Wealth

The oil reserves of the UAE are estimated to be 98 billion barrels, 92 billion of which belong to Abu Dhabi. Within the space of 50 years, oil has transformed the capital from a fishing village into, according to the Sovereign Wealth Fund, the richest city in the world. With US$773 billion in cash in the bank and over US$10 trillion invested, it's little wonder that this wealthy emirate is able to splash the cash. But where does all this oil come from?

Oil's Origins

Extensive flooding millions of years ago led to the remains of marine life being deposited in layers of sediment across Arabia's land mass. When dead organic matter is trapped under the land's surface with a lack of oxygen to prevent it from decaying to water and carbon dioxide, the raw material of hydrocarbons is produced – this is the origin of oil and gas.

The conversion from dead organic matter to a hydrocarbon is subject to many particular conditions including depth and temperature. Arabia's geology is uniquely supportive of these conditions, and 'nodding donkeys' (drilling apparatus, capable of boring holes up to 5km deep) can be seen throughout the interior. In Abu Dhabi's dhow harbour, you can sometimes spot offshore platforms, used for tapping into hidden seams of 'reservoir rock', being towed in for maintenance.

How Long Will it Last?

The media across the region agonise over reserves reaching their peak and whether modern technologies such as fracking will reduce the dependency on Arab oil. Given that the economies of the Gulf rely to a lesser or greater extent on oil and gas, this is one issue that can't be left to *insha'allah* (God's will). As such, Abu Dhabi and the neighbours are busy diversifying their economies and actively exploring alternative technologies (most notably in pioneering Masdar City) to ensure they exchange today's black gold for tomorrow's sound future.

with a staggering debt of at least US$80 billion. When the government announced, in November 2009, that it would seek a six-month delay in repaying its debt, it sent worldwide stock markets into a tailspin.

Markets stabilised quickly after the Abu Dhabi government rode to the rescue with a US$10 billion loan. As a sign of gratitude, in January 2010 Sheikh Mohammed renamed Burj Dubai, the world's tallest building, 'Burj Khalifa', in honour of the UAE president and ruler of Abu Dhabi, Sheikh Khalifa bin Zayed al Nahyan.

Dubai's tourism, some suggest, was built on a clever exploitation of the stop-over market, on the back of an excellent airline. Offering passengers a chance to break their journey and enjoy some tax-free shopping, Dubai has slowly become a destination in its own right.

Dubai climbed quickly out of recession, proving its perennial critics wrong, but the significant drop in oil prices in 2015 is being talked of as the trigger of a new slump. Despite appearances, however, Dubai is playing the long game, investing in enduring strategies that will help it weather future storms. Abu Dhabi has realised the power of this strategy and is catching up on non-oil enterprises, particularly in the tourism sector. Once the capital's cultural district is complete, it will rival Dubai in terms of top sights.

Once a Trader, Always a Trader

Throughout history, trade has been a fundamental part of Dubai's economy. The emirate imports an enormous amount of goods, primarily minerals and chemicals, base metals (including gold), vehicles and machinery, electronics, textiles and foodstuffs. The main importers into Dubai are the US, China, Japan, the UK, South Korea and India.

Exports are mainly oil, natural gas, dates, dried fish, cement and electric cables. Top export destinations are the other Gulf States, India, Japan, Taiwan, Pakistan and the US.

Dubai's re-export trade (where items such as white goods come into Dubai from manufacturers and are then sent onwards) makes up about 80% of the UAE's total re-export business. Dubai's re-exports go mainly to Iran, India, Saudi Arabia, Kuwait, China and Afghanistan.

World's Largest Airport

Dubai never shies away from superlatives, which is why it should be no surprise that it is to have the world's biggest airport. Upon final completion, Al Maktoum International Airport in Jebel Ali will boost the emirate's annual passenger potential to an estimated 160 million by 2035, and be capable of handling over 12 million tonnes of cargo annually. It is costing around US$34 billion to build and will eventually be 10 times the size of Dubai International Airport and Dubai Cargo Village combined.

Dubai is home to the world's largest artificially made harbour and biggest port in the Middle East. Called Jebel Ali, it's at the far western edge of Dubai, en route to Abu Dhabi. And Dubai International Airport has now taken over from London Heathrow as the world's busiest airport.

Abu Dhabi is also building a mega-hub to support the fast-growing national airline, Etihad. Abu Dhabi's Terminal 3 opened in 2009 to accommodate the approximate 12 million annual passengers, with an additional terminal scheduled to open in 2016.

Free Zones

The Jebel Ali Free Zone, established in 1985, is home to 5500 companies from 120 countries and has contributed significantly to Dubai's economic diversification. Companies are enticed here by the promise of full foreign ownership, full repatriation of capital and profits, no corporate tax for 15 years, no currency restrictions, and no personal income tax.

Other industry-specific free zones, such as Dubai Internet City and Dubai Media City, have added a high-tech information and communication stratum to the city's economy. IT firms based here include Google, HP, Dell and Oracle. Reuters, CNN, CNBC, MBC, Sony, Showtime and Bertelsmann are among the media companies that have set up shop in town.

Identity & Culture

A criticism levelled at Dubai and Abu Dhabi is that they are so lacking in national identity 'you could be anywhere'. This must be said by those who've never visited, or by those who mistakenly think high-rise sophistication is the sole preserve of Western cultures. Arrive at the airport of either city with their bold design, extravagant spaces and grand public art; their welcoming, immaculately dressed immigration officers; their prayer rooms, perfumes, nuts and dates, and frankly 'you couldn't be anywhere else'!

Bedouin Heritage

You only have to pay a visit to the Falcon Hospital (p160) in Abu Dhabi to recognise that the Bedouin culture runs deep. Emiratis celebrate their cultural identity through falconry, animal husbandry, horse- and camel-racing and with escapes to the desert. The Bedouin bond with animals may be an obvious indication of a link with the past, but there are more subtle ways in which this heritage is kept alive. Go to a conference and you are likely to be offered coffee and dates, or at the very least offered the welcome that is implicit in those traditional symbols of 'bread and salt'. Visit a neighbour and they will see you to the lift well in a gesture of safe passage.

Sensing that shedding the visible symbols of their old way of life gave the wrong message about their country, the municipalities of Dubai and Abu Dhabi have since worked hard to reinstate them. Forts are being renovated, old buildings preserved, heritage villages and cultural centres promoted, and songs and dances reinstated during national day events. These are not just gestures to attract and entertain tourists: they fulfil a role in educating young Emiratis about the value of their culture and heritage. After all, in the words of Sheikh Zayed, the father of the nation, 'He who does not know his past cannot make the best of his present and future for it is from the past that we learn.'

Presenting the public face of their families remains the traditional prerogative of men. The home is set up with this in mind with a *majlis* (meeting room), used by men to entertain guests. The genders continue to enjoy segregated company, although this should not be misconstrued as subjugation of one gender by another.

Islamic Values

A Life Informed by Religion

If the Bedouin heritage informs one significant strand of the modern identity of the emirates, Islam informs the other. Islam is not just the official religion of Dubai and Abu Dhabi, it is the cultural lifeblood.

Religion in the emirates is more than something performed on a Friday and put aside during the week, it is part of everyday life. It guides the choices an individual makes and frames the general context in which family life, work, leisure, care of the elderly and responsibility towards others take place. As such Islam has played a socially cohesive role in the two rapidly changing cities of Dubai and Abu Dhabi, giving support where old structures (both physical and social) have been dismantled to make way for a new urban experience.

THE FIVE PILLARS OF ISLAM

The general tenets of a Muslim's faith are expressed in the Five Pillars of Islam.

Shahadah The profession of faith: 'There is no god but God, and Mohammed is the messenger of God.'

Salat Muslims are required to pray five times every day: at dawn *(fajr)*, noon *(dhuhr)*, mid-afternoon *(asr)*, sunset *(maghrib)* and twilight *(isha'a)*. During these prayers a Muslim must perform a series of prostrations while facing Mecca. Praying is proceeded by ritual ablutions.

Zakat Muslims must give a portion of their income to help the poor. This is considered an individual duty in Dubai and Abu Dhabi, as opposed to a state-collected income tax redistributed through mosques or religious charities favoured in some communities.

Sawm It was during the month of Ramadan in AD 610 that Mohammed received his first revelation. Muslims mark this event by fasting from sunrise until sunset throughout Ramadan. During the fast a Muslim may not take anything into his or her body. Food, drink, smoking and sex are therefore forbidden.

Hajj All able Muslims are required to make the pilgrimage to Mecca at least once, if possible during a specific few days in the first and second weeks of the Muslim month of Dhul Hijja, although visiting Mecca and performing the prescribed rituals at any other time of the year is also considered spiritually desirable.

Practical Faith

You don't have to be in the two cities long to notice the presence of the 'third party' of Islam in all human interaction. Every official occasion begins with a reading from the holy Quran. A task at work begins with an entreaty for God's help. The words *al-hamdu lillah* (thanks be to God) frequently lace sentences in which good things are related. Equally the words *insha'allah* (God willing) mark all sentences that anticipate the future. These expressions are not merely linguistic decoration, they evidence a deep connection between society and faith.

For the visitor, understanding this link between religion and daily life can help make better sense of often misunderstood practices. Take dress, for example. Islam prescribes modest dress in public places for both men and women. The origin of the custom of covering the body is unclear – it certainly pre-dates Islam and to a large degree makes excellent sense under the ravaging tropical sun. Similarly Muslims are forbidden to consume anything containing pork or alcohol. These strictures traditionally made good sense in a region where tapeworm was a common problem with pork meat and where the effects of alcohol are exaggerated by the extreme climate. They remain sensible precautions today.

Social Interaction

Respect for Elders

Emiratis value the advice of their elders. Traditional tribal leaders, or 'sheikhs', continue to play an important social function in terms of providing for the less well off, settling local disputes and giving patronage where required. The term *wasta*, translated loosely as 'influence', is frequently bandied about. *Wasta* is generally bestowed by sheikhs on family or tribal members and differs little from the cozenage that exists in many Western societies, except that it is more overt and considered more acceptable. Seeking favours from the well-connected has helped consolidate the power of key families, not least the Maktoums and the Nahyans, the ruling dynasties of Dubai and Abu Dhabi.

Marriage

A Muslim man is permitted by Islam to have up to four wives (but a woman may have only one husband). As with many practices within Islam this came about through practical considerations where women were left without a provider through war, natural disasters or divorce. Most Emiratis have only one wife, however, not least because Islam dictates that each spouse must be loved and treated equally. Besides, marriage and housing and child rearing is expensive – perhaps why the average number of children in a modern family has declined from five to two.

Urban life puts a particular strain on city marriages with the high divorce rate (three per day in Dubai alone) revealing a fault line between traditional and modern values. Growing infidelity between partners, unrealistic expectations about living the urban dream, the difficulties of cross-cultural unions and long commutes are some of the many reasons cited for marriage break-ups.

Emirati women in the UAE are employed in the armed forces and police, undertake research and participate in Antarctic exploration. The tally of high-powered women is impressive: four cabinet ministers, three ambassadors, one Consul General, UAE's UN representative, four judges, two public prosecutors, and CEOs of three major trade entities.

Role of Women

Modern life has provided new opportunities for women beyond care of the family, largely thanks to the equitable nature of education in the country. Women now outnumber and often outperform men at many tertiary institutions. They go on to work in a variety of roles, including as doctors, engineers, government ministers, innovators and corporate executives. In fact 66% of the public sector workforce (compared with 48% globally), 30% of senior decision-makers and 17.5% of the partially elected Federal National Council are women. In 2012 the United Arab Emirates (UAE) was the second country in the world to introduce the mandatory appointment of women to UAE boards. Commentators suggest that there is no glass ceiling for women, veil or no veil.

The Workplace

Most Emiratis work in the public sector, as the short hours, good pay, benefits and early pensions make for an attractive lifestyle. The UAE government is actively pursuing a policy of 'Emiratisation', however, which involves encouraging Emiratis to work as entrepreneurs and employees in the private sector.

Until more locals take up the baton of small and medium enterprise, it will be hard for the government to decrease the dependency on an imported labour force, but equally it is hard for this to happen while Emiratis are employed only in a token capacity in the private sector. At some point, a leap in the dark will be inevitable, to allow for local people to assume the roles for which they are being trained – and this includes making mistakes and learning from experience.

Multicultural Population

You can't talk about the identity of the Emirates without factoring in the multinational composition of the population. Across the UAE expats comprise around 80% of the population. In Dubai and Abu Dhabi, therefore, the visitor experience is largely defined by interaction with the myriad nationalities that have been attracted to the Gulf in search of a better (or at least more lucrative) life.

Different nationalities have tended to dominate specific sectors of the workforce: people from the Philippines are employed in health care, construction workers are predominantly from Pakistan, financial advisers are from India, while Western countries have traditionally supplied technical know-how. Discussion prevails as to who benefits most from the contract between employer and employee, with serious concerns about the welfare particularly of construction and domestic workers. Some steps have been taken to right the wrongs of those in low-paid work but it's fair to say that conditions for many remain far from ideal.

On the positive side, the international composition of the resident population of Dubai and Abu Dhabi has resulted in a vibrant multiculturalism. This is expressed in different religious festivals (including Diwali and Christmas), and gives the opportunity to experience the food and customs of each community in restaurants and shops. A visit to either city is likely to involve memorable conversations that allow the visitor to travel the world in an afternoon.

The Environment

It may seem odd to discuss the environment in a guide to two major metropolises, but peer out from the observation decks of Burj Khalifa in Dubai or Etihad Towers in Abu Dhabi and the hinterland immediately makes an impression. The cities are discrete specks in a desert that nips at the heels of civilisation, mocking human attempts to tame it. Exploring the desert is therefore more than just a fun day out – it provides the defining context of each conurbation.

The Land

Geologists speak of the Peninsula in terms of two distinct regions: the Arabian shield and the Arabian shelf. The shield, which consists of volcanic sedimentary rock, makes up the western third of today's Arabian Peninsula. The shelf is made up of the lower-lying areas that slope away from the shield, from central Arabia to the waters of the Gulf. Dubai and Abu Dhabi sit on the very edge of this Arabian shelf.

At 67,340 sq km, Abu Dhabi is the largest emirate in the UAE, occupying more than 80% of the country's total area. Although second-largest of the seven emirates, Dubai is quite small in comparison, extending over only 4114 sq km.

Geologists believe that the Peninsula originally formed part of the larger land mass of Africa. A split in this continent created both Africa's Great Rift Valley and the Red Sea. As Arabia slipped away from Africa, the Peninsula began to 'tilt', with the western side rising and the eastern edge dropping, a process that led to the formation of the Gulf.

There are no permanent rivers in the United Arab Emirates (UAE) but natural springs create oases in the desert. Al Ain and Liwa (both easy to visit as day trips from the city) grew up around the date plantations. Shading citrus trees and grain crops, the plantations are watered via elaborate irrigation networks *(falaj)*. A working *falaj* at the Heritage Village (p137) in Abu Dhabi demonstrates how these channels work for the benefit of the whole community.

Ecosystems

Desert

The harsh lands of Arabia have for centuries attracted travellers from the West, curious to see the great sea of sand known as the 'Empty Quarter' or 'Rub al Khali'. Straddling the UAE, Saudi Arabia, Oman and Yemen, the dunes form a magnificent landscape that changes in colour and texture as the sun and wind project their own dramas on the ridges of sand.

A portion of the Empty Quarter, including one of the highest dunes in the northern sands, lies within the territory of Abu Dhabi, and a sealed road winding from the oasis towns of Liwa to the fringe of the sands makes this environment easily accessible by car from the Gulf cities. For those able to spare the time to camp in this terrain there is the chance to see some of the desert's shy residents. The dunes are home to various reptiles, including vipers, monitor lizards and spiny-tailed agamas.

At dawn, the tracks of hares, hedgehogs and foxes illustrate that many species of mammals have adapted to this unforgiving environment. Many have large ears, giving a broad surface area from which to release heat, and tufts of hair on paws that enable walking on the blistering sands.

To this day, people come to the desert expecting 'sand, sand, sand, still sand, and only sand and sand again'. The Victorian traveller who wrote those words (Kinglake) curiously had only passed through gravel plains at that point, but so strong is the connection between the words 'desert' and 'sand', he felt obliged to comment on what he thought he should see rather than on what was there. For anyone who looks beyond the roadside planting on the drive between Dubai and Abu Dhabi, it will become quickly apparent that the term 'desert' encompasses far more than simply sand. In fact, most of the UAE is comprised of flat gravel plains, punctuated with thorny, flat-topped acacia trees and herbal plants, interrupted by notorious salt flats, known as *sabkha*.

Sabkha is a salt-crusted quagmire of water-saturated land. It looks hard and even polished to the eye but attempt to ride a camel across it or drive a vehicle on it and the surface quickly disintegrates.

Seas

The Gulf has a character all its own, thanks to its largely landlocked location. Flat, calm, and so smooth that at times it looks solid like a piece of shiny coal, it tends to be shallow for up to a kilometre from the shore. With lagoons and creeks edged with valuable mangroves, this is an important habitat for waders and gulls. It is also conducive to human development: much of the rim of the Gulf, particularly surrounding Dubai and Abu Dhabi, has been paved over or reclaimed for land use.

While dredging for this purpose (some 33 million cubic metres of seabed was distributed for the World project alone) has had a detrimental effect on marine life, and particularly on fragile coral reefs, the waters off Dubai and Abu Dhabi still teem with around 300 different species of fish. Kingfish, hammour, tuna, sardines and sharks are regulars of the fish market but thankfully turtles are no longer hunted for food. Green and hawksbill turtles used to nest in some numbers on Dubai's beaches and their tracks can still be seen on the protected beaches of Saadiyat Island in Abu Dhabi. Resorts have understood the value of sharing the beach with these magnificent ocean-going creatures and are contributing to various programs to help with turtle conservation (see www.dubaiturtles.com for more information).

MANGROVES

The Eastern Mangroves off the northeast coast of Abu Dhabi is the largest mangrove forest in the UAE, but Dubai also has an important area of this unique habitat. Some key facts:

What is mangrove? Mangrove is a type of subtropical, low-growing tree with high salt toleration that lives with roots immersed in the high tide.

Are all mangroves the same? No, there are 110 species. The grey mangrove is the most common in Abu Dhabi and Dubai.

Why are they protected? This fragile ecosystem is a haven for wildlife and helpfully protective of shorelines commonly eroded by tides.

What lives in these forests? Mangroves provide a safe breeding ground for shrimps, turtles and some fish species, and habitats for migrating birds.

Any other uses? Historically, they provided a rich source of fuel and building material. The hard wood is resistant to rot and termites, making it ideal for building boats and houses.

Are they endangered? Yes, but thanks to local conservation efforts and deliberate replanting schemes the mangroves have grown in size over recent years.

Are visits possible? Many tour companies organise ecotrips into the mangrove forests. In Abu Dhabi, kayaking trips from Yas Island are a particularly informative way of learning more about this marine environment.

DESERT YES, DESERTED NO

Visiting any wilderness area comes with responsibility and no more so than in a desert, where the slightest interference with the environment can wreak havoc with fragile ecosystems. The rocky plains of the interior may seem like an expanse of nothing, but that is not the case. Red markers along a road, improbable as they may seem on a cloudless summer day, indicate the height of water possible during a flash flood. A month or so later, a flush of tapering grasses marks the spot, temporary home to wasp oil beetles, elevated stalkers and myriad other life forms.

Car tracks scar a rock desert forever, crushing plants and insects not immediately apparent from the driver's seat. Rubbish doesn't biodegrade as it would in a tropical or temperate climate. The flower unwittingly picked in its moment of glory may miss its first and only opportunity for propagation in seven years of drought.

With a bit of common sense, however, and taking care to stick to existing tracks, it's possible to enjoy the desert without damaging the unseen communities it harbours. It also pays to turn off the engine and just sit. At dusk, dramas unfold: a fennec fox chases a hedgehog, a feral dog trots out of the wadi without seeing the snake slithering in the other direction, tightly closed leaves relax in the brief respite of evening and a dung beetle rolls its reward homewards.

City Parks

Perhaps few would consider a city park as part of the natural environment, and in the Gulf states it could be argued there is nothing natural about these landscaped areas. Indeed, most of the planting is imported from neighbouring subtropical countries and each specimen is individually irrigated with piped water.

Despite their artificiality, however, the many city parks dotted around Dubai and particularly Abu Dhabi have proved havens for insects and birds. As islands of fertility in the surrounding desert, these parks attract a whole variety of migrating birds. The Gulf is on the migration path between Europe, Asia and Africa, and more than 320 migratory species pass through in spring and autumn, or spend the winter here. Species native to Arabia include the crab-plover, the Socotra cormorant, the black-crowned finch lark and the purple sunbird – the last of which is a common resident in any park where aloe is grown.

Botanical Reads

Handbook of Arabian Medicinal Plants by S A Ghazanfar

Vegetation of the Arabian Peninsula by S A Ghazanfar & M Fisher (eds)

Environmental Issues

Protected Areas

The idea of setting aside areas for wildlife runs contrary to the nature of traditional life on the Peninsula which was, and to some extent still is, all about maintaining a balance with nature, rather than walling it off. The Bedu flew their hunting falcons only between certain times of the year and moved their camels on to allow pasture to regrow. Fishermen selected only what they wanted from a seasonal catch, and threw the rest back. Farmers let lands lie fallow so as not to exhaust the soil.

Modern practices including sport hunting, trawler fishing and the use of pesticides in modern farming have had an impact on the environment over the past 50 years, however, all governments in the region have recognised the need to protect the fragile ecosystems of their countries. This has resulted in the creation of protected areas (10% of regional land mass), but, with tourism on the increase, there is a strong incentive to do more.

Among its Peninsula neighbours, the UAE leads the way with 5% of the Emirate of Dubai established as a protected area. In addition, the Dubai Desert Conservation Reserve has helped reintroduce the Arabian oryx, hunted almost to extinction in the last century; Sir Bani Yas Island has

LOCAL ENVIRONMENTAL ORGANISATIONS

Emirates Diving Association (EDA; ☎04-393 9390; www.emiratesdiving.com) An active participant in local marine campaigns.

Emirates Environmental Group (☎344 8622; www.eeg-uae.org) Organises educational programs in schools and businesses as well as community programs, such as clean-up drives.

Emirates Wildlife Society (http://uae.panda.org) Works in association with the World Wildlife Fund (WWF) on implementing conservation initiatives to protect local biodiversity and promote sustainable lifestyles.

an important collection of Arabian wildlife, and Al Ain Zoo (p174) has been transformed into a breeding centre and sustainable wildlife park.

Global Footprint

Across the UAE, resources are consumed at a much faster rate than they can be replaced, which is why the ecological footprint of the Gulf cities is so high. It is no easy feat to reverse the trend and achieve environmental sustainability when the UAE relies so heavily on imported goods and urban dwelling has become the norm.

However, the UAE has joined hands with the Global Footprint Network to improve the country's sustainability through practical measures such as the efficient lighting standard, introduced in 2013. This initiative alone reduced energy consumption by 340 to 500 megawatts per year – apparently equivalent to six months' usage of an average gas power station.

Meanwhile, Masdar City (p161), Abu Dhabi's flagship environmental project, is aiming to become the world's first carbon-neutral, zero-waste community powered entirely by renewable energy.

Visitors can play their part in water conservation by taking simple measures, such as showering rather than bathing; cutting down on laundry of towels and bed linen; using the half-flush button, where possible, on toilets; and turning the tap off when brushing teeth.

Water

With their palm-lined avenues, parks and flowerbeds, it may be difficult to remember that Dubai and Abu Dhabi are built in one of the most arid deserts on earth. The cities receive no more than one or two days of rain per year and the ground water is highly saline – almost eight times as saline, in fact, as sea water. Virtually all (98%) of the city's drinking water is supplied, therefore, from desalination.

You'd think that the lack of natural reserves would have led to low water usage but, at 550L per day, the UAE has one of the highest per-capita rates of water consumption in the world. Recognising the challenges involved in indulging the city's seemingly endless thirst for water, the UAE government launches periodic awareness campaigns to encourage citizens to consume less, but the answer may lie with further technology. Ambitious projects to seed clouds in recent years appear to have made an impact, with a slightly increased rainfall being recorded.

Pollution & Rubbish

In a region where oil is the major industry, there is always a concern about spillage and leakage, and the illegal dumping of oil from offshore tankers is a constant concern. Thankfully, the expected ecological disaster after the oil spills of the Gulf War did not materialise. The same cannot be said for the dumping of industrial waste on land. The value of a circular economy is being actively discussed in the region, whereby waste is recycled and biomass harnessed for fuel. Perhaps if waste is shown to have value at a local level it will be easier to persuade industry to dispose of it responsibly.

The Arts

Rightly or wrongly, nations tend to be judged less by their contribution to their own artistic milieu than by their participation in contemporary dialogues that are largely Western in origin. The cities of the Gulf clearly feel this pressure to engage in the globalisation of the arts, as the creation of the Abu Dhabi Louvre amply demonstrates. Go looking only for contemporary exhibitions, however, and you'll run the risk of missing the art that means the most to the locals.

Function & Form

If you chose one feature that distinguishes art in the Arab world from that of the Western tradition, it would have to be the close integration of function with form. In other words, most Arab art has evolved with a purpose. That purpose could be as practical as embellishing the prow of a boat with a cowrie shell to ward off 'evil eye', or as nebulous as creating intricate and beautiful patterns to suggest the presence of God and invite spiritual contemplation. Purpose is an element that threads through all Gulf art, craft, music, architecture and poetry.

Seen on a video at the Dubai Museum or performed live during the Qasr al Hosn festival, *ayyalah* is a typical Bedouin dance. Performed to a simple drumbeat, men link arms, wave camel sticks or swords, sway back and forth and sing of the virtues of bravery in battle.

Craft Heritage

Visiting the Heritage Villages in Dubai or Abu Dhabi is a good way to understand the relationship between function and form reflected in local arts. A woman sitting cross-legged on a rice mat in one of these villages may seem staged, but the mats are bought, sold and used – and that's why they're still being made.

Crafts have traditionally been a notable art form in the Gulf, thanks in part to a partially Bedouin heritage. The nomadic pre-oil lifestyle of part of the population dictated a life refined of excess baggage, and so creativity found its most obvious expression in poetry, song, storytelling and portable, practical craft.

In crafts such as jewellery, silver-smithing, weaving, embroidery and basket-making, function and form combine in artefacts that document a way of life. Take jewellery, for example – the heavy silver so distinctively worn by Bedouin women was designed not just as a personal adornment but as a form of portable wealth. Silver amulets contained rolled pieces of parchment or paper bearing protective inscriptions from the Quran to guarantee the safety of the wearer. These were considered useful against the perils of the 'evil eye' – the envy or malice of others.

At the end of the life of a piece of jewellery the silver was traditionally melted down and traded in as an ultimate gesture of practicality. In the same vein it is a sad fact about practical craft that once the need for it has passed, there is little incentive to maintain the skills. Why bother with clay ewers when everyone drinks water from plastic bottles? Aware of this fact, local craft associations in both Dubai and Abu Dhabi have sprung up in the hope of keeping local craft alive.

Far more vital in this endeavour, however, is finding new opportunities to commission old skills. Sheikh Zayed Grand Mosque is a prime example of this. With its meticulous inlaid marble work, exquisite calligraphy,

THE ORAL TRADITION

If you want to discover what gets the locals clapping, what makes them sway to the beat during national days and holidays, what makes them fall utterly silent after talking all the way through a formal address by a visiting dignitary, it's not classical music or Western visual arts. It's Arabic poetry. When visiting either city, if you get the chance to attend a recitation it shouldn't be missed.

Traditionally dominating Middle Eastern literature, all the best-known figures of classical regional literature are poets, including Omar Khayyam and Abu Nuwas. Poets were regarded as possessing knowledge forbidden to ordinary people and served the purpose of bridging the human and spirit worlds. To this day, even the the TV-watching young are captivated by a skilfully intoned piece of verse.

Poetry is part and parcel of the great oral tradition of storytelling that informs the literature of all Peninsula countries, the roots of which lie with the Bedu. Stories told by nomadic elders served not just as after-dinner entertainment, but as a way of binding generations together in a collective oral history. As such, storytelling disseminated the principles of Islam and of tribal and national identity.

hand-knotted carpet and ceramic tiles commissioned from across the Islamic region, this contemporary masterpiece demonstrates that traditional skills continue to evolve, reflecting the artistic expression of new generations.

Competing Internationally

It's easy to criticise the Emirates for buying into the international arts scene when they invest little in encouraging contemporary arts at home, but they are hardly to blame. There isn't a city to be taken seriously around the globe that doesn't have an opera house or a pavilion at the Venice Biennale, regardless of whether these pieces of imported Western culture are relevant. When the opera house first opened in neighbouring Muscat, a third of the audience left after the interval unaware that the performance continued, underwhelmed by musicians they couldn't see (in the orchestra pit) and mildly offended by the unrobing of the soprano in a brothel scene – a topic so *haram* (forbidden) locally as to be verging on the subversive.

This example serves to show that there is an almost unbridgeable gap between function and form in contemporary arts in the region. This leads one to surmise that the world-class exhibitions and performances on offer are largely there to impress visitors and to prove to cynics abroad that there is a cultural depth to these cities that can only be measured in Western terms.

For the cultural elite of Dubai and Abu Dhabi these are therefore happy days. With the expected opening in 2015 of the Abu Dhabi Louvre in the capital's celebrated Cultural District on Saadiyat Island, the UAE Pavilion hosting international exhibitions, and world-renowned opera and ballet showcased at the Emirates Palace, the city is attracting global attention. Equally in Dubai, the annual Art Dubai festival attracts some of the most celebrated international galleries, artists and dealers to a city associated with innovation and dynamism – as displayed not just in tomorrow's world architecture but also in backstreet workshops around Al Quoz.

For all the criticism, this investment in global arts is to be welcomed as with it comes a greater integration between East and West, and an opportunity to showcase more traditional local art forms to an international audience. This in turn helps preserve the traditions that matter most to local people.

Gulf Galleries & Exhibition Spaces

Third Line (p89)

Gallery Isabelle van den Eynde (p88)

Courtyard (p89)

Manarat al Saadiyat (p156)

UAE Pavilion (p157)

Ghaf Gallery (p144)

Survival Guide

Transport

ARRIVING IN DUBAI & ABU DHABI

Most visitors arrive by air with convenient flights from most major international cities. The approximate duration time from London is seven hours, from Sydney 14 hours, from New York 12 hours and from Ottawa 14 hours. Dubai and Abu Dhabi continue to serve as major stopover hubs between Europe and Asia.

There is road access directly from Oman via Al Ain, Abu Dhabi's southeastern city. You will be required to show your passport and visit visa (if applicable). Travel information is subject to frequent change, so check the www.dubai.ae government website for an update before you go. The United Arab Emirates (UAE) also has a less useful border crossing at Ghuwaifat, Saudi Arabia.

Buses to Abu Dhabi leave from Dubai's Al Ghubaiba station every 40 minutes (single Dh20, return Dh40). The trip takes two hours. Alternatively, it is an easy, direct drive, which takes roughly the same amount of time.

Flights, cars and tours can be booked online at lonelyplanet.com.

Air

All UAE airports have short- and long-term parking facilities. Tariffs range from Dh10 per hour to Dh125 per day in the short-term car park; travellers can leave their cars for up to 10 days in the long-stay car park. Free airport shuttle buses are offered by many hotels.

Dubai

Located in the north of the city, on the border with the Sharjah emirate, **Dubai International Airport** (Map p246; ☎04-224 5555, flight enquiries ☎04-224 5777; www.dubaiairport.com) is the busiest airport in the world, overtaking London Heathrow in early 2015. There are three terminals:

- **Terminal 1** Main terminal used for major international airlines.
- **Terminal 2** For small airlines and charters mainly en route to Iran, Eastern Africa and some Eastern European countries.
- **Terminal 3** Used exclusively by Emirates Airlines.

In 2011, the airport hit the headlines as being the first Middle Eastern airport to offer modular sleep pods called 'Snooze Cubes' for weary visitors. They are located in Terminal 1.

Abu Dhabi

About 30km northeast of the city centre, **Abu Dhabi International Airport** (Map p162; ☎02-575 7500, automated flight information ☎02-505 5555; www.abudhabiairport.ae) has three terminals, including

CLIMATE CHANGE & TRAVEL

Every form of transport that relies on carbon-based fuel generates CO_2, the main cause of human-induced climate change. Modern travel is dependent on aeroplanes, which might use less fuel per kilometre per person than most cars but travel much greater distances. The altitude at which aircraft emit gases (including CO_2) and particles also contributes to their climate change impact. Many websites offer 'carbon calculators' that allow people to estimate the carbon emissions generated by their journey and, for those who wish to do so, to offset the impact of the greenhouse gases emitted with contributions to portfolios of climate-friendly initiatives throughout the world. Lonely Planet offsets the carbon footprint of all staff and author travel.

Etihad Airways' exclusive base, Terminal 3.

Passengers travelling to Abu Dhabi International Airport on Etihad Airways can use free shuttle buses to/from Dubai. Otherwise, there is no direct public transport between the two city airports.

Sharjah

About 15km east of the Dubai–Sharjah border, **Sharjah International Airport** (☎06-558 1111; www.shj-airport.gov.ae) has significantly increased its capacity since becoming the hub of Air Arabia, the region's first budget airline.

To get to/from the airport you have to take a taxi (approximately Dh55 from Dubai), as there's no public transport between the airport and either city.

Intercity Bus

Well-maintained minibuses and air-conditioned (often overcrowded) buses are operated by the Dubai-based **Roads & Transport Authority** (RTA; ☎toll free 800 9090; www.rta.ae) between 6am and 11pm. Only services to Sharjah and Ajman return passengers to Dubai. Maps and timetables are available online and at the two main bus stations.

Abu Dhabi Bus Services (☎800 55 555; dot.abudhabi.ae; within Abu Dhabi Dh2) between Abu Dhabi's main bus terminal and Dubai's Al Ghubaiba station leave every 40 minutes (single/return Dh20/40, two hours). Intercity buses connect the capital with most Emirati destinations.

Al Ittihad Bus Station

Several services depart from **Al Ittihad bus station** (Map p244; cnr Omar ibn al Khattab & Al Rigga Rds), next to the Union metro station. These include buses to Fujairah (Dh25, two to 2½ hours, every 45 minutes), Ajman (Dh7, one to 1½ hours, every 20 minutes), Ras al Khaimah (Dh20, two hours, every 45 minutes), Sharjah (Dh5, 40 to 60 minutes, every 10 minutes) and Umm al Quwain (Dh10, 1½ hours, every 45 minutes).

Al Ghubaiba Bus Station

Bus services from **Al Ghubaiba bus station** (Map p248; Al Ghubaiba Rd, Bur Dubai), next to Carrefour supermarket, include Abu Dhabi (Dh20, two hours, every 40 minutes), Al Ain (Dh20, 1½ hours, hourly) and Sharjah (Dh5, 40 to 50 minutes, every 10 minutes).

GETTING AROUND DUBAI & ABU DHABI

By Foot

Negotiating Dubai by foot, even combined with public transport, is highly challenging due to the lack of pavements, traffic lights and pedestrian crossings. It is not unheard of here to be forced to take a taxi, merely to reach the other side of the road.

In contrast, downtown Abu Dhabi is pedestrian-friendly, with wide, lit pavements, lots of shady parks acting as thoroughfares and corniches with separate bicycle lanes.

Beware of summer heat!

Taxi

Most people get around Dubai and Abu Dhabi via taxis.

In Dubai, taxis are operated by **Dubai Taxi Corporation** (☎04-208 0808; www.dtc.dubai.ae) and are metered, relatively inexpensive and the fastest and most comfortable way to get around, except during rush-hour traffic.

In the capital, **Abu Dhabi Taxi** (☎600-535 353; www.transad.ae) is a government-monitored service operating metered taxis. It also operates a ladies cab service.

Fares

- Daytime (6am to 10pm) flagfall for street taxis is Dh3.50.
- Taxis ordered in advance or from your hotel have a flagfall of Dh6.50.
- The cost is Dh1.60 per kilometre, and Dh1.70 for larger people-carriers.
- From 10pm to 6am the starting fare is Dh4 (Dh7.50 when reserved).
- Trips originating at either airport have a flagfall of Dh25.

Reaching Your Destination

Most taxi drivers speak at least some English but destinations are generally not given via a street address. Instead, mention the nearest landmark (eg a hotel, mall, roundabout, major building). If you're going to a private residence, phone your host and ask them to give the driver directions.

The multiple road names in Abu Dhabi make it particularly challenging to navigate by address.

Taxi Trouble Spots

It's usually fairly easy to catch a taxi, but there are a few places where long waits are common. Expect lengthy queues at the major shopping malls on weekday evenings (especially Thursday) and Friday afternoons.

In Dubai, there's a chronic taxi shortage near the *abra* (water taxi) stations in Deira, by the shopping district of Karama, in Bur Dubai by the bus station, and along The Walk at JBR in Dubai Marina. Finding an available taxi is especially tough between

4pm and 5.30pm when most drivers end their shifts and have to deliver their cars to their partners.

Taxi Companies

DUBAI

Cars Taxis (☎04-269 3344) Blue roof.

Dubai Transport Company (☎04-208 0808) Red roof.

Ladies Taxi (☎04-208 0808) It's perfectly fine for women to ride alone in a taxi, even at night. However, if you prefer, you can also call to request a Ladies Taxi (flagfall Dh7), complete with pink roof and lady drivers.

Metro Taxis (☎04-267 3222) Orange roof.

National Taxis (☎04-339 0002) Yellow roof.

ABU DHABI

Abu Dhabi Taxi (☎600-535 353; www.transad.ae) This government-monitored service runs metered taxis and also operates a ladies cab service.

Al Ghazal (☎02-550 2160; www.alghazalcar-rental.com) Operating from the main bus terminal in Abu Dhabi, Al Ghazal offers an extensive intercity service largely aimed at the residential community, linking universities, oil fields and airports – an alternative to the national bus service. It also runs a fleet of reliable silver taxis in the city.

Car

Car Rental

Well-maintained multi-lane highways, plentiful petrol stations and cheap petrol make car rental a worthwhile option for day trips from the two cities.

To hire a car, you must be over the age of 21 and have a valid credit card and international driving licence, in addition to your home licence.

Daily rates start at about Dh200 for a small manual car, including comprehensive insurance and unlimited mileage. Expect surcharges for airport rentals, additional drivers, one-way hire and drivers under 25 years of age. Most companies have child safety seats for a fee, but these must be reserved. Check for deals with online car-rental brokers such as **Auto Europe** (www.autoeurope.com) and **Holiday Autos** (www.holidayautos.co.uk).

Both cities have scores of car-rental agencies, from major brands to local companies. The former may charge more but give peace of mind with full insurance and round-the-clock assistance included in the price.

The following international agencies have offices in the airport arrivals halls, around town and in major hotels in both cities.

Avis (☎airport 04-224 5219, head office ☎04-295 7121; www.avis.com)

Budget (☎airport 04-224 5192, head office ☎04-282 2727; www.budget-uae.com)

Europcar (☎airport 04-224 5240, head office ☎04-339 4433; www.europcar-dubai.com)

Hertz (☎airport 04-224 5222, head office ☎04-206 0206; www.hertz-uae.com)

Thrifty (☎airport 04-224 5404, head office ☎04-331 8772; www.thrifty.com)

Insurance

You will be offered a choice of insurance plans. If possible, opt for the most comprehensive as minor prangs are common here. If you have a breakdown, contact the **Arabian Automobile Association** (☎800 4900; www.aaauae.com) or the **International Automobile Touring Club** (IATC; ☎800 5200; www.iatcuae.com).

Parking

Increasingly, the busier city streets of both Dubai and Abu Dhabi have a strictly enforced four-hour limit on parking. The following applies to both cities:

- Standard parking zones are indicated by two-tone curb markings (black and turquoise).
- Tickets are purchased from an orange machine and displayed on your dashboard.
- Rates are Dh2 per hour and Dh15 for 24 hours.
- Payment is made by cash or by credit card.
- Parking in the centre of both cities is free on Friday and public holidays.
- Fines for not buying a ticket start at Dh100.

Road Rules

- Driving is on the right.
- The speed limit is 60km/h on city streets, 80km/h on major city roads and 200km/h on dual-lane highways.
- Seatbelts are compulsory and it is illegal to use a handheld mobile phone while driving.

DON'T DRINK & DRIVE!

Drinking and driving are never a good idea but in the United Arab Emirates (UAE) you'd be outright crazy to do so. Let's make it absolutely clear: if you've had as much as one sip, you've had too much. The UAE has a zero-tolerance policy on drink-driving (ie the blood alcohol limit is 0%), and if your vehicle is stopped and you're found to have been driving under the influence of alcohol, you'll be a guest of the police for up to 30 days.

- There's a zero-tolerance policy on drinking and driving (0% is the blood alcohol limit).
- Never make an offensive hand gesture to another driver; it could end in deportation or a prison sentence.
- Tailgating, although common, is illegal and can result in a fine.
- Don't cross yellow lines.
- If you're involved in a traffic accident, it's a case of being guilty until proven innocent, which means you may be held by the police until an investigation determines whose fault the accident was.

NOL CARDS

- Before you can hop aboard a local bus or the metro in Dubai you must purchase a rechargeable Nol Card (*nol* is Arabic for fare), available from ticket offices in any metro and some bus stations. There are also ticket vending machines (with English instructions) in all metro and bus stations, at some bus stops and other places such as malls and the airport.
- There are four categories of Nol Card. If you're only going to use public transport a few times, get a Red Card, which costs Dh2 and may be recharged for up to 10 journeys. Fares depend on distance and are divided into five zones. For Red Cards the cost ranges from Dh2.50 to Dh6.50.
- Day passes for unlimited travel in all zones are Dh14. Children under five years of age travel free.
- For full details, see www.nol.ae.

Rush Hour

If you decide to drive around Dubai, bear in mind that traffic congestion in the city can be a nightmare at peak hours, ie between 7am and 9am, 1pm and 2pm and most of the evening from 5pm onwards. The worst congestion is around the approaches to Al Maktoum and Al Garhoud Bridges and along Al Ittihad Rd towards Sharjah. Accidents are frequent; tune into the radio to get traffic updates.

Traffic in Abu Dhabi is not quite so bad but avoid the main thoroughfares around the same peak hours.

Local Transport

Dubai's local public transport is operated by the **Roads & Transport Authority** (RTA; ☎24-hr hotline 800 9090; www.rta.ae) and consists of the Dubai metro, buses, water buses and *abras* (traditional water taxis). A worthwhile RTA package called 'One Day in Dubai' allows for travel on all public transport covering the main city sights. For trip planning and general information, call the 24-hour hotline or visit the website. See the Abu Dhabi chapter (p129) for information on getting around the capital by public transport.

Abras

Abras are motorised traditional wooden boats linking Bur Dubai and Deira across the Creek on two routes:

Route 1 Bur Dubai Abra Station to Deira Old Souq Abra Station; daily between 5am and midnight.

Route 2 Dubai Old Souq Abra Station to Al Sabkha Abra Station around the clock.

Abras leave when full (around 20 passengers), which rarely takes more than a few minutes. The fare is Dh1 and you pay the driver halfway across the Creek. Chartering your own *abra* costs Dh100 per hour.

Modern *abras* with air-conditioning (minimum fare Dh50) are available for a ride across the Creek between 10am and 10pm.

Dubai Metro

Dubai's **metro** (www.dubaimetro.eu) opened in 2010 and has proved a popular service.

Red Line Runs for 52.1km from near Dubai International Airport to Jebel Ali past Dubai Marina, mostly paralleling Sheikh Zayed Road.

Green Line Runs for 22.5km, linking the Dubai Airport Free Zone with Dubai Healthcare City.

Intersection of Red & Green Lines At Union and Khalid bin al Waleed (next to BurJuman shopping mall) stations.

Onward Journey At each station, cabs and feeder buses stand by to take you to your final destination.

Frequency Trains run roughly every 10 minutes from 6am to midnight Saturday to Wednesday, 6am to 1am on Thursdays, and 1pm to 1am on Fridays.

Cars Each train consists of four standard cars and one car that's divided into a women-only section and a 'Gold Class' section where a double fare buys carpets and leather seats. Women may of course travel in any of the other cars as well.

Tickets *Nol* (fare) cards can be purchased at the station and must be swiped before exit.

Fares These vary from Dh2 for stops within a single zone to Dh6.50 for stops within five zones.

Routes All metro stations stock leaflets, in English, clearly mapping the zones.

Penalties If you exit a station with insufficient credit you will have to pay the equivalent of a day pass (Dh14). Inspectors regularly check cards have been swiped and will issue an on-the-spot Dh200 fine for ticket evasion.

Local Buses

The RTA operates local buses on 79 routes primarily serving the needs of low-income commuters. Buses are clean, comfortable, air-conditioned and cheap (around Dh2 per ride with a prepaid Nol card), but they're slow. The first few rows of seats are generally reserved for women and children.

For information and trip planning check the website www.rta.ae. Free route maps and timetables can also be picked up from major bus stations.

There is a good service of feeder buses that link the Burj Khalifa metro station with the Dubai Mall, and the Mall of the Emirates metro station with the mall (although this is walkable). There are also shuttle buses that connect both malls with a number of local hotels.

Monorail

The elevated, driverless **Palm Jumeirah Monorail** (www.palm-monorail.com) connects the Palm Jumeirah with Dubai Marina. There are only two stations: Gateway Towers near the bottom of the 'trunk' and the Aquaventure Waterpark at the Atlantis hotel. The 5.45km trip takes about five minutes and costs Dh15 (Dh25 round-trip).

Water Buses

Air-conditioned water buses travel along four Creek-crossing routes from 6am to 11pm daily. Routes B1 and B4 operate every 30 minutes, B2 and B3 at 15-minute intervals. Tickets are Dh2.

Route B1 Bur Dubai Station to Al Sabkha Station

Route B2 Dubai Old Souq Station to Baniyas Station

Route B3 Al Seef Station to Al Sabkha via Baniyas

Route B4 Bur Dubai Station to Creek Park Water Bus Station via Al Seef Station

Route B5 Between Shindagha Station near Heritage Village and Creek Park Water Bus Station every 30 minutes, stopping at Bur Dubai Station, Deira Old Souq Station and Al Seef Station.

All-day tickets on Route B5 cost Dh50 (Dh25 for children over six years). The entire journey lasts 45 minutes but you're free to get on and off throughout the ticket's validity (9am to midnight). You can also pay your fare using a prepaid Nol Card.

TOURS

The following reputable companies are all well established and licenced by the Department of Tourism & Commerce Marketing (DTCM). They offer a wide choice of tours, ranging from city excursions of Dubai, Al Ain and Sharjah to more active trips, such as trekking in the Hajar Mountains or overnight desert safaris. Note that some tours only depart with a minimum number of passengers. If you have a choice, Arabian Adventures has a particularly good reputation and repeatedly receives positive feedback from tourists.

Alpha Tours (☎04-294-9888; www.alphatoursdubai.com) Covers dune trips, cruises and helicopter tours.

Arabian Adventures (Map p258;☎04-303 4888; www.arabian-adventures.com; sundowner adult/child Dh330/295) Offers sundowner tours, which include 4WD drives, barbecue and Arab-style entertainment.

Desert Rangers (☎04-456 9944; www.desertrangers.com) This is one of the oldest adventure-sports-and-activities outfits in Dubai. It offers a wide variety of tours, including overnight desert safaris, dhow dinner cruises, mountain safaris and desert driving courses.

Hormuz Tourism (Map p244;☎04-228 0668; www.hormuztourism.com) Specialises in desert safaris but also arranges city tours of Dubai and Abu Dhabi.

Knight Tours (Map p258; ☎04-343 7725; www.knight-tours.co.ae) Offers private camping and tours to the East Coast.

Orient Tours (Map p246; ☎04-282 8238; www.orient-tours-uae.com) Has comprehensive five-night tours of the seven emirates.

Bus Tours

Big Bus Dubai (☎04-340 7709; www.bigbustours.com; ticket adult/child 24hr Dh240/100, 48hr Dh295/130) These 'hop-on hop-off' city tours aboard open-topped double-decker buses are a good way for Dubai first-timers to get their bearings. Buses run on three interlinking routes, stopping at major malls, beaches and landmarks. Tickets are sold online, on the bus or at hotels. There's also a nonstop 2¾-hour Night Tour (adult/child Dh145/75). The tours include taped commentary in 12 languages and such extras as a souq walking tour or a dhow mini-cruise. A similar **Big Bus Tour** (☎02-449 0026; www.bigbustours.com; ticket adult/child 24hr Dh200/100, 48hr Dh260/130; ⏲9am-7pm) is available in Abu Dhabi.

Directory A–Z

Courses

A number of institutes offer Arabic language courses in Dubai and Abu Dhabi; the following centres are popular:

Arabic Language Centre (Map p258; ☎04-331 5600; www.arabiclanguagecentre.com; World Trade Centre, Sheikh Zayed Rd, Dubai) Runs various courses in Arabic from beginner to advanced levels.

Berlitz Language School (Map p254; ☎04-344 0034; www.berlitz.ae; Jumeirah Rd, Dubai) Offers courses in a number of languages, including Arabic and Urdu – the language of most Pakistani expats in the United Arab Emirates (UAE).

Eton Institute (Map p152; ☎02-449 9649; www.etoninstitute.com; Park Rotana Office Complex, Khalifa Park, Abu Dhabi) Has several branches throughout the UAE.

Polyglot Language Institute (Map p244; ☎04-222 3429; www.polyglot.ae; Al Masaeed Bldg, Al Maktoum Rd, Deira, Dubai) Beginners courses and conversation classes in Arabic, French, German and English.

Customs Regulations

Anyone aged over 18 years is allowed to bring in the following duty-free:

- 400 cigarettes plus 50 cigars plus 500g of loose tobacco.
- 4L of alcohol or two cartons (24 cans) of beer (non-Muslims only).
- A total cost of gifts not exceeding Dh3000 in value.

You are *not* allowed to bring in:

- Alcohol if you cross into the UAE by land.
- Materials (ie books) that insult Islam.
- Firearms, pork, pornography or Israeli products.

You must declare to Customs:

- Cash (or equivalent) over Dh40,000.
- A total cost of gifts with a value of more than Dh3000.
- Medicines (you must be able to produce a prescription).

Electricity

The electric voltage is 220V AC. British-style three-pin wall sockets are standard, although most appliances are sold with two-pin plugs. Adaptors are available in supermarkets.

Embassies & Consulates

Embassies usually help in cases of a stolen passport but are not sympathetic to those committing a crime locally, even if their actions are legal back home.

Most countries have embassies in Abu Dhabi, or you can head for the following consulates in Dubai:

Australian Consulate (☎04-508 7100; www.uae.embassy.gov.au; 25th fl, BurJuman Business Tower, Trade Centre Rd, Bur Dubai; ⌚8am-1pm & 1.30-4.30pm Sun-Thu)

Canadian Consulate (☎04-314 5555; dubai@international.gc.ca; 7th fl, Bank St Bldg, Khalid bin al Waleed Rd, Bur Dubai; ⏰8am-4pm Sun-Thu) Next to Citibank.

French Consulate (☎04-332 9040; www.consulfrance-dubai.org; 18th fl, API World Tower, Sheikh Zayed Rd, Trade Centre District; ⏰8am-1pm Sat-Thu)

German Consulate (☎04-397 2333; www.dubai.diplo.de; 1st fl, Sharaf Bldg, Khalid bin al Waleed Rd, Bur Dubai; ⏰8-11am Sun-Thu) Opposite the BurJuman Centre.

Netherlands Consulate (☎04-352 8700; www.netherlands.ae; 5th fl, Royal Bank of Scotland Bldg, Khalid bin al Waleed Rd, Bur Dubai; ⏰9am-noon Sat-Thu)

Omani Consulate (☎04-397 1000; www.ocodubai.com; Consulate Zone, near Khalid bin al Waleed Rd, Umm Hurair; ⏰7.30am-2.30pm Sun-Thu) Issues tourist and business visas.

UK Consulate (☎04-309 4444; www.ukinuae.fco.gov.uk; Consulate Zone, Al Seef Rd, Umm Hurair; ⏰7.30am-2.30pm Sun-Thu)

US Consulate (☎04-309 4000; http://dubai.usconsulate.gov; Consulate General Compound, cnr Al Seef Rd & Sheikh Khalifa bin Zayed Rd, Bur Dubai; ⏰12.30-3pm Sun-Thu)

Emergency

Ambulance (☎999)

Fire Department (☎997)

Police (☎999) If you're involved in a traffic accident, do not move your car until the police arrive. For insurance-claim purposes you must have a police report, and if you move your car, the police may not be able to issue a complete report.

Gay & Lesbian Travellers

A useful read is *Gay Travels in the Muslim World* by Michael Luongo. Check www.al-bab.com for any changes to local laws relating to gay and lesbian issues.

- Homosexual acts are illegal under UAE law and can incur a jail term.
- You will see men walking hand in hand, but that's a sign of friendship and not an indication of sexual orientation.
- You can't access gay- and lesbian-interest websites from inside the UAE.
- Public displays of affection between partners are taboo regardless of sexual orientation.
- Sex outside marriage is against the law.
- Sharing a room is likely to be construed as companionable or cost-cutting but being discreet about your true relationship is advisable.

Internet Access

- Dubai and Abu Dhabi are extremely well wired and you should have no trouble getting online.
- Nearly every hotel offers in-room internet access, either broadband or wireless.
- Etisalat hotspots offer wi-fi access at many cafes, restaurants and shopping malls (see www.etisalat.ae for the full list). You gain access by buying a prepaid card from the venue itself, or by using your credit card (Dh30 for three hours).
- Most shopping malls offer free wi-fi, although you may need a UAE mobile phone number to access this.
- If you don't own a computer, nearly all hotels have business centres, and internet cafes charge as little as Dh2 per hour for access.

Banned Websites

Pornography, gay-interest sites, websites considered critical of Islam or the UAE's leaders, dating and gambling sites, drug-related material and the entire Israeli domain are banned in the UAE, as is software such as Skype.

Legal Matters

Abu Dhabi, and Dubai in particular, may seem to be cities where 'anything goes' but this is absolutely not the case. Locals are tolerant of cultural differences – to a point. Go beyond that point and you could find you are subject to some of the harshest penalties in the region. This section lists the various infringements commonly committed by visitors and the penalties that can be expected.

As ignorance of Emirati law is no defence, check the Dubai Code of Ethics published in March 2009 on www.dubai.ae (relevant to Abu Dhabi, too) to avoid getting into trouble in the first place.

Alcohol-Related Issues

While the drinking of alcohol for non-Muslims is permitted in certain locations, it is against the law to drink in an unlicenced public place. It is also forbidden to buy alcohol from an outlet other than a hotel bar or restaurant without a local liquor licence. You should never offer alcohol to a Muslim, however close your friendship, and drinking and driving is a serious offence.

Cultural Sensitivities

A number of laws and codes of conduct govern personal behaviour.

Sex Avoid public displays of affection, sexual activity outdoors (you are never as unobserved as you may think), indecent public behaviour and indiscreet unmarried cohabitation.

PRACTICALITIES

Currency

The United Arab Emirates (UAE) dirham (Dh) is divided into 100 fils. Notes come in denominations of five, 10, 20, 50, 100, 200, 500 and 1000. There are Dh1, 50 fils, 25 fils, 10 fils and 5 fils coins.

Newspapers & Magazines

English-language newspapers include the long-established dailies (*Gulf News, Khaleej Times* and *Gulf Today*) and the following publications:

➡ *7 Days* (www.7days.ae) Free.

➡ *Emirates Business 24/7* (www.emirates247.com) The government-owned publication covering business news.

➡ *Xpress* (www.xpress4me.com) High-design weekly tabloid.

➡ *The National* (www.thenational.ae) Abu Dhabi's esteemed daily newspaper, launched in 2008.

➡ *Time Out Dubai* (www.timeoutdubai.com) Produced weekly and has detailed listings on upcoming events.

Radio

➡ **BBC Worldwide** (87.9) Broadcasts from 9am to 6pm.

➡ **Channel 4 FM** (104.8) Contemporary Top 40.

➡ **Dubai Eye** (103.8) News, talk and sports.

➡ **Dubai FM** (92) Classic hits from the '80s,'90s etc, as well as dance and lounge on weekends.

➡ **Emirates Radio 1** (104.1) Popular music.

➡ **Emirates Radio 2** (99.3) Eclectic programming.

Smoking

Dubai and Abu Dhabi have a comprehensive smoking ban in all public places, with the exception of nightclubs and enclosed bars. In addition:

➡ There are designated smoking rooms in shopping malls, hotels and restaurants accessible to those over 20 years of age.

➡ Hotels have nonsmoking rooms.

➡ The fine for lighting up in a nonsmoking area can range from Dh1000 to Dh8000.

➡ There are fines for throwing cigarette butts onto the street.

➡ There's a ban on smoking *sheesha* (water pipes) in public-access parks, beaches and recreation areas.

➡ Smoking is not permitted in cars where children are present.

Nudity Do not wear immodest clothing (showing shoulders and knees) or sunbath in non-resort areas in minimal swimwear.

Insults Avoid vulgar language, rude gestures and don't photograph strangers without permission.

Taboo subjects Don't criticise public figures or the government, or discuss politics.

Religion Do not defame Islam or show disrespect towards any religion. Avoid public eating, drinking and smoking during daylight hours in Ramadan.

Public nuisance Spitting, issuing a bounced cheque, loud music in public spaces, pet fouling of public areas and littering are all considered public nuisiance offences.

Drugs & Illegal Substances

Attempting to use drugs in Dubai and Abu Dhabi is simply a bad, bad idea. The UAE has a small but growing drug problem, and the authorities are cracking down hard on it. The minimum penalty for possession of even trace amounts is four years in prison, and the death penalty is still on the books for importing or dealing in drugs (although in fact it usually ends up being a very long jail term). BBC1 radio host and drum-and-bass DJ Grooverider, for example, was sentenced to four years in prison after 2.16g of cannabis was found in his luggage upon arrival at the airport. He was released after 10 months.

Jail sentences for being involved in drugs by association are also fairly common. That means that even if you are in a room where there are drugs, but are not partaking, you could be in as much trouble as those who are. The secret police are pervasive, and they include officers of many nationalities.

Furthermore, if you are attempting to enter the UAE with illegal substances in your bloodstream, this counts as possession, and a urine test could see you found guilty.

Prescription Medications

There are import restrictions for prescription medications that are legal in most countries, such as diazepam (Valium), dextromethorphan (Robitussin), fluoxetine (Prozac) and anything containing codeine. Check with the UAE embassy in your home country for the full list. If you need to take such medications, carry the original prescription and a letter from your doctor.

In case you're thinking not to bother, you may want to bear in mind the case of a British TV producer who was arrested and held for possessing the health supplement melatonin, which is taken to alleviate jet lag and is legal in the UK. After being cleared of importing an illegal substance, he was held for more than a month without charges in a Dubai prison while the rest of his possessions were tested. Similarly, a woman was held in custody for two months before UAE customs officers accepted that the codeine she was using for her back problem had been prescribed by a doctor.

Ignorance No Defence

Penalties for breaching the code of conduct or breaking the law can result in warnings or fines (for littering for example), or jail and deportation (for example for drug possession and criticism of Islam). Ignorance is no defence.

If arrested, you have the right to a phone call, which you should make as soon as possible (ie before you are detained in a police cell or prison pending investigation, where making contact with anyone could be difficult). Call your embassy or consulate first so they can get in touch with your family and possibly recommend a lawyer.

The UAE police have established a **Department of Tourist Security** (toll free 800 243; www.dubaipolice.gov.ae) to help visitors with any legal complications they may face on their trip – this may also be helpful if you get into difficulties.

Medical Services

The standard of medical services in Dubai and Abu Dhabi is good and pharmacies are plentiful (24/7 pharmacies are listed in the newspapers, or call 02-777 929 in Abu Dhabi or 04-223 2323 in Dubai).

Travel insurance that includes health coverage is essential as visitors will be charged for health care.

For house calls, contact **Health Call** (04-363 5343; www.health-call.com; per visit Dh600-800), which sends out Western-trained doctors around the clock.

For information on hospitals, check the government website: www.dha.gov.ae.

Dubai

Al Wasl Hospital (04-219 3000; Oud Metha Rd, south of Al Qataiyat Rd, Za'abeel)

Al Zahra Medical Centre (04-331 5000; www.al-zahra.com; Al Safa Tower, Sheikh Zayed Rd) Near Emirates Towers metro station.

American Hospital (04-336 7777, emergency 04-309 6877; Oud Metha Rd, Bur Dubai; walk-in clinic 10am-5pm) No appointments are needed for the walk-in clinic. The emergency room is open 24 hours.

Dubai Hospital (04-219 5000; Abu Bakar al Siddiq Rd, near cnr Al Khaleej Rd) One of the region's best government hospitals with 24-hour emergency.

Dubai London Clinic (04-344 6663; www.dubai-londonclinic.com; Jumeirah Rd, Umm Suqeim; 8am-7pm Sat-Wed, 8am-5pm Thu)

Rashid Hospital (04-337 4000; off Oud Metha Rd, near Al Maktoum Bridge, Bur Dubai) Main hospital for round-the-clock emergencies.

Abu Dhabi

Gulf Diagnostic Centre (02-665 8090; Al Khaleej al Arabi St; 8am-8.30pm Sat-Wed, to 1pm Thu) Highly regarded private medical centre in Abu Dhabi.

Sheikh Khalifa Medical City (02-610 2000; www.skmc.ae; Al Bateen St) One of many well-equipped hospitals in Abu Dhabi with 24-hour emergency service.

Money

ATMs

Credit and debit cards can be used for withdrawing money from ATMs that display the relevant symbols, such as Visa and MasterCard. A charge (around 1.5% to 2%) on ATM cash withdrawals abroad is levied by some banks.

EXPAT LIFE

If you find you like Dubai or Abu Dhabi well enough to stay, then consider joining the thousands of expats who call these two cities home.

The Rewards

Some expats are drawn to the Gulf in search of tax-free money and the expectation of an easy life. But the days of being paid well for doing little are over while the realities of extreme temperatures and challenging cultural norms remain. So why consider an expat life? For many it's the excitement of being part of something experimental and optimistic in a region where the pace of change is unparalleled. For others it's the prospect of bringing qualifications and experience to bear in a context where those qualities are useful and appreciated.

In addition to high job satisfaction, many expats enjoy the fact that it's safe to leave houses and cars unlocked, for children to play in the streets and talk to strangers, and where neighbours always make time for a chat. Times are changing but on the whole the friendly, safe and tolerant environment of these cities, together with the multicultural nature of the resident population, is a major contributor to the quality of life.

The Challenges

Not everyone is able to cope with the weather. If you're from a cold, wet country, it's hard to imagine getting bored of endless sunshine. But in the summer, the sky is white with heat and the extreme temperatures from April to October (which frequently rise above 45°C) require a complete life adjustment.

The Practicalities

If you have proven skills and preferably qualifications, it's easy to find employment. To secure a three-year residency permit, you need an employer to sponsor you, a spouse with a job, or ownership of freehold property, which comes with a renewable residency permit. Salary packages usually include a relocation allowance, annual plane tickets home, housing, health insurance, children's education allowance and generous paid leave.

For a detailed guide to relocating to the Gulf, see Lonely Planet's *Oman, UAE & the Arabian Peninsula* guide.

Changing Money

If you need to change money, exchange offices tend to offer better rates than banks. Reliable exchanges include **Al Rostamani** (www.alrostamanigroup.ae) and **UAE Exchange** (☎04-229 7373; www.uaeexchange.com), with multiple branches in Dubai and Abu Dhabi.

Currencies of regional countries are all recognised and easily changed, with the exception of the Yemeni rial.

Credit Cards

Visa, MasterCard and American Express are widely accepted at shops, hotels and restaurants throughout Dubai and Abu Dhabi, and debit cards are accepted at bigger retail outlets.

Tipping

By law, only food and beverage outlets in hotels (ie not independent restaurants) are entitled to tack a service charge (usually 10%) on to bills. The service charge rarely ends up in the pockets of the person who served you so a few dirhams is appreciated for a job well done.

Opening Hours

The UAE weekend is on Friday and Saturday. Note that hours are more limited during Ramadan.

Banks 8am to 1pm (some until 3pm) Sunday to Thursday, 8am to noon Saturday.

Government offices 7.30am to 2pm (or 3pm) Sunday to Thursday.

Private offices 8am to 5pm or 9am to 6pm, or split shifts 8am to 1pm and 3pm (or 4pm) to 7pm Sunday to Thursday.

Restaurants noon to 3pm and 7.30pm to midnight.

Shopping malls 10am to 10pm Sunday to Wednesday, 10am to midnight Thursday to Saturday.

Souqs 9am to 1pm and 4pm to 9pm Saturday to Thursday, 4pm to 9pm Friday.

Supermarkets 9am to midnight daily; some open 24 hours.

Post

Stamps are available at local post offices operated by **Emirates Post** (☎600 599

ISLAMIC HOLIDAYS

ISLAMIC YEAR	RAMADAN	EID AL-FITR	EID AL-ADHA
1436 (2015)	19 Jun	19 Jul	25 Sep
1437 (2016)	6 Jun	6 Jul	11 Sep
1438 (2017)	27 May	25 Jun	1 Sep

999; www.emiratespost.com). There are main post offices at both international airports.

Central Post Office (Map p252; ☎04-337 1500; Za'abeel Rd, Bur Dubai, Dubai) In Karama, between Za'abeel and Umm Hurair Rds.

Central Post Office (Map p136; ☎02-610 7101; Sharq/4th St, Abu Dhabi; ⌚7.30am-9pm Sat-Thu, 5-9pm Fri) Main post office.

Public Holidays

Hejira is the Islamic New Year. Eid al-Fitr marks the end of Ramadan fasting and is a three-day celebration spent feasting and visiting friends and family. Eid al-Adha is a four-day celebration following the main pilgrimage to Mecca, the hajj.

Secular holidays are New Year's Day (1 January) and National Day (2 December). If a public holiday falls on a weekend (ie Friday or Saturday), the holiday is usually taken at the beginning of the next working week.

Ramadan

The holy month of Ramadan is considered a time of spiritual reflection. Muslims fast during daylight hours and refrain from sex, swearing, smoking and general indulgence.

During Ramadan, government offices work a shorter day and some sights, attractions and restaurants close. Bars and pubs are closed until 7pm each night, live music is prohibited and dance clubs are closed throughout the month. Some restaurants do not serve alcohol. Everyone, regardless of their religion, is required to observe the fast in public but discreet provisions are made for visitors to eat out of sight of those who are fasting.

Ramadan provides a good opportunity to experience seasonal specialities and sweetmeats, served in Ramadan tents erected for the purpose of breaking the fast each evening.

Safe Travel

Crime On the whole, Dubai and Abu Dhabi are very safe cities, but common sense and caution should still apply.

Terrorism The US Department of State and British Foreign Office periodically warn travellers of a general threat from terrorism but this is due to the UAE's geographical location more than any focused threat.

Traffic accidents Among the highest incidence of road fatalities in the world.

Water hazard The Gulf may look innocuous but currents can be very strong and drownings regularly occur. Swimming, waterskiing or jet-skiing in the Creek is not recommended as the water is semi-stagnant.

Telephone

The UAE has a modern, efficient telephone network.

➡ There are two mobile networks: Etisalat and Du. Both are government-owned.

➡ Local calls (within the same area code) are free.

➡ Coin phones have been almost completely superseded by cardphones. Phonecards are available in various denominations from grocery stores, supermarkets and petrol stations. Do not buy them from street vendors.

➡ To call abroad, dial ☎00 followed by the country code.

➡ When calling the UAE, dial the country code ☎0971.

➡ Useful area codes are ☎04 for Dubai and ☎02 for Abu Dhabi.

➡ Call ☎181 for Directory Enquiries and ☎151 for International Directory Assistance.

Mobile Phones

The UAE mobile network supports the use of mobile phones from abroad that are compatible with the GSM system, providing you have a roaming account.

Mobile numbers begin with either ☎050 (Etisalat) or ☎055 (Du). Prepaid SIM cards are widely available from Duty Free at either international airport, from any Etisalat office or from licenced mobile phone shops.

Recharge cards in denominations of Dh25, Dh50, Dh100, Dh200 and Dh500 are sold at grocery stores, supermarkets and petrol stations. Do not buy them from street vendors.

Time

Dubai and Abu Dhabi are four hours ahead of GMT. The time does not change during the summer. Not taking daylight saving into account, when it's noon in

Dubai, the time elsewhere is as follows:

CITY	TIME
Auckland	8pm
London	8am
Los Angeles	midnight
New York	3am
Paris & Rome	9am
Perth & Hong Kong	4pm
Sydney	6pm

Toilets

Public toilets in shopping centres, museums, restaurants and hotels are Western-style and are generally clean and well maintained.

Toilets in souqs and bus stations are usually only for men.

You'll always find a hose next to the toilet, which is used for rinsing (left hand only if you want to go native): toilet paper is used for drying only and should be thrown in the bin to avoid clogging the toilets.

Tourist Information

The **Department of Tourism & Commerce Marketing** (DTCM; ☎04-223 0000; www.dubaitourism.ae) operates 24-hour information kiosks in the Terminal 1 and 3 arrivals areas of Dubai International Airport, as well as booths at the following malls: Deira City Centre, BurJuman, Wafi Mall, Ibn Battuta and Mercato Mall. Officially, these are open from 10am to 10pm, but are frequently unstaffed and have a meagre assortment of flyers and brochures.

Visit the excellent website of the **Abu Dhabi Tourism Authority** (ADTA; ☎toll free 800 555; www.visitabudhabi.ae) for tourist information on Abu Dhabi.

Travellers with Disabilities

Dubai and Abu Dhabi have made a big effort in recent years to improve services for people with disabilities. The Department of Tourism & Commerce Marketing website (www.dubaitourism.ae) includes a Special Needs Tourism section, which contains information on wheelchair-accessible parks, heritage sites, cinemas, malls and tour operators. Some facilities are outlined here:

International airports Both airports are equipped with low check-in counters, luggage trolleys, automatic doors, lifts and quick check-in. There is a special check-in gate for travellers with special needs and a meet-and-assist service.

Public transport Dubai Taxi (☎04-208 0808, 04-224 5331; www.dubaitaxi.ae) has special vans with wheelchair lifts for Dh50 per hour, but they must be ordered 24 hours in advance. Some local buses and all water taxis are wheelchair-accessible. Dubai's metro has lifts and grooved guidance paths in stations and wheelchair spaces in each train compartment. Most parking areas in both cities contain spaces for drivers with disabilities. The Big Bus Tour (p218) in Abu Dhabi is wheelchair-accessible.

Accommodation Top-end hotels have rooms with extra-wide doors and spacious bathrooms, and even budget hotels have lifts (elevators).

Sights & attractions Wheelchair ramps are still a rarity, even in public buildings and at tourist sights. Exceptions include the Dubai Museum and Heritage Village in Dubai and Sheikh Zayed Grand Mosque, Emirates Palace, Yas Island and Masdar City in Abu Dhabi.

Visas

Visit Visas

Entry requirements to the UAE are in constant flux, which is why you should double-check all information on the official tourism website (www.dubaitourism.ae) before you make final plans.

At the time of research, citizens of 45 countries, including nearly all of Western Europe plus Australia, Brunei, Canada, Hong Kong, Japan, Malaysia, New Zealand, Singapore, South Korea and the USA, were eligible for free on-the-spot visas on arrival in the UAE at air, land and sea ports. Visas are valid for 30 days, with an additional grace period of 10 days. Don't risk outstaying your visa as the fine is Dh100 a day, which can soon add up.

If you're a citizen of a country not included in the list above, a visit visa must be arranged through a sponsor – such as your Dubai hotel or tour operator – prior to your arrival in the UAE. The non-renewable visas cost Dh100 and are valid for 30 days. Citizens of Gulf Cooperative Council (GCC) countries only need a valid passport to enter the UAE and can stay as long

OMAN VISAS

If you are from one of the 34 countries eligible to get an on-the-spot visa at Dubai airport, you won't need to obtain a separate visa for Oman. Everyone else has to apply in advance at the Omani embassy in Abu Dhabi. If you are visiting Oman on a tourist visa, these same 34 nationalities can enter the United Arab Emirates (UAE) by land, air or sea without visa charges.

TOP TIPS FOR WOMEN TRAVELLERS

Dubai and Abu Dhabi are two of the safest Middle East destinations for women travellers but unwanted attention is almost inevitable and lone female travellers are sometimes mistaken for 'working women', regardless of what they are wearing. Although it doesn't officially exist, prostitution catering to both expats and Emiratis is common in clubs, bars and on the backstreets of Deira and Bur Dubai in Dubai, and around the 'Ally Pally' (Al Ain Palace Hotel), just inland from Corniche Rd (East) in Abu Dhabi.

Here are some tips to help ward off unwanted attention and generally make travelling as a woman easier:

- Wear a wedding ring – it will make you appear less 'available' (but be ready for awkward questions about abandoning your home and kids).
- If you're unmarried but travelling in male company, say that you're married rather than girlfriend/boyfriend.
- Avoid direct eye contact with men (dark sunglasses help).
- Don't sit in the front seat of taxis unless the driver is a woman.
- On public transport, sit in the women's section towards the front.
- If you need help for any reason (directions etc), ask a woman first.
- If dining alone, eat at Western-style places or ask to be seated in the 'family' section of local eateries.
- It's perfectly acceptable for women to go straight to the front of a queue (eg at banks or post offices) or ask to be served first before any men who might be waiting.
- If someone follows you in his car, take a picture of his licence plate or just get your mobile phone out (if it doesn't have a camera, simply pretend it does).
- If you're being followed, go to the nearest public place, preferably a hotel lobby. If this doesn't discourage them, ask the receptionist to call the police, which usually makes them slink away.
- Look and be confident. This is the best deterrent for unwanted attention.

as they want. It is generally not possible to enter with an Israeli passport, but there's no problem entering the UAE with an Israeli stamp in a non-Israeli passport.

Note that passports must be valid for at least six months from the date of arrival.

Visa Extensions

Visit visas can be extended once for 30 days by the **Department of Immigration & Naturalisation** (☎04-398 0000; Sheikh Khalifa bin Zayed Rd, near Bur Dubai Police Station) for Dh500 and a fair amount of paperwork. You may be asked to provide proof of funds. It's much easier, and usually cheaper, to leave the country for a few hours and head back for a new stamp.

Visas can only be extended in the city or emirate you arrived in, so if you landed in Abu Dhabi, you can't get your visa extended in Dubai.

Women Travellers

Dispelling the Myths

Many women imagine that travel to the Gulf cities and within the UAE is much more difficult than it is. Some key facts:

- No, you don't have to wear a burka, headscarf or veil.
- No, you won't be constantly harassed.
- Yes, you can drive a car.
- Yes, it's safe to take taxis, stay alone in hotels (although you may want to avoid the fleabag hotels in Deira and Bur Dubai) and walk around on your own in most areas.
- Yes, however, you will receive unwanted male attention and long, lewd stares on public beaches.

Attitudes Towards Women

Some of the biggest misunderstandings between Middle Easterners and Westerners occur over the issue of women. Half-truths and stereotypes exist on both sides: many Westerners assume that all Middle Eastern women are veiled, repressed victims, while a large number of locals see Western women as sex-obsessed and immoral.

Traditionally, the role of a woman in this region is to be a mother and matron of the household, while the man is the financial provider. However, as with any society, the reality is far more nuanced. There are thousands of middle- and upper-middle-class professional women in the UAE who, like their counterparts in the West, juggle work and family responsibilities.

The issue of sex is where the differences between the

cultures are particularly apparent. Premarital sex (or indeed any sex outside marriage) is taboo, although, as with anything forbidden, it still happens. Emirati women are expected to be virgins when they marry, and a family's reputation can rest upon this point. The presence of foreign women provides, in the eyes of some Arab men, a chance to get around these norms with ease and without consequences. Hence the occasional hassle.

What to Wear

Even though you'll see plenty of Western women wearing skimpy shorts and tank-tops in shopping malls and other public places, you should not assume that it's acceptable to do so. While they're too polite as hosts to say anything, most Emiratis find this disrespectful. Despite Dubai's relative liberalism, you are in a country that holds its traditions dear and it's prudent not to parade a different set of values. A bit of common sense (such as covering up to and from a beach party or when taking a taxi to a nightclub) helps keep the peace.

Generally speaking, dressing 'modestly' has the following advantages: it attracts less attention to you; you will get a warmer welcome from locals (who greatly appreciate your willingness to respect their customs); and it'll prove more comfortable in the heat. Dressing modestly means covering your shoulders, knees and neckline. Baggy T-shirts and loose cotton trousers or over-the-knee skirts will not only keep you cool but will also protect your skin from the sun. If you travel outside Dubai and Abu Dhabi, keep in mind that everywhere else in the UAE is far more conservative.

Working in the UAE

Finding Work

While plenty of people turn up in Dubai on a visit visa, decide they like the look of the place and then scout around for a job, this isn't really the most effective way to go about it. First, most employees are on a contract that generally lasts for three years. Secondly, there are a lot of sums to be done before you can really figure out whether the amount you're offered is going to be financially viable.

Employers in Dubai are very fond of people with qualifications and this tends to count for more than the number of years of experience you have in a job. Qualified teachers, nurses and those in engineering are highly valued in Dubai and Abu Dhabi and are well paid.

The *Khaleej Times* and the *Gulf News* publish employment supplements several times a week. When you find a job, you will be offered an employment contract in Arabic and English. Get the one in Arabic translated before you sign it.

Business Aid Centre (☎04-337 5747; www.bacdubai.com)

SOS Recruitment Consultants (☎04-396 5600; www.sosrecruitment.net)

In Country

If you enter the country on a visit visa and then find work, you will have to leave the country for one day and re-enter under your employer's sponsorship.

If you have arranged to work in Dubai in advance, you will enter the country on a visit visa sponsored by your employer while your residence visa is processed. This process involves a blood test for HIV/AIDS and lots of paperwork.

Those on a residence visa who are sponsored by a spouse (who is in turn sponsored by an employer) are not officially permitted to work. They are also subject to other restrictions such as requiring a consent letter from their spouse before applying for a tourist visa to visit another Gulf Arab country, or to apply for a driving licence.

If you obtain your residence visa through an employer and then quit because you've found something better, you may find yourself under a six-month ban from working in the UAE. This rule is designed to stop people from job-hopping.

If you are employed in Dubai or Abu Dhabi and have any work-related problems, you can call the **Ministry of Labour Helpline** (☎800 665; www.mol.gov.ae) for advice.

Language

Arabic is the official language of the United Arab Emirates (UAE), but English is widely understood. Note that there are significant differences between the MSA (Modern Standard Arabic) – the official lingua franca of the Arab world, used in schools, administration and the media – and the colloquial language, ie the everyday spoken version. The Arabic variety spoken in the UAE (and provided in this chapter) is known as Gulf Arabic.

Read our coloured pronunciation guides as if they were English and you'll be understood. Note that a is pronounced as in 'act', aa as the 'a' in 'father', ai as in 'aisle', aw as in 'law', ay as in 'say', ee as in 'see', i as in 'hit', oo as in 'zoo', u as in 'put', gh is a guttural sound (like the Parisian French 'r'), r is rolled, dh is pronounced as the 'th' in 'that', th as in 'thin', ch as in 'cheat' and kh as the 'ch' in the Scottish *loch*. The apostrophe (') indicates the glottal stop (like the pause in the middle of 'uh-oh'). The stressed syllables are indicated with italics, and (m) and (f) refer to the masculine and feminine word forms, respectively.

BASICS

Hello.	اهلا و سهلا.	*ah*·lan was *ah*·lan
Goodbye.	مع السلامة.	ma' sa·*laa*·ma
Yes./No.	نعم./لا.	na·'am/la
Please.	من فضلَك. من فضلِك.	min *fad*·lak (m) min *fad*·lik (f)
Thank you.	شكران.	*shuk*·ran
Excuse me.	اسمح. اسمحي لي.	is·*mah* (m) is·mah·ee lee (f)
Sorry.	مع الاسف.	ma' al·*as*·af

WANT MORE?

For in-depth language information and handy phrases, check out Lonely Planet's *Middle East Phrasebook*. You'll find it at **shop.lonelyplanet.com**, or you can buy Lonely Planet's iPhone phrasebooks at the Apple App Store.

How are you?
كيف حالَك/حالِك؟ kayf *haa*·lak/*haa*·lik (m/f)

Fine, thanks. And you?
بخير الحمد الله. bi·*khayr* il·*ham*·du·li·laa
و انتَ/و انتِ؟ *win*·ta/*win*·ti (m/f)

What's your name?
اش اسمَك/اسمِك؟ aash *is*·mak/*is*·mik (m/f)

My name is ...
اسمي ... *is*·mee ...

Do you speak English?
تتكلم انجليزية؟ tit·*kal*·am in·glee·*zee*·ya (m)
تتكلمي انجليزية؟ tit·*ka*·la·mee in·glee·*zee*·ya (f)

I don't understand.
مو فاهم. moo *faa*·him

Can I take a photo?
ممكن اتصور؟ *mum*·kin at·*saw*·ar

ACCOMMODATION

Where's a ...?	وين ...؟	wayn ...
hotel	فندق	*fun*·dug

Do you have a ... room?	عندك/عندك غرفة ...؟	*'and*·ak/*'and*·ik *ghur*·fa ... (m/f)
single	لشخص واحد	li·*shakhs waa*·hid
double	لشخصين	li·shakh·*sayn*
twin	مع سريرين	ma' sa·ree·*rayn*

How much is it per ...?	بكم كل ...؟	bi·*kam* kul ...
night	ليلة	*lay*·la
person	شخص	shakhs

Can I get another (blanket)?
احتاج الى (برنوس) ah·*taaj* i·*la* (bar·*noos*)
الثاني من فضلك؟ i·*thaa*·nee min *fad*·lak

The (air conditioning) doesn't work.
(الكنديشان) (il·kan·*day*·shan)
ما يشتغل. ma yish·*ta*·ghil

Signs

Entrance	مدخل
Exit	خروج
Open	مفتوح
Closed	مقفول
Information	معلومات
Prohibited	ممنوع
Toilets	المرحاض
Men	رجال
Women	نساء

DIRECTIONS

Where's the ...? من وين ...؟ min wayn ...

bank	البنك	il·*bank*
market	السوق	i·*soog*
post office	مكتب البريد	*mak*·tab il·ba·*reed*

Can you show me (on the map)?
لو سمحت وريني (علخريطة)؟ law sa·*maht* wa·*ree*·nee ('al·kha·*ree*·ta)

What's the address?
ما العنوان؟ ma il·'un·*waan*

Could you please write it down?
لو سمحت اكتبه لي؟ law sa·*maht* ik·ti·*boo* lee (m)
لو سمحت اكتبيه لي؟ law sa·*maht* ik·ti·*bee* lee (f)

How far is it?
كم بعيد؟ kam ba·*'eed*

How do I get there?
كيف ممكن اوصل هناكا؟ kayf *mum*·kin *aw*·sil *hoo*·naak

Turn left/right.
لف يسار/يمين. lif yee·*saar*/yee·*meen* (m)
لفي يسار/يمين. *li*·fee yee·*saar*/yee·*meen* (f)

It's ... هو ... *hoo*·wa ... (m)
هي ... *hee*·ya ... (f)

behind ...	ورا ...	wa·*raa* ...
in front of ...	قدام ...	gu·*daam* ...
near to ...	قريب من ...	ga·*reeb* min ...
next to ...	جنب ...	janb ...
on the corner	علزاوية	'a·*zaa*·wee·ya
opposite ...	مقابل ...	moo·*gaa*·bil ...
straight ahead	سيدا	*see*·da

EATING & DRINKING

Can you recommend a ...? ممكن تنصح/تنصحي ...؟ *mum*·kin *tan*·sah/*tan*·sa·hee ... (m/f)

bar	بار	baar
cafe	قهوة	*gah*·wa
restaurant	مطعم	*ma*·ta'm

I'd like a/the ..., please. اريد ... من فضلك. a·*reed* ... min *fad*·lak

table for (four)	طاولة (اربعة) اشخاص	*taa*·wi·lat (*ar*·ba') ash·*khaas*

What would you recommend?
اش تنصح؟ aash *tan*·sah (m)
اش تنصحي؟ aash *tan*·sa·hee (f)

What's the local speciality?
اش الطبق المحلي؟ aash i·*ta*·bak il·*ma*·ha·lee

Do you have vegetarian food?
عندك طعم نباتي؟ '*an*·dak *ta*·'am na·*baa*·tee

I'd like (the) ..., please. عطني/عطيني الـ ... من فضلك. '*a*·ti·nee/'*a*·*tee*·nee il ... min *fad*·lak (m/f)

bill	قائمة	*kaa*·'i·ma
drink list	قائمة المشروبات	*kaa*·'i·mat il·mash·roo·*baat*
menu	قائمة الطعام	*kaa*·'i·mat i·ta·'*aam*
that dish	الطبق هاذاك	i·*tab*·ak *haa*·dhaa·ka

Could you prepare a meal without ...? ممكن تطبخها/تطبخيها بدون ...؟ *mum*·kin *tat*·bakh·ha/*tat*·bakh·ee·ha bi·*doon* ... (m/f)

butter	زبدة	*zib*·da
eggs	بيض	bayd
meat stock	مرق لهم	ma·*rak la*·ham

I'm allergic to ... عندي حساسية لـ ... '*an*·dee ha·saa·*see*·ya li ...

dairy produce	الألبان	il·al·*baan*
gluten	قمح	*ka*·mah
nuts	كرزات	ka·ra·*zaat*
seafood	السمك و المحارات	i·*sa*·mak wa al·ma·haa·*raat*

coffee ...	نقهوة ...	*kah*·wa ...
tea ...	شاي ...	shay ...
with milk	بالحليب	bil·ha·*leeb*
without sugar	بدون شكر	bi·*doon shi*·ker

bottle/glass of beer	بوتل/قلاس بيرة	*boo*·til/glaas *bee*·ra
(orange) juice	عصير (برتقال)	'*a*·seer (bor·too·*gaal*)
(mineral) water	ماي (معدني)	may (*ma'a*·da·nee)
... wine	... خمر	... *kha*·mar
red	احمر	*ah*·mer
sparkling	فوار	fa·*waar*
white	ابيض	*ab*·yad

EMERGENCIES

Help!	مساعد!	moo·*saa*·'id (m)
	مساعدة!	moo·*saa*·'id·a (f)
Go away!	ابعد!/ابعدي!	*ib*·'ad/*ib*·'ad·ee (m/f)
Call ...!	تصل علي ...!	ti·*sil* 'a·la ... (m)
	تصلي على ...!	*ti*·si·lee 'a·la ... (f)
a doctor	طبيب	ta·*beeb*
the police	الشرطة	i·*shur*·ta

I'm lost.
انا ضعت. *a*·na duht

Where are the toilets?
وين المرحاض؟ wayn il·mir·*haad*

I'm sick.
انا مريض. *a*·na ma·*reed* (m)
انا مريضة. *a*·na ma·*ree*·da (f)

I'm allergic to (antibiotics).
عندي حساسية 'and·ee ha·saa·*see*·ya
لـ (مضاد حيوي). li (moo·*daad hay*·a·we)

SHOPPING & SERVICES

Where's a ...?	من وين ...؟	min wayn ...
department store	محل ضخم	ma·*hal dukh*·um
grocery store	محل ابقالية	ma·*hal* ib·gaa·*lee*·ya
newsagency	محل يبيع جرائد	ma·*hal* yi·*bee*·a' ja·*raa*·id
souvenir shop	محل سياحي	ma·*hal* say·*aa*·hee
supermarket	سوبرمركت	*soo*·ber·mar·ket

I'm looking for ...
مدور علي ... moo·*daw*·ir 'a·la ... (m)
مدورة على ... moo·*daw*·i·ra 'a·la ... (f)

Can I look at it?
ممكن اشوف؟ *mum*·kin a·*shoof*

Do you have any others?
عندَك اخرين؟ '*and*·ak ukh·*reen* (m)
عندِك اخرين؟ '*and*·ik ukh·*reen* (f)

It's faulty.
فيه خلل. fee *kha*·lal

How much is it?
بكم؟ bi·*kam*

Can you write down the price?
ممكن تكتبلي/ *mum*·kin tik·*tib*·lee/
تكتبيلي السعر؟ tik·*tib*·ee·lee i·*si'r* (m/f)

That's too expensive.
غالي جدا. *ghaa*·lee *jid*·an

What's your lowest price?
اش السعر الاخر؟ aash i·*si'r* il·*aa*·khir

There's a mistake in the bill.
فيه غلط في الفطورة. fee *gha*·lat fil fa·*too*·ra

Where's ...?	من وين ...؟	min wayn ...
a foreign exchange office	صراف	si·*raaf*
an ATM	مكينة صرف	ma·*kee*·nat sarf

What's the exchange rate?
ما هو السعر؟ maa *hoo*·wa i·*sa'r*

TIME & DATES

What time is it?
الساعة كم؟ i·*saa*·a' kam

It's one o'clock.
الساعة واحدة. i·*saa*·a' *waa*·hi·da

It's (two) o'clock.
الساعة (ثنتين). i·*saa*·a' (thin·*tayn*)

Half past (two).
الساعة (ثنتين) و نس. i·*saa*·a' (thin·*tayn*) wa nus

At what time ...?
الساعة كم ...؟ i·*saa*·a' kam ...

At ...
الساعة ... i·*saa*·a'...

yesterday ...	البارح ...	il·*baa*·rih ...
tomorrow ...	باكر ...	*baa*·chir ...
morning	صباح	sa·*baah*
afternoon	بعد الظهر	ba'd a·*thuhr*
evening	مساء	*mi*·saa
Monday	يوم الاثنين	yawm al·ith·*nayn*
Tuesday	يوم الثلاثة	yawm a·tha·*laa*·tha
Wednesday	يوم الاربعة	yawm al·*ar*·ba'
Thursday	يوم الخميس	yawm al·kha·*mees*
Friday	يوم الجمعة	yawm al·*jum*·a'
Saturday	يوم السبت	yawm a·*sibt*
Sunday	يوم الاحد	yawm al·*aa*·had

TRANSPORT

Is this the ... (to Riyadh)?	هاذا ال ... يروح (لرياض)؟	*haa*·dha al ... yi·*roh* (li·ree·*yaad*)
boat	سفينة	sa·*fee*·na
bus	باص	baas
plane	طيارة	tay·*aa*·ra
train	قطار	gi·*taar*

Question Words

When?	متى؟	*ma*·ta
Where?	وين؟	wayn
Who?	من؟	man
Why?	لاش؟	laysh

Numbers

1	١	واحد	*waa*·hid
2	٢	اثنين	ith·*nayn*
3	٣	ثلاثة	tha·*laa*·tha
4	٤	اربع	ar·*ba'*
5	٥	خمسة	*kham*·sa
6	٦	ستة	*si*·ta
7	٧	سبعة	*sa*·ba'
8	٨	ثمانية	tha·*maan*·ya
9	٩	تسعة	*tis*·a'
10	١٠	عشرة	*'ash*·ar·a
20	٢٠	عشرين	'ash·*reen*
30	٣٠	ثلاثين	tha·la·*theen*
40	٤٠	اربعين	ar·ba'·*een*
50	٥٠	خمسين	kham·*seen*
60	٦٠	ستين	sit·*een*
70	٧٠	سبعين	sa·ba'·*een*
80	٨٠	ثمانين	tha·ma·*neen*
90	٩٠	تسعين	ti·sa'·*een*
100	١٠٠	مية	*mee*·ya
1000	١٠٠٠	الف	alf

Note that Arabic numerals, unlike letters, are read from left to right.

What time's the ... bus?	الساعة كم الباص ...؟	a·*saa*·a' kam il·*baas* ...
first	الاول	il·*aw*·al
last	الاخر	il·*aa*·khir
next	القادم	il·*gaa*·dim
One ... ticket (to Doha), please.	تذكرة ... (الدوحة) من فضلك.	*tadh*·ka·ra ... (a·*do*·ha) min *fad*·lak
one-way	ذهاب بص	dhee·*haab* bas
return	ذهاب و اياب	dhee·*haab* wa ai·*yaab*

How long does the trip take?
كم الرحلة تستغرق؟ kam i·*rah*·la tis·*tagh*·rik

Is it a direct route?
الرحلة متواصلة؟ i·*rah*·la moo·ta·*waa*·si·la

What station/stop is this?
ما هي المحطة هاذي؟ maa *hee*·ya il·ma·*ha*·ta *haa*·dhee

Please tell me when we get to (Al Ain).
لو سمحت خبرني/خبريني وقت ما نوصل الي (العين). law sa·*maht* kha·*bir*·nee/kha·*bir*·ee·nee wokt ma *noo*·sil i·*la* (al·*'ain*) (m/f)

How much is it to (Sharjah)?
بكم الى (شارقة)؟ bi·*kam* i·*la* (*shaa*·ri·ka)

Please take me to (this address).
من فضلك خذني (علعنوان هاذا). min *fad*·lak *khudh*·nee ('al·'un·*waan haa*·dha)

Please stop here.
لو سمحت وقف هنا. law sa·*maht wa*·gif *hi*·na

Please wait here.
لو سمحت استنا هنا. law sa·*maht* is·*ta*·na *hi*·na

I'd like to hire a ...	اريد استأجر ...	a·*reed* ist·*'aj*·ir ...
4WD	سيارة فيها دبل	say·*aa*·ra *fee*·ha *da*·bal
car	سيارة	say·*aa*·ra

with ...	مع ...	ma' ...
a driver	دريول	*dray*·wil
air conditioning	كنديشان	kan·*day*·shan

How much for ... hire?	كم الإيجار ...؟	kam il·ee·*jaar* ...
daily	كل يوم	kul yawm
weekly	كل اسبوع	kul us·*boo*·a'

Is this the road to (Abu Dhabi)?
هاذا الطريق الى (ابو ظبي)؟ *haa*·dha i·ta·*reeg* i·*la* (a·*boo da*·bee)

I need a mechanic.
احتاج ميكانيك. ah·*taaj* mee·kaa·*neek*

I've run out of petrol.
ينضب البنزين. *yan*·dab al·ban·*zeen*

I have a flat tyre.
عندي بنشار. *'and*·ee *ban*·shar

LANGUAGE TRANSPORT

Behind the Scenes

SEND US YOUR FEEDBACK

We love to hear from travellers – your comments keep us on our toes and help make our books better. Our well-travelled team reads every word on what you loved or loathed about this book. Although we cannot reply individually to your submissions, we always guarantee that your feedback goes straight to the appropriate authors, in time for the next edition. Each person who sends us information is thanked in the next edition – the most useful submissions are rewarded with a selection of digital PDF chapters.

Visit **lonelyplanet.com/contact** to submit your updates and suggestions or to ask for help. Our award-winning website also features inspirational travel stories, news and discussions.

Note: We may edit, reproduce and incorporate your comments in Lonely Planet products such as guidebooks, websites and digital products, so let us know if you don't want your comments reproduced or your name acknowledged. For a copy of our privacy policy visit lonelyplanet.com/privacy.

AUTHOR THANKS

Andrea Schulte-Peevers

Big thanks to the many wonderful people who plied me with tips, insights and ideas and/or opened doors throughout Dubai, including Katie King, Caitriona Gaffney, Sandra Farrero, Sarah Hameister, Melanie Dautry, Nivine William, Sarah Walker-Dufton and Maryam Ganjineh. Special heartfelt thanks to Rashi and Abhi Sen for their friendship and shared culinary passion.

Jenny Walker

Abu Dhabi is a fast-changing city impossible to capture without insightful input from residents. Thanks are due therefore to all our regional friends who have helped with this project. To my beloved husband, Sam Owen, I reserve unqualified thanks for going beyond the call of duty during research and write-up.

ACKNOWLEDGMENTS

Cover photograph: Burj Khalifa, Dubai, Maurizio Rellini/4Corners

THIS BOOK

This 8th edition of Lonely Planet's *Dubai & Abu Dhabi* guidebook was researched and written by Andrea Schulte-Peevers and Jenny Walker. The previous edition was written by Josephine Quintero. The 6th edition was written by Andrea Schulte-Peevers. This guidebook was produced by the following:

Destination Editor Helen Elfer

Product Editors Kate Mathews, Jenna Myers

Senior Cartographer David Kemp

Book Designer Clara Monitto

Assisting Editors Nigel Chin, Melanie Dankel, Christopher Pitts, Martine Power, Gabrielle Stefanos

Cover Researcher Naomi Parker

Thanks to Sasha Baskett, Kate Chapman, Elisabeth Creed, Ryan Evans, Anna Harris, Kate James, Elizabeth Jones, Takis Markopoulos, Claire Naylor, Karyn Noble, Yasar Ozkul, Diana Saengkham, Ellie Simpson, Luna Soo, Angela Tinson, Tony Wheeler, Lauren Wolfe

See also separate subindexes for:
EATING P237
DRINKING & NIGHTLIFE P238
ENTERTAINMENT P239
SHOPPING P239
SPORTS & ACTIVITIES P239
SLEEPING P240

Index

ABBREVIATIONS
AA Al Ain
AD Abu Dhabi

Sights 000
Map Pages **000**
Photo Pages **000**

Sights 000
Map Pages **000**
Photo Pages **000**

DRINKING & NIGHTLIFE

Sights 000
Map Pages **000**
Photo Pages **000**

ENTERTAINMENT

SHOPPING

SPORTS & ACTIVITIES

SLEEPING

Dubai Maps

Sights
- Beach
- Bird Sanctuary
- Buddhist
- Castle/Palace
- Christian
- Confucian
- Hindu
- Islamic
- Jain
- Jewish
- Monument
- Museum/Gallery/Historic Building
- Ruin
- Shinto
- Sikh
- Taoist
- Winery/Vineyard
- Zoo/Wildlife Sanctuary
- Other Sight

Activities, Courses & Tours
- Bodysurfing
- Diving
- Canoeing/Kayaking
- Course/Tour
- Sento Hot Baths/Onsen
- Skiing
- Snorkelling
- Surfing
- Swimming/Pool
- Walking
- Windsurfing
- Other Activity

Sleeping
- Sleeping
- Camping

Eating
- Eating

Drinking & Nightlife
- Drinking & Nightlife
- Cafe

Entertainment
- Entertainment

Shopping
- Shopping

Information
- Bank
- Embassy/Consulate
- Hospital/Medical
- Internet
- Police
- Post Office
- Telephone
- Toilet
- Tourist Information
- Other Information

Geographic
- Beach
- Hut/Shelter
- Lighthouse
- Lookout
- Mountain/Volcano
- Oasis
- Park
- Pass
- Picnic Area
- Waterfall

Population
- Capital (National)
- Capital (State/Province)
- City/Large Town
- Town/Village

Transport
- Airport
- Border crossing
- Bus
- Cable car/Funicular
- Cycling
- Ferry
- Metro station
- Monorail
- Parking
- Petrol station
- Subway station
- Taxi
- Train station/Railway
- Tram
- Underground station
- Other Transport

Note: Not all symbols displayed above appear on the maps in this book

Routes
- Tollway
- Freeway
- Primary
- Secondary
- Tertiary
- Lane
- Unsealed road
- Road under construction
- Plaza/Mall
- Steps
- Tunnel
- Pedestrian overpass
- Walking Tour
- Walking Tour detour
- Path/Walking Trail

Boundaries
- International
- State/Province
- Disputed
- Regional/Suburb
- Marine Park
- Cliff
- Wall

Hydrography
- River, Creek
- Intermittent River
- Canal
- Water
- Dry/Salt/Intermittent Lake
- Reef

Areas
- Airport/Runway
- Beach/Desert
- Cemetery (Christian)
- Cemetery (Other)
- Glacier
- Mudflat
- Park/Forest
- Sight (Building)
- Sportsground
- Swamp/Mangrove

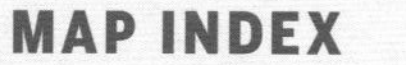

MAP INDEX

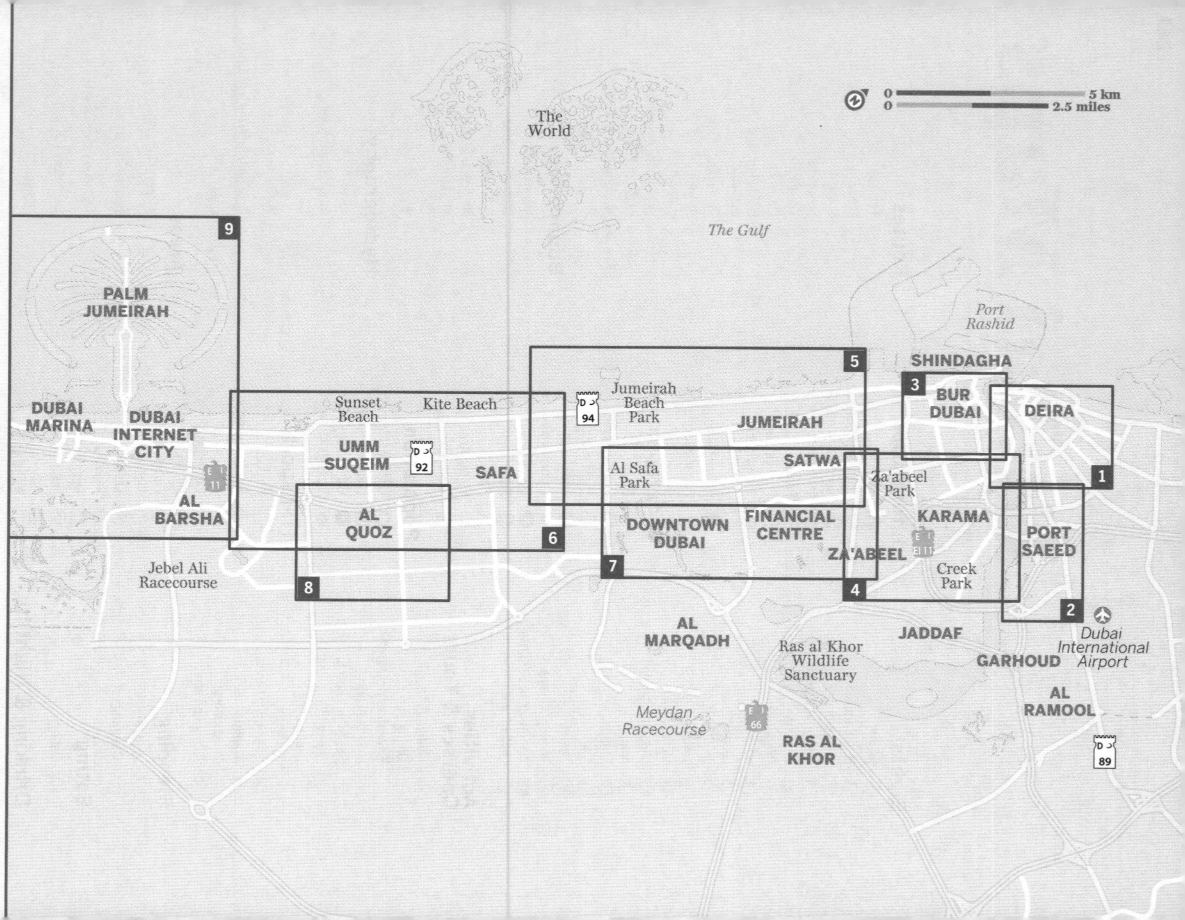

0 5 km
0 2.5 miles
The World
The Gulf
Port Rashid
SHINDAGHA
BUR DUBAI
DEIRA
PALM JUMEIRAH
DUBAI MARINA
DUBAI INTERNET CITY
Sunset Beach
Kite Beach
Jumeirah Beach Park
JUMEIRAH
UMM SUQEIM
SAFA
SATWA
Al Safa Park
Za'abeel Park
KARAMA
AL BARSHA
AL QUOZ
DOWNTOWN DUBAI
FINANCIAL CENTRE
ZA'ABEEL
PORT SAEED
Creek Park
Jebel Ali Racecourse
AL MARQADH
Ras al Khor Wildlife Sanctuary
JADDAF
GARHOUD
Dubai International Airport
AL RAMOOL
Meydan Racecourse
RAS AL KHOR
E11
E66
94
92
89
1
2
3
4
5
6
7
8
9

DEIRA & EASTERN CREEK NORTH *Map on p244*

Key on p243

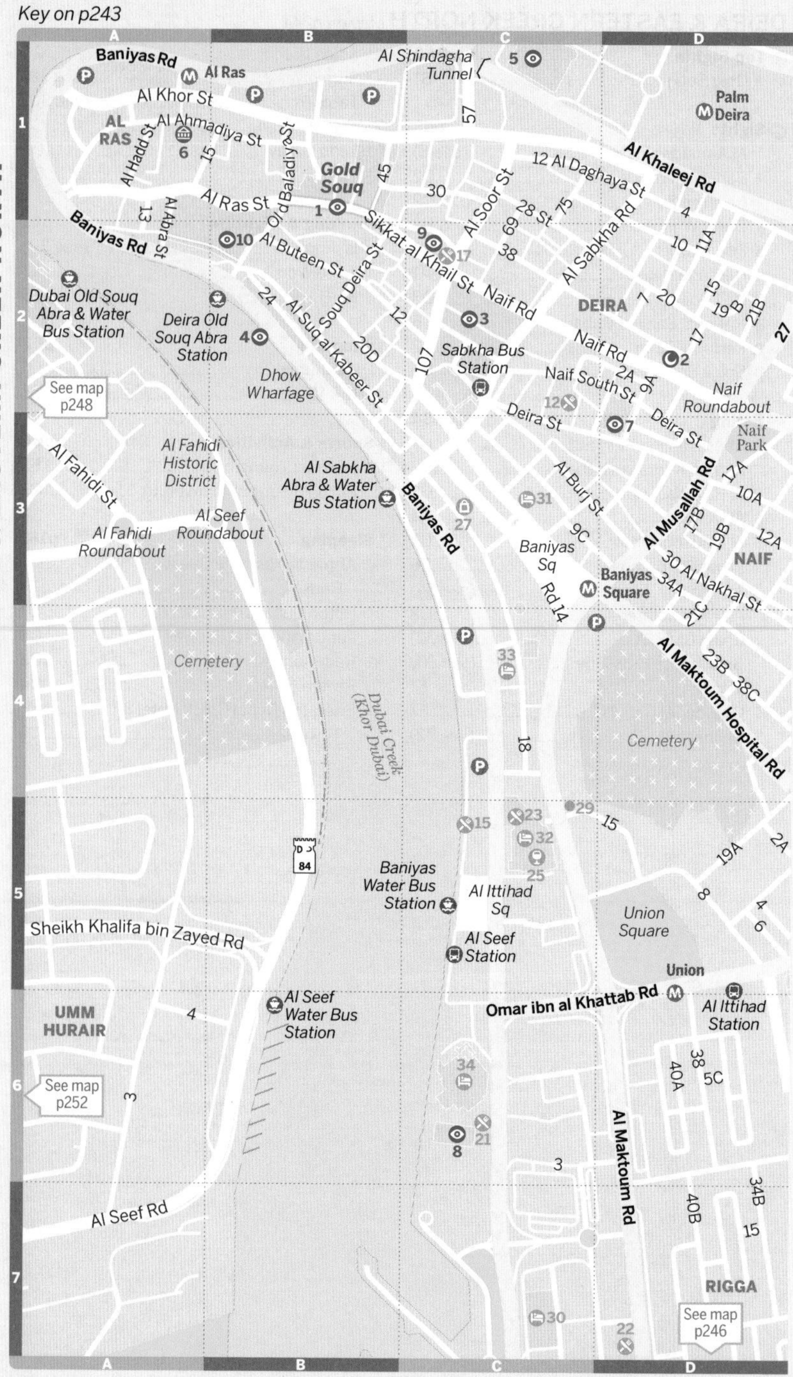

Baniyas Rd
Al Ras
Al Khor St
AL RAS
Al Ahmadiya St
Al Hadd St
Old Baladiya St
Gold Souq
Al Shindagha Tunnel
Palm Deira
Al Khaleej Rd
12 Al Daghaya St
Al Soor St
28 St
Al Sabkha Rd
Al Ras St
Al Abra St
Baniyas Rd
Al Buteen St
Souq Deira St
Sikkat al Khail St
Naif Rd
DEIRA
Dubai Old Souq Abra & Water Bus Station
Deira Old Souq Abra Station
Al Suq al Kabeer St
Sabkha Bus Station
Naif South St
Naif Roundabout
Dhow Wharfage
Deira St
Naif Park
See map p248
Al Fahidi St
Al Fahidi Historic District
Al Sabkha Abra & Water Bus Station
Al Buri St
Al Musallah Rd
Al Seef Roundabout
Al Fahidi Roundabout
Baniyas Sq
Baniyas Square
30 Al Nakhal St
NAIF
Rd 14
Al Maktoum Hospital Rd
Cemetery
Dubai Creek (Khor Dubai)
Cemetery
Baniyas Water Bus Station
Al Ittihad Sq
Union Square
Sheikh Khalifa bin Zayed Rd
Al Seef Station
Union
Omar ibn al Khattab Rd
Al Ittihad Station
UMM HURAIR
Al Seef Water Bus Station
See map p252
Al Maktoum Rd
Al Seef Rd
RIGGA
See map p246

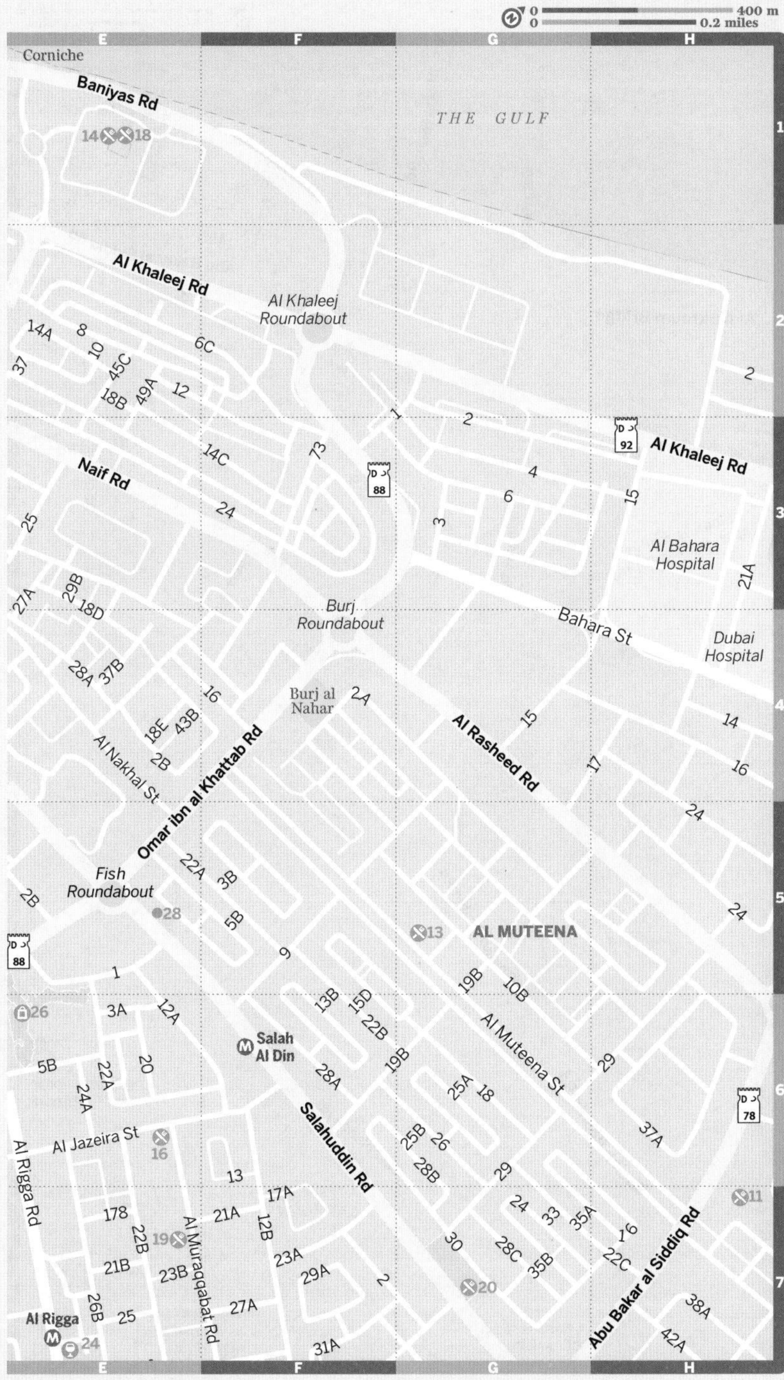

0 400 m
0 0.2 miles
E
F
G
H
1
2
3
4
5
6
7
Corniche
Baniyas Rd
THE GULF
14
18
Al Khaleej Rd
Al Khaleej Roundabout
Naif Rd
Al Bahara Hospital
Burj Roundabout
Bahara St
Dubai Hospital
Burj al Nahar
Al Rasheed Rd
Al Nakhal St
Omar ibn al Khattab Rd
Fish Roundabout
28
13
AL MUTEENA
Al Muteena St
Salah Al Din
Salahuddin Rd
Al Jazeira St
16
Al Rigga Rd
19
Al Muraqqabat Rd
Al Rigga
24
20
Abu Bakar al Siddiq Rd
11
26
88
92
78

DEIRA & EASTERN CREEK SOUTH

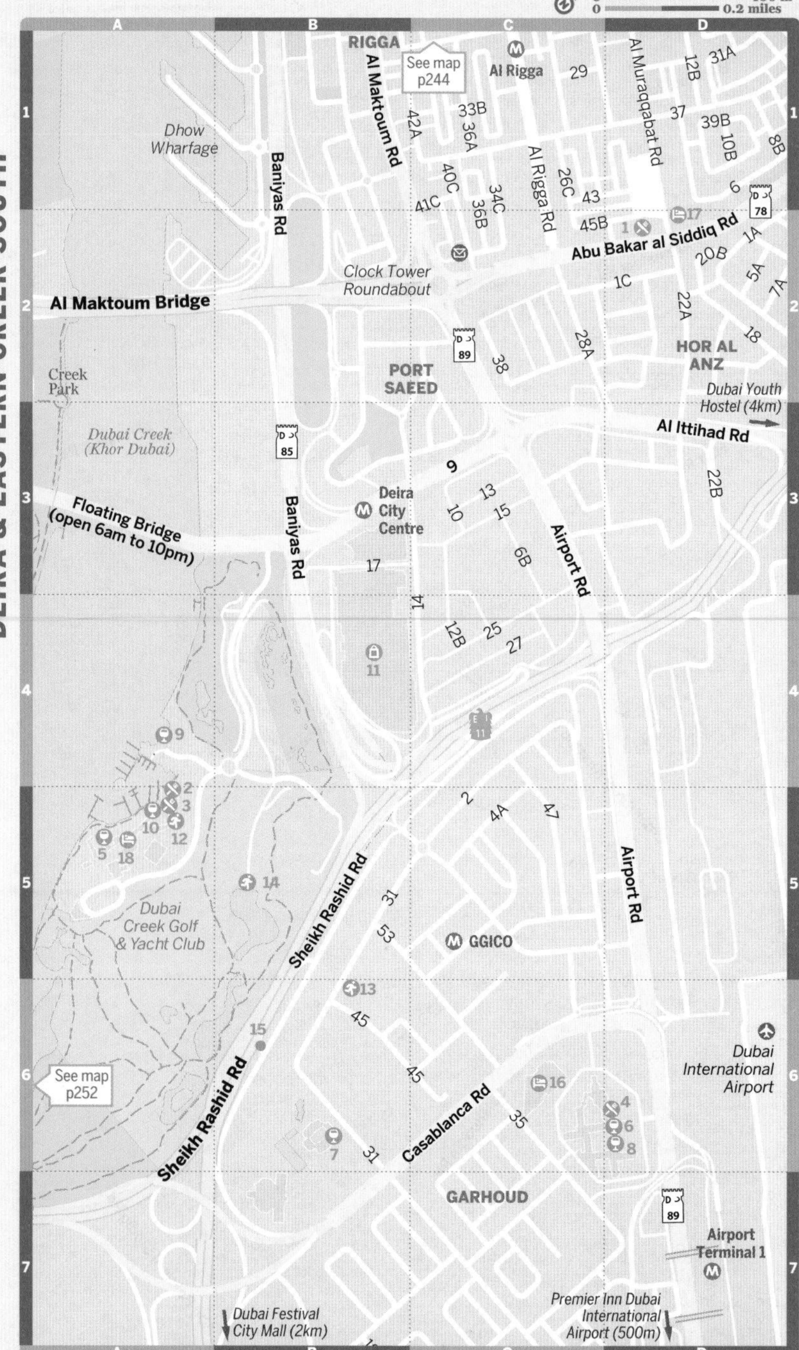

DEIRA & EASTERN CREEK SOUTH

Eating **p54**

1 Al Tawasol D2
2 Thai Kitchen A5
3 Traiteur A5
4 Yalumba D6

Drinking & Nightlife **p61**

5 Cielo Sky Lounge A5
6 Dubliners D6
7 Irish Village B6
8 Jules Bar D6
9 QDs A4
10 Terrace A5

Shopping **p62**

Ajmal .... (see 11)
Al Washia .... (see 11)
Damas .... (see 11)
11 Deira City Centre B4
Early Learning Centre .... (see 11)
Lush .... (see 11)
Mango Touch .... (see 11)
Mikyajy .... (see 11)
Virgin Megastore .... (see 11)
Women's Secret .... (see 11)

Sports & Activities **p64**

12 Amara Spa A5
13 Bliss Relaxology B6
14 Dubai Creek Golf & Yacht Club B5
15 Orient Tours B6

Sleeping **p181**

16 Al Bustan Rotana C6
17 Coral Dubai Deira Hotel D2
18 Park Hyatt Dubai A5

Key on p250

BUR DUBAI & WESTERN CREEK NORTH

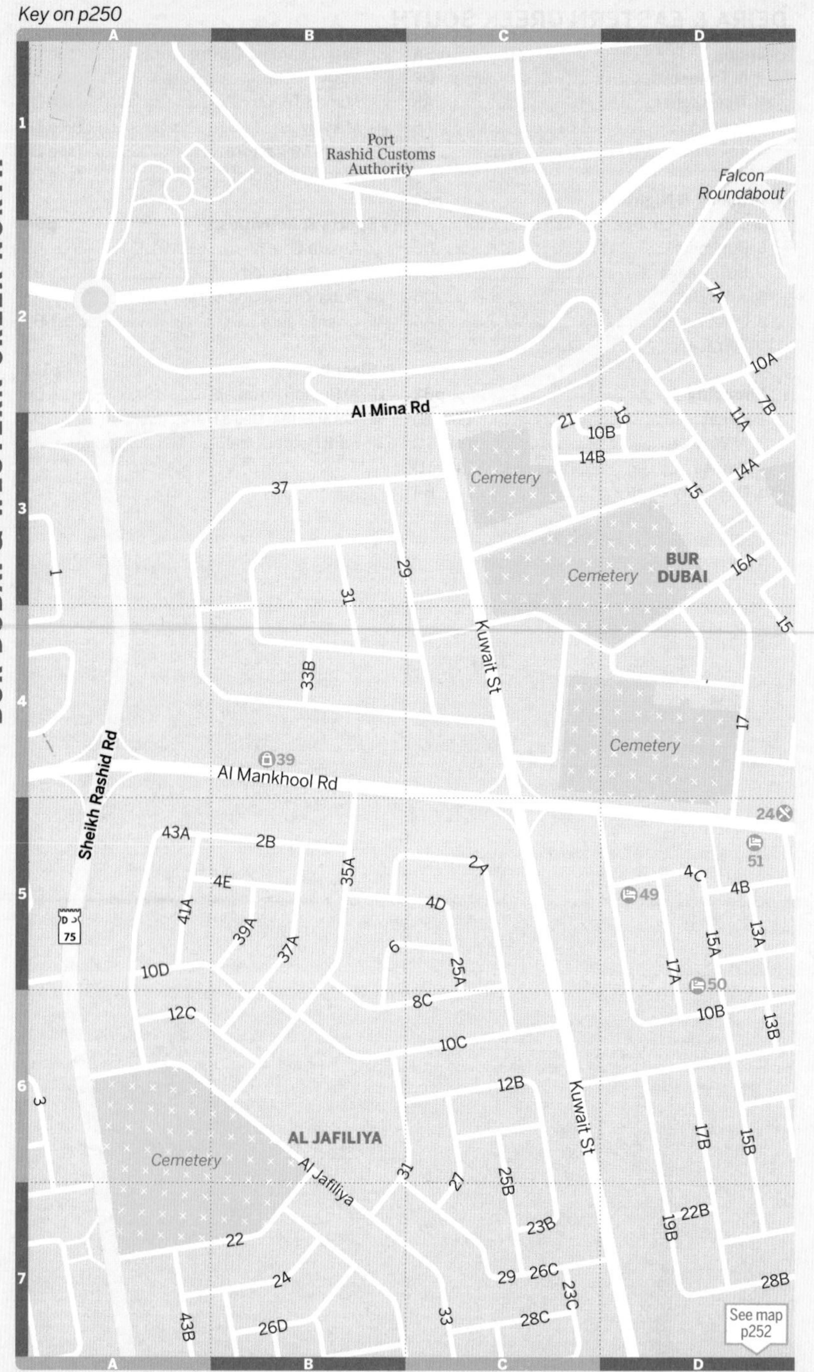

BUR DUBAI & WESTERN CREEK NORTH

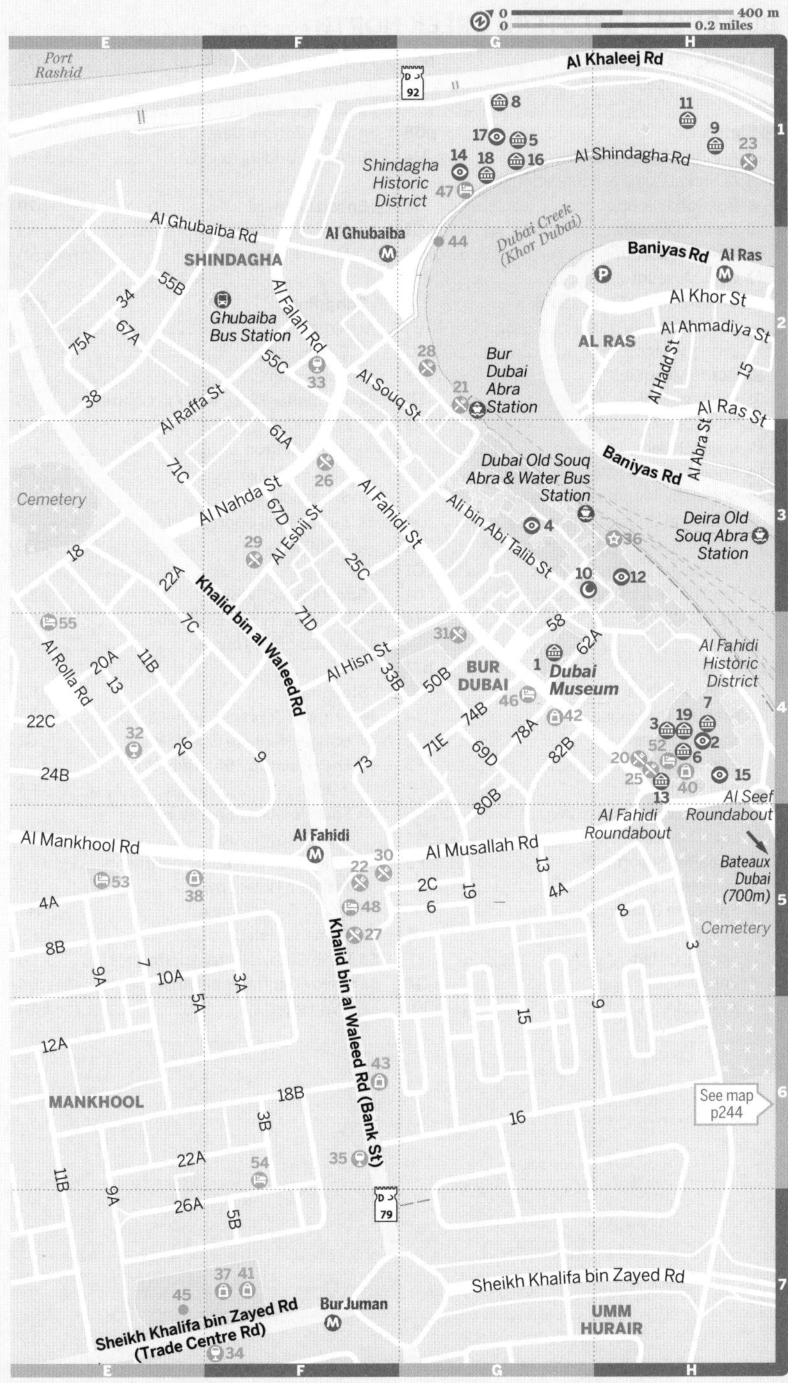

BUR DUBAI & WESTERN CREEK NORTH *Map on p248*

Top Sights p67
1 Dubai Museum G4

Sights p68
2 Al Fahidi Historic District H4
3 Al Serkal Cultural Foundation H4
4 Bur Dubai Souq G3
5 Camel Museum G1
6 Coffee Museum H4
7 Coin Museum H4
8 Crossroads of Civilizations Museum G1
9 Diving Village H1
10 Grand Mosque G3
11 Heritage Village H1
12 Hindi Lane H3
13 Majlis Gallery H4
14 Sheikh Juma Al-Maktoum House G1
15 Sheikh Mohammed Centre for Cultural Understanding H4
16 Sheikh Saeed Al Maktoum House G1
17 Shindagha Historic District G1
18 Traditional Architecture Museum G1
19 XVA Gallery H4

Eating p71
Antique Bazaar .... (see 48)
20 Arabian Tea House H4
21 Bait Al Wakeel G2
22 Curry Leaf F5
23 Kan Zaman H1
24 Lebanese Village Restaurant D5
25 Local House H4
26 Nepaliko Sagarmatha F3
27 Picante F5
28 Saravana Bhavan G2
29 Sind Punjab F3
30 Special Ostadi F5
31 Vaibhav G4
XVA Café .... (see 19)

Drinking & Nightlife p78
32 Box E4
33 George & Dragon F2
34 Rock Bottom Café F7
35 Velvet Underground F6

Entertainment p79
36 Creekside Cafe H3
Music Room .... (see 51)

Shopping p79
Ajmal .... (see 37)
Bateel .... (see 37)
37 BurJuman F7
38 Computer Plaza @ Al Ain Centre E5
39 Fabindia B4
40 Royal Saffron H4
41 Saks Fifth Avenue F7
42 Silk Wonders G4
43 Sun & Sand Sports Factory Outlet F6

Sports & Activities p82
44 Dubai Ferry – Al Ghubaiba G2
45 Wonder Bus Tours E7

Sleeping p182
46 Arabian Courtyard Hotel & Spa G4
47 Barjeel Heritage Guest House G1
48 Four Points by Sheraton Bur Dubai F5
49 Four Points by Sheraton Downtown Dubai D5
50 Golden Sands Hotel Apartments D5
51 Majestic Hotel Tower D5
52 Orient Guest House H4
53 Ramada Hotel E5
54 Rose Garden Hotel Apartments F6
55 Savoy Central Hotel Apartments E4
XVA Hotel .... (see 19)

BUR DUBAI & WESTERN CREEK SOUTH *Map on p252*

Sights p68
1 Children's City G6
2 Creek Park G6
3 Wafi City D6
4 Za'abeel Park C2

Eating p71
5 Asha's E6
Chutneys .... (see 20)
6 Eric's F2
7 Govinda's F1
8 Jaffer Bhai's F2
9 Jambo's Grill F2
10 Karachi Darbar E2
11 Khazana E4
12 Lemongrass D4
Paul .... (see 17)
13 Qbara E6
14 Ripe Food & Craft Market C2
Tomo .... (see 21)

Drinking & Nightlife p78
People by Crystal .... (see 21)

Shopping p79
15 Dubai Flea Market C2
16 Karama Market D3
The One .... (see 17)
17 Wafi Mall E6

Sports & Activities p82
18 Al Nasr Leisureland E4
19 Pharaohs' Club E6

Sleeping p182
20 Mövenpick Hotel & Apartments Bur Dubai D4
21 Raffles Dubai E6

Key on p251

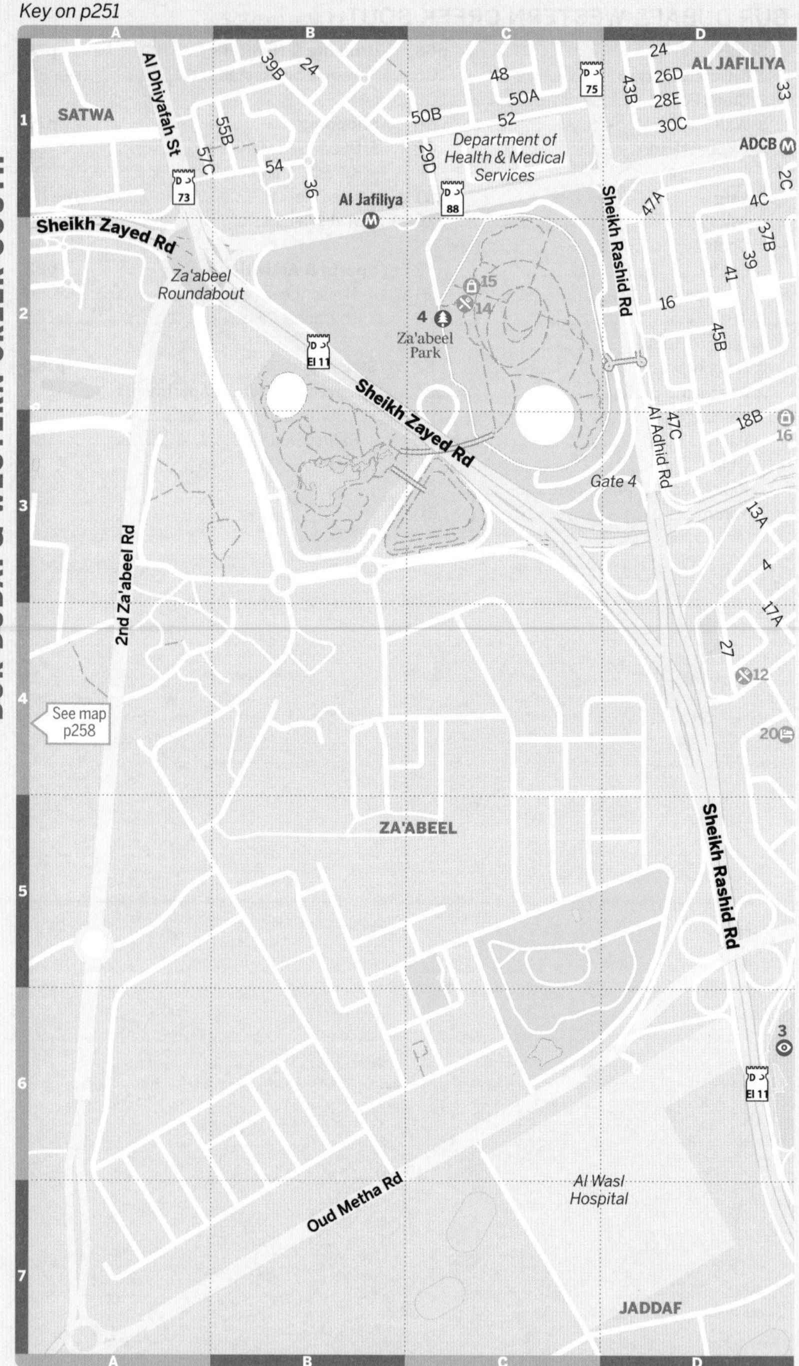

A
B
C
D
1
2
3
4
5
6
7
SATWA
AL JAFILIYA
ZA'ABEEL
JADDAF
Al Dhiyafah St
Sheikh Zayed Rd
Sheikh Rashid Rd
2nd Za'abeel Rd
Oud Metha Rd
Al Adhid Rd
Za'abeel Roundabout
Za'abeel Park
Department of Health & Medical Services
Al Jafiliya
ADCB
Gate 4
Al Wasl Hospital
See map p258
73
88
75
El 11
4
14
15
16
12
20
3
39B
24
55B
57C
54
36
48
50A
50B
52
29D
43B
26D
28E
30C
33
2C
4C
47A
37B
39
41
16
45B
47C
18B
13A
4
17A
27

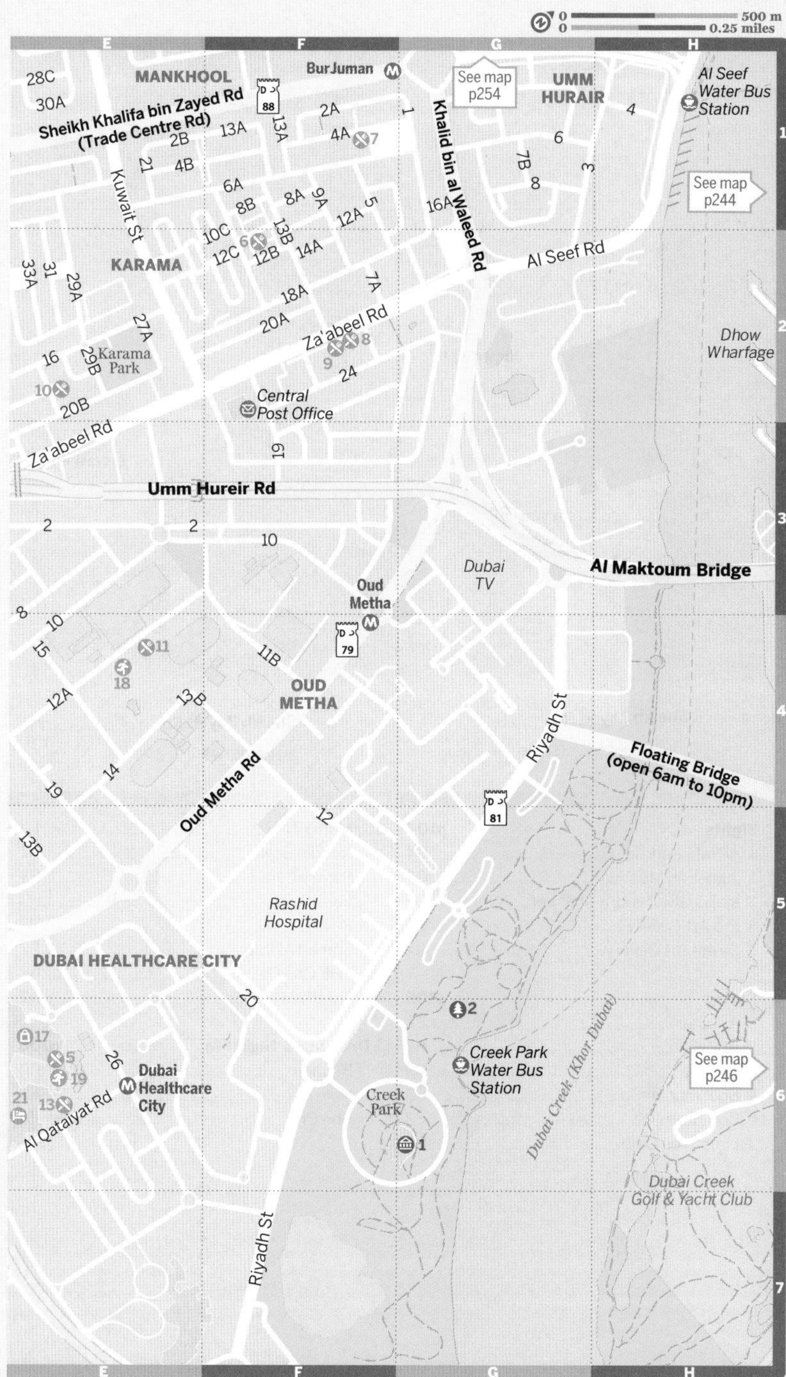
BUR DUBAI & WESTERN CREEK SOUTH
0 500 m
0 0.25 miles
MANKHOOL
BurJuman
See map p254
UMM HURAIR
Al Seef Water Bus Station
Sheikh Khalifa bin Zayed Rd (Trade Centre Rd)
Khalid bin al Waleed Rd
See map p244
Kuwait St
KARAMA
Al Seef Rd
Za'abeel Rd
Karama Park
Dhow Wharfage
Central Post Office
Umm Hureir Rd
Al Maktoum Bridge
Dubai TV
Oud Metha
OUD METHA
Riyadh St
Floating Bridge (open 6am to 10pm)
Oud Metha Rd
Rashid Hospital
DUBAI HEALTHCARE CITY
Creek Park Water Bus Station
Dubai Creek (Khor Dubai)
See map p246
Dubai Healthcare City
Al Qataiyat Rd
Creek Park
Dubai Creek Golf & Yacht Club
Riyadh St

Sights **p104**

1 Al Safa Park C4
2 Jumeirah Mosque G2
3 Majlis Ghorfat Um Al Sheef B2
4 Pro Art Gallery G2
5 Street Art Gallery G2

Eating **p105**

6 Al Fanar E2
7 Al Mallah H2
8 Archive C3
9 BookMunch Cafe B3
10 Comptoir 102 .... F2
11 Lime Tree Cafe G2
12 Mama Tani E2
13 Noodle Bowl H2
14 Pantry Cafe B3
15 Pars H3
16 Ravi H3
17 Samad Al Iraqi C2
18 THE One Deli G2
19 Turath Al Mandi A2

Drinking & Nightlife **p108**

Boudoir .... (see 35)
20 Nar E3
Sho Cho .... (see 35)

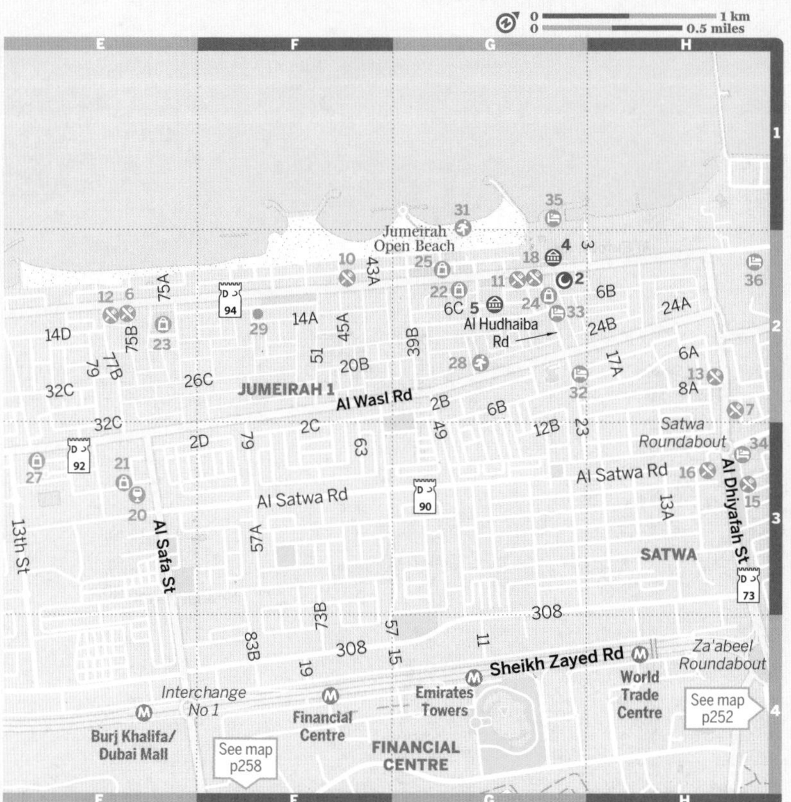

Shopping p110

Sports & Activities p113

Sleeping p186

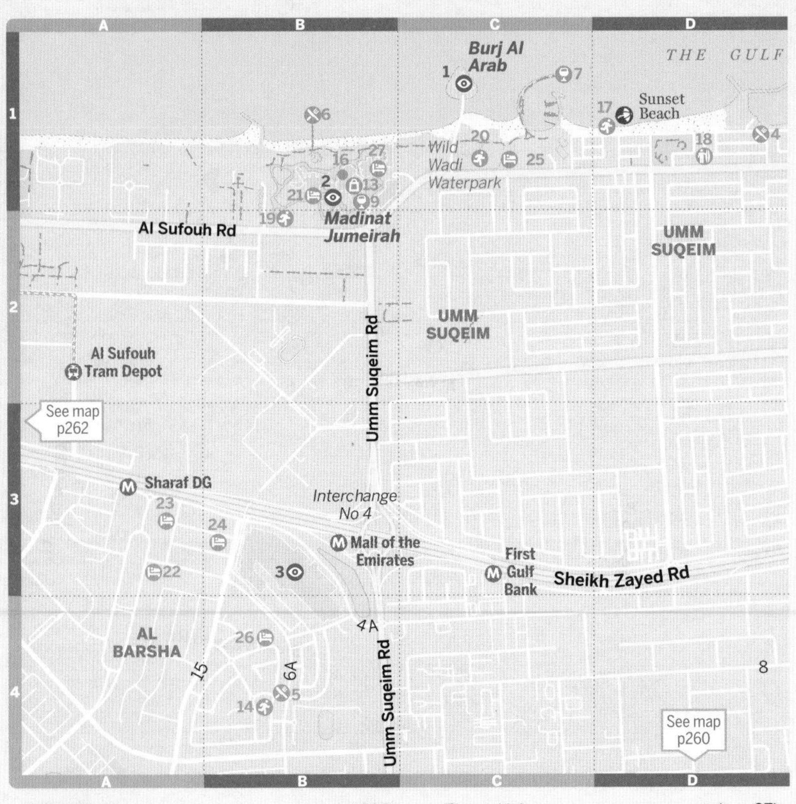

Top Sights p103

1 Burj Al Arab........C1
2 Madinat Jumeirah........B1

Sights p104

3 Mall of the Emirates........B3

Eating p105

Al Fayrooz Lounge........(see 21)
Al Mahara........(see 1)
Al Qasr Friday Brunch........(see 21)
4 Bu Qtair........D1
5 Chicken Tikka Inn........B4
Grand Friday Brunch, Mina A' Salam........(see 27)
Pai Thai........(see 21)
6 Pierchic........B1
The Meat Co........(see 2)
Zheng He's........(see 27)

Drinking & Nightlife p108

7 360°........C1
Agency........(see 2)
Bahri Bar........(see 27)
Koubba........(see 21)
Left Bank........(see 2)
8 Mazology........G1
9 Pacha Ibiza Dubai........B1
Skyview Bar........(see 1)

Entertainment p109

Dubai Community Theatre & Arts Centre........(see 3)
Madinat Theatre........(see 2)
Vox Mall of the Emirates........(see 3)

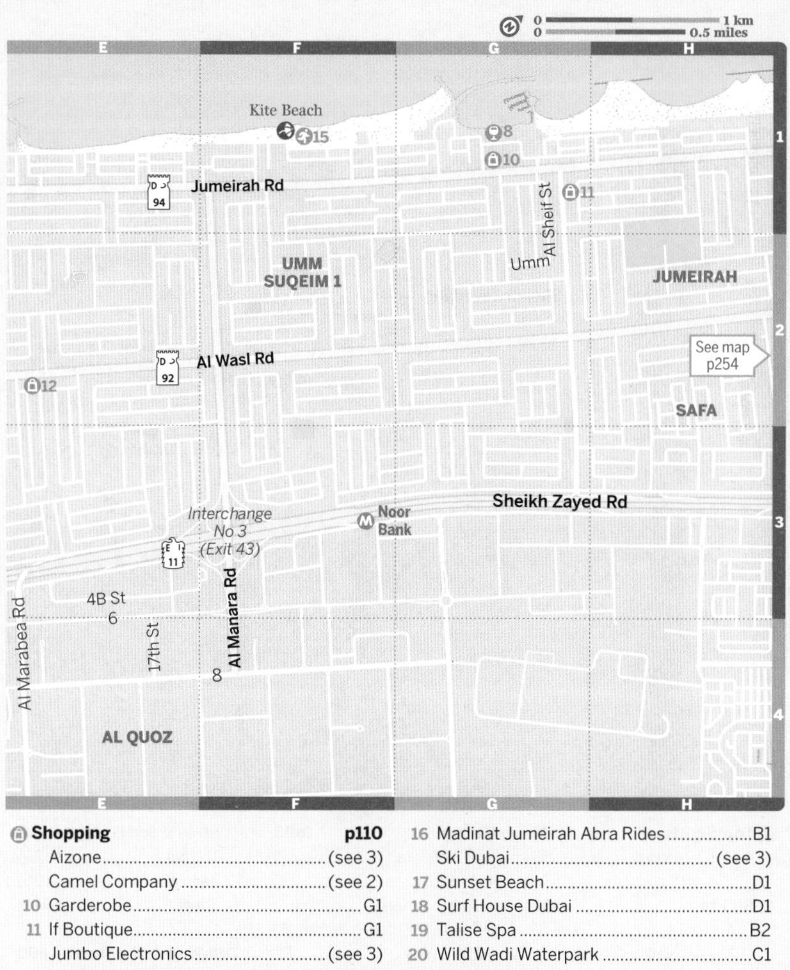

Shopping p110

- Aizone (see 3)
- Camel Company (see 2)
- 10 Garderobe G1
- 11 If Boutique G1
- Jumbo Electronics (see 3)
- Lata's (see 2)
- Mall of the Emirates (see 3)
- Mikyajy (see 3)
- 12 O' de Rose E2
- Rectangle Jaune (see 3)
- 13 Souk Madinat Jumeirah B1
- Yasmine (see 2)

Sports & Activities p113

- 14 Desert Rangers B4
- Dubai Kite School (see 15)
- 15 Kite Beach F1
- 16 Madinat Jumeirah Abra Rides B1
- Ski Dubai (see 3)
- 17 Sunset Beach D1
- 18 Surf House Dubai D1
- 19 Talise Spa B2
- 20 Wild Wadi Waterpark C1

Sleeping p186

- 21 Al Qasr Hotel B1
- Burj Al Arab (see 1)
- 22 Centro Barsha A3
- 23 Donatello Hotel Apartments A3
- 24 Ibis Mall of the Emirates B3
- 25 Jumeirah Beach Hotel C1
- Kempinski Hotel Mall of the Emirates (see 3)
- 26 La Villa Najd Hotel Apartments B4
- 27 Mina A'Salam Hotel B1

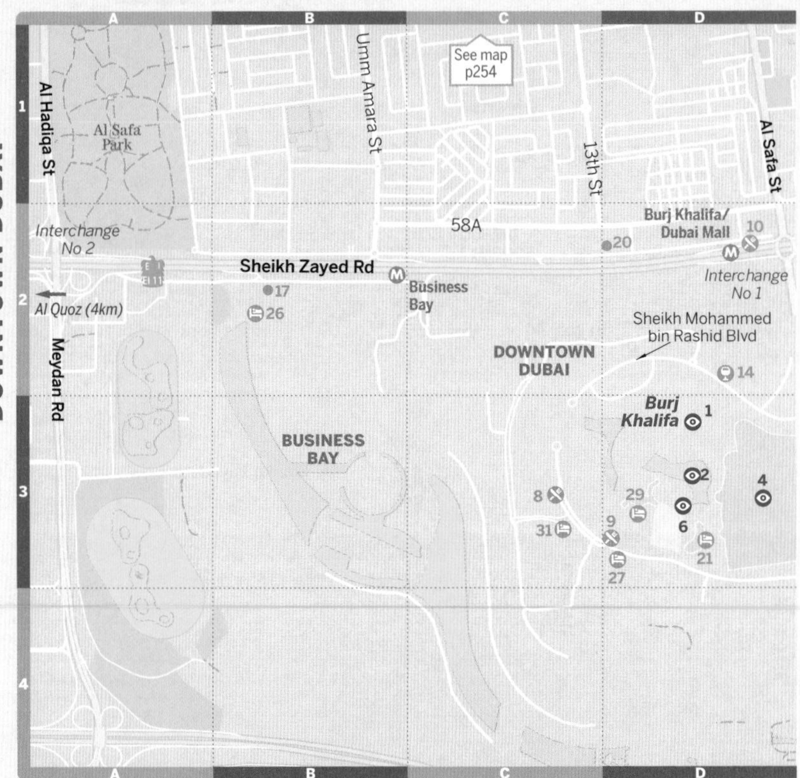

Top Sights p85

1 Burj Khalifa D3

Sights p86

Art Sawa .... (see 5)
Ayyam Gallery .... (see 5)
Cuadro .... (see 5)
Dubai Aquarium & Underwater Zoo .... (see 4)
Dubai Dino .... (see 4)
2 Dubai Fountain D3
3 Dubai International Financial Centre F2
4 Dubai Mall D3
Empty Quarter .... (see 5)
5 Gate Village F2
Opera Gallery .... (see 5)
6 Souk Al Bahar D3

Eating p92

Al Nafoorah .... (see 25)
Asado .... (see 29)
At.mosphere .... (see 1)
Baker & Spice .... (see 6)
7 Clé Dubai F2
Eataly .... (see 4)
Elevation Burger .... (see 4)
Exchange Grill .... (see 23)
Hoi An .... (see 30)
Ivy .... (see 25)
Karma Kafé .... (see 6)
8 Leila C3
9 Mayrig Dubai D3
Milas .... (see 4)
Morelli's Gelato .... (see 4)
Noodle House .... (see 25)
Rib Room .... (see 25)
Rivington Grill .... (see 6)
10 Street Food Festival D2
Thiptara .... (see 29)
Zaroob .... (see 25)
Zuma .... (see 5)

Drinking & Nightlife p95

11 40 Kong H1
Cabana .... (see 4)
Calabar .... (see 21)
Cavalli Club .... (see 23)
12 Double Decker E3
13 Fibber Magee's G1
Harry Ghatto's .... (see 25)
14 Kris Kros D2
Majlis .... (see 4)
Neos .... (see 21)
The Act .... (see 30)
15 Zinc G1

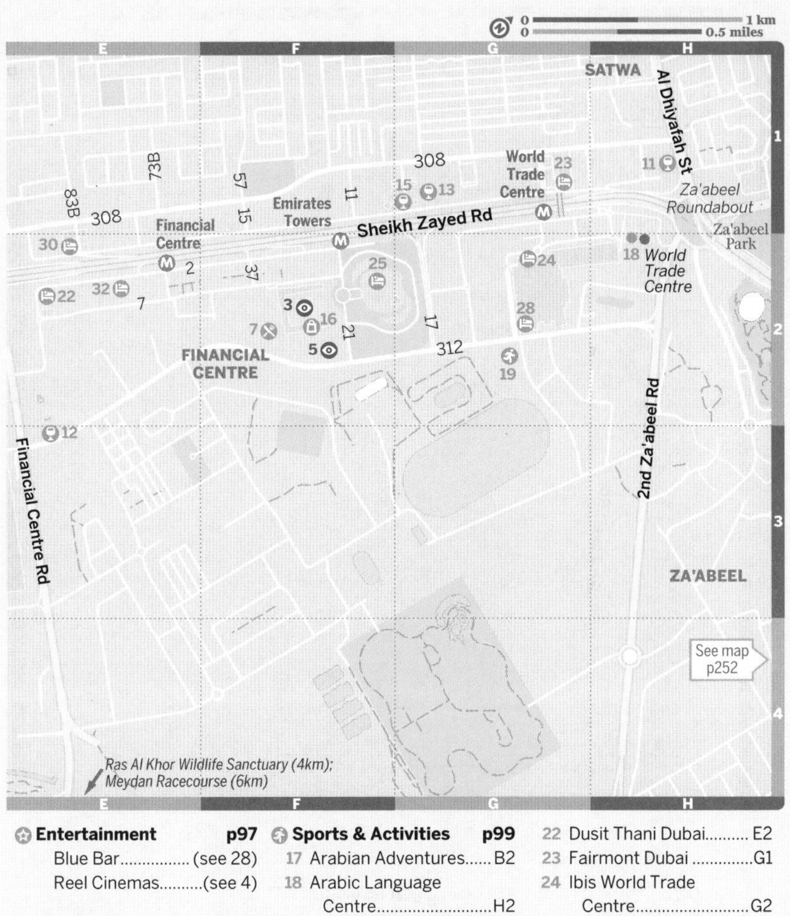
0 1 km
0 0.5 miles
SATWA
Al Dhiyafah St
World Trade Centre
Za'abeel Roundabout
Za'abeel Park
Emirates Towers
Sheikh Zayed Rd
Financial Centre
FINANCIAL CENTRE
World Trade Centre
2nd Za'abeel Rd
Financial Centre Rd
ZA'ABEEL
See map p252
Ras Al Khor Wildlife Sanctuary (4km); Meydan Racecourse (6km)

AL QUOZ

Sights p88

1 1x1 Art Gallery ... D2
2 Alserkal Avenue ... D2
3 Carbon 12 ... E2
4 Cartoon Art Gallery ... E1
5 Courtyard ... E1
6 Gallery Isabelle van den Eynde ... E2
7 Green Art Gallery ... E2
8 Grey Noise ... E2
9 Lawrie Shabibi ... E2
10 Meem Gallery ... A3
11 Salsali Private Museum ... E2
12 Third Line ... D1

Eating p95

13 Lime Tree Cafe ... E1
14 Tom & Serg ... E1

Entertainment p97

15 Bollywood Cinema ... B3
16 Courtyard Playhouse ... E1
17 Fridge ... E2

Shopping p97

18 Gold & Diamond Park ... B1
19 The cARTel ... E2

Sports & Activities p99

20 Desert Rangers ... B1

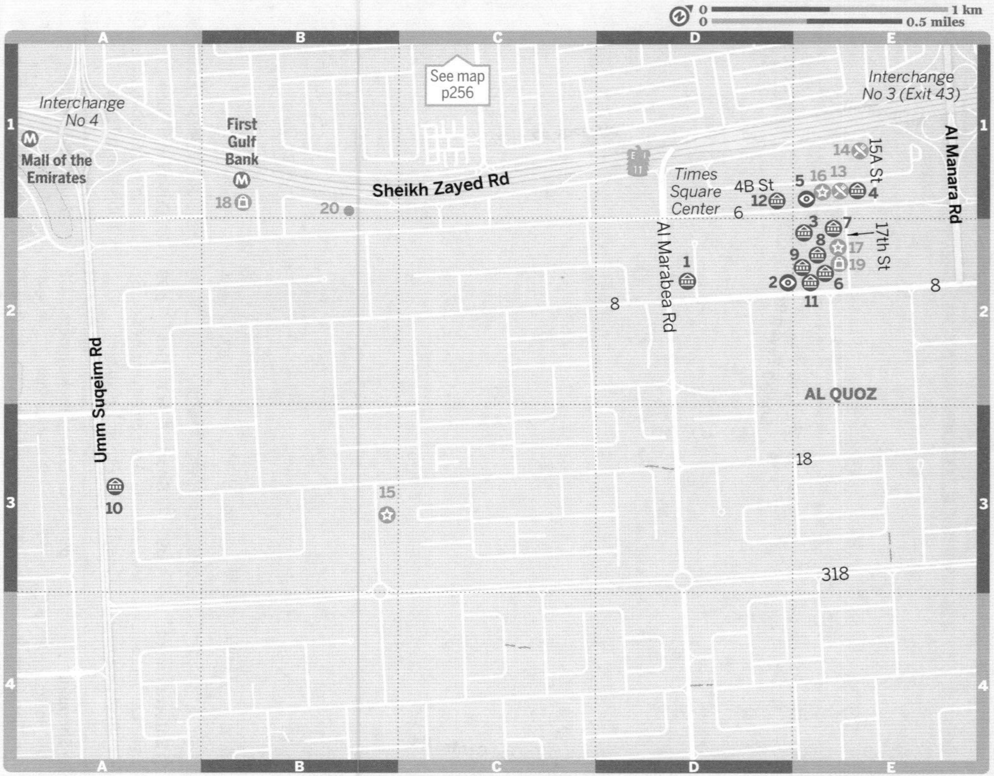

DUBAI MARINA & PALM JUMEIRAH *Map on p262*

Sights p118
1 Ibn Battuta Mall....A6
2 Lost Chambers....F1
3 The Beach at JBR....C5
4 The Walk at JBR....C5

Eating p119
101 Lounge & Bar....(see 48)
Al Khaima....(see 45)
Al Nafoorah....(see 43)
5 Aquara....C5
6 Asia Asia....D5
7 Barracuda....D5
8 BiCE....D5
Bubbalicious, Westin Dubai Mina Seyahi....(see 51)
Buddha Bar....(see 42)
9 Eauzone....F5
10 Frankie's Italian Bar & Grill....D5
Fümé....(see 6)
Indego by Vineet....(see 42)
11 Jazz@PizzaExpress....C6
12 Kcal....C5
13 Massaad....C5
Maya....(see 45)
Rhodes W1....(see 42)
14 Saladicious Deli....D5
Simsim....(see 14)
Splendido....(see 50)
Stay....(see 48)
15 Sushi Art....C5
Tagine....(see 47)
16 The Counter....C5
Toro Toro....(see 42)
17 Zero Gravity....D5

Drinking & Nightlife p123
Atelier M....(see 6)
Barasti....(see 44)
18 Basement....G6
Blends....(see 39)
19 Bliss Lounge....C5
Buddha Bar....(see 42)
20 Casa Latina....H6
Dek on 8....(see 46)
21 Jetty Lounge....F5
Library Bar....(see 50)
Maya Lounge....(see 45)
22 Nasimi Beach....F1
23 N'Dulge....F1
24 Observatory....E5
Pure Sky Lounge....(see 8)
25 Reem Al Bawadi....E5
26 Rooftop Terrace & Sports Lounge....F5
Siddharta....(see 42)
27 Tamanya Terrace....F5
The Courtyards....(see 47)

Entertainment p125
Jazz@PizzaExpress....(see 11)
Music Hall....(see 43)

Shopping p126
Bauhaus....(see 1)
28 Boutique 1....D5
29 Dubai Marina Mall....D5
Gallery One....(see 28)
Ginger & Lace....(see 1)
Ibn Battuta Mall....(see 1)
Marina Market....(see 29)

Sports & Activities p127
30 25' Beach Club....F4
31 Aquaventure Waterpark....G1
32 Beach Water Park....C5
33 Black Palace Beach....H5
Club Mina....(see 51)
Dolphin Bay....(see 31)
34 Dubai Ferry....D5
35 Emirates Golf Club....E6
Favourite Things....(see 29)
36 JBR Open Beach....D5
37 Meydan Beach Club....D5
One&Only Spa....(see 47)
Oriental Hammam....(see 47)
Skydive Dubai....(see 17)
38 Tour Dubai....D5
Zero Gravity....(see 17)

Sleeping p187
39 Address Dubai Marina....D5
40 Gloria Hotel....G6
41 Grand Midwest Tower....G6
42 Grosvenor House....E5
43 Jumeirah Zabeel Saray....E3
44 Le Meridien Mina Seyahi Beach Resort & Marina....E5
45 Le Royal Meridien Beach Resort & Spa....D5
46 Media One Hotel....E5
47 One&Only Royal Mirage....E5
48 One&Only The Palm....E4
49 Pearl Marina Hotel Apartments....C5
50 Ritz-Carlton Dubai....D5
51 Westin Dubai Mina Seyahi Beach Resort & Marina....E5

Key on p261

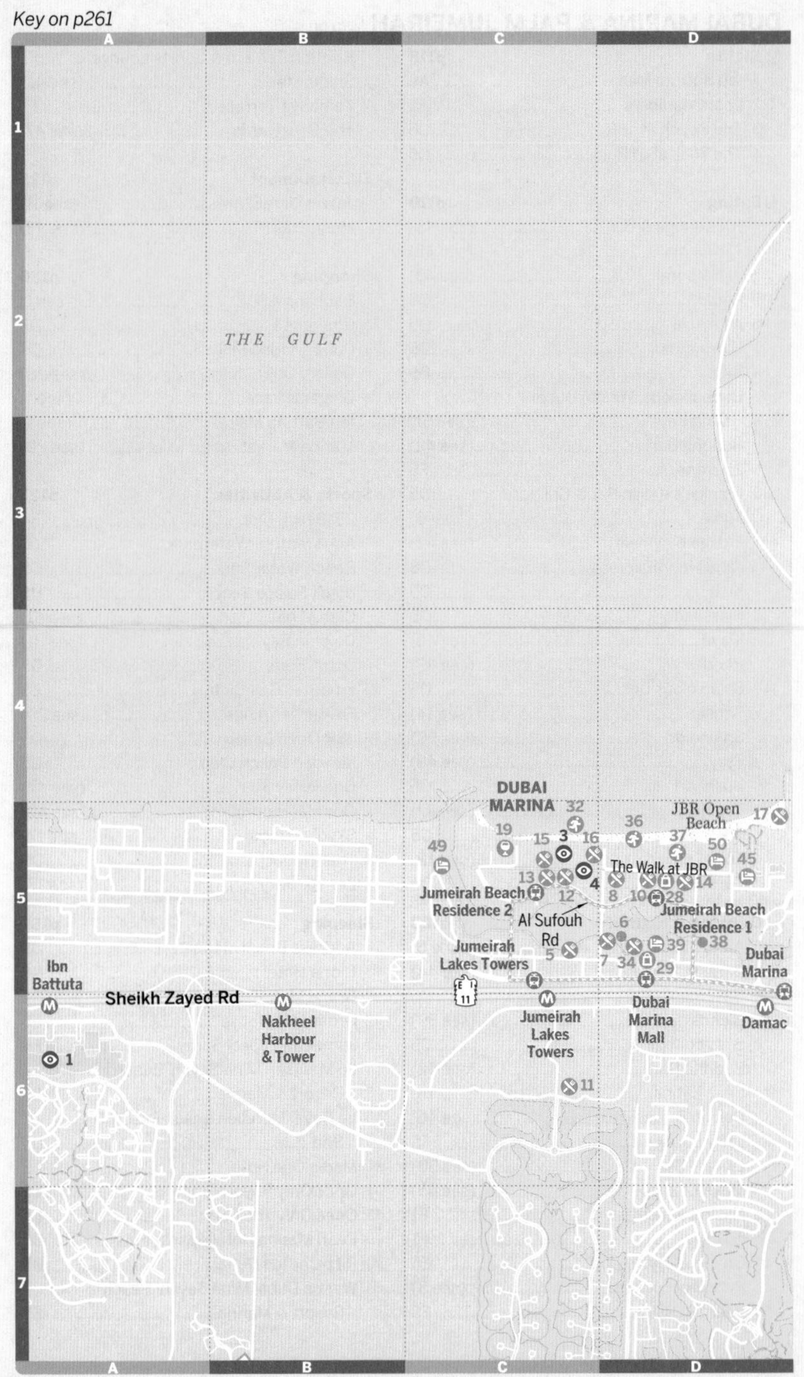
A
B
C
D
1
2
3
4
5
6
7
THE GULF
DUBAI MARINA
JBR Open Beach
The Walk at JBR
Jumeirah Beach Residence 2
Jumeirah Beach Residence 1
Al Sufouh Rd
Jumeirah Lakes Towers
Dubai Marina
Ibn Battuta
Sheikh Zayed Rd
Nakheel Harbour & Tower
Jumeirah Lakes Towers
Dubai Marina Mall
Damac
E 11
1
3
4
5
6
7
8
10
11
12
13
14
15
16
17
19
28
29
32
34
36
37
38
39
45
49
50

Our Story

A beat-up old car, a few dollars in the pocket and a sense of adventure. In 1972 that's all Tony and Maureen Wheeler needed for the trip of a lifetime – across Europe and Asia overland to Australia. It took several months, and at the end – broke but inspired – they sat at their kitchen table writing and stapling together their first travel guide, *Across Asia on the Cheap*. Within a week they'd sold 1500 copies. Lonely Planet was born.

Today, Lonely Planet has offices in Franklin, London, Melbourne, Oakland, Beijing and Delhi, with more than 600 staff and writers. We share Tony's belief that 'a great guidebook should do three things: inform, educate and amuse'.

Our Writers

Andrea Schulte-Peevers

Dubai Born and raised in Germany and educated in London and at UCLA, Andrea has travelled the distance to the moon and back in her visits to dozens of countries, including several in North Africa and the Middle East. She's authored or contributed to some 80 Lonely Planet titles, including the 6th edition of this guide, the *Pocket Dubai* guide and the *Oman, UAE & the Arabian Peninsula* guide. After years of living in LA, Andrea now happily makes her home in Berlin. Andrea also wrote the Plan section and the Sleeping chapter.

Jenny Walker

Abu Dhabi, Day Trips from Dubai & Abu Dhabi For over a decade Jenny Walker has written extensively on the Middle East in many Lonely Planet publications and is a member of the British Guild of Travel Writers. She has a long academic engagement in the region (dissertation on Doughty and Lawrence, MPhil thesis from Oxford University on the perception of the Arabic Orient and current PhD studies at NTU). Associate Dean at an engineering college in Oman since 2008, she has travelled in 110 countries from Mexico to Mongolia. Jenny also wrote the Understand and Survival Guide sections.

Published by Lonely Planet Publications Pty Ltd
ABN 36 005 607 983
8th edition – Sep 2015
ISBN 978 1 74220 885 5

10 9 8 7 6 5 4 3 2 1
Printed in China

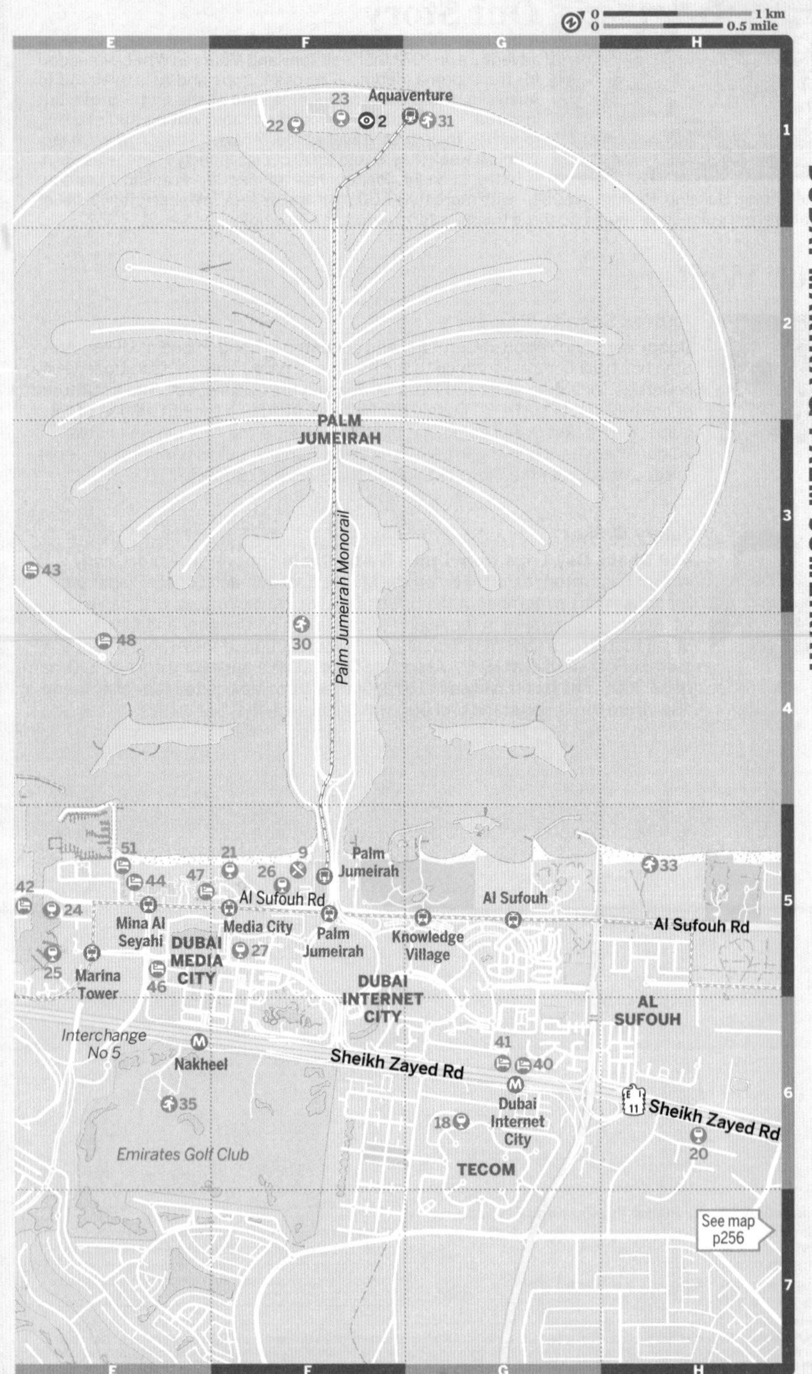

0 1 km
0 0.5 mile
E
F
G
H
1
2
3
4
5
6
7
Aquaventure
23
22
2
31
PALM
JUMEIRAH
Palm Jumeirah Monorail
43
48
30
51
21
9
Palm
Jumeirah
33
42
44
47
26
Al Sufouh Rd
Al Sufouh
24
Mina Al
Seyahi
Media City
Palm
Jumeirah
Knowledge
Village
Al Sufouh Rd
25
Marina
Tower
DUBAI
MEDIA
CITY
46
27
DUBAI
INTERNET
CITY
AL
SUFOUH
Interchange
No 5
Nakheel
Sheikh Zayed Rd
41
40
35
Dubai
Internet
City
E 11
Sheikh Zayed Rd
18
20
Emirates Golf Club
TECOM
See map
p256